VIRTUAL ORGANIZATIONS
SYSTEMS AND PRACTICES

This page intentionally left blank

VIRTUAL ORGANIZATIONS
Systems and Practices

Edited by

Luis M. Camarinha-Matos
New University of Lisbon, Portugal

Hamideh Afsarmanesh
University of Amsterdam, The Netherlands

and

Martin Ollus
VTT Industrial Systems, Finland

Springer

ISBN: 978-1-4419-3657-8
eBook ISBN: 978-0-387-23757-2
eBook ISBN: 0-387-23757-7

Visit Springer's eBookstore at: http://ebooks.springerlink.com
and the Springer Global Website Online at: http://www.springeronline.com

TABLE OF CONTENTS

TECHNICAL SPONSOR:

VOSTER

European Commission IST-2001-32031 Project
Virtual Organizations Cluster

PARTNERS

- **VTT** – Research Center of Finland, Finland [Coordinator]
- **IAO** – Fraunhofer-Gesellschaft zur Forderung der Angewandten Forschung e.V., Germany
- **CeTIM** – Centre for Technology and Innovation Management, Germany / The Netherlands
- **UNINOVA** – Instituto de Desenvolvimento de Novas Tecnologias, Portugal
- **FIR** – Research Institute for Rationalization and Operations Management at Aachen University of Technology, Germany
- **LoU** – Loughborough University, UK
- **DUT** – Dresden University of Technology, Germany
- **USal** – University of Salford, UK
- **UvA** – Universiteit van Amsterdam, The Netherlands
- **Computas AS**, Norway
- **CEC** – Concurrent Engineering Consulting, Italy
- **SUT** – Silesian University of Technology, Poland

http://voster.vtt.fi

PEER REVIEWERS

Adam Pawlak, PL
Adrian Plüss, CH
Andrea Bifulco, IT
Arturo Molina, MX
Dimitris Assimakopoulos, FR
Eoin Banahan, UK
Eugénio Oliveira, PT
Frank Lillehagen, NO
George Kovacs, HU
Gus Olling, US
Hermann Loeh, DE
Ian Wilson, UK
Iris Karvonen, FI
Istvan Meszgar, HU
Jorge Pinho Sousa, PT
Karsten Menzel, DE
Kim Jansson, FI
Kurt Kosanke, DE
Laszlo Nemes, AU
Maria Anastasiou, GR
Martin Keller, DE
Martin Ollus, FI
Martin Weidemann, DE
Matti Hannus, FI
Nada Lavrac, SI
Peter Bernus, AU
Ricardo Rabelo, BR
Roberto Santoro, IT
Simon Field, UK
Tarek Hassan, UK
Ted Goranson, US
Tomasz Janowski, PL
Toshiya Kaihara, JP
Vladimir Marik, CZ
Volker Tschammer, DE
Weiming Shen, CA

FOREWORD

Towards a consolidation of empiric knowledge on virtual organizations

Purpose. During the last decade, considerable investments have been made worldwide in a large number of research projects fostering new organizational forms. These projects have on one hand produced an abundant variety of specific solutions and on the other hand broad awareness about the necessary organizational changes. The area of *Virtual Organizations* as a main component of the new discipline of *Collaborative Networks* has been particularly active in Europe where a large number of R&D projects have been funded. The fast evolution of the information and communication technologies and in particular the so-called Internet technologies, also represents an important motivator for the emergence of new forms of collaboration. However, the research in many of these cases is highly fragmented. Each project is focused on solving specific problems and, by applying Information and Communication Technology, partially designs and develops its proprietary minimal business-to-business interaction mechanism according to its basic needs. As such, there is no effective consolidation/harmonization/continuity among them in order to have an effective impact. Trying to improve this situation, this book represents an attempt to contribute to a consolidation of existing empiric knowledge and experiences in this area.

Intended audience. Given the nature of the book, focused on the consolidation of the state of the art, it is mainly intended for researchers, PhD students, engineers, and managers entering the field of virtual organizations. It can also be useful for those already involved in specific areas of virtual organizations and those who want to get a broader view of the field of collaborative networks.

Style. This is a multi-author book and therefore, although an attempt is made by the editors to achieve minimal uniformity, the reader should expect to find different styles of writing along the various chapters. Furthermore, the reader needs to be aware of the fact that the VO paradigm is a highly multi-disciplinary area for research, and comprising contributions from a large number of experts from different research communities. This situation by itself introduces a new level of heterogeneity in the styles, as different communities have different ways of expressions, different literary styles, and different inherent semantics are associated to the terminology used in each discipline.

Sources. This book was prepared in the context of VOSTER, the European Virtual Organizations Cluster project. The overall aim of VOSTER was to collect, analyze and synthesize the results from a number of leading European research projects on Virtual Organizations, i.e. "geographically distributed, functionally and culturally diverse, dynamic and agile organizational entities linked through ICT". In addition to the European projects, and although constrained by the limited resources available, VOSTER also made an attempt to consider results from some relevant projects from other geographical areas (e.g. USA, Canada, Australia, Mexico, Brazil, Japan).

Book structure. In summary, the book sections include the following:
Section 1 presents a summary of the main concepts, definitions, and models used in this area. Section 2 introduces the ICT requirements and support infrastructures. Section 3 is devoted to implementation aspects such as legal, socio-organizational, and performance measurement issues. Section 4 includes a collection of case studies in various application domains. Finally, Section 5 presents some concluding remarks. Additionally, an Annex presents a brief summary of the main projects considered in the VOSTER study.

The editors would like to thank the large community of experts involved in this work – authors and referees - for their many valuable opinions, suggestions, and recommendations. On behalf of the VOSTER consortium we also thank the European Commission, the Commission's project officer Joel Bacquet, and the review team, Alberto Bonetti and Olivier Rerolle, for their valuable support and suggestions.

We hope that the result of this work can constitute a valuable input for those who want to get a better understanding of virtual organizations and collaborative networks.

The editors

Luis M. Camarinha-Matos, *New University of Lisbon, Portugal*
Hamideh Afsarmanesh, *University of Amsterdam, The Netherlands*
Martin Ollus, *VTT Automation, Finland*

<table>
<tr><td>1.</td><td></td></tr>
</table>

CONCEPTS AND MODELS

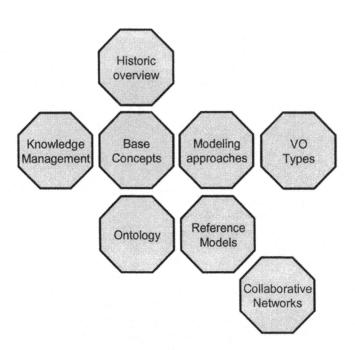

This page intentionally left blank

BRIEF HISTORICAL PERSPECTIVE FOR VIRTUAL ORGANIZATIONS

Luis M. Camarinha-Matos
New University of Lisbon / Uninova, Portugal, cam@uninova.pt
Hamideh Afsarmanesh
University of Amsterdam, The Netherlands, hamideh@science.uva.nl

Emergence of the virtual enterprise / virtual organization paradigm falls within the natural sequence of the restructuring processes in traditional industrial paradigms that is enabled by advances in information and communication technologies. In parallel with the outsourcing tendency, another transformation observed in large companies is their reorganization as a "federation" of relatively autonomous departments. The idea of VE/VO was not "invented" by a single researcher; rather it is a concept that has matured through a long evolution process. The history of industrial enterprise integration, as well as the integration technologies and paradigms in the last three decades are briefly introduced. The position of the VE/VO in the e-movement is identified.

1. INTRODUCTION

Several new industrial paradigms have emerged in recent years as an answer to the fast changing socio-economic challenges, such as the virtual manufacturing, lean enterprise, agile manufacturing, fractal company, and holonic manufacturing. Introduction of these concepts in enterprises has made them face successive "waves of restructuring" during the last decades. Emergence of the virtual enterprise / virtual organization paradigm falls in the natural sequence of these restructuring processes, enabled by the "explosive" developments in the information and communication technologies. The need to remain competitive in the open market forces companies to seek "world class" status and therefore, to concentrate on their core competencies while searching for alliances when additional skills / resources are needed to fulfil business opportunities.

Some authors see the roots of this paradigm in early works of economists like Oliver Williamson in the 1970s. Along his very prolific work, and in particular in the "Markets and Hierarchies" (Williamson, 1975) Williamson established the study of Transaction Cost Economics as one of the first and most influential attempts to develop an economic theory of organizations. He defends that manufacturing firms should make much greater use of externally purchased goods and services, rather than those internally supplied. Williamson discusses the business transaction costs at the same level as the production costs. While production costs are considered as being analogous to the costs of building and running an "ideal" machine, transaction costs covers those that incur by deviation from perfection. For instance he argues that the lack of information about the alternative suppliers might lead to paying too high a price for a good or service. Through identifying the important variables that determine the transaction costs, the work of Williamson contributed to the better understanding of business interactions among enterprises.

These ideas had a more evident impact with the booming of the "outsourcing" wave in the 1980s. Outsourcing became very attractive when managers had to reduce the organization overheads and eliminate the internal inefficient services, the so called lean manufacturing, as it transfers the problem to the outside, namely other efficient service providers. For many enterprises, outsourcing some services allows them to concentrate on their core competencies. For others, outside contractors simply provide complementary services for which the company lacks adequate internal resources or skills.

Among many factors that justify the outsourcing strategy, the reduction of costs, and elimination of poor performance units, can be pointed out, particularly in the case of those units that do not represent core capabilities or when better and cheaper alternatives can be identified in the market.

In parallel with the outsourcing tendency, another transformation can be observed in large companies that reorganize themselves in terms of their production lines, leading to some "federation" of relatively autonomous departments.

These transformations, putting the emphasis on networking and partnership / cooperation have raised a large interest for new disciplines such as the coordination theory, organizational theory, and sociology of the industrial organizations.

The idea of virtual enterprise (VE) / virtual organization (VO) was not "invented" by a single researcher, rather it is a concept that has matured through a long evolution process. Some of the early references first introducing the terms like virtual company, virtual enterprise, or virtual corporation go back to the early 1990s, including the work of Jan Hopland, Nagel and Dove, and Davidow and Malone [3,4]. Since then a large but disjoint body of literature has been produced mainly in two communities, the Information and Communications Technology community and the Management community.

However, concepts and definitions related to the VE/VO paradigm are still evolving, and the terminology is not yet fixed. There is still not even a common definition for the VE/VO that is agreed by the community of researchers in this area. Nevertheless, many real examples of VE/VO are already available and functional in different regions of the world, which indicates the importance of this area and the need for stabilizing the terminology and definitions for this paradigm, as well as research in developing a model of their life cycle, behavior, and evolution.

The area of VE/VO is particularly active in Europe, not only in terms of research and development, but also in terms of the emergence of various forms of enterprise networking at regional level. This "movement" is consistent with the process of European integration, which represents a push towards a "culture of cooperation", but also with the very nature of the European business landscape that is mostly based on small and medium size enterprises (SME) that need to join efforts in order to be competitive in open and turbulent market scenarios.

2. VIRTUAL ORGANIZATIONS AND SYSTEMS INTEGRATION

The emergence of virtual enterprise / virtual organization paradigm can also be seen as another step in the systems integration process. As an example, let us consider the context of industrial companies. Systems integration can be addressed and instantiated at different levels of complexity and abstraction (Fig. 1), as follows:

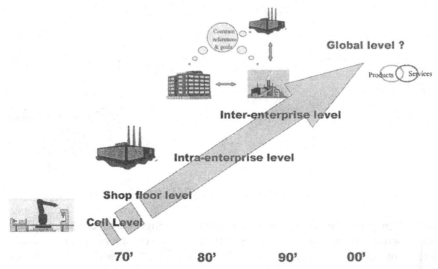

Figure 1 - Levels of integration in manufacturing enterprises

– <u>Cell level</u> – when basic resources (robots, NC machines, conveyors, etc.) and their local controllers need to be integrated in order to build a cell dedicated to a specific function or a set of functions (assembly, painting, inspection, etc.).

– <u>Shop-floor level</u> – when various cells, transportation subsystems and warehouses are integrated within one manufacturing system.

– <u>Intra-enterprise level</u> – when the objective is to integrate all areas of the enterprise, including not only the shop-floor but also other departments e.g. marketing, planning, engineering, etc. and their interactions.

– <u>Inter-enterprise level</u> – when cooperation among various enterprises is envisaged. The manufacturing processes or complex services are not performed by isolated companies. On the contrary, in a network of collaborating enterprises (virtual enterprise) each node contributes with some value to the value chain. The materialization of this paradigm requires the definition of a reference architecture for the cooperation process and the development of a support infrastructure, including the protocols and services for information exchange, communication and cooperation.

Furthermore, the need for a new level of integration (integration at global level) is emerging, emphasizing the role and opportunities for collaborative networked environments. The inclusion of processing capabilities (local intelligence) is many components is spreading all over the living environments, both in the professional environment and at home (Fig. 2), leading to the idea of pervasive or ubiquitous computing. The working methods change, making it possible to perform professional activities from different locations (tele-work).

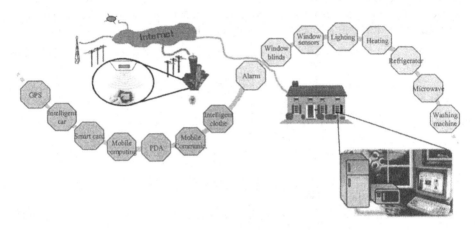

Figure 2 – Ubiquitous computing and global integration

This tendency is reflected by the proliferation of intelligent devices such as: PDAs, mobile phones, smart cards, embedded networks in the car, processors embedded in clothes of athletes or patients to monitor their status, elevators, safety and surveillance systems, traffic control systems, intelligent and Internet-enabled home appliances, among many others, which open new opportunities for collaborative networks. An important challenge is the interoperability among all these components and the development of appropriate integration approaches among their processing capabilities.

Systems integration, even if under different names, has been a major topic of research and development during the last three decades.

A simplified vision of the "history" of industrial enterprise integration can be the one shown in Fig. 3, where in fact the integration work at the various levels of abstraction continues through the three decades. This picture is not intended to be complete showing all the paradigms and development areas in systems integration. Neither it is strictly accurate in terms of the exact time span for each paradigm. Rather, the purpose is instead to provide a general and simplified overview of relative relationships among different integration developments. For instance, the ellipsis representing CIM does not mean that this topic "finished" in the early 1990's, rather representing the fact that it has received less attention since then and the developments slowed down or was replaced by more appropriate concepts. Similarly, the idea is to show that the second half of the 1980's were the most active years for this paradigm.

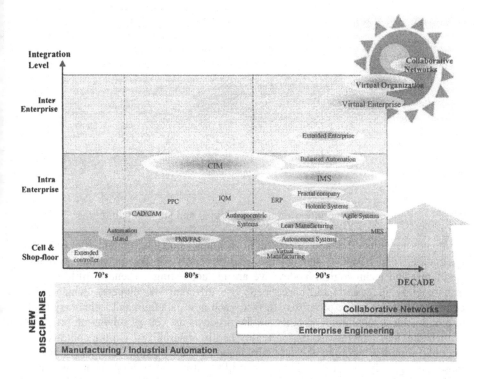

Figure 3 – Main phases in manufacturing systems integration

Also, as can be seen in the same figure, in recent years increasing attention is being devoted to the integration of more complex systems towards the creation of a global system. However, meanwhile the integration issues at the cell or shop-floor levels still remain in the agenda and not resolved.

A similar picture could be drawn for other areas such as the service industry or governmental organizations.

The paradigm of virtual enterprise / virtual organization, and more generically collaborative networks, appear naturally in this sequence of "systems integration", addressing the most comprehensive scope of integration of autonomous, heterogeneous, and distributed entities.

As illustrated in Fig. 3, the emergence and evolution of paradigms and concepts is also leading to the foundation of new scientific disciplines that try to capture the essence of this domain of study and build the foundations for further progress.

The actual implementation tools used for systems integration depend on the technologies available during each historic phase both for components development and for integration support. A very simplified overview of the main paradigms and technologies used in industrial systems integration during the last three decades is shown in Fig. 4.

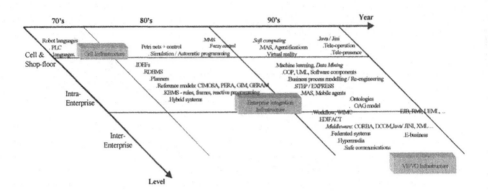

Figure 4 – Some integration technologies and support paradigms

It should be noted that the increase in systems' complexity and the foreseen integration scope results an increase and diversity of the potential available paradigms and technologies. Today, we are in fact facing a scenario of too many technologies suggested and produced by different developers, which also corresponds to too many promises! In fact, each new paradigm and technology tends to promise most capabilities of other similar products as well as solving all problems of their previous generations, that in reality hardly materializes! On the contrary, the multiplication of all tools by the fast introduction of new versions and generations of those tools greatly increases the incompatibility ratio among components, which in turn justifies the question "To what extent are these technologies and tools enablers, or are they in fact disablers of systems integration and cooperation among distinct entities?"

In addition to the diversity of paradigms and technologies available at a given historic phase, in each enterprise or network of enterprises there is also always a co-existence of diverse technology generations and components with different life cycles and in different phases of their life cycles. Therefore, systems integrator must not only master the tools and technologies of the current time frame, but also take into account the legacy systems and how to promote their technologic migration.

3. VIRTUAL ORGANIZATIONS IN THE *e-MOVEMENT*

Generalized access to Internet that is available through multiple channels and the fast developments around the world-wide-web has led to the proliferation of many terms such as the e-commerce, e-business, e-work, e-government, etc. To put it in a more emphatic way it seems that in the first years of this decade everything became *e-something*. Similarly, Business-to-customer (B2C) and Business-to-Business (B2B) are other examples of popularized terms.

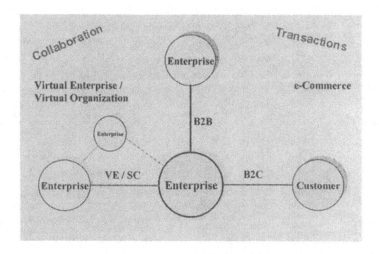

Figure 5 – Virtual Organization vs. e-Commerce

So the question remains: since virtual organizations are also supported by the Internet and the web, where do they fit in this "e-movement"?

Fig. 5 shows an attempt to put things into perspective, showing that e-Commerce is mostly about B2C relationships and mainly concerned with buy-sell **transactions** among the involved entities. Virtual organizations on the other hand, go far beyond simple transactions, and are focused on **collaboration** *among a number of enterprises* and *doing things together.*

4. VIRTUAL ORGANIZATION AND RESEARCH PROJECTS

During the last 10~15 years a large number of R&D projects tried to establish some technological foundations as well as operating practices for the support of Virtual Enterprises /Virtual Organizations. This effort is particularly visible in Europe through the European Commission funded programs (e.g. ESPRIT, IST, INCO), but also in the USA and other geographical regions (Australia, Brazil, Mexico, Japan, to name a few). Programs such as IMS (Intelligent Manufacturing Systems) also supported various projects in this area involving organizations from various continents. Fig. 6 gives some examples of this R&D effort.

All these initiatives, together with practical realizations of many variations of virtual organizations, have generated a large amount of empiric knowledge that is however still disperse and fragmented. The IST VOSTER project, whose main results are synthesized in this book, represented an attempt to consolidate some of this existing knowledge.

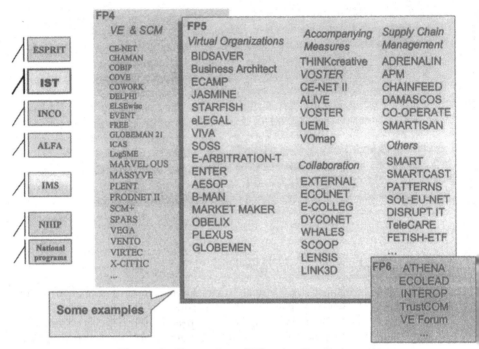

Figure 6 – Examples of VO-related projects

More recently, in part as a result of initiatives such as the THINKcreative and VOmap projects among others, the need for investing on more fundamental research towards the creation of a sound theoretical foundation for virtual organizations became more evident. The 6th Framework research program of the European Commission also includes in its objectives to pursuing more integrated and fundamental research in the area. The ECOLEAD project is an example in this direction.

5. REFERENCES

1. Camarinha-Matos, L. M.; Afsarmanesh, H. - Tendencies and general requirements for virtual enterprises, in Infrastructures for Virtual Enterprises, Kluwer Academic Publishers, 1999.
2. Camarinha-Matos, L. M.; Afsarmanesh, H. - Designing the information technology subsystem, in Handbook on Enterprise Architecture, P. Bernus, L. Nemes, G. Schmidt (Eds.), Springer, 2003.
3. Davidow, W.; Malone, T. – The virtual corporation, Harper Business, 1992.
4. Introna, L.D.; More, H.; Cushman, M. - The virtual organization – Technical or social innovation ? Lessons from the film industry, Working paper N° 72, 1999, London School of Economics, Department of Information Systems, http://is.lse.ac.uk/wp/pdf/wp72.pdf.

Mehmet Kürümlüoglu, Rita Nøstdal
Fraunhofer IAO, Germany, mehmet.kueruemlueoglu@iao.fhg.de, Rita.Noestdal@iao.fhg.de
Iris Karvonen
VTT, Finland, iris.karvonen@vtt.fi

In literature numerous definitions and characteristics of virtual organizations are available. A large number of research initiatives and industry cases have been developing concepts, methods and enabling IT for virtual organizations. This chapter presents a synopsis of results from more than 60 national, European, and global research projects (including IMS), as well as US research and road-mapping activities (IMTI and FIATECH). The first part describes common definitions, characteristics and core concepts for networks and virtual organisations. In the second part expectations, potentials and management issues in virtual organizations are discussed.

1. INTRODUCTION

In the past years a large amount of new virtual organization (VO) concepts and approaches have been developed. The motive is based on the changing business situation of companies and customer needs. Main drivers for the rise of organization networks are mass-customization, extension of products, globalization, and agility (cf. Saabeel et al, 2002).

There are basically two different types of concepts for the inter-enterprise organization. Different terms have been used for both of them:

- **Network / source network / support network / breeding environment** is a more stable, though not static, group of organizational entities which have developed a *preparedness* to co-operate in case of a specific task / customer demand.

- **Virtual organization / virtual enterprise** is a temporary consortium of partners from different organizations established to fulfill *a value adding task,* for example a product or service to a customer. The lifetime of a VO is typically restricted: it is created from the network for a definite task and dissolved after the task has been completed.

Both of these concepts thus presume the participation of different organizations, for example different enterprises. The main features distinguishing them are the temporal nature and the operational mode of the organization. A network operates developing, maintaining and managing the preparedness for value creation and setting up a VO/VE for a customer delivery. The timeframe of the VO/VE is restricted by its task it has been set up for, but may extend from a few hours to some years. As the base concepts have been developed simultaneously with the development of information technology, the utilization of modern ICT is often seen as an enabler for the VOs. Figure 1 presents a description of the core concepts and their relations.

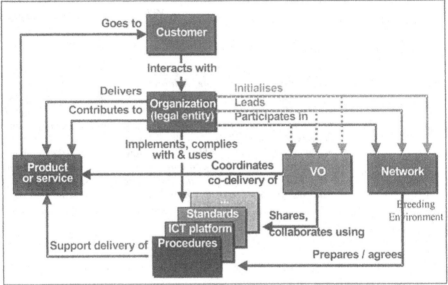

Figure 1: *Core concepts of VOs*

2. VIRTUAL ORGANIZATION - DEFINITIONS AND CHARACTERISTICS

In literature numerous definitions and characteristics of virtual organizations are available. Important definitions and characteristics are manifested in the following sections.

2.1   Definitions of virtual organizations

2.1.1   Virtual organization and virtual enterprise

A virtual organization is a set of co-operating (legally) independent organizations, which to the outside world provide a set of services and act as if they were one organization[1]. The set of co-operating organizations can change with time; it can be

---

[1]

Supported by a computer network.

a dynamic configuration depending on the function / service to be provided at that point in time. It can also be a more stable configuration with a sizeable time span and a stable set of services and functions.

A virtual organization consists of semi-independent entities with separate core competencies, who band together to achieve a prescribed or subscribed business objective supported by information and communication technologies. The most common industries for virtual organizations are information technology, manufacturing and consulting, but VOs can exist in any industry where the marketplace desires multi-faceted services or products that require very costly logistic or infrastructure investments (cf. MBDA, 2001).

A virtual enterprise is a "customer solutions delivery system created by a temporary and reconfigurable ICT enabled aggregation of core competencies" (Globmen-Project, 2000). Camarinha-Matos, Afsarmanesh (1999) defines a virtual enterprise as "a temporary alliance of enterprises that come together to share skills or core competencies and resources in order to better respond to business opportunism, and whose co-operation is supported by computer networks".

Filos, Ozounis (2004) define a virtual enterprise as a "particular case of virtual organization. An example of a virtual organization could be a "virtual municipality", associating via a computer network, all the organizations of a municipality, e.g. city hall, municipal water distribution services, internal revenue services, public leisure facilities, cadastre services, etc.".

A virtual enterprise may hence be seen as a subset of virtual organizations. In the following the two terms are not distinguished.

2.1.2 Extended enterprise, virtual teams and workspaces

The concept of extended enterprise (EE), the closest rival term to virtual enterprise, is usually applied to an organization in which a dominant enterprise extends its boundaries to all or some of its suppliers and / or customers[2] [Camarinha-Matos, Afsarmanesh (1999)]. In some cases, it is used for continuous manufacturing collaborations (mass production). Sometimes, extensions cover geographical constraints and creation of distributed, virtual teams is associated with extended enterprises.

The extended enterprise collaborates with suppliers, partners and customers to streamline business processes - going beyond traditional boundaries and enhancing benefits for all. The traditional workplace is no longer bound to a physical location. Offices give way to cubes, cubes become open spaces, and open spaces are turning into a network of distance workers. A workspace is the virtual version of a workplace. And a natural consequence of working anywhere and anytime is working for anyone, hence, the virtual organization, virtual teams and virtual workers. Vitality is associated with activities that can take place anytime, anywhere and anyway one desires, without physical, geographical or structural constraints. In short, the virtual organization is becoming a strategic characteristic applicable to any organization. The new possibilities provided by virtual workspaces in the communication web are realized through use of communication and IT. In an electronic environment, new social structures can appear, be modified and

---

[2] A typical situation in the automotive industry.

experimented on with a speed and to an extent that was not possible in the traditional organization (Karlsson, Eklund; 2002).

2.1.3   Smart organization

The concept of smart organization brings new perspectives to management decision making through an organization. It identifies the key practices that enable successful organizations to deliver a stream of winning products and services. Matheson (1998) describes in his book "The smart organization" that smart organizations have internalized nine interlocking principles essential for creating corporate cultures emphasizing on making the right strategic decisions at the right time. These principles - among them, embracing uncertainty, disciplined decision making and value creation culture - enable companies to make appropriate choices about their R&D planning, portfolio management and product strategies. As far as we know, the leading companies in any industry today are the "smartest" organizations. They absorb knowledge like a sponge from the work they do, the customers they see and the suppliers and partners they deal with. Smart organizations collect and use information. An organization can concentrate on mass production but it cannot stand still as an organization. If a company figure out how to do things better, and those ideas can be shared throughout the company, this company will become smarter and smarter. Matheson also writes that the most effective way to get the return on investments is to present real life conditions and generate conversations where managers can see for themselves what it is they need to do.

Comparing these descriptions of smart organizations with VOs, it may be concluded that VOs supported by networks (see next chapter) enable the realization of the smart organization concept, but do not guarantee it.

2.1.4   The Source of VOs - Networks / Breeding environment

The long-term supporting network forms the underlying environment enabling efficient collaboration in virtual organizations. The term "breeding environment", introduced by Camarinha-Matos, Afsarmanesh (2003), is used for a long term network to emphasize its importance as a basis for VO activities. Typical preparation actions for a network are the development of procedures, standards, common processes and ICT to support the customer deliveries. This preparation is necessary to be able to react quickly to potential business opportunities; that is, to set up a virtual organization to fulfill a customer task.

In addition of configuring and creating virtual organizations, the preparation is needed for the smooth operation and lean management of the VO. Preparation and previous experience contribute to the building of trust between the VO partners. Trust - again - enables faster operation in the inter-enterprise relationships.

Networks or breeding environments are partly created around a specific product / product family / brand and a leading enterprise. Another type of networks, is the case in which the network is formed by organizations located in a common region, although geography is not a major facet when co-operation is supported by computer networks. Nevertheless, the geographical closeness has some advantages for co-operation, as it may facilitate better adaptation to local (culture) needs and an easier creation of a "sense of community". Cultural ties, even particular human relationships, are motivating factors to form such networks which represent in fact the VO breeding environments (VBE) for the dynamic formation of VOs. For each business opportunity found by one of the VBE members, acting as a broker, a subset of the VBE enterprises may be chosen to form a VO for that specific business opportunity.

2.2 Characteristics of virtual organizations

Even though the definitions for virtual organizations and virtual enterprises vary in several senses, some basic characteristics of the virtual organization are often referred to (cf. Eckstein, Albiez, 2002):

- Dematerialization

- Delocalization

- Asynchronization

- Integrative Atomization

- Temporalization

- Non-Institutionalization

- Individualization.

2.2.1 Dematerialization

The term "virtualization" relates to the dematerialization process. With increasing virtualization products become *potential immaterial*. Dematerialization has the following virtual manifestations along the development of the virtualization. A virtual organization has forms such as virtual products and services, telework, virtual teams, virtual workspaces and virtual communities.

Potentially immaterial
Potentially immaterial in this context means, that all object areas are immaterial. An ideal VO defines itself by,

- Common Characteristics
  - uniform manner towards the customer
  - total optimization of the whole value chain
- Absence of physical attributes
  - no common legal roof
  - no common administration/head office
- Special auxiliary specifications
  - matured information technology
  - absolute mutual confidence
  - presence of individual core authority
  - no internal competition
- Utilization effects
  - flexibility and adaptability
  - use of a common synergy potential

2.2.2   Delocalization

Delocalization is one of the most important developments in the globalization process and relates to the dimensions of virtuality. The delocalization is potentially space independent - beyond the decentralization efforts - as virtual areas (the cyberspace) replaces physical locations. Enterprises become independent off space / capacity. It eliminates the need for a particular location.

2.2.3   Asynchronization

The release of time, which takes place in the context of innovations in an organization and is used innovatively for more communication and interactions, is called asynchronization. Asynchronization makes a contribution to the uncoupling of temporal and spatial conditions (virtualization). Traditional enterprises use asynchronization, in order to increase flexibility and stability in their organization.

Potentially time-independent (24-hours organization):
The information technology has paved the way to form an organization for the production of "economy of speed" under the criterion of competitive advantage in the global market. Time has become an important accelerating factor in the context of product innovation, production times, logistics processes etc. These times, which are set free here, can be used for the interaction with the customers (temporal asynchronization). For example, development times of vehicles and software can be reduced substantially by utilizing different time zones. Leading companies like DaimlerChrysler and Hewlett-Packard are thriving on globalization through working "in three shifts" between Europe, America, and Asia. This asynchronous division of labor enables the necessary flexibility. For common communication and coordination information and communication technologies (such as email, voice mail, conferencing systems, etc) are deployed.

2.2.4   Integrative Atomization

The consequent focus on core competences entails the atomization of the value chain. For each individual task in the enterprise a specialized bidder can be found, who often offers a world market standard. The difference to the classical outsourcing is, that here, the integration of all atomized and out-differentiated value-added activities is considered to create processes achieving customer satisfaction - and this not only up to the next customer within the value chain, but up to the last customer, the final consumer. Such initiatives are often made by the enterprises, whose core interest consists of central coordinating of the external value chain.

Physical and virtual creation of value added networks
The virtualization dimensions regarding the optimization of the value-added network have three important consequences in relation to the outsourcing:

1. Focus on core competences

2. Threatening risks and avoiding the fast, unproductive end of the enterprise

3. Integration of the value chain of the customer.

Vertical disintegration and virtual reintegration

Vertical disintegration and virtual reintegration refers to the relationship of supplier and manufacturer. The suppliers were traditionally regarded as "supporters" or as "extended work benches". The virtual revolution now makes them to value chain partners. Manufacturers are forced to assign exclusive manufacturing rights to supplier. But suppliers again are also increasingly dependent on their customer, the manufacturers. This bond of trust is expressed world-wide, in the increase of virtual cross-linking. The information technology compatibility, in particular via Internet, creates more confidence, because of the increase of communication and limited restrictions.

2.2.5 Temporalization

The term temporalization is named with the aspect of time and the temporal limitation of intra- and inter-organizational virtual organizations. The interdependence is described in the life cycle stages of virtual organizations as a circular process of creation, operation, evaluation and dissolution.

The temporalization refers thereby to the inter-organizational relations and to the internal process organization, in the sense of the modular and fractal organization.

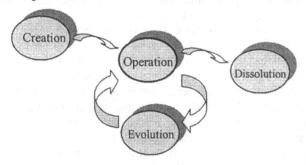

Figure 2: Life cycle stages of a virtual enterprise (Camarinha-Matos, Afsarmanesh, 1999)

2.2.6 Non-Institutionalization

By the renouncement of headquarters and by increasing relocation of the work from office work to telework, the typical physical attributes of an enterprise is becoming virtual. Virtual enterprises, to a large extent, waive the costly and time-intensive institutionalization of their inter-organizational relationships.

2.2.7 Individualization

Individualization is the idea of combining low cost mass production with personalization of products and services. The main reason for this is increasing consumer demands: the consumer requires more and more individualized products, satisfying their personal needs and desires. Mass Customization is one approach for manufacturers to fulfill customer demands, improve competitiveness and capture new markets or market sectors by introducing new products. But, this re-orientation from mass produced to mass customized (individualized) products are challenging. Such a radical change in the product nature forces a revision of the product itself, the processes/organization and the supporting ICT systems within an 'Extended Mass Customizing Enterprise'.

3. VO CORE CONCEPTS – STATE-OF-THE-ART

Within the VOSTER project more than 60 national, European, and global research projects (including IMS), as well as US research and road-mapping activities (IMTI and FIATECH) with focus on state of the art approaches and concepts of virtual organizations/virtual enterprises have been analyzed and consolidated. The main purpose of surveyed VO concepts is to understand the basic elements in the co-operation between enterprises.

The level of preparedness of a network and the tightness of the linkages between the organizations may vary, ranging from an almost open market setting with just some knowledge about the entities between them to entities within a large company or other organization. The preparedness includes defining core competences, harmonizing procedures and interfaces, creating and sharing common knowledge etc. The preparedness makes it possible to set up a VO/VE quickly and operate efficiently over organizational borders. To achieve the preparedness an investment to the network development is needed. In case of different companies the co-operating network can be called an "enterprise network". Other terms sometimes used are enterprise constellations and enterprise associations.

The practical purpose of concepts has in many projects been the business process redesign in the inter-organizational environment. Different projects have addressed different product life cycle phases, different environments and different issues (organizational, human, business, legal, ICT).

Many surveyed research projects present the expected benefits of operating in VOs compared to more traditional forms. It is not analyzed if there are differences between the divergent (outsourcing) and convergent (coming closer) creation of VOs. The implementations do not go far enough to get empirical data of the benefits. As the objectives of the projects have mainly been in developing the tools, processes and methods, there is no sufficient analysis of the prerequisites, realization or dependencies of the success factors in the projects. Thus it is not possible to make a synthesis of them based on the cluster projects. A critical study of the success factors and business drivers of VOs can be seen as a requirement for further VO research.

In the surveyed VO concepts and approaches, the characteristics of virtual organizations (section 2.2) are identifiable. But, the listed characteristics are not alike. Part of them link to the product/ service characteristics (dematerialization, individualization), part of them are linked to the environment or conditions of the VO (delocalization, asynchronization). Atomization and participation are linked to how the VOs operate. It seems that all these characteristics are important in the VO environment, as they have quite commonly been considered. It is easily understood that the requirements of regional distribution and customized products may be better solved by VOs. However, it is not to be interpreted, that these characteristics and

VOs exclusively belong together. That is, the characteristics may appear also in case of non-VO forms and VO-forms may appear without all of these characteristics.

3.1 Management concepts for source network

The main process considered at the source network level is the inclusion of a new partner to the network (rules, policies, tools). Typically in the industrial cases (chapter 4.1) the source network has already existed at some level of co-operation and thus there has not been a need to create the network from the beginning. Another process is the development of the network preparation: procedures, tools and services for the existing network. Product development within the source network is also mentioned.

Nearly all the surveyed projects address the development of information sharing and ICT infrastructures at the source network level. Typically web-based tools and services like organizational models, cost and performance monitoring, have been created for sharing different kinds of information: documentation, product information within the total life cycle. In addition the support for teamwork, design, partner management and tools have been developed.

The main modifications for the implementation of VO management concepts for source network of the VO enterprises were the redesign of business processes, organizations and roles, human resource development and dissemination of quality standards. It has been clearly understood, that it is not enough to develop the IT tools, to make them beneficial also process improvements and redesign are needed.

3.2 VO management concepts

At the VO level the processes considered are set up and configuration of a specific VO and operation and management of VOs (including project management). At this level information sharing is developed for a specific task and VO; supporting also the coordination, people and relationship management. The modifications needed are similar to the source network level: socio-organizational, process and technological redesign. Evaluation and dissolution of VOs were only minor issues.

3.3 VO operational Concept

Concerning the VO operation there is an overlapping with the VO management. This relates to VO phases, the modifications required and ICT infrastructures. The operational processes considered cover the total product life cycle from sales and marketing, product development, engineering, manufacturing (including scheduling and order management) to product operation, service and renewal.

A special question analyzed within VO operation was how individualization correlates with VO operational processes. The main forms of individualization are the mass customization and one-of-kind products, in which not the same resources and capabilities are needed in each project. Thus the VO must be configured separately for each case. In addition individual considerations are needed in different market areas and regionally and culturally distributed environments. The analysis does not clearly explain how these one-to-one features are handled in the surveyed concepts, but probably they must be taken into account in the configuration phase of the VO.

3.4   Structures of virtual organizations

The structures of the source network and VO have been viewed using three different types of topologies: "supply-chain topology", "star/consortia topology" and "peer-to-peer topology". For VOs the structure is viewed separately for operation and governance.

Part of them addressed only the structures of source network or VO, which is depending on the scope of the surveyed projects. The projects, which address all the three types, mainly have the same topology for all of them. In some of the projects more than one topology is possible and even configurable.

The "peer-to-peer" topology appears most often in the projects closely followed by the "Star/consortia" topology while the "supply-chain topology" seems to be less used. At the source network level the "star"-topology refers to networks, which are lead by a strong enterprise. This is often the case in product-centric networks, which are built around a specific product or product family. In "peer-to-peer" networks the enterprises are typically more equal. However, the management structure of a VO created from a "peer-to-peer" network may be "star-like". The equality of the partners means that not always the same company is the leader of the VO.

It looks natural that distributed operations, which aim to a common objective (for example a product), cannot achieve the goal without centralized management. Most used is a hierarchic structure, in which at each level, the level below is managed in the "star"-topology.

3.5   Management roles of source networks and virtual organizations

Management roles are addressed for different product life cycle phases as well as for different network and VO lifecycle phases. Most of the surveyed projects have not considered the management roles at the source network level. This may be the result, because the networks operating in the "peer-to-peer" topology do not have so clear management roles. In the network of "star-like" topology a management role is more stable. Some of the projects mention brokers and broker services supporting the management of the VO.

In the management of source networks and operational VOs the organization or department has a management role. In addition a single person is mentioned in most cases. In some cases an individual is in the background of an organization and in some cases the organization is in the background of a single person. Though a single person seems to be important in the VO management, it cannot live alone without the background support of an organization especially in cases, where high responsibilities and risks exist.

4. VIRTUAL ORGANIZATION CONCEPTS VERSUS TRADITIONAL ORGANIZATIONAL CONCEPTS

4.1   Reasons for and potentials of virtual organizations

Co-operation between enterprises or organizations is not a new phenomenon. For example manufacturing companies have been purchasing raw material, equipment and components from other companies. In some industrial fields, like construction, it has been typical to subcontract also part of the work / tasks to external companies, even within the same job site. This has happened far before the terms network and VO were launched.

Networking can be seen as a more systematic way to build up co-operation with other organizations. In companies it has been seen as an answer to tightening requirements of competitiveness relative to cost-effectiveness, time and quality. In addition it is expected that networking contributes to flexibility, agility, customer orientation and management of risks.

For complete comprehension of collaboration in the virtual organization, it is essential to understand the reasons and motives for the decisions to form co-operation or the building of a VO. Approaching business problems or seeing business opportunities – both can lead the way to the establishment of networks. The motives can come from within the company or from outside, for example internal cost problems versus new market developments. Reasons for collaborating in a VO may include (Büchel a.o., 1998), (Bullinger, 2002), (Balling, 1997), (Harrigan, 1985), (Sell, 2002):

1. Tie down resources which are hard to get on the market
2. Save time, for example reducing development process, time to market
3. Spreading costs and risks with partners
4. Improving access to financial resources
5. Benefits of economies of scale and advantage of size
6. Access to new technology and new customers
7. Access to new markets through partnership
8. Access to innovative managerial practices
9. Diversification, approaching new product or market segments with the help of partners
10. Improve capacity utilization
11. Know-how exchange and sharing of information
12. Creation and exploitation of synergies
13. Ease political tension (overcome trade barriers)
14. Gain access to global networks

In most cases a mixture of these will be the driver for operating and doing business in networks. But the partners' reasons do not need to be the same. This leads to different expectations on all sides of the partnerships. Therefore the definition of the goal of the alliances is essential to the success and the satisfaction of the enterprises involved. There are competitive goals like cost saving, outrival competitors, influencing structural evolution of the industry or the creation of stronger competitive units. Strategic goals can be the creation of synergies, the transfer of technology or diversification.

Potentials of networks are not self-fulfilling; they must be developed and fostered. Thriving on the virtual organization necessitates an efficient management of collaborative tasks and business and a basic, common foundation of the virtual organization.

A virtual organization is always a form of a partnership. Managing partners and the handling of partnerships is crucial, not trivial. There are certain attributes which are very basic for working together with other people and those have to be considered. The first two of them are derived from a business perspective and the following six are basic principles of human interaction. Business partnerships are partnerships – interacting individuals – and therefore the same patterns apply. The important attributes for good partnerships are (Mariotti, 1996):

Business perspectives:

1. Self-interest of both partners – there must be "something in it" of an economic or otherwise beneficial nature for both partners

2. Balance of rewards vs. risks and/ or resources required – the partnership cannot be too lopsided

Basic principles of human interaction:

3. Character – the combination of qualities of features that distinguishes one person, group, or thing from another

4. Integrity – steadfast adherence to a strict moral or ethical code

5. Honesty – marked by or displaying integrity, upright; not deceptive or fraudulent, genuine; characterized by truth, not false, sincere, and frank

6. Trust – firm reliance on the integrity, ability, or character of a person or thing

7. Open communication – a process by which information and ideas are exchanged freely between two parties

8. Fairness – having or exhibiting a disposition that is free of favoritism or bias, impartial; just to all parties, equitable

These are essentials of networking and the foundation for a collaborative edge. We may say, these are the ethics and policy layer of virtual organizations. The following chapter discusses strategy, organization and management of virtual organizations.

4.2   What is new? – Issues in managing virtual organizations

One of the most debated questions about virtual organizations is *"What replaces hierarchy"*. As far as the analyzed partnership is a co-operative organization of parity, the linking type is contractual and *every hierarchy is banned.* The agreeing on the same policy mostly consists of mutual support and advantage, therefore the alignment of actions and stated values requires a common agreement, even if not always completely explicit.

Hierarchies should not exist among the collaborating partners because (Martin, 1995):

- Hierarchies *tend to build barriers* between functional areas, so that a cross functional communication raised in one branch, is channeled into the bottleneck of the high level hierarchical branch and only then can flow down the other branch.

- Hierarchies tend to filter and *distort information* as it is passed upward

- Hierarchies tend to create rules and controls that *increase complexity.* Often the hierarchies multiply themselves creating obsolete heavy mechanisms that are against the peculiar agility of the VO

- Teams *close to the customer* know what actions to take to delight the customer; higher management does not. Teams doing work know better than anyone else how to improve the work process.

Due to the special multi–site configuration of the VO, some additional issues in the collaboration can occur. As found in literature and in previous researches (MUSCLES, 1999) associated to a distributed collaboration (geographic and cultural distances) there are some typical situations that can be avoided with simple advices. A preliminary categorization of the problems groups them into issues associated with:

- People
- Technology
- Process
- Context

The first ones are the issues due to Human Factors: maturity, experience, culture. The issues related to the behavior of mangers, employees, and people in general and are the most difficult to solve. Only a slow, evolving process can change habitudes and let working cultures grow together.

The issues due to technology often relate to the tools utilized by the collaborators. The development and *utilization of ICT* is a critical element in the current networking. It can be seen as an enabler for distributed co-operation - even if its potential is currently still underused. Incompatibility of data formats, non-availability of network links, different platforms, can not only slow down the processes – the bottle neck is in the data exchange, so in communication – but also can lead to errors – like approximations and losing of information.

The issues related with processes are often found in particularly complex collaborative processes. The main issue in this case is the co-ordination. Bad timings, not clear operations, incompatibility and low interoperability always lead to delays and additional costs. Often a common planning is missing, so the need of a common project management and project strategy, becomes vital.

Adding to these problems there are all the issues due to the context, less controllable but often foreseeable. It is about the market stability, the demand fluctuations, but often the problems are still into the companies, like structural problems and lack of resources. The context in this case is no more external but internal and maybe within the VO.

The table below shows the most common issues in a collaborative work environment:

PEOPLE
Unaccustomed to teamwork: Team members may be experts in their own technical fields but unaccustomed to the particular requirements of collaborative work. Building teams of mixed experiences, special team-trainings and support from team externals in early phases are adequate countermeasures.

Different management styles: If management styles don't fit, dysfunctionalities must be expected. Identifying and understanding of differences in management style is the basis for evolvement of common culture and decision making. Oral or written agreements widely communicated supports the acceptance of a joint decision culture.

Team building: The difficulty of tracing the boundaries of a team and its tasks can lead to various problems. Teams and tasks are often not defined well enough. A successful team needs a set of common goals and values, shared responsibility, relationship and trust. Ensuring a shared vision, providing an adequate infrastructure and an accurate selection and assessment of the team increase team .

Cultural and language barriers: A feeling of discomfort and distance increased by language barriers. Different professional cultures, different corporate cultures, nationality barriers are often a problem. Promoting team awareness and support of adequate communication media should help to establish a "team climate". Shared values of each of the cultures; finding a new team-based culture, use of agreed codes, protocols, and cross-cultural training are further means to overcome cultural barriers.

Team trust: One of the most difficult issues to be obtained within collaborating people. A lack of team trust can lead to information hiding and stop in communication. Trust tends to be built over team performance. Face to face meetings can consolidate the team trust at the beginning of the project, when significant personnel changes, or for critical decisions.

TECHNOLOGY

Data compatibility: Distributed information can often not be used because of format incompatibility. Many costless software systems can transform the data produced into files of a standard format (pdf, html, java). A minimum hardware support is needed. As migration to new standard may be costing, format translators can be found in commerce.

Availability of appropriate communication networks: Slow and inappropriate networks are one of the greatest lack in collaborating companies.
The problem issue becomes a problem of cost and planning of a reasonable commercial solution, in order to ensure the respect of all the requirements. The solution covers both the infrastructure and the work structure planning.

PROCESS

Project complexity: The project articulation can leave out some responsibilities and the horizon of the task can be too wide. Often the project status and the progress are not clear. Communication lacks are very sensible. A good communication structure can support difficulties in complex projects. The use of a forum with a dedicated "war room" can be set up. In this forum the status, the progress and all the changes are regularly updated.

CONTEXT

Different Working practices: Some of the behaviors found in distributed teams arising from local conditions require management strategies. A lack of a strategy to handle working practices may lead to emphasize the national and cultural barriers. The strategies should be documented and available to all the team members. Study the probable workflow and optimize the working practices.

Resources: The availability of skilled workers, adequate time to undertake tasks and an appropriate communication infrastructure are the most important resource issues. In the planning phase it is essential to consult people experienced in multi site-operations, so that they can provide realistic estimates of the resources that will be needed.
Industry stability: Turbulence and transition in the industry can seriously hamper multi –site operations, especially with international collaborating groups. It is important to maintain trust within the team during periods of instability. Good communications should be ensured and a equitable distribution of power.
Insufficient corporate structures: The maturity level and the structure of the companies affect the good project behavior. The use of project oriented teams, but above all project management solutions in order to establish an order in the organizational structure.

Table 1: Issues and solutions within multi-site collaborations
(adapted from MUSCLES, 1999)

4.3 Management areas

A recent case study research (cf. Dold et al, 2004) shows typical management topics in collaborative environments and allows deduction of the relevant management areas. Topics covered in the case study include the strategic backbone of the collaborations, overall collaborative business processes, collaboration mechanisms, structures and procedures for knowledge transfer as well as problems encountered during the collaboration. The analysis of the interviewed networks highlighted typical problems for the management and operation of critical issues in different thematic areas:

- *Integration strategy:* The main finding is an overall lack of a common strategic approach and of a formal agreement that establishes the sharing of benefits and risks between partners.

- *Collaboration:* Language and cultural issues play a fundamental role: different languages and working cultures can hinder the daily activities. Difficulties in establishing a community spirit and in changing from a competitive attitude to a collaborative one. For VOs as well as for global organizations there is an increasing need to get groups of people sometimes from different nationalities to work together effectively either as enduring management teams or to resource specific projects addressing key business objectives. The cultural management in VOs has the tasks of building awareness of the cultural differences, developing knowledge about the impact on the business of those differences and - most important - building skills to over-come cultural caused problems and to benefit from the cultural diversity.

- *Knowledge sharing:* No knowledge management strategy is currently performed in any of the analyzed case studies; this implies a dispersion of distinctive know-how and competences and difficulties in the exchange of information (the excess of paper based information flow). An effective knowledge/information transfer can only be achieved by different coherent means: the fostering of relationship and trust building, the activation of formal communication channels in parallel with informal ones and the overcoming of rigid hierarchical communication procedures. VOs still experience the lack of adequate tools for knowledge/document base management and an excess of paper based information flow. One of the possible reasons to collaborate is to gain knowledge the partners already have, so to complement each other by collaborating. The knowledge transfer is therefore especially in technology intensive industries of essential importance. The learning capacity of organizations becomes a sustainable competitive advantage.

- *Technology and Information Technology:* In this area the necessity of bridging the gap in technical expertise, technological infrastructure and IT tools (software integration and compatibility) is the first need of each virtual organization. The partners need the same or similar technology levels for all relevant interaction areas. This covers collaboration/ communication tools, project management tools as well as logistic-supporting ICT-systems. Best and up-to date communication, knowledge exchange and development tools available, accessible and ex-changeable for every team member. Highly educated employees at all partners are essential for successful collaboration.

- *Organization:* Different standards for production and product development technology within VOs are a frequent source of inefficient processes and redundant work. Need for common working procedures and wide cross-organizational labor mobility aiming at assimilating common practices. Legal and organizational structure should be clear and should not give cause for misunderstandings. This includes the legal structure of the VO and the operational management of the day-to-day tasks. Organization includes the implementation of coherent and common management procedures strategic aspects and operational management and collaboration.

- *Logistics:* Lack in common planning and warehouses managing, difficulties in coordinating and tracking deliveries.

- *Project Management:* A strong necessity of improving co-operation and project management processes has emerged, due to insufficient visibility on partner's activities and lack of inter-functional coordination.

In order to tackle the expressed issues and needs a framework for the management of the virtual organizations has been conceived (see Figure 4). The framework includes the main topics that need to be addressed and can be seen as a cluster of methodologies that has been developed with the aim of accompanying companies along their evolution path towards the efficient and competitive virtual organization.

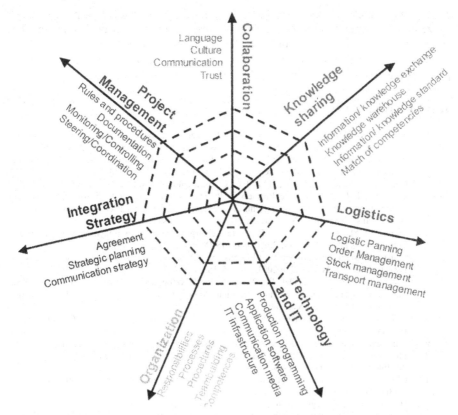

Figure 3: Framework for the management of the virtual organizations (Boer et al, 2002)

The planned evolution of a virtual organization is a complex management matter of several dimensions. An integrative approach for the management of these dimensions, based on a mutual and agreed development path towards a certain collaboration level, may support VOs in identifying and exploring a common competitive edge. The basis for such a development is trust. Here we would like to quote from one case study: *"...trust in the virtual organization means predictability of behavior and reactions in common issues. This can only be achieved within a win-win situation. This is the foundation for any collaboration".*

5. CONCLUSION

In the context of inter-enterprise co-operations, there exist two basic types of concepts 'network/source network/support network/breeding environment' and 'virtual organization/virtual enterprise'. Most of the analyzed research projects/initiatives/etc. has focused on the development of methods, tools and infrastructures for specific business processes, starting from an existing network and focusing on the creation and operation of the virtual organizations. VO concepts and approaches for the evaluation phase and dissolution phase of virtual organizations was not main focus of research. There is not sufficient analysis of prerequisites, realization, or dependencies of the VO success factors. A critical study of the success factors and business drivers of virtual organizations can be seen as a requirement for further VO research. As a final conclusion, there are still many open questions and research needs in the field of virtual organizations!

6. REFERENCES

1. Balling, R.: Kooperationen, Strategische Allianzen, Netzwerke, Joint-Ventures und andere Organisationsformen zwischenbetrieblicher Zusammenarbeit in Theorie und Praxis, 1997.
2. Boer, C.; Bosani, R.; Dold, C.; Nøstdal, R.; Pierpaoli, F.; Ristol Jorba, S.: The Prominence Project. In: Proceedings of the ACS'02 – SCM Conference, October 23-25, Poland, 2002
3. Büchel, B.; Prange, C.; Probst, G.; Rüling, C.: International Joint Venture Management, 1998.
4. Bullinger, H.J.: Collaborative Business – Unternehmensübergreifende Wertschöpfungsketten organisatorisch und informationstechnisch unterstützen, Forum mit Fachausstellung am 9. Juli 2002 am Institutszentrum Stuttgart der Fraunhofer Gesellschaft, 2002.
5. Camarinha-Matos, Afsarmanesh; The virtual enterprise concept; in Infrastructures for Virtual Enterprises, Kluwer Academic Publishers, ISBN 0-7923-8639-6, 1999.
6. Camarinha-Matos, Afsarmanesh; Elements of a base VE infrastructure; J. Computers in Industry, Vol. 51, Issue 2, Jun 2003, pp. 139-163.
7. Dold, C.; Mauro, P.; Nøstdal, R.; Pierpaoli, F.: Development and management of East-West European extended enterprises. In: Camarinha-Matos, L.M.; Afsarmanesh, H.: Processes and foundations for virtual organizations, 2004
8. Eckstein, Albiez; E-Organisations: Life Cycle Support für Virtuelle Organisationen, Fraunhofer IAO; 2002.
9. European Commission; http://europa.eu.int/ISPO/ecommerce/books/aecev2/2_1.htm.
10. Filos, Ozounis; Virtual organisations Technologies, Trends, Standards and the Contribution of the European RTD Programmes, 2004.
11. Globmen-Project, Global Engineering and Manufacturing in Enterprise Networks [IST-1999-60002 IMS 99004], 2000.
12. Harrigan, K.R.: Strategies for Joint Ventures, 1985.
13. Karlsson, Eklund; Managing the Extended Enterprise; http://www.abo.fi/~jonkarls/mit.htm, 2002.
14. Mariotti, J.L.: The Power of Partnership – The Next Step beyond TQM, Reengineering and Lean Production, 1996.
15. Martin, James: The Great Transition: Using the seven disciplines of enterprise engineering to align people, technology and strategy (1995)- New York: Amacom.
16. Matheson, James E.: The Smart Organization: Creating Value Through Strategic R&D, Harvard Business School Press; ISBN: 087584765X, 1998.
17. MBDA, 2001, http://www.mbda.gov/templates/ printer.php?content_id=538.
18. MUSCLES: Multi-site concurrent engineering for large aircraft engineering and support. Project funded by the European commission in the Industrial and Material Technologies Program, 1999.
19. Saabeel, W.; Verduijn, T.M.; Hagdorn, L.; Kumar, K: A model of Virtual Organisation: A structure and process perspective, in: Electronic Journal of Organizational Virtualness, Vol. 4, No. 1, 2002.
20. Sell, A.: Internationale Unternehmenskooperationen, 2002.

MODELING FOR VIRTUAL ORGANIZATIONS

1.3

Hermann Löh, Chunyan Zhang, Bernhard Katzy
CeTIM– Centre for Technology and Innovation Management
Werner-Heisenberg- Weg 39, 85579 Munich-Neubiberg, Germany
hermann.loeh@cetim.org, chunyan.zhang@cetim.org, prof.katzy@cetim.org

The development of virtual organizations, but also their introduction in practice requires models depicting the concepts and supporting communication and understanding. Most research and development projects for virtual organizations have focused on modeling for system design and used related models and tools. However, these approaches are not well suited to capture the underlying VO business architecture and concepts resulting in less progress in this field. This chapter discusses a broader spectrum of modeling approaches from management-oriented, conceptual models to system design and enactment. It proposes a staged modeling process both for practical VO implementation and for research and tool development. This approach should support advancing the conceptual, technical and practical state of the art in the virtual organization domain.

1. INTRODUCTION

Virtual Organizations can take a broad variety of different forms such as collaborative supply chains, project organizations or networks of small and medium sized enterprises. They all employ some characteristics of virtual organizing to gain competitive advantage as outlined in the previous chapter:

- Combination of competences and resources from different partners (Integrative Atomization)
- Project-oriented organization with fast recombination of partners, roles and processes (Temporalization)
- No legal or other formal structures (Dematerialization, Non-institutionalization)
- Geographically dispersed working (Delocalization)

Usually, the search or need for agility and innovation (Goldman, Nagel et al. 1995; Walker, Kogut et al. 1997) are the main drivers towards more virtual or networked organizations – implying that they need to constantly readjust to changing business requirements. But despite the potential flux, some organizational design has to be done and made explicit. Modeling is a very suitable means to aid designing, communicating, and implementing virtual organizations.

Managers wanting to introduce a virtual organization or are operating in them require models especially for understanding and communication. Since different partners with different ideas and mental models come together in a VO, they need a common basis for discussing and negotiating structures and processes, and also for training the people operating in them. In the future, models might even directly drive transactions and workflows in model based IT systems, allowing faster changes in processes.

Researchers and designers developing tools and methods for virtual organizations require blueprints of organizational architecture and processes as basis for their work. Models help to make assumptions explicit and allow evaluation and comparison of different forms of virtual organizations as well as of the solutions developed.

The objective of the chapter is to present modeling approaches for the design and implementation of virtual organizations and for developing tools and methods for them. Other applications such as modeling for analyzing specific organizations or for detailed software design and interoperability support require different models (e.g. graph models, entity relationship diagrams), even though researchers and developers working in these fields should also consider especially the architectural and process models presented here as first steps for their work.

The chapter is structured as follows: the next section introduces the research method used for deriving the methods and recommendations presented in this chapter, followed by a short general introduction to models and purposes for modeling. This provides a framework for the different modeling approaches portrayed in the subsequent section. A critical analysis of the approaches used in business implementation and European research projects are the basis for recommending a practical process for modeling in these contexts, but also for suggesting future work to advance modeling methodologies.

2.   RESEARCH METHOD

The authors have reviewed various modeling methodologies and models proposed in the literature. This was the basis for a semi-structured questionnaire on modeling methods employed, models developed, and experiences from the modeling process. The questionnaire was used in a survey among 29 research projects funded by the EU IST program with 22 valid questionnaire returns. The other projects did not pursue any modeling activities. Additionally, the projects provided project overviews, publications, and reports and allowed clarification of any issues through telephone interviews.

Further, about 100 papers on virtual organizations presented at the ICE-conferences 2001, 2002 and 2003 and at the PRO-VE-conferences 2002 (Camarinha-Matos 2002) and 2003 (Camarinha-Matos & Afsarmanesh 2003) were evaluated regarding their modeling approaches and related model results.

Additionally, the authors have first hand practical experience in the development and implementation of about ten virtual organizations, which allowed a critical reflection of the literature review and survey results, as well as the suggestion of tested modeling approaches.

3. INTRODUCTION TO MODELS

Models and modeling are an integral part of human understanding and thinking. Since reality is usually too complex to understand and influence directly, we develop models of reality either in our minds (mental models) or formally using drawings or other representations including computer models. Imagine the activities in a company to achieve a business purpose such as the fulfillment of a customer order. For modeling this order fulfillment process, one would capture the typical activities, combine directly related ones into a "process step" and describe the link between these steps or alternative routes. Depending on the purpose of the modeling, the most useful model can vary considerably, e.g. by:

- Summarizing a group of activities under one heading or describing each individually
- Capturing only the "standard" process of activities, or exemptions with alternative routes
- Describing only the activities, or also responsibilities, input and output of each step, or the required resources
- Being noted as a text or simple graphic, or in the format of a formal modeling language such as IDEF0, UML flow diagram, or event driven process chain (ARIS).

In any case, such model represents only some aspects of reality — the ones most relevant for the purpose at hand.

To differentiate modeling approaches and the resulting models, it is necessary to understand the purpose for which they are used. But even the same modeling framework and language might yield very different and not compatible or interoperable results if used for different purposes. The following is a list of purposes of enterprise modeling, which is derived from a number of recent references on enterprise modeling (Kosanke 1997; Bacquet 2002; Bernus, Baltrusch et al. 2002; Chen, Vallespir et al. 2002; Tølle, Bernus et al. 2002):

- Support the development and understanding of the organizational structure and processes for the management
- Define and document ways how partners collaborate in virtual organisations for the human actors involved
- Support enterprise and business process reengineering
- Document the solution domain (e.g. actors, objects, standard processes)
- Document software requirements (e.g. system processes, entity relationships)
- Document computer systems (e.g. system architecture, system objects)
- Allow computer enactment of the models
- Define standards for data exchange and process behaviours
- Establish system interoperability requirements

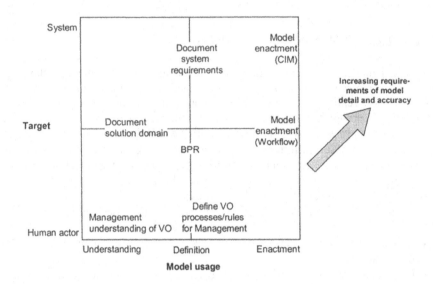

Figure 1: Positioning framework for purposes of modeling

Figure 1 positions the different purposes for modeling in a matrix with one dimension being the target user (human actors use the model or it is targeted to be used in the context of computer system) and the second being the type of usage (understanding the enterprise or system, defining it, or enacting elements of it through the model).

The lower and further left the objective for the modeling is positioned, the simpler and easier to understand the models should be. A model to support management requires a very simple notation and less detail. It can therefore usually not directly be used for system designs, as it lacks the definition of the full system behavior and any process exemptions. On the other hand, the further the objective is placed in the upper and right corner, the more detailed and accurate the models must be. Correspondingly, the effort for modeling will increase, while the flexibility to change the models decreases. Such model would also not well support human understanding or communication due to its complexity.

4. EXAMPLES OF MODEL APPROACHES

This section intends to illustrate how enterprise models can support the definition, implementation, and operation of virtual organizations. As introduced in the last section, different model approaches exist for different application areas (e.g. information system design, business process reengineering). We have selected and grouped them into four different categories which have proved to be most relevant for supporting the VO life cycle. Figure 2 positions the different enterprise models according to their main purpose.

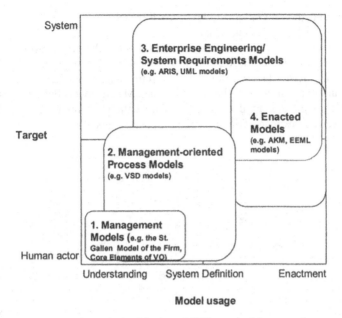

Figure 2: Positioning of different model approaches

The following sections introduce the model approaches in more detail and relate them to their usage in a VO context.

4.1. Management Models

Management models depict the core concepts and elements of the (virtual) organization. They usually set the frame of reference or high-level architecture of the VO, and thus support understanding and discussing the main principles. There are two types of management models: framework models which are used as checklists or structures to design organizations, and concept models which depict the principles of structure and operations.

Due to their high-level and conceptual nature, management models need subsequent detailing with process models or enterprise integration models. However, the project survey and paper analysis has shown that the limited usage of management models especially by researchers and system developers is a major impediment for advancing the state of the art in the VO domain.

4.1.1. Framework Models

The main purpose of framework models is to provide a structure for thinking about and defining organizations. As such, they are primarily an "empty shell" with different place holders and their relationships. These serve as a checklist of what elements should be defined by management or discussed in order to make assumptions about them explicit.

This model approach understands an organization and its development as a complex system and process, which can only partly be "designed" and is more the result of the negotiations and actions of the people involved.

Figure 3 depicts the St. Gallen Model of the Firm (Rüegg-Stürm 2002) as an example for such model. At the centre stands the operative core of different processes, which are however influenced by strategies, structures and the organizational culture and changed over time either through optimization or through steps of renewal. Further internal and external factors, but also different stakeholders have influence on the behavior and opportunities of the organization. Management, but also researchers should go through such model and either define the elements or discuss the potential influence or relevance of them for the purpose at hand.

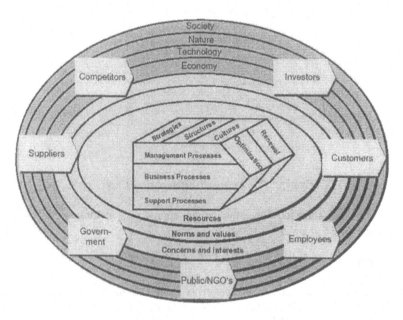

Figure 3: St. Gallen Model of the Firm

A number of such models can be found in literature, of which Friedli (2000) and Klein et al. (2004) are specifically geared towards virtual organizations.

4.1.2. Concept Models

Concept models depict the main principles and elements of the virtual organization, which could include for example: How do the different partners relate to one another, what is the structure of the business processes, what are the main roles, how are business and IT systems related? Such concept models depict the high-level business architecture.

Figure 4 shows as example a model of the core elements of a VO (Katzy and Schuh 1997) pursuing short-term business opportunities: Different companies, depicted through their core competencies as potential process contributions, are members of a network. To pursue a business opportunity, they combine the required contributions to a process chain within a short-term project.

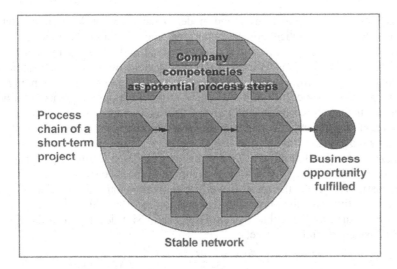

Figure 4: the core elements of the VO

As people in a VO usually come from different organizational and sometimes even cultural background, they will have different understanding of the purposes and functioning of the VO. The model above implies for example:

- Companies should analyze and "model" their core competencies, e.g. in a common database for the network.
- There need to be mechanisms – processes, people and tools – that can describe a business opportunity in terms of required competencies, select the right companies, and combine them to a process chain.

Concept models thus allow better understanding and discussion of the new ways of operating. They also provide a necessary basis for the further development of processes or IT systems.

Such concept models would be well suited to build a library of architectural reference models for different types of virtual organizations. However, only very few projects have provided contributions in this area.

4.2. Management-oriented Process Models

Operative work in organizations is nowadays usually understood as business and management processes. Such processes define the order and relationships between activities necessary to reach a business objective such as fulfilling a customer order or developing a new product. Since the collaboration and specific products in a VO change from project to project, it is of great importance that the people involved in the operations and management have a common understanding of the processes and responsibilities.

We term models suitable for this purpose management-oriented process models. They often do not need to be very detailed as the persons involved usually know their own activities, but the model should especially depict the collaboration and coordination spanning different locations or organizations. Similarly, they provide blueprints which do not need to cover all exemptions and special cases that could occur; should such case occur, it is often less effort in a VO to discuss the situation and actions than to try to foresee and model all possibilities. More important than detail is thus the simplicity of designing and understanding the models, as they should be developed by the people actively involved in the VO, not by specialists.

Consequently, the models are not directly suitable for systems development or system enactment. However, such models can contribute to the understanding of the overall process – especially as they can be better developed together with people involved in managing and operating VOs than when more complex modeling approaches are used – and thus speed up the system definition process.

Many modeling methodologies and languages used in enterprise engineering and system requirement definition could also be (and are) used for management-oriented process models, such as ARIS's event controlled process chains or UML's process flow charts. However, the tools as well as the notation are not as simple to use as would be optimal for the purpose. A better alternative are purpose designed model approaches such as the Value System Designer (VSD) developed in the European BAP (Business Architect Project).

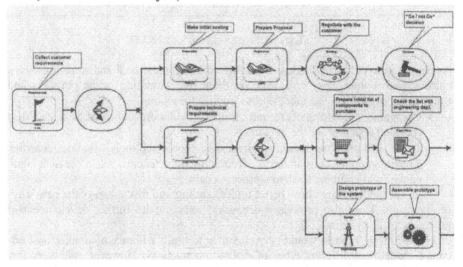

Figure 5: Example of process model created with VSD

Figure 5 shows an example of a Management-oriented Process Model created through VSD. The primary activities in the process, as well as the coordination and communication points are visualized by easy to understand graphical constructs. The models can be directly published to e.g. a VO collaboration space for joint viewing and discussion, but also for training the people involved in the VO. In a VO project done by the authors, employees could develop own processes with the tool after 15-30 minutes training, and received process feedback from others who never had any training or explanation of business process models.

The management-oriented process models are also best suited to build reference process libraries for VO processes. They capture the core principles of the different processes, but are much easier to generalize and transfer than more complex enterprise engineering oriented models. Other users can understand them quite easily and adapt them to their specific applications.

4.3. Enterprise Engineering/System Requirements Models

Most researchers and developers active in the field of information systems and technologies think first of this type of models when discussing VO modeling. Different systematics and methodologies such as CIMOSA (CIM Open System Architecturewww.cimosa.de)or GERAM (Generalized Enterprise Reference Architecture and Methodology, www.cit.gu.edu.au/~bernus/taskforce/geram/versions/geram1-6-2/), model notations such as the IDEF (Integrated DEFinition, www.idef.com) family or UML (Unified Modeling Language, www.uml.org) and modeling tools such as ARIS or RationalRose were developed to support the translation of the business domain and its requirements into suitable system designs and configurations.

The requirements of these model approaches are driven by system engineering, not by management or worker understanding and training. The aforementioned management models do not provide the comprehensive data and rules to completely define a system.

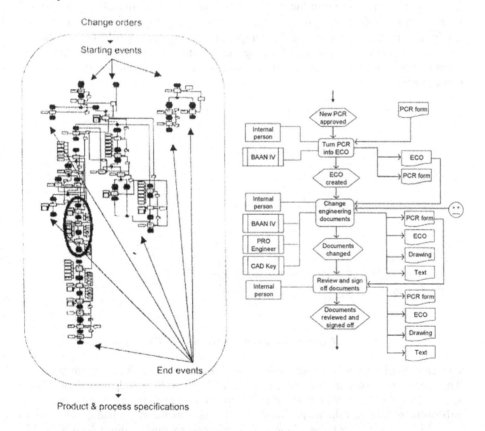

Figure 6a: Engineering change order (ECO)   Figure 6b: Excerpt from ECO process model
process model (ARIS)

Figure 6 depicts an engineering change order (ECO) process model created using ARIS (Sousa, Van Aken et al. 2002) both as full process, and as excerpt. This process view shows also the roles, systems and related information objects. It is only one part or view of a model required for a system definition, which would also include data (entity relationship) and object views. A developer can derive from this model the requirements for the system design.

These types of models tend to become very complex and thus difficult to comprehend and change. Usually the support of specialists is required to develop these models, because of which they are not well suited for supporting the fast configuration and implementation of virtual organizations. Instead their domain lies in defining e.g. tools and applications for supporting VOs.

4.4. Enacted Models

The main idea of enacted model approaches is to capture the business activities, necessary data, and related logic in suitable models that can be directly used to drive IT applications and tools. Instead of the need for reprogramming the application logic by IT specialists, business analysts together with the users could make changes in the collaboration set-up or the workflow through changing models that are somewhat easier to work with. This technology can be used within a single company, but is of course more appropriate for the changing requirements of virtual organizations.

Figure 7 shows a task model for usage in an enacted system environment. Also Chapter 1.5 in this book expounds in more detail this model approach and gives further examples.

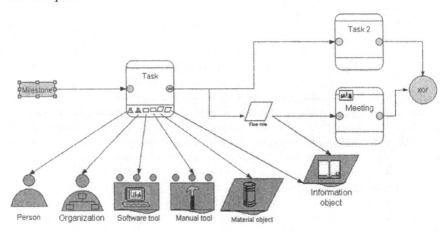

Figure 7: A process model created through EEML for enactment

Currently applications enacting models in a VO context are still in a prototype stage. Therefore, their potential for future usage cannot yet be fully judged. There is however a strong push towards model driven application development as this would significantly reduce development times and efforts. On the other hand, only certain parts or activities of VO operations lend themselves to support through workflow or other enacted model driven applications. A certain element of standardization and repetition are required, such that e.g. many management or governance processes, but also product development or research are not well suited. On the other hand, complex data requirements and business logic still entails very careful and time-consuming development work.

In any case, the organizational architecture and business model of the VO need to be defined before enacted model approaches should be employed.

5. ANALYSIS OF THE VO MODELLING APPROACHES IN RESEARCH PROJECTS

This section analyzes which model approaches the different research projects have used for their purposes, and the results and experiences with the approach chosen. The results are based on the returned surveys from 22 projects plus the evaluation of related conference papers.

Figure 8 gives an overview of the different modeling purposes of the projects. The figure shows that most of the projects have focused on system requirements and engineering, which is to be expected from projects of the European IST research program. Some have explored model enactment for directly supporting VOs. Few projects have focused on human understanding and management of VOs and on organizational reference models.

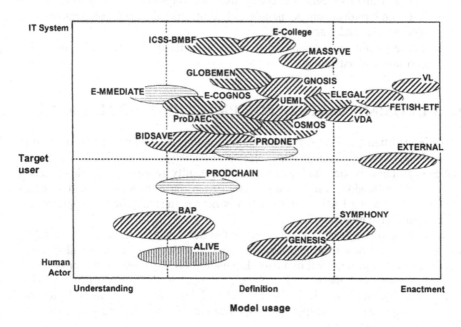

Figure 8: overview of VO modeling purpose

The projects focusing on system requirements all used enterprise engineering or integration model approaches, e.g. ARIS or UML. The analysis of the research projects and conference papers showed that almost 75% of projects have used such detailed models from the beginning, without first defining the organizational structure, high-level processes and main operational principles using management-oriented models. However a project management process and related tools for example need to be designed very differently in a supply-chain oriented VO compared to a large construction project VO with a main contractor, or a laterally organized research project. Without making the assumptions of the organizational context and its requirements explicit, the solutions developed are often not well adapted to the real business needs. Additionally, this lack of organizational reference models and grounding (see also Chapter 1.4 for a systematic of reference models) also fosters a tendency to reinvent the wheel and not building on the VO principles and solutions already available.

Another area of analysis focused on the practical modeling process, the responsibility for modeling, and experiences. The majority of the projects indicated that the research institutes did the actual model development, while companies provided user requirements and feedback. Half of the projects pointed out that a major problem in modeling was the limited experience of both, the industrial users and research institutes, not in formally using the tools or the modeling notations, but in practical modeling know-how: e.g. choosing the right level of detail, placing good questions to understand the business domain, or discerning the standard process from the exception. Another significant problem was the absence of organizational reference architectures and process models as basis for the specific modeling activities.

Lessons learnt from the modeling processes emphasized especially:

- Early user involvement is extremely important for successful modeling.
- Start with top-level, simple models with limited detail before going into detailed process and data models.
- Choose suitable model approaches and tools to minimize efforts and support good user understanding.

6. RECOMMENDATION FOR PRACTICAL VO MODELING

Modeling is often a critical part in both practical VO implementation projects and in research and system development projects. The analysis of past modeling efforts indicates that practitioners and researchers are not fully aware of a suitable modeling process and methodologies. Or they stick – often out of principle – with one approach such as using UML even though it is not the most appropriate approach for all or a part of the modeling effort.

Therefore we suggest a practical and at the same time systematic VO modeling process which moves from high-level architectural design to more detailed levels according to the project requirements. Depending on the needs of the project, the process can stop with the second step – e.g. in a practical VO implementation context – or include the third step – e.g. for VO tool development. Figure 9 depicts the different steps and an example of the application of this modeling process can be found e.g. in (Loeh 2000).

Step 1: Develop business architecture for VO or adopt it from reference models
The first step in the VO definition process should be the development or adoption of a suitable business architecture. This includes the high-level organizational structure and roles, the logic of business processes and cooperation mechanisms. Relatively simple conceptual management models – e.g. as graphical drawings – are usually sufficient for this purpose. Framework models or conceptual reference models as presented in Chapter 1.4 support this step. The VO management team or the re-

search project team should discuss and iterate these models until they have reached understanding and agreement.

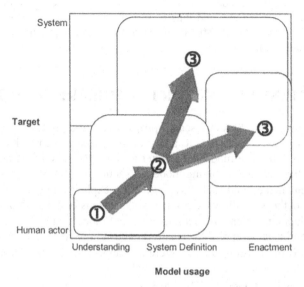

Figure 9: Suggested VO modeling process

Step 2: Detail processes and roles to a level sufficient for employees or researchers to understand (and operate in) new organization

Based on the high-level business architecture, management and people involved in the operations can detail the relevant processes depicting the flow and relationship of the activities. The detail should be sufficient to show the main hand-over and co-ordination steps especially between partners in a VO, but not each working step. For most processes, 15 to 30 steps are a suitable level of detail, allowing people to still keep the overview.

This stage in the modeling activity should be strongly driven by people involved in the processes, although a coach familiar with the modeling methodology is usu-ally necessary as support. Nevertheless, it is advisable to employ a simple to use management-oriented process modeling language to foster user involvement, fast changes and broad communication. Especially in VOs, the different partners need to be able to understand, discuss and adapt the models.

Many practical VO implementation projects do not need to proceed further, but also system development projects should not omit this step, as they gain a thorough understanding and grounding for the further development work.

Step 3: Detail processes, data requirements and views for system development or system enactment

With the business architecture and process models available, there is a good basis for further system requirements engineering. In this step, modeling is driven by sys-tem architects or analysts, but still needs user involvement to clarify critical issues. Iteratively detail is added to the different models. However, as detail increases, models become more and more complex and thus more difficult to change. Errors are sometimes difficult to track as they can propagate through the different models. Inexperienced modelers can easily get lost in too much detail and loose tack of the actual business purposes.

Enacted Model approaches seem to be quite promising to speed the process from definition to system deployment and thus to support fast reconfiguration and learning cycles. As the technology is still quite early in its development little practical experience is already available.

7. RECOMMENDATIONS FOR FURTHER RESEARCH

The analysis of more than 20 VO research projects and 100 conference papers has shown the need for a more systematic and professional approach to modeling and the development of reference models. To better advance the state of the art in virtual organizations, future research applying modeling should:

- Ground their method and tool development on explicit architectural and process models of the VO, allowing comparison and transfer of the solutions.
- Review, adopt and extend available (reference) models and VO concepts suitable for their business application instead of designing from scratch.
- Contribute to the development of reference models for Virtual Organizations; make modeling results more broadly available.
- Carefully plan the modeling steps and select suitable tools for each step.
- Engage the people practically involved in the VO in the modeling effort.
- Plan for training and expertise development as modeling is a skill.

But also modeling methodologies require further research and developments, from a VO perspective especially in the areas:

- Most enterprise and system requirements engineering methodologies have a mathematical and informatics background, which are strongly concerned with formal notations and algorithm validity. Simpler to use, business focused methodologies and notations are required.
- Modeling tools should better support distributed modeling efforts, discussion of models and fast changes – requirements imposed by the nature of VOs.
- Reference model libraries for VO architectures and processes, which allow the selection and application of the solutions based on different VO business models and configurations, should be systematically built.

8. CONCLUSIONS

Modeling can provide important support for the implementation of virtual organizations and the development of new methods and tools for them. We have presented a number of different model approaches and positioned them according to their purpose and application. The analysis of recent research and development efforts has led to recommendations both for practical modeling activities in developing and implementing virtual organizations and for directing future research activities.

A book chapter cannot provide a complete training guide but it should have sensitized practitioners and researchers for current limitations and the opportunities of modeling for VO implementation and research.

9. REFERENCES

Bacquet, J. (2002). "Plug and Do Business" and the European R&D Programmes. Collaborative Business Ecosystems and Virtual Enterprises. L. Camarinha-Matos, Kluwer Publisher: 283-292.

Bernus, P., R. Baltrusch, et al. (2002). Fast Tracking ICT Infrastructure Requirements and Design Based on Enterprise Reference Architecture and Matching Reference Models. Collaborative Business Ecosystems and Virtual Enterprises. L. Camarinha-Matos, Kluwer Publisher: 293-302.

Camarinha-Matos, L. M. (Ed.) (2002). Collaborative Business Ecosystems and Virtual Enterprises, Kluwer Academic Publishers, ISBN 1-4020-7020-9.

Camarinha-Matos, L. M., Afsarmanesh, H. (Ed.s) (2003). Processes and foundations for virtual organizations, Kluwer Academic Publishers, ISBN 1-4020-7638-X.

Chen, D., B. Vallespir, et al. (2002). Developing an Unified Enterprise Modelling Language (UEML) - Requirements and Roadmap. Collaborative Business Ecosystems and Virtual Enterprises. L. Camarinha-Matos, Kluwer Publisher: 247-254.

Friedli, T. (2000). Die Architektur von Kooperationen. Bamberg, Difo-Druck.

Goldman, S. L., R. N. Nagel, et al. (1995). Agile Competitors and Virtual Organizations - Strategies for Enriching the Customer. New York, Van Nostrand Reinhold.

Katzy, B. R. and G. Schuh (1997). The Virtual Enterprise. Handbook of Life Cycle Engineering: Concepts, Methods and Tools. A. Molina, J. M. Sanchez and A. Kusiak. New York, Chapman & Hall.

Klein, S., A. Poulymenakou, et al. (2004). IOIS and interfirm networks - interdependencies and managerial challenges. Inter-Organizational Information Systems in the Internet Age. S. B. Eom. Hershey, Idea Publishing.

Kosanke, K. (1997). Comparison of enterprise modelling methodologies. Information infrastructure systems for manufacturing, proceedings of DIISM'96, international conference on the design of information infrastructure systems for manufactureing. J. Goossenaerts, F. Kimura and H. Wortmann, Chapman and Hall.

Loeh, H. (2000). A Coordination Framework for Complex Production Networks. Imperial College. London, University of London.

Rüegg-Stürm, J. (2002). Das neue St. Galler Management-Modell, Haupt.

Sousa, G. W. L., E. M. Van Aken, et al. (2002). "Applying an enterprise engineering approach to engineering work: a focus on business process modeling." Engineerig Management Journal 14(3): 15.

Tølle, M., P. Bernus, et al. (2002). Reference Models for Virtual Enterprises. Collaborative Business Ecosystems and Virtual Enterprises. L. Camarinha-Matos, Kluwer Publisher: 3-10.

Walker, G., B. Kogut, et al. (1997). "Social Capital, Structural Holes and the Formation of an Industry Network." Organizational Science 8(2): 109-125.

www.cimosa.de Computer Integrated Manufacturing Open System Architecture, Cimosa Association.

www.cit.gu.edu.au/~bernus/taskforce/geram/versions/geram1-6-2/ Generalised Enterprise Reference Architecture and Methodology, Peter Bernus.

www.idef.com Integrated Definition Language, Knowledge Based Systems, Inc.

www.uml.org Unified Modeling Language, Object Management Group.

This page intentionally left blank

REFERENCE MODELS FOR VIRTUAL ORGANISATIONS

Bernhard Katzy, Chunyan Zhang, Herman Löh

CeTIM-Center for Technology and Innovation Management, Germany
Prof.Katzy@CeTIM.org, chunyan.zhang@cetim.org, hermann.loeh@cetim.org

General consensus on a limited set of hierarchical organization types has propelled the development of the industrial organization at the beginning of the 20th century. This paper presents a study of organizational patterns across 20 projects that could be early descriptions of possible types of virtual organizations at the beginning of the 21st century. We look at information systems, and more important, coordination roles, network structure, and strategies as complementary elements of a consistent structure and propose three distinct basic types of virtual organizations: supply chain, lead contractor, and peer projects.

1. INTRODUCTION

Much research has been conducted on Virtual Organizations (VOs) as an emerging organizational form. In this chapter we review 20 projects in the VO domain that were funded by the European Community. Our aim is to understand what organizational models researchers, software developers, and practitioners did associate with VOs, and whether there is one common model and what the specific characteristics of a VO are.

This an important research question in its own rights, because generally accepted reference models for VOs do not yet exist. Development work, especially for enterprise systems for industrial enterprises relies on well-established organizational models such as the bureaucratic organization by Weber (1947) or Mintzberg (1979). For VOs such organizational models are not yet available or systematically developed. Yet, there is an emerging body of literature on the organizational specifics of VOs, which we will use to explore elements of such reference model.

The purpose of this chapter therefore is to extract organizational insights from the research projects studied and to present the essence of this work in a structure of an early draft of a reference model for VO. Taking an organizational approach towards a reference model for VO is a choice. Current VO models stem from many different disciplines and backgrounds. Many VO models stem from IT system design while other VO models are based in operations management or business strategy. Given the early state of VO research many such models describe what is new and different to the industrial organization of the 20th century, but in doing so, are using the concepts of the traditional organizations with hierarchical structures or central control (Barley and Kunda, 2001). As in the early days of organizational studies, we therefore favor the study of work and how it is coordinated to guide research and practice on VO in their own rights.

The chapter aims to contribute a structuring framework of virtual organization configurations to academia. To practice the paper contributes guidance and reference on how to structure a VO consistently in strategy, partnership, coordination, organization and finally, information systems.

The chapter is structured as follows: we first introduce the basic elements and relations of the VO reference model derived from the literature. We then propose a further classification of VOs into three model types which imply specific instantiations of the reference model elements. After a short description of the research and analysis method, we present how the projects surveyed relate to the reference model and what specific elements they contribute. At last we draw some conclusions based on this analysis and recommend future research directions.

2. VO REFERENCE MODEL

If VO is to emerge as a sustainable domain of scientific interest, reference models would be needed to foster common understanding and communication amongst members of the scientific community. It would equally be helpful in identifying what additional work is most needed, and explain how different research results relate. A reference model documents the emerging consensus within the scientific and industrial community, but should not constrain future work. It therefore is by nature generic, and not applicable to a concrete case.

In this section, we propose elements for a VO reference model based on the literature in the VO domain. It is an organizational model intended to present the underlying concepts and principles of the VO, not a model oriented towards IT system design. Any generally accepted reference model offers a choice of the characteristics of its object that are regarded as more important. From the concepts developed in the projects and presented in this book, we construct the VO reference model from (1) the short-term project which is set up to exploit a (2) fast changing business opportunity. Such a temporary configuration of mostly independent, cooperating business units in most cases emerges from a breeding environment (Camarinha-Matos, Afsarmanesh 2003), usually (3) a more stable network. A VO thus covers permanent restructuring processes, the creation of new short-term projects from the network until their dissolution at the end of their life-cycle. VOs build dedicated (4) dynamic capabilities for governance, management, and organizational and information system structures that allow for cooperation in the network and the constant restructuring. Figure 1 graphically summarizes the elements of the VO reference model.

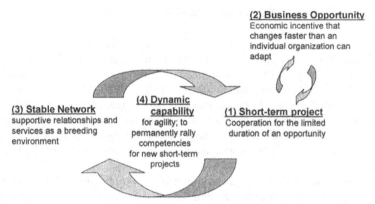

Figure 1: VO reference model

In the next sections we sketch some trends in literature, which point to a set of research questions for VO that are addressed by the here studied projects.

2.1. Stable network

2.1.1. What are the functions of the stable network?

Under time constraints setting up resources and processes from scratch and building the necessary competencies can limit market penetration. The more agile (Goldman et al., 1997) a VO is, the more rapidly it can configure short-term projects and the more these profit from underlying structures and capabilities to restructure. In line with literature we summarize the more stable relationships of VOs as Networks (e.g. Thorelli, 1986, Sydow, 1992). Networks serve as the breeding environment of temporary organizational structures in which the life cycles of short-term projects are embedded. Networks can have many different forms such as the business units of a holding company, SMEs in a regional network, or preferred suppliers in a supply chain network. They typically have certain membership criteria and are relatively stable because members' investments in the relationships only pay on a long-term basis. Due to the stability of the network, it can offer supportive services to the VO, like competence development of both the individual member and the network, knowledge management and learning, innovation capabilities, financial services, culture and trust building, or IT infrastructure development.

At Stockholm School of Economics, researchers have studied the success of comparably small Swedish firms in global markets since the 1960s. Hakansson and Johanson (1992) explain their success by networks, which they describe as the competence in building, maintaining and using relationships with customers and suppliers. These networks have no boundaries or lifecycle. Instead, they evolve as the memory of all activities among the business partners as a valuable, scarce and difficult-to-imitate business capital. This type of network can be exploited in two ways. First, close relationships or intense networks allow for virtual size and second, collaboration can be restructured to fill "structural holes" (Walker, Kogut et al., 1997) for innovation, for example in the Silicon Valley (Saxenian, 1991).

2.1.2. What is the origin of networks and how do they evolve?

Fast growing businesses often draw on existing industrial structures to feed their growth. Electrolux, for example, made its way from a regional SME to a world class company through acquisition of undermanaged white goods companies, restructuring and integrating them into the Electrolux distribution system (Pümpin, 1995). Textile companies, such as Diesel or Benetton, do not manufacture themselves, but draw on the regional network of Prato in northern Italy to select from some 7000 small suppliers, enabling them to provide four collections per year (Ritaine, 1990). The origin of networks can be geographic regions, industry sectors or multinational companies.

As we have seen from Prato, the region is a relevant boundary for the networks of small companies. Piore and Sable (Piore and Sabel, 1984) have rediscovered traditional European craft traditions as models for the post mass production structure of industry. Popular as well as historical examples of regional industrial structures are reported from the Japanese keiretsu, the Italian industrial districts, and the German guilds. Within a region or cluster, business often is a heritage from ancestors in long chains of tradition. This distinction reduces workforce mobility for the business. A strongly-coupled system of manufacturers, suppliers, toolmakers, professional schools, and entrepreneur organizations with frequent and intense contacts as well as a similar cultural background creates an idiosyncratic regional competence that cannot be easily copied elsewhere.

Networks can also emerge inside large firms as decentralized form of the (former) integrated (multinational) company. ABB, Nike, Puma and IBM are frequently-cited examples of this phenomenon. From this perspective, the network organization marks a further step in the development towards more organic organizational forms, from the integrated, divisionalized, or matrix organization to the new or networked N-form.

Networks as clusters are often described as a source for innovation. Silicon Valley and Hollywood are further examples of highly innovative regions, illustrating that regional clusters can emerge in short periods of time. In the information age, this model regains importance, leading managerial and organizational theorists to exploit it as a source of continuing global success (Piore and Sabel, 1984). Miles and Snow (Miles and Snow, 1986) generally re-interpret industry structures as dynamic networks to develop a strategic framework for the identification of additional strategic possibilities from co-operation within the industry. In their eyes comparative advantages of successful companies stems from specialization in one of three types of generic innovation strategies: the prospector who creates new products, the analyzer who concentrates on growth, and the defender who maintains stable efficient business at the later stage of the life-cycle. The dynamic network model builds on the widespread model of competitive advantage (Porter, 1985). From a distinct strategic position, the broker uses the instrument of the network as an effective organizational form to create value in the industry (in new niches, demand pockets) and to capture value for the individual company. Dynamic networks, like VOs, therefore are no new phenomenon, but a new way of interpreting industrial reality with the objective to revitalize (Miles and Snow, 1986) the industry, to restructure it from within.

2.2. Short-term project

Short-term projects within the VO framework are temporary organizations of partners, which are created in response to a market opportunity. Short-term projects are sustained for the duration of a single order or a limited period of time to be dissolved after completion to free resources for another short-term project. Some spectacular examples are the teams that create Hollywood film (Goransson, 1999) or open source programmers, who work entirely computer based.

2.2.1. What are the activities in managing the life cycle of short-term projects?

By definition short-term projects have a limited time span and thus run through a life-cycle from their initial conception to completion. Short-term, however, can mean very different time spans, from only seconds for a one-click combination of a credit card company, a logistics company and the web store, to days or weeks of collaborative work in creative projects, to many years in aerospace projects. In all these cases though, virtual cooperation is advantageous because business does change faster than the individual partner firm could internally change or adapt. For the purpose of this paper we discuss relevant questions in three phases along the life-cycle.

Creation
Important questions in the creation phase of short term projects are how the business opportunity can be identified and how the best competencies can be identified and marshaled to form an effective partnership. It further includes the organizational design of the cooperative project. Which partners are selected from within the network, or in which cases partners from outside the network. In this phase, the common rules of cooperation, risk and profit sharing are defined and the partner companies establish commitment to the common efforts. This commitment can stem from sources ranging from pure opportunism (Byrne, 1993) to a win-win mentality (Preiss, Goldman et al., 1996). Regardless of the reason, maintaining this commitment to the goal is the core of management competence for virtual operation integration (Bleicher, 1995).

Operation
Successful operation in projects represents effective and efficient integration of partner activity. Cooperation mechanisms and performance measurement play important roles in the operation, in addition, the effectiveness and efficiency of VO operation can be facilitated by several methods. Existing methods, such as business process re-engineering are proposed to be re-used in the context of VO. Within the organization, business process re-engineering (Hammer and Champy, 1993) overcomes functional silos through the re-design of business processes that cut across existing departmental boundaries. This approach applies as well to co-operations with suppliers and customers across existing organizational boundaries in inter-organizational processes (Brooks and Reast, 1996). A second main driver is automation through the application of IT, which as well is the common ground for all chapters of this book. Information Technology has developed from early local automation of isolated business functions with stand-alone applications to network-wide

integrated information infrastructures. Entire new business processes now become possible from the perspective of information management.

Dissolution
Because projects within a VO have a limited life span, they do end and need to be dissolved with fulfillment of the market opportunity. Partner companies, however, remain being connected to each other in the network where the knowledge and the relationship gained during operation are preserved for a next cycle of restructuring. Research question to be addressed in this phase are sharing of intellectual property rights, financial risks, and rewards.

2.3.   Dynamic Capability of VO

Mowshowitz (2002) identifies the "switching principle" as the distinctive difference between virtual and other organizations. Information technology is one mechanism to switch between partners that can satisfy a need from a business opportunity, for example when an online customer makes his or her choice for one of the possible credit card companies to complete the transaction. Miles and Snow (1992) raise the expectation that encompassing information systems would be a sufficient switching and coordination solution for dynamic organizations,

Yet another expectation is that virtual organizations can reduce technical and organizational coordination and simply use market mechanisms. (Electronic) markets serve as an efficient means to allocate resources to evolving business opportunities with no hierarchical overhead or central management. Transaction cost economics (Williamson, 1975) calculates the cost for market transactions, such as searching the right partner or specifying the transaction and Information and communication technology will reduce this kind of transaction cost, leading to more market coordination in virtual organizations (Miles and Snow, 1986).

Others argue that since the member companies within the network and the VO are legally independent entities, governance cannot build on hierarchical command and central control or market mechanisms alone. Instead, shared values (Goldman, Nagel et al., 1995), trust (Byrne, 1993) or general harmony (Taylor, 1911) contribute to the governance of network. In addition, some governance instruments like common boards (Davies, 1995), administration structures, or management roles (Katzy, Schuh et al., 1998) have been suggested as organizational capabilities that are built into networks for successful dynamic change.

Different names of the management roles have been proposed, like broker (Snow and Miles, 1992), 'architect', lead operator (Snow and Miles, 1992), caretaker (Snow and Miles, 1992), integrator, or project manager (Laurikkala, Vilkman et al., 2002). Some of these descriptions address similar management functions. Based on the industrial practice and the synthesis of the different names for the management roles, Katzy, Schuh and Millarg (1998) have identified one list that illustrates management roles in VO (Figure 3).

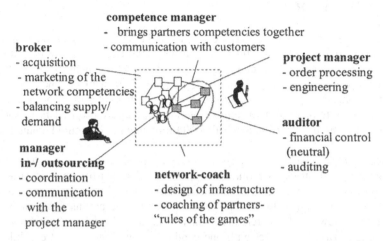

competence manager
- brings partners competencies together
- communication with customers

broker
- acquisition
- marketing of the
  network competencies
- balancing supply/
  demand

project manager
- order processing
- engineering

auditor
- financial control
  (neutral)
- auditing

manager
in-/ outsourcing
- coordination
- communication
  with the
  project manager

network-coach
- design of infrastructure
- coaching of partners-
  "rules of the games"

Figure 3: Examples for management roles (Katzy, Schuh et al., 1998)

The broker: He is responsible for the marketing and for the sale of the competencies of the VO. He is the entrepreneurial person responsible in the early phase of a market opportunity, functioning as a broker between customer and production in the acquisition of new project products.

The competence manager: He provides knowledge about available technologies and competencies in the network to the customers. He defines the services that are necessary to fill the order. Moreover, he is responsible for the selection of the best partners for the given order and the configuration of the short-term project organization.

The project manager: He is the manager of the operations in the project. He leads the project management and replaces partners who do not perform or produce on time. Internally, he communicates with the in-/outsourcing-managers and guarantees the quality, target cost and delivery dates of the products to the customers.

The manager of in-/outsourcing: He offers the technological know-how of his enterprise, the resources and the technology to the VO. He is responsible for a step in the value chain of the project and represents the interest of his company to the other partners.

The network-coach: He coaches the network, caring for a minimal technological infrastructure and managing relationships.

The auditor: He serves the VO as a neutral, independent financial auditor, providing objectivity and solidity when no track record can be presented.

More research is needed to decide when to use which coordination mechanism and how to combine information technology, market mechanisms and organizational capabilities. Organizational capabilities, which were illustrated as management roles probably are the least studied of the three coordination mechanisms and further research is need to understand how these are performed, e.g. by a single person or an organizational entity (partner, department, etc.). Very little is known in literature about how VOs learn and build such capabilities.

3. VO TYPOLOGY

So far we have considered four basic elements of the VO reference model and identified some initial research questions that further detail and generalize the reference
model. In this section we introduce typologies as a complementary description of
reference models which show similar patterns in all their elements and can be used
across multiple settings, such as regional clusters, global enterprises or professional
communities. Enterprise system implementation has largely profited from such enterprise types, and the question is whether VO implementation could be equally propelled.

Three VO types seem to appear frequently in literature: supply-chain VO in
manufacturing industries, star (main contractor) VO in construction industries, and
peer-to-peer VO in creative and knowledge industries. These types are based on
basic network topologies. In a supply-chain topology, the partners' interaction pattern mainly follows a chain, relating mainly to its upper and lower neighbors. In a
star topology, partners interact with one central hub or strategic centre, while partners in peer-to-peer topology have multiple relationships between all nodes without
hierarchy.

| Supply-chain | Hub and Spoke | Peer-to-peer |
| (Process oriented) | (Main contractor) | (Project oriented) |

Figure 2: Types of VO

From an organizational perspective these VO types describe the main coordination structure that governs information and material flows as well as the power relationships and decision making within the network and projects. Generally speaking,
the relationship topology of a VO therefore has impact on its management, business
processes and IT structure at the same time. VOs, which adopt a supply chain topology, usually use Supply Chain Management (Christopher, 1992) and Efficient Consumer Response (ECR) to improve inter-organizational co-ordination and control.
Integration of information flow (e.g. EDI) and material flow creates transparency in
the entire value chain and reduces waste and doubles effort in the virtual enterprise.
In contrast, VOs with peer-to-peer topology are built on self-organization. For example, in Hollywood, a number of agents provide the solution for each task in a
film. Using professional standards as a basis, workers self-coordinate (Goranson,
1999). There is no central planning or management. Instead, co-operation emerges
spontaneously from markets.

If nodes represent partners and edges represent the most relevant relationships,
the question arises on how such macro structures translate into information, decision, and material flow. Networks are more ambivalent than hierarchies and it is
possible that the graph of contracts is hub and spoke while the material flow is a
supply chain while scheduling & planning information is exchanged in a peer to
peer negotiation. More research is needed to address the organizational micro structure of VO in order to decide on the requirement of effective information systems.

4. RESEARCH METHOD

On the basis of published results the VOSTER project has selected 29 relevant projects in VO domain from a larger list of several hundred projects that have been funded under the European fifths research program on Information Society Technology (IST) between 1998 and 2002. We have collected information of these projects from various sources, such as technical deliverables, public web sites, project plans and conference papers. Based on the VO reference model, we reviewed these projects in the first round to study the state of science in the field of VO. After the initial review, 20 projects among these 29 projects (see Appendix 1, the Acronyms identify each project in the search engine of the EU research portal www.cordis.lu) for a more detailed questionnaire survey to obtain complementary information. The authors know all project coordinators allowing for occasional phone interviews where clarification was necessary. The survey was undertaken between May and November 2002.

5. OVERVIEW OF PROJECTS IN THE VO FIELD AND DIS-CUSSION OF SURVEY RESULTS

5.1. Network and collaboration as one research focus

Almost 90% of the projects make explicit or implicit reference to the existence of a more stable network of companies or individuals to select partners from within.

From the review we found that almost all projects focus on ICT support for collaboration in networks. They develop systems or internet-based platforms to provide supportive services to the members. For example, the project e-COGNOS offers a generic, modular and open solution (methodology, tools and architectures) for knowledge management in the construction domain based on ICT infrastructure. The project eLEGAL defines a framework for legal conditions and contracts regarding the use of ICT in project business. The project SYMPHONY aims to equip SMEs with a dynamic management methodology and a modular-structured software toolbox to increase the competitiveness of SMEs in turbulent environments.

We found networks that stem from all sources identified in literature, be it regional clusters, globally dispersed enterprises in a supply chain, companies and individuals registered on a common platform. Projects address networks in almost all industries such as manufacturing, IT, construction, or tourism, just to name a few. Given the strategic objective of the funding mechanism, it does not surprise that all projects address information systems in one way or the other. It however became obvious that all projects combined their development with research on organizational, managerial, process management, or legal issues, often motivated by solving problems that related to the commercial exploitation of their technical results.

5.2. Solutions for restructuring and short-term projects

Most of the projects (except SYMPHONY, which has a different focus) confirm that the VO aims at creating temporary short-term projects for a specific order, product, or service development and to dissolve the team after delivery. All projects highlight the role of IT in support of configuring short-term projects. Again, it does not surprise that the projects, while all were selected under the e Business innovation program of the European Union, either develop systems or internet-based platforms, or employ existing software tools to support the life cycle of the short-term projects.

Half of the projects offer more or less complex solutions for the set-up of short-term projects. For example, BAP has developed a team configuration approach and tools to find right partners, PRODNET II and MASSYVE have either tools or databases to support partner selection, the e-business platform developed by e-MMEDI-ATE can offer negotiation service to match demands and offers, and eLEGAL supports contract editing and configuration. In terms of supportive services, BAP presents a value qualification methodology and tools to identify business opportunities as "real options" and to characterize the specific risks and chances associated with them. ISTforCE and OSMOS respectively have developed open platforms, into which various service providers can plug services, such as for financial management or human resource management.

To support configuration of short-term projects GENESIS and PRODNET II, have developed either methodologies or systems for general business process management. GENESIS has developed a continuous process management methodology and tools to support the management team of VOs to design, change and control business processes and to react to changes in a dynamic environment. PRODNET II has focused on the distributed nature of operation in VOs and developed a Distributed Business Process Management System (DBPMS) tool to support business process planning, monitoring, simulation and assessment of alternative process designs. Some projects have developed solutions for concrete activities during the operation of short-term projects. For example, GNOSIS developed a web-based Client-Server architecture for online production scheduling and manufacturing tasks delivering as short-term projects. MASSYVE employs a Production Planning and Control system (PPC) to plan and monitor manufacturing, and e-business platforms developed by e-MMEDIATE support tracking orders.

In conclusion, numerous systems have been developed by the projects surveyed that can support building to order supply chains with order / production management and work flow management. Multiple aspects of effective creation of short-term projects are addressed by this basic research. However, the few reported real life cases let assume that integration of the results into commercially workable solutions still has to be achieved.

PRODCHAIN and GENESIS have developed tools for performance measurement, which could guide further applied research and development to focus on economically rewarding fields. PRODCHAIN, for example has developed techniques to optimize value chains of a global production network by analyzing the gap between the objective and the performance.

In general, the economically most relevant exit scenarios of VO are not adequately addressed. With the exception of the project EXTERNAL, which develops methodology, infrastructure/tools and business solutions for VO modeling, analysis, engineering and operation, no projects have studied the dissolution of short-term projects.

5.3.   VO topology

Projects reviewed show that all three VO types can easily be identified and all projects can be categorized into one of them (see Appendix 2). Professional networks, tourism industry, and SME clusters tend to have multiple peer-to-peer relationships and distributed management roles, while lead-contractor networks, e.g. in the construction industry usually adopt a star typology with the lead contractor in the central role. Globally distributed production networks are typically chain networks as supply chain configurations.

The solutions presented by these projects can usually be applied into the specific VO topology. However, about a fourth of the projects did not make an assumption of a VO topology or at least did not show any awareness for the relevance of such models.

5.4.   Management roles

Since most of the projects focus on ICT system and infrastructure development, less than half of the projects modeled distinct management roles in the VO. Yet, based on the functionality that the developed information systems offer they can be mapped into the management roles in the reference model. For example, the business integrator in BIDSAVER conducts the responsibilities of the roles of a competence manager, and a project manager. GLOBEMEN has developed a detailed activity model both for managing cooperation in the network and to operate short-term projects.

6.   CONCLUSION

The review and the survey results of 20 projects under the European IST funding scheme that are relevant to the VO domain support relevance of the here chosen elements to establish a VO reference model. Although discussions still are intense and usage of different terms will continue for the time being, consensus seems to emerge on some main characteristics of the VO: Networks exist as the breeding environment for short-term projects that are created to exploit concrete market opportunities. Yet there is potential for improvement by the projects if they adapt results of network research in literature. Although most of the projects assume a network as an essential element of VOs, few projects later include the network in the description of their solution. This seems understandable in a situation where agility and rapid reconfiguration is the innovation driver for the developed applications. In the next phase, however, understanding of the dynamic capabilities and the necessary learning in the network during take-up of virtual organizations would deserve more attention for wider VO adoption.

We have broadly classified VOs into three types of supply chain, star, and peer-to-peer based on the basic topology of their cooperative relations. More typology related research is needed to design concrete and consistent industry-specific reference models for VOs. Little – in our eyes too little – attention has been put into socio-economic dimensions of VOs and to include consistency of business models, governance and management, and organizational structures into encompassing business architectures for VOs. An example for such research could be industry models that have been instrumental in the take-up of ERP and enterprise systems.

Since most of the here studied projects developed information systems management aspects of the VO, management roles could be re-engineered from requirements analysis reports or implicit assumptions of the developers. Generally speaking more research is needed about many management roles und functions to populate the VO reference model with validated high quality modules.

Overall, the VO domain appears to be driven by academic research and therefore is in a technology-push situation of advanced solutions and technological knowledge that does not always fit industrial demand. Yet, there is little doubt about the general need for VO in a globalizing, increasingly turbulent environment. More research on performance management in/of VOs could be a way to address the gap between economic needs and technical solutions.

7. BIBLIOGRAPHY

1. Barley, S. and G. Kunda (2001). "Bringing work back in." Organization Science 12(1): 76.
2. Bleicher, K. (1995). Das Konzept integriertes Management Frankfurt, Campus Verlag
3. Brooks, I. and J. Reast (1996). "Re-designing the Value Chain at Scania Trucks." Long Range Planning 29(4): 514-525.
4. Byrne, J. (1993). "The virtual Corporation." Business Week: 36-41.
5. Camarinha-Matos, L. M., Afsarmanesh, H. (2003). Elements of a base VE infrastructure, J. Computers in Industry. Vol. 51, Issue 2, Jun 2003, pp. 139-163
6. Christopher, M. (1992). Logistics and Supply Chain Management - Strategies for Reducing Costs and Improving Services. London, Pitman.
7. Davies, P. (1995). "Case study - Global Supply-chain Management." Logistics Focus(5): 2-7.
8. Flaig, L. S. (1993). "The Virtual Enterprise": Your New Model for Success - Vertical Integration is Out. Today's Markets Require a Broad Fabric of Alliances for Managing the Entire Value Chain." Electronic Business(3): 153-155.
9. Goldman, S. L., R. N. Nagel, et al. (1995). Agile Competitors and Virtual Organizations - Strategies for Enriching the Customer. New York, Van Nostrand Reinhold.
10. Goranson, H. T. (1999). The Agile Virtual Enterprise, Westport, Quorum Books.
11. Hakansson, H. and J. Johanson (1992)."A Model of Industrial Networks". In: B. Axelsson and G. Easton (Ed.) Industrial Networks - A New View of Reality.,London, Routledge: 28-36.
12. Hammer, M. and J. Champy (1993). Reengineering the Corporation - A Manifesto for Business Revolution. London, Nicholas Brealey Publishing.
13. Katzy, B. R., G. Schuh (1998). "The Virtual Enterprise", in: Molina, A., Sanchez, J.M., Kusiak, A. (Ed.), Handbooks of Life-cycle Engineering: Concepts. Methods, and Tools, Dordrecht, Kluwer Academic Publisher
14. Miles, R. and C. C. Snow (1986). "Organizations: New Concepts for New Forms." Sloan Management Review, No.3, p.62-73.
15. Mintzberg, H. (1979). The Structuring of Organizations - A Synthesis of the Research. Englewood Cliffs, Prentice-Hill.
16 Mowshowitz, A. (2002) Virtual Organization; Toward a Theory of Societal Transofrmation Stimulated by Information Technology, Westport, Quorum Books.
17. Piore, M. J. and C. F. Sabel (1984). The second industrial divide - Possibilities for prosperity. Basic Books.
18. Porter, M. E. (1985). Competitive advantage - Creating and sustaining superior performance. New York, The Free Press.
19. Preiss, K., S. L. Goldman, et al. (1996). Cooperate to Compete. New York, van Nostrand Reinhold.
20. Pümpin, C. (1995). Corporate Dynamism - How World Class Companies Became World Class. Bombay, Jaico Publishing House.

21. Ritaine, E.(1990). "Prato: An Extreme Case of Diffuse Industrialization." International Studies of Management and Organization 20: 61-76.

22. Saxenian, A. (1991). The origins and dynamics of production networks in Silicon Valley, Research Policy, p. 423-437

23. Snow, C. C. and R. Miles (1992). "Managing 21st century network organisations." Organizational Science: 5-20.

24. Sydow,, J. (1992). Strategische Netzwerke, Wiesbaden Gabler Verlag.

25. Taylor, F. W. (1911). The Principles of Scientific Management. New York, London, Norton & Company.

26. Thorelli, H.B. (1986). Networks: Between markets and hierarchies, Strategic Management Journal, p.37-51

27. Walker, G., B. Kogut, et al. (1997). "Social Capital, Structural Holes and the Formation of an Industry Network." Organizational Science 8(2): 109-125.

28. Weber, M. (1947). The Theory of Social and Economic Organization. NY, The Free Press.

29. Williamson, O. E. (1975). Markets and Hierarchies: Analysis and Antitrust Implication. New York, Free Press.

Appendix 1: Projects

Number	Project
1	BAP
2	BIDSAVER
3	e-COGNOS
4	ELEGAL
5	e-MMEDIATE
6	EXTERNAL
7	FETISH-ETF
8	GENESIS
9	GLOBEMEN
10	GNOSIS
11	ICSS-BMBF
12	ISTforCE
13	MASSYVE
14	OSMOS
15	ProDAEC
16	PRODCHAIN
17	PRODNET II
18	SYMPHONY
19	VDA
20	VL

Appendix 2: Overview of VE topology

Topology	Project
Supply-Chain	e-MMEDIATE
	PRODCHAIN
	PRODNET II
Star/Consortia	e-COGNOS
	ELEGAL
	GLOBEMEN
	ICSS-BMBF
	ISTforCE
	OSMOS
	ProDAEC
Peer-to-Peer	BAP
	BIDSAVER
	EXTERNAL
	FETISH-ETF
	GENESIS
	GNOSIS
	MASSYVE
	SYMPHONY
	VDA
	VL

Appendix 3: Examples of management roles

Role	Responsibility	Project
Broker	• Acquisition of new customers • Coordination of assignments • As a permanent contact person for the customers	VDA
Business Architect	• Initiation of new business cooperation • Selection of partners • Facilitation of strategy and operational plans formulation	BAP
Business Integrator	• Negotiation of contractual agreements • Project Management/administration • Process analysis and simulation • Analysis of ICT solution • Engineering competencies	BIDSAVER
Contract negotiator & checker	• Contract negotiation and check	ELEGAL
VE coordinator	• Origination of VO • Distribution of VO configuration • Monitoring progress of tasks	RRODNET II MASSYVE
Product manager	• Management of product development and related product model data	ICSS-BMBF ISTforCE

ONTOLOGY AND KNOWLEDGE MANAGEMENT

Frank Lillehagen

Computas AS, Norway, fli@computas.com

This chapter gives an insight into ontology and knowledge management approaches as applied to Virtual Organizations. It focuses on research efforts from the mid-nineties, and briefly describes approaches, implementations, and innovative achievements.

The dominant approach is for VO projects to develop application systems and tools and to integrate them through common databases and ICT architectures. Ontology tools and structures, knowledge management systems and knowledge elements are developed and managed disjoint from operational systems.

However, recent model-based approaches, creating ontology and knowledge services as reusable task and meta-models, are indicating a paradigm-shift in solutions design and systems architecting and engineering approaches.

1. BACKGROUND WORK

Research on ontology and knowledge engineering and management as technologies contributing towards developing quality virtual organizations and extended enterprises goes back to the provision of the first web-servers in the early nineties.

Both areas and technologies have been researched as potential contributors to new industrial approaches to systems development and engineering, process and product design, organizational development and solutions delivery. The recent development of many new innovative technologies is adding to the visions of an entirely new approach to industrial computing, solutions design and collaboration.

The technologies that give rise to the coming paradigm-shift involving Model Designed Solutions and Model Generated Workplaces are:

- Web technologies with services, repositories and standards
- Agent technologies with plug-and-play ICT architectures
- Portal-based Ontology and Knowledge Engineering Environments
- The Active Knowledge Modeling technology and visual knowledge spaces

The first generation of Knowledge Engineering (KE) tools targeted the reconstruction of semantic space of human expertise, and repertory grid-centered tools like the Expertise Transfer System (ETS), AQUINAS and others. The second generation KE tools - visual knowledge engineering - provides ideas of CASE technology to AI. These early tools did not fit into any sustainable approach or architecture so they were bound to fail, but they did contribute to our understanding.

In the mid-nineties industry was flooded with Knowledge Management Systems (KMSs). They were, as many other systems, sold with the promise to support creative work, and thus were dramatically oversold. The knowledge elements, or nuggets as some chose to call them, were stored as entities in traditional databases. Storage and retrieval of content depended on carefully defined identity schemes and categorization structures, and the context for reuse was not adequately captured and represented. These KM systems were nothing more than advanced information and file management systems, but they did provide novel methods for navigation and retrieval of contents.

KE tools recently developed enable knowledge processes such as generation, structuring and reuse, and help cut down the revise and review cycle-times. They promise to refine, structure and test human knowledge and expertise in the form of ontology [PROTEGE, WebOnto, OntoEdit, 2001-2003], but they are still standalone tools with no support for services and service composition and orchestration..

Since the mid-nineties Enterprise Modeling has provided tools and templates for capturing, expressing and sharing enterprise knowledge. Some projects have created prototypes that demonstrate the possibility of achieving model-designed solutions for execution. Knowledge-model driven approaches are becoming available from leading tool vendors [Computas AS, Ptech Inc., and MEGA, 2000-2003]. Some of them also provide modeling and execution platforms integrating methodologies, infrastructures and services to support knowledge model reuse and cultivation.

1.1 The role of Ontology and Knowledge Engineering

The role of ontology and knowledge management in VO development and operations is to express and share knowledge that can be extended and adapted to support model-designed solutions and operations. Capturing situated knowledge, achieving interoperable solutions, and providing interactive views are important for increased stakeholder participation. To support innovative work the ICT and KE architectures, integrating IT components and web-services, must be dynamically extended and adapted. Capabilities needed to enable this are:
- Visual capture, expression and management of knowledge
- Concurrent modeling, model management, execution and management
- Separating Enterprise Architecture (EA) into distinctly manageable layers
- Integrating layers and legacy systems through cascaded meta-modeling

Ontology and knowledge modeling must provide integrated services to enable model extension and adaptation. Models are reused from enterprise knowledge repositories. Abstract enterprise models are pure ontology structures, but there are many types and kinds of ontology structures that must be aligned, re-designed and combined.

2. APPROACHES AND IMPLEMENTATIONS

The dominant approach for VO projects so far has been to develop overlapping application systems and tools and to integrate them towards common databases and ICT architectures. Ontology tools and ontology structures, knowledge management systems and knowledge elements are developed and managed disjoint from other application systems and tools. Most approaches are based on fairly traditional client-server architectures, but some novel web-based service architectures have been prototyped. Moving to the web and exploiting web-standards some projects have developed comprehensive architectures. These projects have been able to demonstrate plug-and play capabilities of software components [e-Colleeg, 2001-

2003]. One project [EXTERNAL, 2000-2002] has experimented with a layered architecture, and a model-driven approach to systems development and engineering. The layered architecture is further described in section 4.

2.1 State-of-the-art

There is a wide spectrum of VO approaches, methodologies and achieved prototypes that have been researched. However, the practical solutions are based on standardized IT architectures and interfaces, rigidly integrating existing applications, databases and tools. More recent approaches cover top-down business-process modeling and simulation, off-line enterprise knowledge modeling and management services development, and bottom-up ICT architecture development and component generation for service-oriented architectures. The middle-out approach developing service-oriented knowledge architectures of models and meta-models to integrate many business models and ICT architectures and platforms is being researched. Ontology tools are used and manifested as topic-maps and concept maps.

Knowledge processing and management is dependent on the encoder's proximity to actions and events, on the medium, on method and language of encoding, and on users being able to concurrently capture knowledge, design solutions and perform work. Designing and developing working environments, workplaces, rules and habits, and generating operational solutions are interactive tasks performed by users while executing work. Knowledge engineering should focus on company core competencies and activities, that is strategy, business, human capital, architectures, platforms, operational solutions, and infrastructure services.

Use of ontology to design VOs
Ontology defines the basic terminology and relations comprising the structured vocabulary of a topic area. Ontology has to do with naming conventions for industrial nomenclature of all types of core knowledge structures of any enterprise. This is illustrated in figure 1.
"Ontology is an explicit specification of a conceptualization or a hierarchically structured set of terms for describing a domain that can be used as a skeletal foundation for a knowledge base".

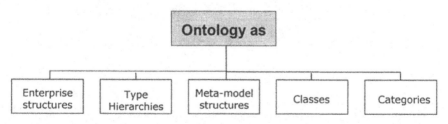

Figure 1 - An ontology is a structure relating concepts and artefacts by their identity, enhancing the total meaning.

Ontology tools are becoming available as web services, but the structures to be semantically and logically transformed are not easily imported and exported out of traditional systems and databases.

Model-driven solutions
OMG and many other institutions are pushing model-driven approaches to systems architecture and systems development. The models referred to are pure diagrams comparable to functional views. When executing these models there is no feedback or services enacted to update the models based on execution and performance experiences. The cyclic behavior of model-generated task solutions, and task execution-driven model development is only enabled by the AKM technology [7]. By the AKM approach a closed loop is created between visual modeling, execution, value-creation and experience gathering, thus implementing learning by doing.

Knowledge Spaces and AKM technology
Active Knowledge Modeling (AKM) technology [5] is an innovative way of representing and continuously developing layered enterprise architectures, separating business operations from ICT platforms by introducing interactive enterprise knowledge architecture. The AKM technology is built on the paradigm-shifting concept that enterprises and working organizations are cascaded knowledge spaces that should be implemented as pro-active visual scenes.

2.2 Ontology tools

Ontology tools and ontology structures created are currently not part of the operational enterprise systems, except for ontology structures embedded in entity relationship diagrams and modeling languages. There is no support for interactive development and adaptation of ontology structures. Enterprise structures, flows and working rules must be modeled and embedded in active models driving operational architectures and solutions, integrating all enterprise knowledge spaces.

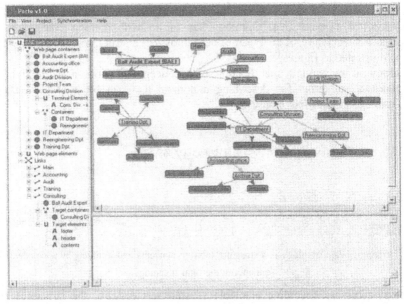

Figure 2 - the Porto BAE portal ontology

Go to: http://xml.com/2002/11/06/Ontology_Editor_Survey.html for a tool survey.

2.3 KM systems and KE tools

Knowledge engineering and management cannot be achieved by introducing KM systems and ontology tools alone. Knowledge engineers, workers and systems analysts, designers of information systems in the different subject domains, must be directly engaged in expressing, embedding and executing their knowledge.

3. SCIENTIFIC FOUNDATIONS

Ontology and knowledge structures and processes are created, used and supported by most cognitive sciences. It is therefore an integral part of all our sciences and solutions. So expressing knowledge and building enterprise and VO knowledge spaces and active models are major challenges faced by IT providers and users when attempting to converge and integrate dispersed enterprise knowledge, and when exploiting the new digital multi-media. The ontology of the physical world or the structures existing in static disjoint media encoded by use of natural languages does not necessarily apply as a basis for knowledge engineering [8].

3.1 Pedagogic and Epistemological Views

Ontology is not only a philosophical discipline studying the being. It should also cover epistemological (about knowing and knowledge evolution) aspects. Ontolgy is about knowledge artifact naming, identity, identification, coding schemes, categorization, classification, thesauruses, taxonomies and glossary. It is about the entire enterprise logical description, the meta- and operational views of the enterprise. Epistemology on the other hand is about the logical evolution and meaning of enterprise concepts. The challenge of knowledge modeling is thus manifold when we integrate across enterprises to form evolving VOs, and when we start expressing and representing the meta-knowledse of enterprise practitioners.

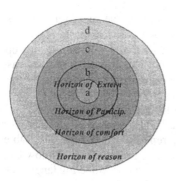

4 Layers of Knowledge:

Expert knowledge - internal and tacit - a

Participative knowledge social and external -- b

Sensed knowledge - our real world percept.- c

General acquired knowledge - d

Proximity, media and encoding is vital for knowledge representation.

Figure 3 - Existence of knowledge as defined by pedagogy and epistemology.

Figure 3 defines four zones of knowledge perception and representation, each delimited by a perceptive horizon or border, defining knowledge existence, form and value as dependent on proximity to action and method of knowledge encoding and diffusion. The innermost zone is only expressed in collaborative visual scenes.

3.3 Knowledge Spaces

Visual organization of subjective space [3], the perception and evaluation of its coordinates, colors and shapes are different in the right and left halves of the human brain. The right provides isomorphic reflection of objects and scenes, while the left introduces an object into generalized classes of phenomena and episodes, and provides for logical context and operations. Therefore visual techniques and graphical approaches, activating right-half functions, work as versatile cognitive tools for more transparent and effective data/knowledge base design procedures.

The AKM technology and way of thinking [5] opens up for model designed approaches, methodologies, intelligent infrastructures and dynamically generated solutions. This implies that in all enterprise activity there are four major knowledge dimensions involved. This discovery is termed the AMIS principle: Approach, Methodology, Infrastructure and Solution. (AMIS).

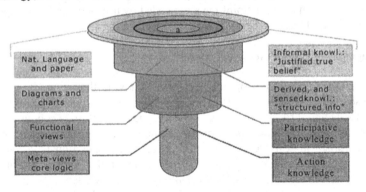

Figure 4 - the value of knowledge according to existence and form.

These four-dimensional spaces are the source of the four logical flows of process as discovered by Hugh Ross as far back as 1969 [13].

Enterprises have many knowledge spaces; the innovative, the operational, the governing, the strategic, the cultural, and a multitude of smaller cascaded spaces. The enterprise knowledge spaces, called industrial war-rooms by their innovators, define the foundations of the AKM technology. [5-8]. The core knowledge of these knowledge spaces is the knowledge within the two inner zones shown in figure 4.

Action or situated knowledge typically has a set of intrinsic properties; such as: reflective views, recursive processes, repetitive tasks and replicable meta-views. These do not exist in the two outer zones. Expressing action knowledge, often tacit to humans, is still a major challenge for Enterprise Modeling languages and tools.

4. ENTERPRISE ARCHITECTURES

Enterprise model-designed architectures supporting execution will play an increasingly important role in future VOs. They will be a source of precise knowledge for managers and users as well as systems engineers and IT providers as regards all aspects of user model-designed solutions, support and maintenance.

In figure 5 there are three layers that are glued together by an intelligent infrastructure visualized as barrels and the customizable EKA box. The architecture of the infrastructure is, contrary to the remaining architectures, independent of industrial sectors, applications and user solutions, it is generic. The two barrels denote services that are stored in the process repository as repeatable tasks. These services can be re-activated and adapted to any given platform and solution.

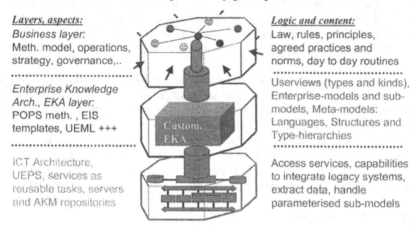

Layers, aspects:
Business layer:
Meth. model, operations,
strategy, governance,..
....

Enterprise Knowledge
Arch., EKA layer:
POPS meth. , EIS
templates, UEML +++
....

ICT Architecture,
UEPS, services as
reusable tasks, servers
and AKM repositories

Logic and content:
Law, rules, principles,
agreed practices and
norms, day to day routines
....
Userviews (types and kinds),
Enterprise-models and sub-
models, Meta-models:
Languages, Structures and
Type-hierarchies
....
Access services, capabilities
to integrate legacy systems,
extract data, handle
parameterised sub-models

Figure 5 - Layers of Enterprise Architecture – integrated by an Intelligent Infrastructure.

4.1 The Business Operational Architecture (BOA)

The concepts at the core of the Business Operational Architecture concern the integrated representation of law, business rules, project norms, project and working rules and habits, and new rules of collaborative practices. Support to define and assess the adherence to these rules and regulations must be available in an e-Business network. Law, contracted values, rules and obligations are controls on business processes. Business rules are typically agreements on value and risk sharing, division of tasks and responsibilities, and agreements on liabilities and life-cycle support. These mutual expectations and controls must be expressed in a separate business model and correlated with program and project performance indicators. Being able to predict and track performance, and assess the degree of adherence to contract and key performance indicators, are important properties for successful collaboration. These capabilities all warrant a separate set of models where rules and regulations of working together apart must be continuously refined and managed, and where the rules of collaboration are continuously changed to fit local practices and habits.

4.2 The Enterprise Knowledge Architecture (EKA)

The Enterprise Knowledge Architecture is a set of inter-dependent knowledge structures that allow us to de-couple, engineer and manage enterprise knowledge constructs, methodologies and operational solutions. The six major enterprise knowledge structures are composed of these structural elements and constructs:

1. User enterprise views (types and kinds), the kinds of views are comparable to many Extended Enterprises frameworks (Zachman, Cimosa, and GERAM), but the types are not described and explained by these frameworks,
2. Enterprise models and sub-models, and structures of integrated solution models, supporting distributed working environments,
3. Partial meta-models of many types and supporting many kinds of services,
4. POPS languages, core visual constructs, the basis of modeling languages,
5. Structures of meta-model objects and constructs, and finally,
6. Type-hierarchies representing standardized industrial knowledge.

These enterprise knowledge structures are vital for the formation, integration and operation of intelligent enterprises and smart organizations, and must be visually editable and manageable in order to harvest the full benefits of models of knowledge spaces as visual scenes. The EKA is the most important and common knowledge asset of any enterprise, integrating mental models and augmenting the minds of all employees, for which the EKA is an active visual support system. The EKA represents the nervous or logic centre and the communication central of the enterprise. It is the main source of manageable Enterprise Intellectual Capital.

4.3 The ICT Architecture

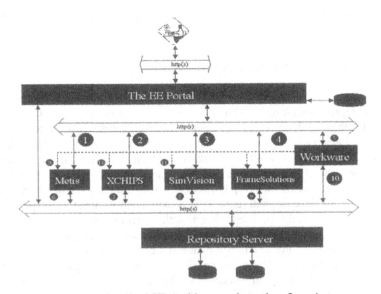

Figure 6 - The ICT Architecture layer has four tiers

Figure 6 illustrates the ICT architecture as implemented in the EXTERNAL project. It shows that the user meets the infrastructure through a portal-based project engineering and management environment. This provides a set of web services to support modelling, model-designed solutions engineering, work execution, value-metrics and experience gathering. The project environment acts as an integrator and as a platform to plug in and perform all kinds of services: software, tasks and applications. Among the services provided are services to build knowledge models (Metis), services to cooperate and collaborate (XCHIPS), services to do project simulation (SimVision), services to do work management (Workware) and services to perform work, enactment and execution (FrameSolutions). The portal-based technology used was prototyped in the project. As a front end, it has the main objective of generating a dynamic and personalized user interfaces, bridging the gaps among the available systems, tools and functions, and the users.

Combining the Intelligent Infrastructure with techniques enabling dynamic generation of user interfaces, we are able to describe, implement, and deploy software platforms capable of generating operational solutions, driven and managed by knowledge models.

5. SUPPORTING DESIGN AND ENGINEERING

The AMIS knowledge space of four main extensively dependent dimensions was discovered by industrial practitioners and not by researchers. The figure below, termed the "Railway-crossing Diagram" is from the Globeman 21 project. Japanese industry partners directed our attention to the fact that the project, the plant, the production and the building site (infrastructure) were actually designed, engineered and evolving in parallel, but that current methods and systems are not able to adequately support concurrent engineering of these flows. With enterprise knowledge spaces and the AKM technology, implementing the spaces as visual scenes, performing concurrent knowledge engineering work will be possible.

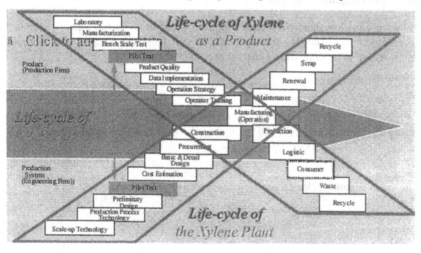

Figure 7 - The four knowledge dimensions of construction industry.

The AKM technology and the holistic AMIS approach have the potential to support concurrent knowledge engineering and execution of project-oriented work.

5.1 Active Knowledge Models

AKM technology will enable model-designed solutions, and work-driven active model development and knowledge engineering. This means that ontology and Enterprise Modeling tools must be integrated in the ICT architecture and described as tasks to work on the structures of the EKA, in order that semantic ambiguities and flaws may be detected and corrected. Ontology engineering is an integral service of active knowledge modeling. This means that most Enterprise Modeling approaches also have to open up, and recognize the true nature of enterprise knowledge. Enterprise Modeling has to capture and engineer structures and support work execution in knowledge spaces. "Enterprise Modeling is externalizing situated knowledge (4th horizon KM) and building the Enterprise Knowledge Architecture."

Interoperability, integration and reuse are facilitated by the layered architecture, and the services supported and provided by the EKA. Situated knowledge always involves knowledge spaces of four major inter-dependent knowledge dimensions. This has long been accepted in problem-solving and design theories.

By this approach all systems are federated and integrated systems, embedded in the VO knowledge space and all its cascaded knowledge spaces for innovation, business operation, strategy governance and balanced values assessment.

6. THE FUTURE OF ONTOLOGY AND KNOWLEDGE MANAGEMENT

Work to develop the three layers of the described Enterprise Architecture integrated by the Intelligent Infrastructure and its services is underway [8].

6.1 Model Designed Solutions

Knowledge models should have web components and user environments defined in their meta-models. Then the knowledge that is externalized and managed in models can be reused to generate truly dynamic user interfaces.

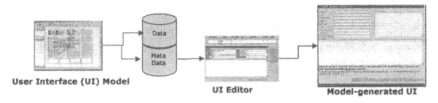

Figure 8 - Model-generated workplaces and task execution views.

Once a user environment has been built and its behavior defined, we still need to guide the users in performing tasks and in having new tasks assigned.

6.2 The powers of knowledge spaces and visual scenes

Knowledge spaces implemented by AKM technology as visual scenes have unique properties, such as reflective views, recursive tasks, repeatable templates and replicable meta-models. These properties support capabilities that are not obtainable in other settings than visual scenes:

- Continuous knowledge development and capture, modeling processes and views, executing tasks, and aggregating values and experiences,
- Knowledge creation and processing, meta-modeling, executing and monitoring task execution as adaptive services,
- Knowledge use and value creation, performing model interrogations and task and method executions, and providing value metrics,
- Knowledge management, developing meta-models, reflective meta-model views, handling architectures, and generating governance views,
- Cognitive and Generative Learning, preparing knowledge for practical use as competence and skill profiles.
- Support pro-active learning and collaboration by the sharing of knowledge and mental.models, augmenting the human brain in performing creative work.

7. RECOMMENDATIONS

Enterprise interoperability is concerned about how to express, share, represent and manage enterprise knowledge. Software is nothing but knowledge encoded for the digital multi-media and for computers to execute, so it is our challenge to de-couple the knowledge that will be compiled to executable code, from the enterprise logic needing interactive enhancement by users, from that which has to be simple but yet powerful in supporting on-demand business opportunities. Enterprise logic as meta-models has to be created by designers, engineers and knowledge workers continuously interacting with active knowledge models throughout the design and engineering phases of any development project.

Continuously being able to express, refine and represent situated knowledge, generating new views and language constructs, is still not understood by solution providers. Creative design work is all about interactively developing the solution languages and views. Any stakeholder should also be able to continuously interact with project knowledge through the lifecycles. This requires that IT providers deliver integrated modeling and execution platforms, and develop news ways of performing work management and delivering workplaces for work execution.

Enterprise Architecture (EA) development is still only able to capture descriptive legacy views and limited dependencies, but there are initiatives underway towards also supporting operational solution architectures,

Situated knowledge drives behavior and human actions, work yields values, values yield experiences and new behavior, and experiences drive enhanced knowledge. This human learning cycle must be closed in order to support creative work. The degree of interaction with the contents of the enterprise knowledge architecture will vary across sectors, type of knowledge work, and platforms, and the ambition of the foreseen solutions.

7.1 Future research directions

Business Models, Business Architectures and Enterprise Knowledge Architectures still require a lot of research and experimentation to become viable industrial solutions. To get business people involved in modelling, the user interface must be truly simple to use and the value contributed by the models and the platform supporting them must be substantial. Business case analyses must be easily performed. Enterprise Modelling must be enhanced to support the capturing of knowledge in enterprise knowledge spaces, and to exploit the services of intelligent infrastructures turning models into executable workplaces and task lists.

The layered Enterprise Architecture is no doubt a major break-through, separating business behaviour and execution platforms from enterprise ICT –architectures by introducing the Enterprise Knowledge Architecture..

Semi-automatic Knowledge management
Extending the services of the Enterprise Knowledge Architecture it is possible to start researching the objective of automating knowledge management in the area of design and knowledge engineering. Intelligent Infrastructures act as a "reflective enterprise visual memory", supporting the intrinsic properties of knowledge, and will allow us to also collapse the temporal dimension. This means cycles are represented by task patterns and we may be relieved of revisions and nested versioning.

Integrating Enterprise Modeling and Ontology
Integrating ontology tools and services to: - edit ontology structures of the enterprise knowledge architecture, - transform ontology structures between cultures and many global enterprise architectures, - compare ontology structures to validate changes and incompliance, and propose corrective actions, and finally to manage ontology structures as part of the enterprise Knowledge Architecture and its life-cycles.

Work Execution and Management
Project engineering and management environments (PEME), supporting model generated workplaces and tasks execution, are needed to move knowledge work to the web. Web services will be of at least four types: software services, dynamic agents, adaptive work process tasks and application capabilities,
Enterprise Visual Scenes (EVS) hold the key to a new style of computing that will enhance creativity, reduce complexity, and augment human capacity.

Enterprise Knowledge Architectures
Structures of dependent views, cascaded models, coherent meta-model structures, partial meta-models, type-hierarchies, the EKA and its services, seamlessly integrate enterprises; creating situated semantics, syntax and work action context,

Systems Development
System Engineering is transforming to Solutions Design and System Engineering, separating business, enterprise and IT specific logic and views. The solutions will be model designed, and all solutions will be embedded in knowledge spaces.

Support for Governing Networked Organizations
In any research project use-cases must be modeled as knowledge spaces as early as possible. VO research needs true industrial user involvement and good user environments for concurrent modeling, meta-modeling, work execution and monitoring.
   Some key lessons learned from the most recent R&D projects:
- Each use-case meta-knowledge integrates and validates the results,
- Specific enterprise knowledge architectures yield interoperable solutions,
- Knowledge models and architectures are major results of the project,
- Services of many types and kinds will have to be developed.

Enterprise Modeling as services adapts and extends the generic architectures. Knowledge Management means building knowledge architecture solutions. Semantics alone is not the key to interoperability. Patterns of work in reproducing contexts will be needed. Interoperability is all about knowledge architectures and services for extending and adapting models in order to capture the situations in which we execute work.

Acknowledgements. The results included in this paper are partially developed in the context of the European IST VOSTER project. The author thanks the contributions from his partners.

8. REFERENCES

1. Dehli,, Einar, Smith-Meyer Henrik and Lillehagen Frank, July 2003, Metis LEARN, Enterprise Architecture paper presented at CE 2003, Madeira, Portugal; see http://www.ce2003.org/.
2. Camarinha-Matos, Luis and Afsarmanesh, H.; Virtual Organization systems and Practices, Springer, 2004.
3. Fox, Mark and Grueninger M., September 1997, The TOVE Ontologies, presentations at the Globeman 21 project workshop, Japan, see also http://www.eil.utoronto.ca/enterprise-modelling/tove/.
4. Gavrilova, Tatiana and Gorovoi, Vladimir, October 2003; "Ontological Engineering for Knowledge Portal Design", Slides presented at the PROVE 2003 conference in Lugano, Italy.
5. Lillehagen, Frank, Computas, 1997 and 2002, The Foundations of the AKM technology, last presented at the CE 2004 conference, Madeira July, 2003, see also www.akmii.net.
6. Lillehagen, Frank and others, July 2003, IDEAS report D 2.4: Visions of 2010, for IDEAS project, see also www.ideas-roadmap.net.
7. Lillehagen, Frank:, February 2004; Enterprise Modeling Tutorial, presented at the Athena project kick-off meeting; Valencia, Spain. Go to: www.athena-ip.com.
8. Lillehagen, Frank, Solheim Helge and Tinella, Stefano, Enterprise Knowledge Spaces, providing scenes for new approaches to SE and KM, Paper to be presented.
9. McElroy, Mark and Firestone Joe, The New Knowledge Management, Book published by Butterworth Heineman, ISBN: 0-7506-7608-6.
10. Noy, Natalia F. and McGuinness, Deborah L., Summer 2003, Ontology Development 101: A Guide to Creating Your First Ontology http://protege.stanford.edu/publications/ontology_development/ontology101.pdf.
11. Petit, Michael and all, April 2003, State-of-the-art in Enterprise Modeling. UEML project report and presentation; see www.UEML.org.
12. Rohlenko, Oleg, Spring 2002, Ontology Seminar, Given at the Interop NoE project Kick-off; Bordeaux, France.
13. Ross, Hugh, " SADT – Structural Analyses and Development Tool", presentation at IFIP seminar Røros, Norway, 1969.

<table>
<tr><td>1.6</td></tr>
</table>

COLLABORATIVE NETWORKS: A NEW SCIENTIFIC DISCIPLINE

Luis M. Camarinha-Matos
New University of Lisbon / Uninova, Portugal, cam@uninova.pt
Hamideh Afsarmanesh
University of Amsterdam, The Netherlands, hamideh@science.uva.nl

*Collaborative networks manifest in a large variety of forms, including virtual organizations, virtual enterprises, dynamic supply chains, professional virtual communities, collaborative virtual laboratories, etc. A large body of empiric knowledge related to collaborative networks is becoming available, but there is an urgent need to consolidate this knowledge and **build the foundations** for sustainable and solid research and development in this area. Establishment of a scientific discipline for collaborative networks is a strong instrument in achieving this purpose.*

1. INTRODUCTION

During the last years both the business and the scientific world have faced many emerging challenges, requiring the emergence of a variety of collaborative networks, enabled by the continuous advances in the information and communication technologies. Advanced and highly integrated supply chains, virtual enterprises / virtual organizations, professional virtual communities, value constellations, and collaborative virtual laboratories, represent only the tip of a major trend in which enterprises and professionals seek complementarities and joint activities that allow them to participate in competitive business opportunities in new markets and / or scientific excellence for innovative developments.

A large number of research projects are carried out worldwide[1] and a growing number of practical cases[2] on different forms of collaborative networks are being reported. This has so far led to an extensive amount of empirical base knowledge that now needs to be leveraged. In addition to the identification of many required components, tools, and the base infrastructure functionalities, an awareness is now being built, and partially studied, regarding the fundamental configuration and operational rules, as well as the behavioral patterns that emerge, even in traditional collaborative organizations. It is now urgent to consolidate and synthesize the existing knowledge, setting a sound foundation for the future research and development in this area. In fact, one of the main weaknesses in the area is the lack of appropriate **definitions** and **formal theories, consistent modeling paradigms** and **formal modeling tools**. Dramatically enough, there is not yet even a common

---

[1] See Annex A of this book for an extended list of examples.
[2] Several practical cases are described in part 4 of this book.

definition of the basic examples of collaborative networks such as the virtual organization, professional virtual communities, breeding environments, virtual enterprise, or collaborative virtual laboratories. This situation constitutes a major obstacle for interaction among experts from multiple disciplines, involved in this area, and creates an obstacle for the recognition of collaborative networks as a new scientific paradigm. The reader should not conclude that researchers in this domain are working on "something" they do not know what it is. Certainly each research group or even each project consortium agrees on a number of basic definitions. In some cases these definitions are not too distinct from group to group, representing some intuitive understanding of the area[3]. Nevertheless, the lack of formal and widely accepted definitions and models frequently leads to discussions and debate whenever different groups meet (Fig. 1).

Figure 1 – A recurrent question

We are now in the stage that Kuhn [1] would call a pre-paradigmatic phase, in which the collaborative networks phenomenon is described and interpreted in many different ways, depending on the background of the researcher.

The acceptance of a new paradigm is not a pacific process [1], as the established sciences and paradigms tend to resist the introduction of another new paradigm, and rather prefer to extend the existing science or paradigm and its associated rules to explain the new phenomena. This tension situation is increased by the multi-disciplinartiy of the phenomena, namely in the case where multiple traditional disciplines / branches of organized knowledge and professionals compete to master the new area. This is the clear case for collaborative networks, where its related disciplines involve: computer science, industrial engineering, management, economy, social sciences, etc. As a good example of this strained behavior, so far several of the established branches of science have tried to use / extend the definition and behavior of the single enterprise paradigm to explain the collaborative networks; e.g. the attempts in the direction of "enterprise engineering" and "enterprise architect", among others. However, the *anomaly* appears when the existing enterprise-centric models and their extensions fall short of capturing the key facets and specificities intrinsic in networked organizations, as well as when realizing that the base facilities of the applied discipline is not sufficient to properly represent and model all aspects of collaborative networks' behavior. In the history of science, the recognition and acknowledgement of anomalies has resulted in "crises", that are the necessary preconditions for the emergence of novel theories and for a paradigm change or even the rise of a new discipline.

---

[3] Chapters 1.2 and 1.3 in this book illustrate some of the "working definitions" used in various projects.

As in all other past paradigm changes, considerable research efforts have been focused on identification of "anomaly" aspects, i.e. the identification of what is new in the collaborative networks in reference to the established body of knowledge, leading to the induction and progressive characterization of a new scientific paradigm. A **new scientific discipline** emerges once: (1) the new paradigm is adjusted to cover the various manifestations of the emerging collaborative forms, (2) the consolidated set of basic knowledge is organized, and (3) the various multi-disciplinary researchers involved in this work start to identify themselves as members of this new community rather than doing research on collaborative networks while staying as members of their original communities. A discipline represents therefore a branch of knowledge and a systematic and ordered method, based upon clearly defined models and rules, and provides a foundation for practice [4].

As it happened many times in the past history of sciences [1], it is natural that at the beginning of this process various formulations / interpretations / theories compete (e.g. the various existing definitions of virtual organization in the literature). This process continues until a comprehensive definition becomes accepted by a large majority, namely when eventually the one that better explains the various manifestations of collaborative networks will be settled in this position.

Furthermore, this process, leading to the establishment of a scientific discipline, is likely to bring a number of advantages to the progress of the area:

- In order to gain strength, when free from the assumptions of other specific disciplines that were contributing to the area, the associated body of knowledge will get more focused and organized.
- Researchers will dedicate their energy on many challenging issues raised by the new area instead of fighting their colleagues from other disciplines, trying either to claim the ownership of the area or to prove the primacy for their former base discipline in tackling these challenges.
- Researchers will get / build new instruments to get their work recognized and respected in the established academia such as:
  - A well delimited scope of their activity. Nowadays, due to its multi-disciplinarity, research on collaborative network tends to not be well accepted by "traditional" disciplines. For instance, the computer science area has not fully accepted this research area because it involves social sciences, management, manufacturing, and industrial engineering. At the same time, for instance the management area has not fully accepted it because it has strong involvement with technology and the computer science area. A scientific discipline to be recognized needs to have unique principles and practices, and a research community that generates its own literature and supports its education.
  - Well-established communication and interaction channels. Conferences, journals, praxis, professional associations, etc. shall form the basis for sustaining the associated research community.

Which name should be given to this new scientific discipline? In the literature, a large variety of terms have been suggested to represent the various *manifestations* of collaborative networks. Some of these terms have a very short life, simply due to the "anxiety" observed in some research groups to always generate new names. Some other terms are better established that in fact address and distinguish different forms of this phenomenon. When establishing a discipline we should however aim at a name that can represent the widest set of manifestations, not being linked to any particular sub-group or application domain, and also being a term that intuitively gives a first idea of the main elements of the wide paradigm. Therefore, we suggest the term *"collaborative networks"* (**CN**) as a suitable name for this new discipline.

The remaining sections of this chapter summarize some important results from the two European projects of THINKcreative and VOmap that contribute to the purpose of establishing a sound theoretical foundation for research and development in the collaborative networks area.

2. CONTRIBUTING AREAS

Like in any other scientific discipline or engineering branch, collaborative networks require the development of formal theories and models of their structure and life cycle behavior, not only as a help to better understand the area, but also as the basis for the development of methods and tools for better intelligent and calculated decision-making. In fact decision-making in all phases of the future CN life cycle need to be based on well developed and verified models and methodologies. These models and methodologies constitute the basis for the growth and development of the area, for building ICT-based support infrastructures for business and organizational development and operation, as well as serving the base for education, training, and active operation of the CNs.

Disciplines, like the proposed one, certainly rely and are based upon other earlier disciplines, including the reference and / or adjacent disciplines [4]. Some theories and paradigms defined elsewhere have already been suggested by several research groups as promising tools to help understand and characterize emerging collaborative organizational forms. Examples are: multi-agent theories, coordination models, federated systems paradigm, game theory, theories of complexity, graph theory, etc. More recently researchers are also starting to look into the "soft computing" area in order to find suitable approaches for modeling aspects related to human behavior in collaborative organizations and to handle the issues of decision making and behavior management in the contexts of incomplete and imprecise knowledge.

As a result of the THINKcreative project [2] various disciplines and theories that are likely to have a positive contribution to the foundation of the *collaborative networks* were identified and briefly analyzed. Table 1 summarizes the main findings of this work as follows:

Table 1 – Contributing theories to the foundation of collaborative networks

Potential applicability	Limitations & Challenges
Formal theories and modeling of dynamic networks	
▪ Solve design problems: architecture, protocols, network creation ▪ Specify systems, verify specifications according to correctness and completeness ▪ Test and verification implementations versus specifications or standards	▪ Lack of knowledge of formal methods in the current engineering community ▪ Need to consider developments in communication networks

Graph theory	
▪ Represent networks of relationships – topology, routing, activity, flow ▪ Perform computations on flows ▪ Optimization	▪ Basic theory is very rigid - needs extensions to represent non tangible, qualitative relationships (fuzzy dimensions), and multi-criteria
Formal engineering methods	

▪ Best applicable to description of
  - operational behavior of CN
  - formulating operational plans that bind partners (consumers/suppliers) in CN
  - verifying formally that the plans are indeed satisfied by the operational behavior
▪ Economic and social aspects cannot be represented.
	▪ Difficult to develop and understand
	▪ Lack of intermediate-level formalisms linking the abstract approach to direct software development
	▪ Need practical application methodology
	▪ Need methods to bridge the gap between abstract formalism and IT implementation

Semiotics, normative models and multi-agents	
▪ Model responsibility relationships and commitments ▪ Prescribe norms and roles, legal support ▪ Capture system requirements	▪ Reasoning in deontic logic may lead to paradoxes; difficult to automate reasoning ▪ An promising approach: integration with agent logic
Network analysis and game theory	
▪ Non cooperative game theory: good for selecting partners, sustaining cooperation and trust ▪ Cooperative game theory: distribution of responsibility and resources ▪ Network exchange theory: coordination, efficiency, power relationships; maintenance of ties and reputation	▪ Practical results are not available yet ▪ Evolving structures generate emergent responses so an updating of the model based on continuous data collection would be necessary ▪ Weak capture of subjective relationships
Temporal and modal logic	
▪ Model the operational phase aspects ▪ Synthesis of processes	▪ Complex, as any formal method ▪ Need to integrate structure descriptions
Metaphors	
▪ Quick description for human communication (a possible help in expressing complex ill-defined concepts) ▪ Use in early stages (conceptual design)	Risk of taking metaphors too strictly ▪ Need further evaluation and research in consistent understanding in the creation and interpretation of metaphors ▪ Need to combine with formal methods
Theories of complexity	
▪ Analysis of self-organizing behavior ▪ Learn how to manage chaotic dynamics ▪ Insights on CN behavior ("small-worlds")	▪ Models from other domains (e.g. biology, physics) are difficult to apply to CNs ▪ Need further work on complex systems with social actors (humans)
Dynamic ontologies	
▪ Unlike static ontologies, dynamic ones can capture the evolution of mutual understanding among members of the network.	▪ Building them is still more of an art ▪ So far, only first limited experiences on distributed and evolving ontology creation and interoperation

Suggestions in the same direction start to appear in the literature (see [5], for instance). Perhaps surprisingly, some important contributions to the study and understanding of complex dynamic networks come nowadays from the area of Physics [6], [7].

3. A ROADMAP FOR A THEORETICAL FOUNDATION

Another research project recognizing the urgent need for the development of a more sound theoretical foundation for collaborative networks in general, and virtual organizations in particular, is the IST VOmap that elaborated a strategic research roadmap including a detailed plan for the required further research in this area.

The assumption in VOmap is that a sound theoretical foundation is a key requirement for the progress in the area of Virtual Organizations (VO). In specific it is necessary to design rigorous reference models to properly define VOs from the point of view of different disciplines. There is also a need for the integration /interoperation of these reference models and for the definition of associated metrics.

In summary, the roadmap suggested by VOmap for the development of a theoretical foundation for collaborative networks can be characterized by 6 key elements as shown in Fig. 2.

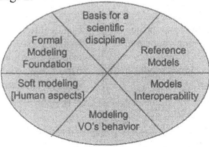

Figure 2 - Key elements of a roadmap for a theoretical foundation for CN

Based on these elements, the following strategic research actions are proposed by VOmap from the formal models and theories point of view [3]:

1. *Establish a formal theoretical foundation and methodology for modeling dynamic collaborative networks.* This action shall include:
   - Hands-on assessment of promising modeling approaches: formal languages, graph theory, multi-agent models, game theory, modal logics, etc.
   - Identification and characterization of the necessary modeling *purposes*
   - Establishment of a map between needed modeling purposes and promising modeling tools ("shopping list")
   - Formalization of existing empirical knowledge based on selected representative cases
   - Promotion of education and increasing awareness for the need of a theoretical foundation.
2. *Define basic formal reference models (including ontologies) for collaborative networks at general and focused-area levels.* This action shall include:

- Consolidation of results and their abstraction in terms of a general reference model (semi-formal and easily understandable by humans)
- Development of an engineering methodology for application of the reference model
- Advanced reference models and guidelines for development of advanced collaborative, networked organizations.

3. *Elaborate soft modeling approaches and soft models to both handle incomplete / imprecise knowledge and capture the social/human aspects in collaborative networks.* Action including:
   - Combination of soft engineering models and social theories
   - Combination of game theory and social networks
   - Development of soft reasoning models and decision-making support
   - Development of graphical visualization and simulation tools
   - Understanding of leadership, actors' roles, and social bodies roles.

4. *Devise mechanisms for evolution and maintenance of reference models for collaborative networks.* This action shall include:
   - Identification of actors responsible for models maintenance
   - Elaboration of mechanisms to support models evolution.

5. *Elaborate approaches for models interoperability, supporting multiple modeling perspectives (e.g. structure, behavior) at generic and focused area levels.* Action involving:
   - Characterization of multi-level modeling perspectives and their needs
   - Devising approaches for models interoperability and integration, starting with bilateral work for each two pairs of inter-related modeling approaches (to digest the commonalities and identify the necessary extensions).

VOmap also suggests tentative schedules for the development of the proposed actions (Fig. 3).

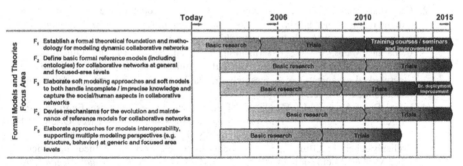

Figure 3 – Actions for the formal models and theories focus area

In addition to the formal models and theories, other areas are also covered by the VOmap roadmap [2]. The implementation of the suggested actions will have a great contribution to the consolidation of the scientific basis of the collaborative networks area.

4. CONCLUSIONS

A growing number of collaborative networked organizational forms are emerging as a result of the advances in the information and communication technologies, the industrial, market and societal needs, and the progress achieved in a large number of international research and development projects. The accumulated body of already achieved empiric knowledge and the size of the involved research and development community, guarantee important pre-conditions for the foundation of a new scientific discipline for collaborative networks as suggested by some pioneering projects and initiatives and guarantee its future achievements and success. At the end of a phase mainly characterized by ad-hoc initiatives too focused on obtaining immediate practical solutions, there is a growing awareness of the need for a more theoretical-oriented foundational work.. The organization and promotion of such discipline is foreseen to have a boosting effect in the development and consolidation of the area, both in terms of research, and practical sustainable implantation.

Acknowledgements. The results included in this paper are partially developed in the context of the European IST VOSTER, THINKcreative, and VOmap projects. The authors thank the contributions from their partners.

5. REFERENCES

1. Kuhn, T. S. – The structure of scientific revolutions, Univ. of Chicago Press, 2nd edition, 1975.
2. Camarinha-Matos, L. M.; Afsarmanesh, H. - New collaborative organizations and their research needs, in *Processes and Foundations for Virtual Organizations*, Kluwer Academic Publishers, Oct 2003.
3. Camarinha-Matos, L. M.; Afsarmanesh, H.; Löh, H.; Sturm, F.; Ollus, M. – A strategic roadmap for advanced virtual organizations, chap 7.2 in Collaborative networked organizations: A research agenda for emerging business models, Kluwer Academic Publishers, 2004.
4. Liles, D.; Johnson, M.; Meade, L.; Underdown, D. – Enterprise Engineering: A discipline?, Society for Enterprise Engineering (SEE) Conference, Orlando, FL, 1995, http://www.webs.twsu.edu/enteng/ENTENG1.html
5. Eschenbaecher, J.; Ellmann, S. – Foundations for Networking: A theoretical view on the virtual organization, in_Processes and Foundations for Virtual Organizations, Kluwer Academic Publishers, Oct 2003.
6. Dorogovtsev, S. N.; Mendes, J. F. – Evolution of networks - From Biological Nets to the Internet and WWW, Oxford University Press, 2003.
7. Barabási, A.-L. - Linked: The New Science of Networks, Perseus Books Group, 2002.

| 2. | **INFRASTRUCTURES** |

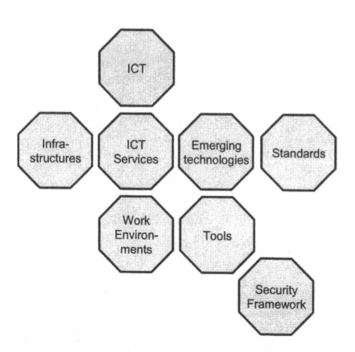

This page intentionally left blank

ICT INFRASTRUCTURES FOR VO

Luis M. Camarinha-Matos

New University of Lisbon / Uninova, Portugal, cam@uninova.pt

The design and development of a transparent, easy to use and affordable ICT infrastructure is a key pre-requisite for the effective large-scale implementation of the collaborative network organizations such as virtual organizations, professional virtual communities, e-science communities, etc. This chapter introduces an overview of the main classes of infrastructures required by different types of virtual organizations and summarizes the main approaches followed by a number of research projects in the area.

1. INTRODUCTION

In recent years a large number of new collaborative, networked organizations have emerged, mainly as a result of the progress on computer networks and communication systems, but also as a reaction to market turbulence when companies seek complementarities to increase their competitiveness and reduce risks. Advanced and highly integrated supply chains, virtual enterprises (VE) / virtual organizations (VO), professional virtual communities (PVC), and new specialized collaborative organizations such as e-science and e-government, are some examples of this trend. The design and development of **transparent, easy to use** and **affordable ICT infrastructures** is a key pre-requisite for the effective large-scale implementation of the collaborative networks paradigm. Ideally this infrastructure should also be self-adaptive to different operating conditions. The ICT infrastructure is usually aimed to play an *intermediary* role as an enabler of the **interoperation** among components. In this context it is intended as the enabler for safe and coordinated interactions among the members of the collaborative networks [6], [2], [3].

In terms of research projects, Fig. 1 summarizes the various levels of required infrastructure to support not only inter-enterprise collaborative networks but also more human-oriented networks, i.e. professional virtual communities and virtual research communities [7].

The "typical" VO (and Virtual Enterprise) projects have been mostly focused on the basic interactions to support business collaboration among enterprises, including: safe communications, distributed information management and information sharing (eventually using specific standards such as EDIFACT, STEP, or XML-based standards), coordination, and (minimal) distributed business process management, with little focus on the human collaboration.

The second class of infrastructures is mostly dedicated to support collaboration among humans, although some of the projects also consider the organizations behind the professional virtual communities. Examples are infrastructures to support Concurrent / Collaborative Engineering in networked organizations, networks of consultants, and other professional virtual communities.

The third class is focused on a special case of human collaboration. It combines both inter-organizational and human collaboration, but including the access to remote equipment (e.g. machines, sensors, equipment for scientific experiments), collaborative experiments involving teams located close to the equipment and teams located remotely.

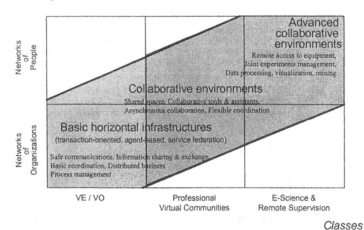

Figure 1 – Main classes of collaborative networks and corresponding infrastructures

This chapter summarizes the main findings of an analysis of 38 research projects in terms of their contribution to the ICT infrastructures. A first attempt to structure and classify the multiple developments in the area is made. Some of the remaining key research challenges are also pointed out.

2. INFORMATION SOURCES

As the initial basis for the analysis of the current situation and trends, a portfolio of several international projects, most of them funded by the European Commission, were considered. In a second phase some additional projects and other non-European results were also analyzed, mainly resorting to published results in major VO-related conferences (e.g. PRO-VE, BASYS, ICE) or special issues of journals (e.g. J. Intelligent Manufacturing, Computers in Industry, Communications of ACM, Int. J. Networking and Virtual Organizations).

The following diagram gives a qualitative overview of the main areas covered by the analyzed projects in terms of ICT infrastructure development. In this diagram contributions were classified as horizontal or base infrastructures and (vertical) support services for the various phases of the VO's life cycle.

As it can be observed, most projects had to devote considerable efforts to the establishment of a minimal horizontal infrastructure even when such development was not part of the project's goals. This situation is mainly due to the lack of common ICT reference architectures and truly plug-and-play infrastructures. This leads to duplication of efforts and usually results in minimal infrastructures hardly re-utilizable.

Project	"Horizontal" Infrastructures					VO Creation functionalities						VO operation functionalities					VO dissolution functionalities		
	Info & knowl Sharing	Coordin ation support	Safety & Security	Interoper ab & legacy integr.	Collabor ative environ ments	VE planning	Partner search/s elect	Enterpri se catalog	Cluster / marketpl ace	Contract negotiati on	Distribut BP plan & sched.	Distrib BP supervisi on	Perform ance assessme nt	Process assessme nt	Speciali zed Model/ Simul	Distrib domain funct	Liability definitio n	Prod/Ser v lifecycle supp.	Perform ance history data
From VOSTER portfolio																			
BAP																			
BIDSAVER																			
COVE																			
e-COGNOS																			
ECOLLEG																			
ELEGAL																			
EXPIDE																			
EXTERNAL																			
FETISH-ETF																			
GENESIS																			
GLOBEMEN																			
GNOSIS																			
ICCI																			
iCSS																			
ISTforCE																			
KM Forum																			
MASSYVE																			
NGMS																			
NIMCube																			
NIITM																			
OSMOS																			
ProDAEC																			
PRODCHAIN																			
PRODNET II																			
Symphony																			
TeleCARE																			
THINKcreative																			
UEML																			
VDA																			
VL																			
Other projects (with VOSTER members)																			
EPICE																			
eHUBS																			
ENBI																			
eSharing																			
ProServ																			
RAPTIL																			
Other projects (without VOSTER members)																			
AIM																			
Spars / Spars SC																			

Figure 2 – Qualitative overview of projects' contributions to ICT infrastructures

In terms of functionalities to support the VO's life cycle, it can be observed that considerable activity has been done regarding the creation and operation phases but very little attention has been devoted to the dissolution phase and proper handling of the VO's legacy (i.e. what remains after the VO dissolves).

The following sections analyze in more detail the state of achievements as observed in the studied projects. It shall be noted that this analysis was naturally limited by the availability of public information on those projects.

3. HORIZONTAL INFRASTRUCTURE

Three main approaches have been followed in the development of horizontal infrastructures for VO/VE:

- ❑ Layer-based or transaction-oriented approach, which adds a cooperation layer to the existing IT platforms of the enterprises. Inter-enterprise cooperation is then performed via the interaction through these layers.

❑ Agent-based approach, including the cases that represent enterprises as agents and the inter-enterprise cooperation as interactions in a distributed multi-agent system.

❑ Service-federation / service-market approach - according to which enterprises publish their services in service directories, representing their potential "offer" to the cooperation processes. By means of proper "standard" service interface, the interoperability with other (service requesting) enterprises, regardless of the heterogeneity associated with the actual implementation of the services themselves, is supported.

Although not all projects aim at developing horizontal infrastructures, the lack of a common and widely accepted **reference model** and reference architecture for the ICT infrastructure is forcing almost every project to design and implement its own mini-infrastructures, deviating some resources from its main focus, while generating something only applicable to that project.

Interoperability remains as a critical topic in the agenda of VO supporting infrastructures. Furthermore, the fast evolution of ICT technologies with reduced life cycles and the need to cope with technologies with different life cycles and at different stages of the corresponding life cycle represent a major difficulty. Furthermore, some efforts are too biased by short-term technologies, which might represent an obstacle for non-ICT SMEs.

It is also important to notice that emerging infrastructures induce new organizational forms, but emerging organizational forms will require new support infrastructures (co-evolution principle).

A. Layer-based / transaction-oriented infrastructure

Early infrastructures in this group have identified the need to exchange business and technical data through the use of standards (e.g. EDIFACT, STEP). An adequate coordination functionality and proper interaction with the enterprise's ERP/PPC and PDM systems are necessary in each enterprise in order to "guarantee" its proper participation in the VO/VE-business process. Further functionality includes safe communication to guarantee the privacy and authentication of the business interactions, and federated / distributed information management to support the information visibility rights and sharing of production status data.

Table 1.

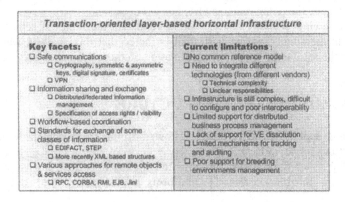

Transaction-oriented layer-based horizontal infrastructure	
Key facets:	**Current limitations:**
❑ Safe communications ❑ Cryptography, symmetric & asymmetric keys, digital signature, certificates ❑ VPN ❑ Information sharing and exchange ❑ Distributed/federated information management ❑ Specification of access rights / visibility ❑ Workflow-based coordination ❑ Standards for exchange of some classes of information ❑ EDIFACT, STEP ❑ More recently XML based structures ❑ Various approaches for remote objects & services access ❑ RPC, CORBA, RMI, EJB, Jini	❑ No common reference model ❑ Need to integrate different technologies (from different vendors) ❑ Technical complexity ❑ Unclear responsibilities ❑ Infrastructure is still complex, difficult to configure and poor interoperability ❑ Limited support for distributed business process management ❑ Lack of support for VE dissolution ❑ Limited mechanisms for tracking and auditing ❑ Poor support for breeding environments management

Table 1 summarizes the main facets addressed by VOSTER projects and also the current limitations of the proposed solutions in the layer-based approach.

PRODNET II

One of the earlier examples of a layer-based / transaction-oriented infrastructures.

The infrastructure extends the functionalities of each VE member (represented by the enterprise applications such as ERP/PPC, PDM, CAD, etc.) with a *Cooperation Layer* responsible to handle all inter-enterprises transactions and cooperation events.

Central to this cooperation layer are a Distributed/Federated Information Management System (DIMS) and a workflow-based Coordination Engine (LCM). A safe Communications Infrastructure (PCI) and a library of support services (EDIFACT, STEP/PDM) complete the Cooperation Layer.

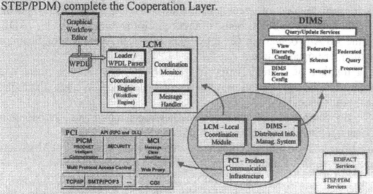

Typical services for an industrial VE, as offered by the PRODNET platform, include:
- Exchange of commercial data via EDIFACT messages.
- Exchange of technical product data using STEP.
- Federated information management, supporting not only the administrative information about the VE, but also the information the enterprise shares with other VE members.
- Coordination module, handling all cooperation-related events (execution of a local activity flow plan).
- Configuration module, allowing the definition and parameterization of the VE and the behavior of each node.
- Safe communications, including cryptography services, digital signature, certificates, auditing mechanisms, etc.
- Monitoring of orders and production status.
- Quality related information exchange.
- Extended ERP/PPC system adapted to interact with a VE environment.

www.uninova.pt/~prodnet

Figure 3 – The PRODNET II example

It shall be noted that infrastructures combining heterogeneous components from different vendors are potentially unstable, it being difficult to determine which component (or tool) provider is responsible when something goes wrong with such complex systems. In spite of the fast growing technological developments, lack of proper interoperability mechanisms among enterprise applications is a major obstacle to agile VO/VEs.

Setting up an infrastructure for VO/VE based on multiple technologies still requires a large engineering effort, which represents a major obstacle for the implantation of this new organizational paradigm. Furthermore, the fast evolution of the information technologies often presents a disturbing factor for non-IT companies.

B. Agent-based infrastructure

Although at an abstract level there are similarities between agent-based and layer-based approaches, from the underlying technology / software development point of view they are quite different. We are assuming here an AI notion of agent as an encapsulated computational system, that is situated in some environment, and that is capable of flexible, autonomous behavior in order to meet its design objective. There are nowadays a large number of development platforms for multi-agents systems (MAS), most of them based on Java. Some of these platforms, e.g. FIPA OS, JADE, ZEUS, follow the FIPA (Foundation for Intelligent Physical Agents) specifications and several of them are open-source.

There are a number of characteristics in the VE/VO domain that make it a suitable candidate for the application of multi-agent systems approaches. Examples of such characteristics include:

- A VE is composed of distributed, heterogeneous and autonomous components, a situation easily mapped into MAS.
- Coordination and distributed problem solving also tackled by MAS are critical problems in VE management.
- Decision making with incomplete information, and involvement of network members as autonomous entities, that although willing to cooperate in order to reach a common goal might be competitors regarding other business goals, is another common point.
- The effective execution and supervision of distributed business processes requires quick reactions from enterprise members. Computer networks being the privileged media for communication, there is a need for each company having a "representative" in (or "listening" to) the network. Agents can support this need.
- Recent developments in VE are changing the focus from information modeling and exchange to role modeling, addressing aspects of distribution of responsibilities, capabilities and knowledge.
- The phase of VE formation in which it is necessary to select partners and distribute tasks, shows market characteristics and negotiation needs that have been research issues for years in the MAS community (coalition formation).
- A VE consortium is a dynamic organization that might require re-configurations – e.g. replacement of partners, changes in partners' roles, etc., for which a flexible modeling paradigm is necessary.
- VE supporting functionalities need to interact with the "local" environment (legacy applications and humans). Interaction with the environment is one of the defining attributes of agents.
- The scalability property of MAS seems particularly adequate to support dynamic VEs in which different levels of cooperation with different sets of partners might be established at different phases. On the other hand, each enterprise might itself be seen as composed by a network of semi-autonomous entities (departments).

- More flexibility than in a client-server model is required to support dynamic change of roles of the VE members.
- Continuous evolution of business models, technologies, organizational paradigms, and market conditions require effective support for evolution and a high level of modularity of the infrastructures.
- New forms of teamwork, namely cooperative concurrent engineering or Virtual Communities of Practice (VCP), are emerging in the context of VEs. Agents can play an important role as "assistants" to the human actors in such environments.
- There is a need to handle the requirements of autonomy vs. cooperative behavior for which federated MAS approaches may provide a balanced solution.
- On the other hand, as agents are designed and developed independently, it is quite difficult to guarantee coordination unless common rules ("social laws" and standards) are adopted. Theoretical foundations on agents' sociability can be combined with current developments of a legal framework for VE/VOs.

It shall be noted that in spite of these strong motivating elements, the application of MAS technology to VE/VO infrastructures is still limited to research projects.

Table 2 summarizes the main facets addressed by VOSTER projects and also the current limitations of the proposed solutions in the agent-based approach.

Table 2.

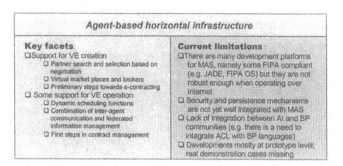

A growing number of research prototypes on the application of multi-agent systems and market-oriented negotiation mechanisms for the VO/VE formation are being developed. Early MAS applications to VO/VE are mainly focused on the creation phase. In many cases it is assumed that simple mechanisms of inter-agent cooperation are sufficient to support the operation phase of VO/VE. The decision-making in a VO/VE is however a complex process where it is important to combine human decision with some automatic functionalities. It is even likely that the level of automatic decision-making will evolve as the trust of humans in the systems increases. But independently of the ultimate decision making center, there is a need to provide mechanisms to support process coordination, supervision, and controlled information exchange and sharing.

With deeper studies of VO application domains however this paradigm reveals many specific aspects that cannot be simply supported by basic MAS approaches. In the VO community interoperation / cooperation must be regulated by the following requirements that need further extensions to the basic MAS technologies:

-Cooperation agreements and contracts that establish a framework for the

general operating conditions must be established.
-   Distributed business process models and mechanisms that establish the allocation and sequence of tasks to be performed by the community must exist.
-   Efficient data exchange and communication services, distributed service management functionalities, support for nodes autonomy / privacy, high level of service quality, auditability, and accountability, etc., have to be guaranteed.

MASSYVE

An example of application of a multi-agent approach in VO/VE infrastructures.

The figure illustrates a practical example of the application of MASSYVE to VE creation in the context of an industry cluster formed by twelve companies in the domain of moulds and die-casting [10]. The cluster is legally represented by a broker entity that supports a human expert responsible for getting and analyzing business opportunities. By means of a *broker agent* a business opportunity is transformed into a distributed business process that is then distributed (through a contract-net protocol) to the (potentially interested) enterprises within the cluster. In the end of the whole process, a set of possible teams of enterprises ("potential" VEs) that can carry out that business opportunity is formed and the most suitable team is proposed (but the ultimate decision is made by the human expert). In this example, there are three VEs capable of accomplishing the business process but VE1 was the selected team.

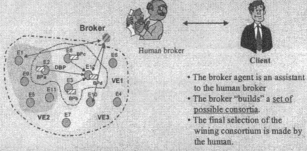

Moulds industry cluster [Rabelo, Camarinha-Matos, Vallejos 2000]
MASSYVE Project

Based on a real scenario: cluster of 12 mould and die industries in the south of Brazil

- The broker agent is an assistant to the human broker
- The broker "builds" a set of possible consortia.
- The final selection of the wining consortium is made by the human.

The Contract-net Protocol coordination mechanism is used to support the task assignment among agents, and the Negotiation method is used to overcome conflicts taking place during planning or execution phases, both at intra-enterprise and inter-enterprise levels.

In MASSYVE an integration of MAS and federated information management is proposed. Each agent is enhanced with a Federated Information Management System (FIMS), through which it seamlessly interoperates and exchanges information with other agents. However, considering the autonomy of agents, the access to information is strongly controlled by the information visibility rights defined among them that in turn preserve their autonomy. Therefore, a MASSYVE agent is seen as a kind of tandem architecture composed of a "normal" agent and its FIMS. An essential concept introduced in this architecture is that the *data* elements are not sent from one agent to the other via a high-level protocol (e.g. ACL language), as in the traditional *push* strategy case, but rather through a *pull* strategy, via accessing to the respective agents' FIMS. Thus, the high-level protocol is only used for the control/coordination purposes.

www.gsigma.ufsc.br/massyve

Figure 4 – MASSYVE example

A number of recent research works have addressed the issues of contract modeling and electronic contracting processes.

C. Service federation infrastructure

Figure 5 illustrates the basic principles behind the service federation approach. Regardless the different implementation approaches the general three steps – publish, discover, invoke – are usually considered.

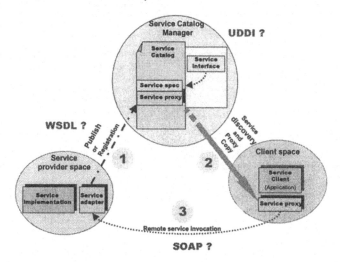

Figure 5 – Service federation approach

According to this model, companies (potential members of the virtual organization) are considered as "service providers", i.e. the potential collaborative behavior of each company is "materialized" by a set of services. The approach assumes the existence of one entity that keeps a catalog of services where service provider companies publish their service offers. This entity is sometimes called a "service market", a "service promoter node", or even "service portal". Services are published in the catalog through a "service specification" record that also includes a "proxy" or representative of the service to allow transparent remote invocation of the service. Client companies can then use the functionality provided by the catalog manager to "discover" existing services (and their providers). Once a service is selected, the client gets a copy of the corresponding proxy and can invoke it remotely in a transparent way, i.e. without caring about the actual location of the service or even its implementation language.

An early example of this approach is represented by the JINI technology. Perhaps earlier ideas in the same direction can be traced back to CORBA. More recently vendor-independent efforts have been trying to establish a number of *de facto* standards to facilitate the creation of such infrastructures: UDDI, WSDL, SOAP.

The implementation of a harmonized representation of services in the service catalog does not necessarily mean that all members have access to all services all the time. Service providers shall keep their autonomy and the right to specify whom and under which conditions, has access rights to their registered services.

Table 3 summarizes the main facets addressed by VOSTER projects and also the current limitations of the proposed solutions in the service federation approach.

Table 3.

Service federation horizontal infrastructure	
Key facets:	**Current limitations**:
❑ Basic architectures for service federation ❑ Mechanisms for remote service invocation ❑ Preliminary standards for service description and cataloguing: UDDI, WSDL, SOAP, ... ❑ Basic service search mechanisms ❑ Preliminary mechanisms for Value Added Service composition	❑ Poor integration of service federation and VO concept ❑ Poor integration of security / privacy mechanisms ❑ Search mechanisms still too basic ❑ Ad-hoc concept of portal

FETISH-ETF

FETISH-ETF is an example of application of a service federation approach to establish a horizontal infrastructure to support VOs in tourism. Clustering is a typical phenomenon in this sector, especially at regional level. Regional tourism promotion organizations try to offer an integrated view of the local resources (service promoter node). In order to reduce the fragmentation and dispersion of information some trends to form networks of service promoter nodes are emerging.

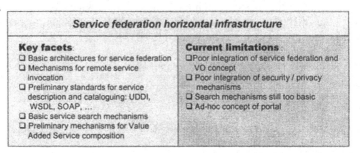

The developed infrastructure is based on Java/JINI, extending the service federation mechanisms of JINI to a wide area network. Services are specified using WSDL.
Services implementation can be done in any language provided that a wrapper (proxy) for transparent remote access is developed in Java.
The tourism services can be provided in two levels. The lower level contains the basic tourism services, which represent *atomic* services created by a tourism operator. On top of this level, it is possible to create another level in which the basic services are used as components of a *Value Added Service (VAS)*. An example of a VAS is a holiday package. The "materialization" of such a value-added service involves a process – business process (BP) – requiring the invocation and coordination of other services that may be provided by different service providers. In such a case of distributed execution the BP becomes a distributed business process (DBP). The contributing members can therefore form a temporary organization or virtual enterprise. FETISH-ETF provides a tool for composing VAS, specifying the corresponding workflow and selecting service providers from the catalogue. A selection of a set of service providers to satisfy the needs of a particular VAS leads to the formation of a VO to attend the business opportunity given by each instantiation of that VAS [4].

Figure 6 – The FETISH-ETF example

A "popular" term - ***portal*** – could be considered a special case of service federation infrastructure. This term is often used in the literature to represent rather different structures, from (i) a simple web entry point to a number of resources without any other form of collaboration among the resource providers, to (ii) some form of virtual organization. In this latter case, the basic idea is the existence of a "centralized access point", where the various VO members are "represented" and that might offer a "joint representation" to the outside, as well as a platform for interactions among the VO members.

4. VO LIFE CYCLE SUPPORT

In terms of VO life cycle support there is a clear focus on the "creation" and "operation"phases.

While in earlier projects the emphasis was mostly on supporting the operation phase, it can be noticed that in running projects the creation phase is becoming as important.

The "dissolution" phase remains almost untouched. Even though a few projects claim they address this phase, the actual functionality supported is rather limited.

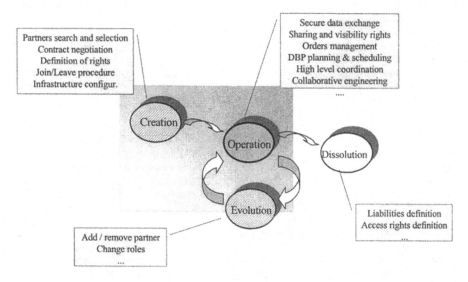

Figure 7 – Functions in VO life cycle support

VO creation. Some of the functionalities addressed in different projects include: VO planning, partners search and selection (perhaps the most addressed area), enterprise catalogues, contract negotiation, etc. It shall be noted that the fact that several projects address one topic this does not mean the topic is extensively treated. For instance, the issue of partners search is, in some cases, meant as a facility to help search by humans based on HTML pages. Only a few projects progressed towards computer-assisted (e.g. based on agents) partners search. One of the problems in partners search for VO creation is the availability of directories of companies / organizations where their profile (skills, resources, performance history, etc.) are represented in a standard format. The unavailability of a standard to represent these profiles has been a major obstacle. Recent developments (UDDI, WSDL) represent promising steps in this direction. Nevertheless if the catalog is confined to a cluster or VO breeding environment it is easier to reach a common representation of profiles.

VO operation. Coordination of distributed business processes (DBP) and activities is an important element in the VO operation. Most of the early approaches took a workflow-based approach, starting with the WfMC reference architecture and experimenting with extensions for supervision of distributed processes (cross-organizational workflow) including some preliminary but very limited works on exception handling, multi-level coordination and its relationship to coordination roles of the VO members, and flexible workflow models to support less structured processes.

---

eLEGAL
One of the most important aspects to consider in the creation of the VO is the ICT contract between the partners. The eLEGAL project has considered this and has developed a number of tools to enable the contract creation and negotiation to take place over the WWW. The figure shows the typical contracts needed in order for online collaboration to take place.

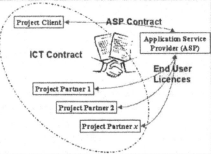

From extensive user requirements capture and analysis, an architecture for assisting tools to enable online contract creation and negotiation was developed. The tools include:
1. The *Contract Wizard* and
2. The *Virtual Negotiation Room* (VNR)

The contract wizard is an editing tool for electronic contracts, which are represented in XML. It allows the signing of the contractual parts of the document and access to a contract database, which holds text clauses imported from a library of clauses. The Contract Wizard allows validating, visualizing and printing contracts as well as storing them locally or on the VNR.

The second component is the VNR, which serves document management purposes like upload/download of contracts, version control, access control and multi-user support. The VNR is accessed via WebDAV protocol for document management and via SOAP for administration.

http://cic.vtt.fi/projects/elegal/

Figure 8 – The eLEGAL example

In terms of DBP planning and modeling some graphical languages have been suggested but a standard is still necessary in order to allow effective distribution / sharing of business processes. Proposals like PIF and PSL have been discussed in the USA but there is still more work to do. A recent European initiative, the UEML network, might contribute to some harmonization in the modeling area. Another initiative is BPEL4WS (Business Process Execution Language for Web Services).

In terms of business support functions, most of the projects have addressed application specific cases. ERP vendors have been extending their monolithic single-enterprise-centric systems in order to comply with more dynamic supply chains and networks, but this is an area requiring more investment on generic functionalities.

VO evolution and dissolution. During the life cycle of a VO it is natural that some partner leaves the consortium and be replaced by a new organization. The termination of this collaboration process or even the ending of a VO, are subjects not properly addressed yet. The consequences of the operation of a VO/VE cannot be simply discarded when the VO/VE dissolves. Most of these consequences are of a legal nature and shall be regulated by the cooperation agreements. That is the case, for instance, of the responsibility of customer support / product maintenance during the life cycle of the product / service generated by a VO/VE.

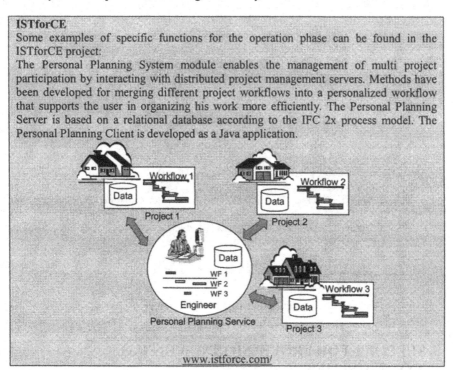

ISTforCE
Some examples of specific functions for the operation phase can be found in the ISTforCE project:
The Personal Planning System module enables the management of multi project participation by interacting with distributed project management servers. Methods have been developed for merging different project workflows into a personalized workflow that supports the user in organizing his work more efficiently. The Personal Planning Server is based on a relational database according to the IFC 2x process model. The Personal Planning Client is developed as a Java application.

www.istforce.com/

Figure 9 – The ISTforCE example

Environment regulations are also forcing companies to plan provisions regarding the product disposal and recycling after its end of life. Recent regulations in some countries also state that the liabilities regarding each component of a product may ultimately lie with the component's supplier. In the case of a network chain type of manufacturing this forces each node in the chain to keep track of the history of each component/sub-product that "passed by" this node. This is a functionality that is properly supported by most of the more advanced ERP systems, but not by most of the scheduling systems, for instance. There are, however, several other less "material" issues which are more difficult to handle. One of these issues is the Intellectual Property Rights policy, namely for the post-dissolution phase and its consequences in terms of information accesses by the VE members. In some cases there is also the possibility that the VE evolves into a more permanent organization, a joint venture enterprise created by the VE members, to exploit the intellectual and industrial property results developed in cooperation. There is also considerable knowledge that can be elicited from the ending cooperation experience, namely the knowledge about what went right, what went wrong, partners performance / reliability, jointly defined business process templates, etc. Defining the ownership and access rights to this knowledge is not an easy task and requires further investigation.

BIDSAVER
• The VE contract establishes, through a dedicated technical section, rules for:
  – Computing partners' rights on the final product and on related profits: reference algorithm based on pro-rata ownership of profits, based on a development mortgaging mechanism with asymptotic royalty and on the subdivision of profit according to effort and financial risk
  – Assessing liability of individual partners on the final product, through the reference to responsibility on product parts and processes.
• The ICT environment of BIDSAVER accommodates:
  – Management of dynamic composition of partnership
  – Establishment of responsibilities
  – Tracking of activities and costs (effort + expenditures).
• It supports for VE termination:
  – The enacting of principles for product liability allocation to partners down to the end of liability period
  – The computation of rights and due profits to individual partners upon VE termination, through the valorization of assets and of residual industrial risks.

www.vive-ig.net/projects/bidsaver/

Figure 10 - BIDSAVER example

5. SUPPORT FOR PROFESSIONAL VIRTUAL COMMUNITIES

When a proper cooperation environment is in place, **professional virtual communities** (PVC) / virtual teams emerge within such environment, constituting a fundamental element of value creation, innovation and sustainability. Virtual Communities and Communities of Practice are not new concepts but they acquire specific characteristics and increased importance when considered in the context of the collaborative networked organizations. These communities, although spontaneously created, are bound to certain social rules resulting from the commitment of their members to the underlying organizations (new concept of *social-bound PVCs*).

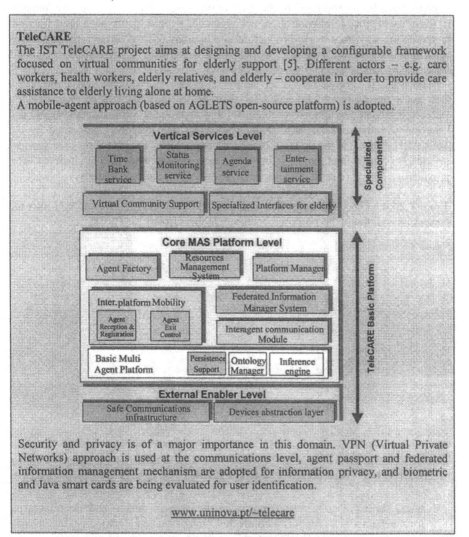

TeleCARE
The IST TeleCARE project aims at designing and developing a configurable framework focused on virtual communities for elderly support [5]. Different actors – e.g. care workers, health workers, elderly relatives, and elderly – cooperate in order to provide care assistance to elderly living alone at home.
A mobile-agent approach (based on AGLETS open-source platform) is adopted.

Security and privacy is of a major importance in this domain. VPN (Virtual Private Networks) approach is used at the communications level, agent passport and federated information management mechanism are adopted for information privacy, and biometric and Java smart cards are being evaluated for user identification.

www.uninova.pt/~telecare

Figure 11 – TeleCARE example

This is the case, for instance, in *concurrent* or *collaborative engineering* where teams of engineers, possibly located in different enterprises, cooperate in a joint project such as the co-design of a new product. A large number of computer supported cooperative tools are becoming widely available for synchronous cooperation. Some examples are teleconference, and chat tools combined with application-sharing mechanisms. Considering the geographical distribution, the autonomy of the VE members, the local corporate cultures, and also the individual working preferences of the team members, it is likely that most of the activities will be carried out in an asynchronous way, which requires new assisting tools.

In terms of coordination, several approaches to develop *flexible workflow* systems have been proposed. In the case of processes mainly executed by humans, rigid forms of procedural control are not adequate. People like to keep their freedom regarding the way they work. Product design, like any other creative process evolves according to a kind of "arbitrary" workflow. It is therefore necessary to also support *loosely constrained* sets of *business processes.*

The trend is followed by other communities of professionals (e.g. consultants) that share the body of knowledge of their professions such as similar working cultures, problem perceptions, problem-solving techniques, professional values, and behavior. Another special area of application, as for instance represented by the TeleCARE project, is the creation of virtual communities for providing care services to elderly. These communities involve organizations and people such as care providers, health care professionals, relatives of elderly, and the elderly.

Table 4 summarizes the main facets addressed by VOSTER projects and also the current limitations of the proposed solutions in the support for PVCs.

Table 4.

PVC-support infrastructure	
❑ First steps towards "shared working spaces" ❑ Large number of "small" tools (e.g. chat, instant messaging, teleconference, CSCW) ❑ Some application sharing mechanisms ❑ First steps towards flexible workflow and asynchronous coordination of activities, notification mechanisms ❑ Basic PVC management	❑ Very limited integration of tools and mechanisms ❑ Limited coordination facilities ❑ No adequate PVC management for professional communities (Virtual Communities of Practice) able to capture multi-level relationships ❑ No integration of IPR issues in the PVC management services ❑ Limited support for mobile contexts

6. SUPPORT FOR REMOTE OPERATION AND E-SCIENCE

Advanced forms of cooperation mostly in the area of design and manufacturing require mechanisms to support a controlled "intrusion" of a company, for instance the VE coordinator, into the "territory" of its partners. An initial example of this "intrusion", which is properly supported by the federated database paradigm, is the access to selected (authorized by the cooperation agreements) subsets of the information (for instance, the orders' status, stock levels, etc.). But this process may assume more extensive forms. Consider the case that a company wishes to "open a window" over the shop-floor of its partner (according to contractual rules) to monitor the manufacturing process of the ordered parts and even have an interference on the shop-floor processes, i.e. supervise these processes from distance and in cooperation with the local people. The local supervision functionalities installed in each production site shall interact / cooperate with the global VE (network-wide) supervision, providing controlled levels of transparency.

Mobile computing also suggests new forms of tele-operation and tele-supervision of processes.

A Virtual Laboratory (VL) is another form of collaborative network, representing a heterogeneous, distributed problem-solving environment that enables a group of researchers located in different geographical places to work together, sharing resources (equipments, tools, experimental data, etc.), i.e. a specialized form of VO.

Virtual Laboratories are attracting growing interest due to their potential applications in areas such as education, research, medicine, etc., in order to operate tools and equipment in remote locations or hazardous environments, among others. A typical VL involves scientific equipment connected to a network, large-scale simulations, visualization, data reduction and data summarization capabilities, application-specific databases, collaboration tools e.g. teleconferencing, federated data exchange, chat, shared electronic-whiteboard, notepad, etc., application-dependent software tools and interfaces, safe communications, and large network bandwidth.

Therefore, the concept of Virtual Laboratory has to be supported by the following main requirement classes:

(i)   *Remote operation*: in order to have access and manipulate tools and equipment located at a remote workshop;

(ii) *Information management:* to store information and data generated by the experiments realized;

(iii) *Simulation*: to visualize and reproduce the actions on the remote workshop, and

(iv) *Collaborative tools:* in order to share and coordinate the experiments among different partners around the world. A more recent term – **e-science** – is likely to replace the term virtual laboratory.

Collaborative remote supervision in manufacturing shares many requirements and challenges with the e-science environment, among which the following can be mentioned: Operation of remote instruments / equipment, remote diagnosis, team discussion, virtual meetings, sharing data at highly interpreted level, tele-mentoring (e.g. explaining a new process), what-if analysis / simulation, exclusive and shared accesses (to data, tools, and devices), access rights definition (to data, tools, and devices), visual checks and video link (conferencing), support for un-experienced users (the supervision partner does not necessarily know the details of the remote environment), and the need to automate many adjustments that were previously done manually (if not assisted by local operators in the physical equipment place).

VL

The VL (*Virtual Laboratory*) project aims at the design and development of an open, flexible, scalable, and configurable framework providing necessary GRID-based hardware and software, enabling scientists and engineers in different areas of research to work on their problems via experimentation (a virtual scientific community) [1], [9]. The VL provides a distributed high performance computing and communication Virtual Laboratory infrastructure with advanced information management functionalities, addressing in specific the experimentation requirements in the scientific domains of biology, physics, and systems engineering.

The VL makes it possible to attach a wide range of software tools to the laboratory; from basic tools such as simulation, visualization, data storage / manipulation, to advanced facilities. The main functionalities of the VL middleware include: remote controlling of devices (COMCOL), visualization in a virtual reality environment (VISE), and federated advanced information management (VIMCO). The VL solves various technical problems that scientists face, hence enabling them to focus better on their experiments, while using the GRID infrastructure, simultaneously reducing the costs of experimentation by sharing the expensive resources among them.

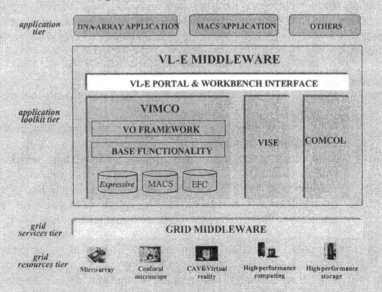

The GRID infrastructure is promising for the Virtual Laboratory environments supporting scientists and engineers with their complex collaborative experimentation. VL nodes in a network *register* themselves and become GRID nodes. The GRID-based nodes will then share their full computational and storage capacity, properly managed by the GRID resource management facility. As such, collaborating scientific nodes are supported by a close-to-standard communication infrastructure, empowering them with high-performance and/or high-throughput computing machinery, which is extendable with more resources, as other nodes join the GRID. Another advantage of using GRID for the scientific community is the possibility to share the free *published data* among the nodes.

http://carol.wins.uva.nl/~netpeer/projects/VirtualLaboratory/VirtualLaboratory.html

Figure 12 – The VL example

Table 5 summarizes the main facets addressed by VOSTER projects and also the current limitations of the proposed solutions in the remote operation and e-science.

Table 5.

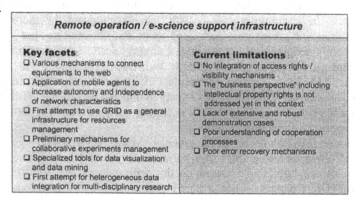

Remote operation / e-science support infrastructure	
Key facets:	**Current limitations:**
❑ Various mechanisms to connect equipments to the web	❑ No integration of access rights / visibility mechanisms
❑ Application of mobile agents to increase autonomy and independence of network characteristics	❑ The "business perspective" including intellectual property rights is not addressed yet in this context
❑ First attempt to use GRID as a general infrastructure for resources management	❑ Lack of extensive and robust demonstration cases
❑ Preliminary mechanisms for collaborative experiments management	❑ Poor understanding of cooperation processes
❑ Specialized tools for data visualization and data mining	❑ Poor error recovery mechanisms
❑ First attempt for heterogeneous data integration for multi-disciplinary research	

7. VO BREEDING ENVIRONMENT SUPPORT

Early proposals, too much technology-driven, underestimated the difficulties of the VE/VO creation process and suggested very dynamic scenarios but the agility and dynamism required for VOs are limited by the process of trust building. Even if flexible support infrastructures become widely available, the aspects of trust building and the required reorganization at the enterprise level are hard to cope with in cooperative business processes. "Trusting your partner" is a gradual and long process. The definition of "business rules", contracts for VE/VO or even common ontologies also take time, especially when different business cultures are involved. In this sense, very dynamic organizations formed by enterprises without previous experience of collaborating together might be limited to scenarios of simple commerce transactions (e.g. buy-sell).

The creation of long term clusters of industry or service enterprises represent an approach to overcome these obstacles and can support the rapid formation of VE / VO according to the business opportunities. The concept of cluster of enterprises, which should not be confused with a VO, represents an association or pool of enterprises and related supporting institutions that have both the potential and the will to cooperate with each other through the establishment of a long-term cooperation agreement. Buyer-supplier relationships, common technologies, common markets or distribution channels, common resources, or even common labor pools are elements that typically bind the cluster together. This is not a new concept as a large number of related initiatives have emerged during the last decades, namely in Europe and USA. But the advances in information and communication technologies now bring new opportunities to leverage the potential of this concept, namely by providing the adequate environment for the rapid formation of agile virtual enterprises.

The more frequent situation is the case in which the cluster is formed by organizations located in a common region, although geography is not a major facet when cooperation is supported by computer networks.

Nevertheless, the geographical closeness has some advantages for cooperation as it may facilitate better adaptation to the local (culture) needs and an easier creation of a "sense of community". But with the development of more effective communication infrastructures such long-term associations are not necessarily motivated by geographical closeness. Cultural ties, even particular human relationships are also motivating factors to form such associations which represent in fact the **VO Breeding Environments** (VBE) for the dynamic formation of VE/VOs [7]. For each business opportunity found by one of the VBE members, acting as a **broker,** a subset of the VBE enterprises may be chosen to form a VO/VE for that specific business opportunity.

The enterprises involved in a given breeding environment are normally "registered" in a directory (part of a portal or service market), where their core competencies are "declared". Based on this information, the VO/VE initiator / creator can select partners when a new business opportunity is detected. Clearly, several VOs can co-exist at the same time within a VBE, even with some members in common. A VBE, being a long-term organization, presents an adequate environment for the establishment of cooperation agreements, common infrastructures, common ontologies, and mutual trust, which are the facilitating elements when building a new VE.

Although not well understood in earlier projects, it is now clear to many of the analyzed projects that the formation of dynamic VE/VOs requires an appropriate "breeding" or "nesting" environment.

Table 6.

Breeding environment support infrastructure	
Key facets	**Current limitations**
□ Various practical cases of breeding environments (clusters, industrial districts) exist, with limited ICT support	□ Very limited VBE management functionalities
	□ No integrated framework for VO creation in the VBE context
□ Basic needed functionalities identified	□ Poor models of VBE and its working mechanisms, value systems, and trust building process
□ Some basic tools and methods for partners' profiling and selection	
□ Basic negotiation algorithms (namely following agent-based approaches) for coalition formation.	□ No tools / mechanisms for performance management
	□ Lack of integrated tools for contract negotiation and management

8. CONCLUSIONS

Considerable progress has been made in terms of design and development of infrastructures and support services for VOs but there are still a large number of challenging issues requiring further research.

In parallel with technological developments it is mandatory to reach some level of harmonization of models and approaches in order to reach interoperability and to reduce the engineering efforts still required to launch an operative VO. The lack of common reference models and widely accepted reference infrastructures still constitutes a major obstacle for the practical implementation of the VO paradigm. Today any VO project still needs to struggle with the development of its own basic infrastructure.

The interoperability problem, although an old issue in systems integration, remains on the agenda.

The fast evolution of ICT technology also calls for the need of a strong theoretical technology-independent foundation.

Acknowledgements. The results included in this paper are partially developed in the context of the European IST VOSTER project. The author thanks the comments and contributions from his partners.

9. REFERENCES

[1] H. Afsarmanesh, E. C. Kaletas, L. O. Hertzberger, "A Reference Architecture for Scientific Virtual Laboratories", *Future Generation Computer Systems*, vol. 17, 2001.

[2] P. Bernus, R. Baltrusch, J. Vesterager, M. Tolle, "Fast tracking ICT infrastructure requirements and design, based on enterprise reference architecture and matching reference models", *in: L.M. Camarinha-Matos, ed., Collaborative Business Ecosystems and Virtual Enterprises,* (Kluwer Academic Publishers, Boston), 2002.

[3] L. M. Camarinha-Matos, H. Afsarmanesh, "Virtual Enterprise Modeling and Support Infrastructures: Applying Multi-Agent Systems Approaches", in Multi-Agent Systems and Applications, M. Luck, V. Marik, O. Stpankova, R. Trappl (eds.), *Lecture Notes in Artificial Intelligence LNAI 2086,* pp.335-364, Springer, ISBN 3-540-42312-5, July 2001.

[4] L. M. Camarinha-Matos, H. Afsarmanesh, "Service Federation in Virtual Organizations", in *Proceedings of PROLAMAT'01,* 7-10 Nov 2001, Budapest, Hungary.

[5] L. M. Camarinha-Matos, H. Afsarmanesh, "Design of a virtual community infrastructure for elderly care", *in: L.M. Camarinha-Matos, ed., Collaborative Business Ecosystems and Virtual Enterprises,* (Kluwer Academic Publishers, Boston, 2002).

[6] L. M. Camarinha-Matos, H. Afsarmanesh, "Dynamic Virtual Organizations, or not so dynamic?", in *Proceedings of BASYS'02 - Knowledge and technology integration in production and services,* Kluwer Academic Publishers, ISBN 1-4020-7211-2, pp. 111-124, Sept 2002.

[7] L. M. Camarinha-Matos, H. Afsarmanesh, "Elements of a base VE infrastructure", to appear in *Computers in Industry, 2003.*

[8] L. M. Camarinha-Matos, K. Menzel, T. Cardoso, "ICT support infrastructures and interoperability for VOs", Deliverable D44, VOSTER. March 2003.

[9] E. C. Kaletas, H. Afsarmanesh, and L. O. Hertzberger, "Virtual Laboratories and Virtual Organizations Supporting Biosciences", in *Collaborative Business Ecosystems and Virtual Enterprises, Kluwer Academic Publishers, May 2002.*

[10] R. J. Rabelo, L. M. Camarinha-Matos, R. Vallejos., "Agent-based brokerage for virtual enterprise creation in the moulds industry", in *E-business and Virtual Enterprises,* L.M. Camarinha-Matos, H. Afsarmanesh, R. Rabelo (Eds.), Kluwer Academic Publishers, ISBN 0-7923-7205-0, pp. 281-290, 2000.

EMERGING TECHNOLOGIES AND STANDARDS

Ersin C. Kaletas
University of Amsterdam, The Netherlands, kaletas@science.uva.nl
Hamideh Afsarmanesh
University of Amsterdam, The Netherlands, hamideh@science.uva.nl
Maria Anastasiou
INTRACOM, Greece, mana@intracom.gr
Luis M. Camarinha-Matos
New University of Lisbon / Uninova, Portugal, cam@uninova.pt

*In response to VO challenges, research and development efforts shall address different features and components of VO, that cover a wide spectrum of areas. Considering the complexity of building technical support infrastructures and applications for VOs, clearly **at the time of such developments**, the choice of best approach, standards, technology, commercial tools/systems, or R&D developed prototypes plays a major role in their efficiency and sustainability. To assist developers in this challenging process, this chapter suggests a careful and systematic study of the problem/solution areas. This study discusses the properties required for technical support of VOs, the main related R&D focus areas, commercial development efforts, and the current trends in these areas.*

1. INTRODUCTION

A large number of emerging technologies and standards address some of the technical requirements identified in the paradigm of Virtual Organizations (VOs). These technologies and standards can thus be applied to supporting certain features and components of the base infrastructure and/or applications for networked collaborations. In fact the emergence of these elements is mainly driven by two factors. On one hand, due to the many existing collaborative application cases with challenging characteristics, coming from a wide range of business, science, and engineering domains, the need for such technologies and standards is already established. On the other hand, this need is continuously increasing, since due to the availability of these technologies and standards, the development of support environments for collaborative networks has increased, and at the same time many other new collaboration possibilities have risen, each identifying other new technical requirements.

Considering the complexity involved in building technical support infrastructures and/or applications for VOs, ***choosing the best approach, standards, technology, commercial tools/systems, or R&D developed prototypes,*** plays a major role in efficiency and sustainability of such developments. However, these elements are widely varied in their characteristics (e.g. public/proprietary), and considerably different in the features they provide. Furthermore, some of these elements have a very short life span, while other new elements are continuously emerging; hence, making it a real challenge to choose the right elements for building new technical developments for VOs. Therefore, we acknowledge that there is *no generic best set of elements* for future technical developments in the area of VOs. At the same time, we suggest that a careful and *systematic study of the current promising elements* and their features is a necessity to facilitate any infrastructure and/or application developments. Such a systematic study must consider: (1) the properties required for the technical VO support environments, (2) the main focus areas of the R&D as well as the commercial development efforts, and (3) the current trends in these areas. At this point, we must emphasize that solutions or recommendations are very much specific per application (area). Therefore the primary aim of this chapter is to provide a structure for the systematic study of existing and emerging technologies and standards as well as the results of such a study, together with an overall view of some of these technologies and standards, rather than proposing solutions or recommendations. Examples are excluded for similar reasons.

The remaining of this section provides a high-level structure for the systematic study presented in the paper, and classification of existing / emerging technologies and standards that support the VO paradigm, their features, and their components.

1.1 Structure of the Study

An overview of the classification structure, introduced in the paper, is depicted in Figure 1. The columns in this figure represent: (1) the addressed problem areas from the VO paradigm, (2) technical challenges, open questions, and classification of the technologies and standards providing solutions, and (3) the current enabling technologies and standards considered in the paper. Different columns of the figure also represent the topics covered in this chapter and hence correspond to the outline of the chapter. A summary of the study and classification structure is given below:

- **Problem areas** (Section 2): This part focuses on the target support environment for VOs, and briefly describes its main features and components. This part is itself divided into three sub-sections:
  - *Horizontal support infrastructure:* Features and components of the base horizontal infrastructure, focusing on the required base functionality necessary to support higher-level VO functionality.
  - *VO life cycle:* Features and components of the VO, which are related to required functionality to support its life cycle.
  - *Non-technical related disciplines:* Features and components of the VO that are related to other non-technical disciplines, e.g. the legal and organizational features.

  This chapter provides a summary of these features and components. More detailed descriptions of these areas are provided in other chapters of this book.
- **Challenges & solution areas – classification of enabling technologies** (Section 3): This part constitutes the main contribution of the chapter. First it identifies key challenges and open questions for VO support environments and related technologies and standards. Then it introduces focus areas and features addressed in current research and development efforts, and the current trends in these areas. Finally, a classification of related technologies and standards is presented, including a mapping from each technology or standard to the features and components mentioned above.

- **Current enabling technologies and standards** (Section 4): This part enumerates and exemplifies a number of promising - existing and emerging - technologies and standards applicable to the focus areas mentioned before, and provides a brief description of these technologies and standards.

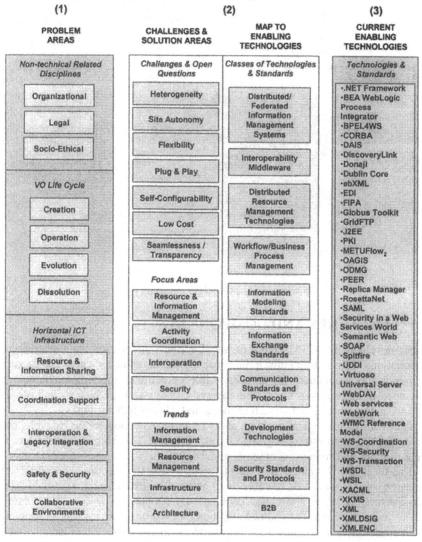

Figure 1. Structure of the study

The classification structure presented in Figure 1 is exemplified in Figure 2, where circles in each rectangle represent examples of topics in that rectangle. For instance, a circle in the problem area rectangle represents a feature or component of the VO that needs to be supported (e.g. safety & security). Similarly, a circle in the solution areas rectangle represents a focus area in current research and development efforts, while a circle in the rightmost rectangle represents an example technology or standard. Arrows connecting different circles represent inter-relationships between these areas. For instance, arrows from the solution areas to problem areas link these focus areas to those VO features and components that they support.

Classification Structure

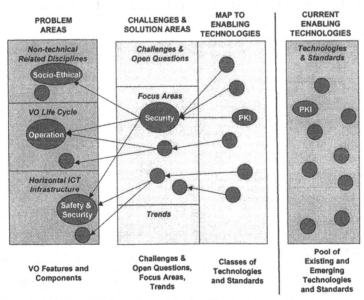

Figure 2. Overview of the classification structure

2. VO FEATURES AND COMPONENTS

Proper development of VOs requires an effective combination and integration of contributions from multiple disciplines, namely the computer science, management, sociology and organizational sciences, while sometimes applying methodologies developed in other fields, from economy and ecology to even biology and physics, but also taking other aspects - such as moral and ethics - into account.

The main technological problem areas requiring attention for VO development can be grouped into three categories: the horizontal ICT infrastructure, the VO life cycle support, and supporting other related disciplines.

The so called "horizontal ICT infrastructure" for VOs focuses on building and provision of as much as possible a generic, transparent, and affordable base infrastructure to support safe and coordinated interoperation among VO members. This infrastructure is usually aimed at playing an *intermediary* role, as an enabler of the interoperation among different VO members. In this context, it is intended as the enabler for safe and coordinated interactions among different organizations. The main components of this horizontal infrastructure are depicted under "Horizontal ICT Infrastructure" in Figure 1.

When analyzing the features and components of a VO, it is important to consider various phases of its life cycle and the functionalities required to support these phases. Figure 3 represents a minimal life cycle model including: the creation, operation, evolution, and dissolution phases, along with the main activities performed in each one of these phases. A detailed presentation of each phase and the research support it has received so far is provided in a previous chapter of this book.

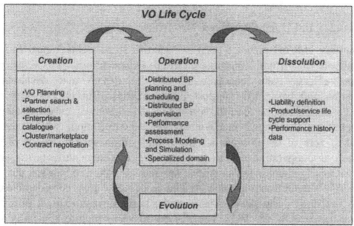

Figure 3. Phases of a VO life cycle and some of their main activities

As mentioned earlier, the main features and components of VOs are of different nature, requiring innovative solutions from different disciplines. In [1], three main disciplines are distinguished, classified here as **other related disciplines** for the VO research; namely the organizational, legal, and socio-ethical areas. The contributions of these disciplines to the VO are exemplified in Figure 4 and discussed in detail in Part 3 of this book. In order to support these features, new ICT tools are required.

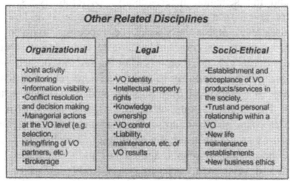

Figure 4. Features and components of VO related to the other disciplines

3. CHALLENGES, FOCUS AREAS AND TRENDS

The last years have been quite fertile in terms of development of new technologies and standards to support e-business and distributed/collaborative applications, but several challenges still remain to be overcome and some open questions left to be answered. In this direction, this section first identifies and discusses some of these challenges and open questions, then presents the main focus areas of the current VO development efforts. The most representative examples of (existing and emerging) technologies and standards are named next in this section, which are then classified and mapped onto the focus areas. Then a mapping of the focus areas onto the problem areas is provided. Finally, the current trends in these areas are summarized.

3.1 Challenges and Open Questions

A large number of R&D projects tried to establish some technological foundations for the support of Virtual Enterprises/Virtual Organizations [2]. Many of these development efforts were concentrated on the design and development of infrastructures and basic VO support functionalities. But only a few of these initiatives correspond to the required *horizontal developments,* aimed at establishing the base platform, tools and mechanisms for VO operation, while most others correspond to vertical developments, addressing certain specific needs of specific sectors, such as cooperative design (and engineering) in manufacturing, dynamic supply chain management in agribusiness, service federation in tourism, etc.

Although it is natural that in the early phases of a new area, considerable effort is devoted to the design and development of the basic infrastructures, unfortunately this was not the case for the VOs. The ICT-based infrastructure is usually aimed at playing an *intermediary* role as an enabler for interoperation, e.g. for safe and coordinated interactions among the VO partners. Furthermore, and from another perspective, the generic infrastructure should play the role of VO's "operating system" or executor, hiding the details of the collaborative network "machinery", and thus achieving collaboration/communication **transparency.**

Transparency is required to hide **heterogeneity and complexity of collaboration.** Different types of heterogeneity arise in a complex environment such as the VO. Among these, one can mention the system heterogeneity, the syntactic heterogeneity, and the semantic heterogeneity. Different types of heterogeneity occur at different levels in a VO: at the communication level, hardware/software platform level, data level, and activity level (i.e. processes involved in the VO life cycle). In addition, enterprises, although willing to cooperate with others to fulfill the common goals of the VO, insist on ensuring the security of their information and resources, preserving their **autonomy** to make decisions related to what part of their resources to share, at which level of granularity and with which partners inside or outside the VO. The study of state of the art reveals a lack of mature standard definitions and mechanisms to address these requirements, leaving the smooth integration of security and collaboration technologies as a challenge.

Furthermore, most available related approaches and technologies are still in their infancy and under development, requiring considerable effort to implement and configure comprehensive VO support infrastructures. Also, even the most advanced infrastructures coming out of the leading R&D projects still require complex configuration and customization processes, which are hardly manageable by SMEs. At the same time, **reducing the cost** of solutions development, and their deployment and integration is another challenge set by most enterprises, that needs to be achieved in order to facilitate and promote their collaboration in VO environments.

Moreover, when infrastructures comprise components from different technologies and vendors, it is also difficult to determine which component (or tool provider) is responsible when something goes wrong with such complex systems. **"Plug and play"** is a buzzword used today that expresses the vision where all systems will be seamlessly plug compatible, such that a software module or a new piece of equipment could be inserted into a process or an operation and be up and running immediately with zero integration costs [3].

In conclusion, setting up a VO infrastructure still requires a large engineering effort, which represents a major obstacle for the implantation of this new paradigm. Furthermore, the fast evolution of the information technologies often presents a disturbing factor for non-IT companies. In order to leverage the potential benefits of the VO paradigm, flexible and generic infrastructures need to be designed and implemented. **Flexibility,** usually understood as the capability of a system to rapidly adapt to new needed processes, is a requirement to cope with the variety of emerging and evolving behaviors in collaborative organizations. **Generality** is another requirement to cope with the needs of different application domains. **Self configurability** is an additional requirement to deal with the variety of user needs and situations that the infrastructure should address in collaborative organizations and refers to the ability of the system to adapt its capabilities according to user needs by selecting the right components for the situation. Some further challenges regarding the interoperability is addressed in Section 3.3 below.

Figure 5 summarizes the research challenges and open questions to be answered.

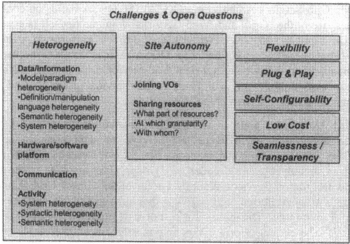

Figure 5. Challenges and open questions

3.2 Solution Focus Areas

From the technology development perspective some focus areas of research can be distinguished as important contributors / enablers for VO environments, including those represented in Figure 3, which are further addressed below.

3.2.1 Distributed Resource & Information Management

In the early VO cases, resources comprise data/information, software tools (e.g. workflow systems, CAD/CAM tools), and in some cases hardware facilities (e.g. computing nodes). With the emerging VOs, however, new types of resources are being considered. For instance, the emerging virtual laboratory paradigm in e-science allows applications and scientists to share instrumentation, networking and storage facilities in addition to software and hardware. In some cases, even entire physical facilities (e.g. a biology laboratory) are considered as resources and shared among collaborators. In geographically distributed, large, complex collaborative environments like VO, management and sharing of resources is an essential issue.

Distributed Resource Management

In this section, two related resource management technologies are presented and analyzed: Grid for the management of computing and networking resources; and Data Grid for the management of storage resources.

Grid Computing: In the late 90s, Grid computing [4] was proposed as a distributed computing infrastructure for advanced sciences and engineering fields. Grid computing enables coordinated and dynamic resource sharing for collaborative problem solving in large scale distributed computing environments. Although a relatively recent technology, Grid is a promising distributed resource management technology. It provides mechanisms and develops standards for security, allocation and monitoring of resources, and submission, monitoring and management of remote jobs relying on these resources. Next generation of Grid architecture is based on the Open Grid Services Architecture (OGSA) [5]. OGSA builds on concepts and technologies from the Grid and Web services communities. It supports Web Services Description Language (WSDL) and defines uniform exposed service semantics (the Grid service). Furthermore, OGSA defines standard mechanisms for creating, naming and discovering transient Grid service instances, provides location transparency and multiple protocol bindings for service instances, and supports integration with underlying native platform facilities.

Data Grid: Data Grid aims to define an integrated architecture that allows coordinated application of different technologies to data-intensive application domains. It is a specialization and extension of the Grid. Research efforts related to Data Grid are mainly organized under two groups. The first one is the Database Access and Integration Services Working Group of the Global Grid Forum (GGF-DAIS) (http: //www.gridforum.org/6_ DAT A/dais.htm). and the second one is the UK e-Science Programme Database Task Force (http://www.cs.man.ac.uk/grid-db/dbtf.html). The current efforts in this field mostly concentrate on identifying the requirements and proposing mechanisms for accessing storage facilities from the Grid environment. In this direction, a layered architecture is designed, which aims to provide varying services: replica management and replica selection; data and metadata access; authorization and authentication; resource reservation and co-allocation; performance measurement; and instrumentation.

Considering the horizontal infrastructure for VO, this technology can be considered for all categories except for the coordination tasks. Specifically, Grid/Data Grid can support the following requirements of VO: a) general information and knowledge sharing; b) safety/security; c) interoperability and legacy systems integration; and d) collaborative environments.

In terms of functionality support, the Grid/Data Grid technology has the potential to also fit some categories of the required VO creation and operation functionality: a) partners search and selection/e-procurement; b) contract/agreement negotiation; c) distributed BP planning and scheduling; and d) dynamic performance assessment. Nevertheless this potential still requires further developments in order to be leveraged.

Distributed/Federated Information Management

Distributed information management addresses issues related to the management of geographically distributed information. A distributed database consists of a collection of logically inter-related databases [6]. The distribution is mainly for better performance reasons. A distributed database is typically designed as a whole and managed centrally [7].

In a fully federated database on the other hand, many databases contribute data and resources to a multi-database federation, while each participant has full local autonomy [7]. Federated information management [8, 9, 10, 11] can enable sharing and exchange of information among collaborating sites, while preserving the autonomy of the sites and ensuring the security of proprietary information. Federated access to data from diverse sources provides users the possibility of securely accessing all data made available by these sources, while hiding heterogeneity of the underlying platforms with respect to their data modeling approaches, data manipulation languages, and distinct schemas [10].

Figure 6 shows a classification of federated database systems as described in [10]. In loosely-coupled systems, every user in the system is responsible for developing the integration mechanisms suited to her/his requirements. Generally, there is no integrated schema in loosely coupled systems, and users directly access the information that they need from the respective data source and adapt it to their view of data. Tightly-coupled systems, on the other hand, provide common integrated schemas in a single database environment for all users, where accessing the local data sources is transparent to the users. In single-federations within tightly-coupled systems, there is only one global integrated schema visible to the federation members [9], while in multiple-federations every federation member generates its own integrated schema as its view of available information [8, 10].

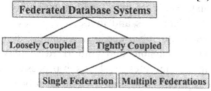

Figure 6. Classification of federated database systems

Other classifications for federated database systems can be found in [8]. A specific type of federated database system can be more suitable for a certain type of VO. For instance, a single federation tightly-coupled system can better represent the data architecture in a VO with star-like coordination. In [12] the heterogeneity and interoperability issues involved in information brokering through a metadata-based architecture are discussed.

Data/Information Modeling & Exchange

Information models provide a means for describing entities and concepts involved in a domain in a structured way, whereas standards allow collaborators to share and exchange information. Availability of such models will enable the development of generic and uniform mechanisms for managing the information represented by these models. Standards, on the other hand, further allow to overcome semantic heterogeneity (e.g. by standardizing elements and their meanings), syntactic heterogeneity (e.g. by standardizing data models, query and manipulation languages, and exchange formats), and systematic heterogeneity (e.g. by using standard communication/interoperability mechanisms) that may occur among the information models and information management systems of collaborators.

3.2.2 Activity Coordination – Workflow Management Systems

A workflow is defined as a collection of processing steps (activities) organized to accomplish some business process [13]. An activity can be performed either by one or more software systems or machines, by a person or a team, or a combination of these. In addition to activities, a workflow defines the order of activity invocations or condition(s) under which activities must be invoked (i.e. flow control) and data-flow between these activities. Activities within a workflow can themselves be workflows. A Workflow Management System is defined by the Workflow Management Coalition (WfMC) (http://www.wfmc.org/) as a set of tools providing support for process definition, workflow enactment, and administration and monitoring of workflow processes [14].

With the rise of the Web, inter-organizational workflows became a crucial issue. In [37], Bernauer et.al. identify three major characteristics of inter-organizational workflows as *interoperability* (which requires agreements on interfaces and common understanding of data and services exchanged), different levels of *autonomy* (design autonomy at build-time, communication and execution autonomy at run-time, and association autonomy at agreement time), and *openness* of the environment (concerning legality, security, trust, etc).

Dayal et.al., on the other hand, provide a framework in [36] for business process management. According to this framework, business processes are typically of long duration, involve coordination across many manual and automated tasks, and require access to several different databases and invocation of several application systems. Business rules trigger tasks and sub-processes, which are assigned to *resources,* i.e. organizational units that are capable and authorized to play specific *roles* in the processes. The scripting of the rules, tasks, sub-processes, and resource policies constitute a process description. Commonly, business processes are defined prior to their execution. Most systems allow graphical editors to model the business process as a flow diagram, with rules determining the next step in the flow. Some other systems use a collection of rules to represent the process without explicitly delineating the flows. In order to tackle the long-running and distributed nature of business processes, a number of (extended) transaction models have been proposed. Some of the transaction models summarized in [36] allow long-running transactions to be chained, nested, or both. In case of failure, either the sub-transactions are rolled back using their semantic inverses, or an alternate task (contingency) is executed, or the failure is propagated to higher levels in the transaction hierarchy where the appropriate failure recovery mechanism is chosen and implemented.

Another aspect related to inter-organizational workflows is the specification language. Several specification languages have been proposed, each having different origins and pursuing different goals. [37] describes a framework for comparing specification languages. In this framework, there are seven perspectives: **Functional perspective** describes *what* has to be done in a workflow, as specified by a *workflow type,* and focuses on inter-organizational workflow types, information hiding, and activity semantics. **Operational perspective** describes *how* activities are implemented, focusing on activity implementation. **Behavioral perspective** is concerned about *when* activities have to be performed, and focuses on control flow primitives, timing constraints, and exception handling. **Informational perspective** comprises data structures and data flow between activities, focusing on data types, reusability of data types, and data flow. **Interaction perspective** deals with the interactions among participants to coordinate the execution of workflow fragments, and focuses on interaction primitives, interaction implementation, and implementation independence. **Organizational perspective** is concerned about *who* participates in which role in a workflow, and focuses on roles, organization profiles, agreements, and dynamic participation. Finally, **transactional perspective** describes which parts of a workflow exhibit which transactional properties. Seven specification languages are compared in [37] based on the perspectives defined in this framework, namely WSDL, WSFL, ebXML, BPML, XLANG, BPEL, WSCL, WSCI and WPDL. Results of the comparison of these workflow specification languages can be found in [37].

3.2.3 Interoperation

Interoperability is defined as "the ability of two or more systems or components to exchange information and to use the information that has been exchanged" [15]. However, interoperability is not related to ICT only. According to IDEAS project [16], in order to achieve meaningful interoperation between enterprises, interoperability must be achieved in all the layers of the enterprise including the business environment and the business processes, the organizational roles, skills and competences of employees and knowledge assets in the knowledge layer, the application, data and communication components related to ICT layer. In addition, semantic descriptions at all levels can be used to create the necessary mutual understanding between enterprises that want to collaborate.

The three layers and the various interoperability aspects on each layer are integrated into an interoperability framework [3] that IDEAS project has developed. Figure 7 presents a simplified version of the interoperability framework with an emphasis on ICT layer, as this is the scope of this chapter.

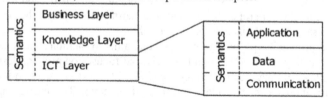

Figure 7. Simplified IDEAS interoperability Framework with a focus on ICT layer

In order to address all layers and the various interoperability aspects, the contribution of three research domains is required [16]:

- Architecture/Platform (A&P) for defining a framework for interoperability.
- Enterprise Modeling (EM) as the art of "externalizing" enterprise knowledge, i.e. representing the enterprise in terms of its organization and operations [20]. The finality is to make explicit facts and knowledge that add value to the enterprise or can be shared by business applications and

users in order to improve the performance of the enterprise. EM role in interoperability could be considered in at least the following dimensions: (a) to help establishing interoperability between existing heterogeneous applications and software (b) to elaborate specifications to choose interoperable applications & software on the market, and (c) to provide new approaches to solutions and system development.

- Ontology (ON) to address the semantics necessary to assure interoperability. An ontology refers to the set of logical definitions that express the meaning of terms for a particular domain. These conceptual definitions make use of explicit assumptions and may include semantics as well [33]. Ontologies are based on the understanding of the members of a particular domain, and help to reduce ambiguity in human-computer, human-human, and computer-computer interactions [34]. Considering ontology's influence to interoperability [20], the focus is on using ontology in achieving application system interoperability.

Enterprises have been facing interoperability problems since a long time but these problems became even more critical and important in the context of networked enterprises and VOs. The problems stem from the heterogeneous hardware and software platforms in use, the lack of standards but also the oversupply of standards. Indicatively, in spite of the large number of existing and emerging standards for enterprise data exchange, most of them have been developed using divergent methodologies and without concern to have their models interoperable with other standards, in the same or complementary scopes of usage [17]. Therefore, there is no global plan for these standards to be interoperable with others.

In addition, VO participants require having diverse local solutions that better suit their unique local conditions and interconnect to the other nodes preserving their autonomy. This implies that even if there are global standards sufficient for every business need, there will be incompatible systems either by choice or because of proprietary solutions (legacy) [16]. Consequently, there is a need for some interoperation approach rather than a tight integration [18].

The current state of the art on infrastructures provides good support for the integration solution paradigm, according to which there is a standard format for all constituent systems [19]. Business issues, however, are still to be addressed [20]. Considering semantic interoperability and the harmonization of the enterprise models is necessary for real business interoperability.

The UEML project (http://www.ueml.org) that aims to facilitate interoperability at enterprise modeling level, STEP standard [21] that focuses on product design data exchange and Process Specification Language (PSL) [22] that is process oriented are state of the art approaches that adapt the unified scenario. The unified approach assumes that there is a common meta-level structure across constituent models, providing a means for establishing semantic equivalence [19]. ebXML (http://www.ebxml.org) is also considered to support the unified approach.

The federated model scenario may exist if no agent successfully or globally can impose requirements for semantic equivalence across all models of an enterprise [19]. Interoperability requires that models be dynamically accommodated rather than having a predetermined meta-model. This assumes that concept mapping is done at an ontology level. The federated situation seems to be the most adequate scenario for full interoperability in a network of heterogeneous and autonomous pre-existing enterprises wherein most models will not be in a standardized or common form. However, currently available infrastructures that support the federated paradigm are limited to the information layer only.

In addition, there is also a set of open issues relating to migration from existing implementations of platforms to any future ones that meet the objectives and criteria for interoperability [20]. A further issue is that few platforms have been developed with due consideration of the re-structuring of inter- and intra- organizational relations, the changing market structures, and the transitioning from traditional organizational models to networked organizations.

Ontology state of the art, in perspective of ontology based application system interoperability, reveals a limited level of maturity of existing solutions [20]. The key point is represented by ontology languages, and in particular their semantic adequacy for modeling mentioned concepts such as business entities, transactions, goals, processes, and related notions. Current languages are more than adequate to model static aspects of the reality. However, functions and processes are much more difficult to be ontologically defined. The main problem resides in the availability of modeling constructs able to capture the deep nature of a business process. A business function has the effect of changing the reality and, even worse, a process need to relate a collection of functions from a logical and temporal perspective. Current ontology languages are not adequate to represent the latter concepts (i.e., logical and temporal sequences)

3.2.4 Security

Security of a system indicates that the system is free from danger, damage or risk. In [23], some representative examples of the risks include: a) Violation of the access policy (e.g. unauthorized access); b) Violation of security privileges (e.g. a user that damages the system); c) Violation of communications integrity and/or confidentiality (e.g. an insecure cryptographic algorithm); and d) System crashes. Different security mechanisms can be applied to address these risks; for instance firewalls (http://www.interhack.net/pubs/fwfaq/) can be applied at the edge of the system network to prevent some unauthorized access to protected systems, or redundant physical servers can be employed within the main system to increase the system availability [23]. Some of the main related mechanisms addressed below include authentication, encryption, digital signature, digital certificates and VPN.

User **authentication** mechanisms and systems can be divided into three large groups: based on something known (a password), based on something owned (a smart card (http://www.rainbow.com/ikey/index.html), or based on biometric systems (characteristics of particular individuals, for example the strokes of a signature or a fingerprint) (http://www.computer.org/itpro/homepage/Jan_Feb/ security3.htm). Typically, authentication systems combine several of these mechanisms in order to increase the security level. The authentication process, as well as the authorization and access control processes are discussed in more detail in Chapter 2.3.

Today, the state of the art in **data encryption** uses of a combination of symmetric and asymmetric systems [11]. Encryption consists of obscuring data of any type for everybody except those authorized to see the contents. The encryption and decryption operations may be carried out by hardware systems (smart cards) or software (computer programs). The advantages of **digital signatures** include: (1) its *authenticity,* since the signature indicates that the document has been signed deliberately; (2) its *non-repudiation,* since the signer cannot deny that the signature is his or hers; and (3) the signature cannot be re-used, since a different signature is generated for every document.

One of the problems of asymmetric cryptosystems is that it is difficult to know whether the public key of an entity really belongs to that entity and not to another entity that is impersonating it. **Digital certificates** solve this problem (http://www.verisign.com/whitepaper/enterprise/overview/index.html). The certificate is no more than a public key together with certain information about the person or organization to whom the key belongs, and an entity trusted by the whole community - a **certification authority** or the CA - that digitally signs both documents. Namely, what the certification authority does is to link the key to the data of the owner, so that we know to whom the public key really belongs.

In fact, a certificate is a credential, the same as a passport or an identity document; all of these contain information, which identify individuals, here, also the organizations, which certifies that the document is correct and that we are who we say we are. However, the certificate alone cannot guarantee the authenticity of the personal data of the owner; it simply links a key with data, and therefore, before a certificate is issued by a CA it is necessary to investigate the identity of the person or organization requesting it.

A **Virtual Private Network (VPN)** consists of the software and hardware, which allows mobile users, tele-workers and remote nodes to use an insecure public network (such as Internet) to establish a secure, private connection to other nodes in the network (http://www.fatelabs.com). From the user's point of view, a VPN connection is a point-to-point connection between the user's computer and a remote server or another node. These point-to-point connections however, can easily be extended for use with more clients and servers, to the point where it appears that we have a very large and secure local network with many clients and servers, but over an insecure public network (usually Internet). Therefore, there can also be many isolated, private, local sub-networks interconnected over a public network (Internet) that in turn also lowers costs. Advantages of the VPN include the following: confidentiality, integrity, authentication, protection against replay attacks, application independence, IP address routing, compliance with standards, multiple hardware and software implementations, existence of support hardware (cryptographic accelerators).

Besides the security issues at the system level (i.e. accessing hardware, such as server machines or disks) and at the software level (i.e. accessing software, such as database management systems - DBMSs), another level of security is required at the data/information level. At this level, the security must address **data/information visibility rights,** which means who can see the data/information and what portion of it is visible to each user. Today, almost all DBMSs allow the definition of roles and grouping of users in these roles with specific views defined on the data/information for every user role. However, VOs introduce new challenges for the security at the data/information level. For instance, an enterprise can be a member of more than one VO, where every VO's information must be treated proprietary and secure from the other VOs. But, an enterprise may also have the right to share some of the information within the context of one VO with another partner from another VO. Furthermore, in some cases, it might be necessary for a VO member to define restrictions on some data sets which are not stored at its local servers, but available from another member. In such complicated cases, federated information management systems can offer the necessary functionality for the definition and enforcement of information visibility and access rights.

3.3 Current Trends

This section provides an overview of the current trends in some of the focus areas, namely infrastructure/architecture, and information and resource management.

In parallel to the improvements in the networking and communication technologies, and availability of widespread facilities, the terms *distribution, mobility,* and *dynamic* have arisen as the keywords to represent the current trends.

The trend in infrastructure/architecture can be summarized as infrastructures moving from client/server over the Intranet towards P2P over the Internet, and at the same time architectures moving from transaction/layer-based towards service-based and agent-based approaches. Please refer to Chapter 2.1 of this book for a detailed elaboration of the infrastructure/architecture related issues.

A similar trend can be observed in the area of information and resource management. Most existing information management systems are built on top of pre-defined structured data models that are at the same time static. In these systems, applications are information-oriented, and built with a bottom-up approach to basically support only the current application needs. In these applications, data/information is generally modeled using the relational model for storage, while for instance complex applications require object-oriented modeling of their structures. Research trends in support of the emerging applications, especially in the area of scientific research, are towards semi-structured, dynamic models. The main factor behind this transition is that these applications are usually of *ad-hoc* nature, and gradually generate different types of information as the result of each process execution. In order to cope with this behavior, semi-structured and more dynamic data models are suggested to be used for representing information, using for instance XML and WebDAV. Information is usually represented as the name-value pairs in these models. Specific libraries are also being developed to manipulate and query information in these models.

In resource management, the trend of moving from centralized systems to distributed systems is now changing towards the application of networked clusters. One can see networked clusters as 'distributed systems', where a number of distributed facilities are connected to each other. In general, these facilities are geographically distributed all over the world, and comprise facilities from many organizations. Availability, and eventually maturity, of the distributed resource and information management systems, such as Grid and federated information management, will serve as pushing factors for this trend.

As mentioned in Section 3.1, autonomy still remains as a challenge in collaborative environments, where participating organizations require full control on their resources. In some distributed and highly heterogeneous environments, autonomy is preserved and enforced through a set of mappings from global users to local users and from global permissions to local permissions. In the Grid, for example, every Grid user (i.e. a global user) has a certificate which uniquely identifies this user. Each organization participating in the Grid maintains mapping files that map this global user to a local user on each resource (e.g. to a database user). Furthermore, certain permissions are given to these local users on each resource. Therefore, while sharing its resources in a collaborative Grid environment, the participating organization still preserves its autonomy on deciding who can use its resources and how. Two related aspects in Grid are transparent access (i.e. single sign-on) and sharing permissions in the context of a virtual organization [35].

Some new research trends on development of VO support environment address the need for new disciplines providing more generic and intelligent tools; for instance, replacing the cumbersome programming tasks related to implantation / configuration - now needed to be performed by developers - with the careful parameterization of complex pre-defined structures. Also the new trends in support of interoperability are heavily focused on using and management of web-services and W3C standards and tools, e.g. the more use of WSDL and UDDI.

One other current trend is related to semantics. Many research efforts focus on provision, representation and usage of semantic information about resources. As mentioned in Section 3.2.3, ontologies are used to store and maintain semantic information, such as descriptions of entities involved in a specific domain with a well-defined boundary, and the relationships between the entities. Several applications of semantic information are emerging, among which one can mention information integration and inter-linking, collaborating (intelligent) agents, (intelligent) assisting tools/user interfaces (e.g. that allow users to formulate their questions, possibly in native language, in more formal terms so that they can be translated into queries over multiple sources). Semantic Web is an example here, which will allow the development of intelligent agents to discover relevant information and services, understand the information and process it using the available services. Since such agents can change their behavior at run-time, they can perform ad-hoc tasks and even modify pre-defined procedures with such ad-hoc tasks and/or information.

3.4 Classification of Technologies and Standards

The existing and emerging technologies and standards presented in this chapter are categorized into nine groups:

- **Resource management technologies** address sharing of resources in the VO, where the resources can be information, hardware or software.
- **Distributed/federated information management systems** provide generic mechanisms for sharing and exchange of information among multiple information centers, which may at the same time be autonomous and involve different types of heterogeneity.
- **Workflow management systems** address the organization of activities required to accomplish a task, and specify rules for the correct execution and successful completion of the activities.
- **Interoperability middleware** addresses the system heterogeneity. In order to share resources among multiple organizations and organize tasks whose execution may span multiple organizations, interoperability comes up as a very important issue.
- **Development technologies** providing the software environment suitable for large distributed system development.

- **Information modeling standards** address the representational aspects of information. Standardization is among the most important constituents for interoperability. One specific need for interoperability rises when sharing and exchanging information among multiple sites.
- **Information exchange standards** focus on the syntactic aspects of information.
- **Communication standards and protocols** addressing distributed object access protocol.
- **Security standards and protocols** focusing on different aspects of security in distributed networks.
- **Technologies and standards related to B2B** focused on framework definitions and tools for business-to-business collaboration.

Figure 8 graphically illustrates the classification of the technologies and standards, and names some of the most representative examples for each class. The mapping between the focus areas and the classes of technologies and standards is also given in Figure 8, indicating which class of technology and standard can be used to support which focus area. Another mapping provided in this figure is the mapping of focus areas to problem areas, showing which focus area addresses which problem area (i.e. VO features and components).

4. EXITING AND EMERGING TECHNOLOGIES AND STANDARDS

This section provides a survey of some representative example systems of so far existing technologies and standards that can be used to support the VOs. Please notice that for every item in the list only a brief description and some references are provided. And it should be highlighted that given the highly dynamic pace of the emerging technologies and standards, the following list is not exhaustive. The objective here is rather to provide examples of the main publicly available elements, for which the interested readers can find an overview specification.

IBM's **DiscoveryLink** [27] is a wrapper-based relational federated system originally developed for life sciences. Version 7.2 supports read-only access to data sources. Specific wrappers are developed for different data sources (e.g. Oracle, SQL Server, comma-separated text files, MS Excel files). Structures in data sources are exposed to DiscoveryLink as tables by importing their definitions. There is no integrated schema; semantic integration is left to the applications, which can be realized to some extent through views. When a query arrives on the imported structures, the query is decomposed into sub-queries, which are then executed by the data sources.

Virtuoso Universal Server from OpenLink Software is a data middleware which provides transparent access to heterogeneous data resources. Virtuoso approach is similar to the one of DiscoveryLink; it imports table definitions from underlying data sources to Virtuoso server and allows users to issue queries against these imported table definitions. Virtuoso supports accessing data from Native Virtuoso SQL Database, different SQL databases, and native XML databases. It provides different access mechanisms including Web services, SOAP, and HTTP (http://www.openlinksw.com/virtuoso/index.htm).

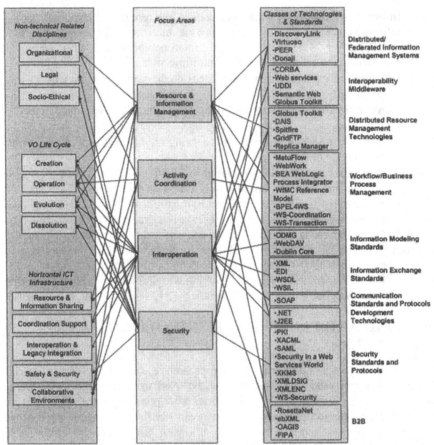

Figure 8. Classification of technologies and standards; mapping of technologies and standards to focus areas; mapping of focus areas to problem areas

PEER is an object-oriented multiple-federation system. Its architecture is based on a *global data model* and a *global language* [25], supporting the full autonomy and heterogeneity of every involved database. Several schemas co-exist in every node in a PEER federation, including local, export, import, and the integrated schemas, together representing the world of information accessible by users through this node. Therefore, users can issue queries against any schema (local and remote) accessible by their node. When a query arrives at a node, the federated query processor of the node handles it. The query is first converted into its source (derived) specifications. It will then get decomposed into sub-queries on the local and/or remote information sources. The necessary sub-queries are then submitted to, and evaluated against, schemas at those sources. Finally the query results are returned to the requester and merged. The entire process of federated queries is transparent to the users.

Donaji has a tightly-coupled single-federation architecture [26]. The metadata model in Donaji is based on the ODMG2.0 object model. The AQUA query algebra is used as the global query language. Among its components, *conceptual mediators* support access to the metadata and mappings between global and local sources, decomposition of global queries into local ones, and translation from global conceptual schema structures to local schema structures. *Query processor* is the logical unit for handling user's global queries. *Operational mediators* translate the sub-queries into the query languages of the local data sources and place the local query results into the temporary object repository, and resolve terminology conflicts.

CORBA (Common Object Request Broker Architecture) is an industry standard that defines a higher-level facility for distributed computing. CORBA is defined by the Object Management Group (OMG). OMG is a not-for-profit consortium that produces and maintains computer industry specifications for interoperable enterprise applications. OMG defines CORBA consisting of four groups of entities: (1) the Object Request Broker, which is a specification for distributed objects communication, (2) Object Services that support the life-cycle management of objects, (3) Common Facilities that are generic functions such as printing, electronic mail, (4) Domain Interfaces that provide functionality of direct interest to end-users. CORBA specifications are available at OMG web site: http://www.omg.org.

Web Services. The ongoing efforts in the Web services area are mainly carried out by the W3C Web Services Architecture Group, which defines a web service as "a software application identified by a URI, whose interfaces and bindings are capable of being defined, described, and discovered as XML artifacts. A web service supports direct interactions via Internet-based protocols". Web Services are self-contained, self-describing, modular applications that can be published, located, and invoked across the Web. Once a Web service is deployed, other applications (and other Web Services) can discover and invoke the deployed service.

In this context a number of standards are being proposed, for instance, the WSDL, UDDI, SOAP, etc. (see below). The security aspects are being standardized by OASIS. QoS infrastructures are still at a very early stage of development.

UDDI. The Universal Description Discovery Integration (UDDI) creates a platform-independent, open framework for describing services, discovering businesses, and integrating business services using the Internet, as well as an operational registry that is available today.

The UDDI business registry includes three kinds of information: *white pages, yellow pages* and *green pages*. The *white pages* component is a listing of business entities and ability to search companies by their name. The *yellow pages* categorize business entities into their business categories and other sorts of applicable categories. The *green pages* add the ability to understand a service definition and its access requirements. Providing all these information enables an online application such as a web service an automated way to find and access other services as well as the distribution of the service itself. Using such servers enables companies and organizations to publish and retrieve web services and enables collaborative working inside a company, between companies, or both.

Semantic Web targets at a A global mesh of information linked up in such a way that can be easily processed by machines. The main idea behind Semantic Web is two folds: 1) Allow anybody to say anything about anything, 2) Publish information in a machine-processable manner. Main components of the Semantic Web are *identifiers* (URI – Uniform Resource Identifier), *documents* (XML – Extensible Markup Language), *statements* (RDF – Resource Description Framework), *meaning & relationships* (schemas & ontologies), *computer reasoning* (logic), *proving logic statements* (proof), and *trust* (digital signatures).

URI, XML and RDF allow machines to read data/information (about published resources). Ontologies provide the meanings of resources (within a given context) and their relationships to other resources, and allow programs to understand the resource, and if necessary, change their behavior to process the data based on its ontology description and relationships. This way, many complex tasks formulated and assigned by humans can be automated and executed by agents working on the Semantic Web. For more information on Semantic Web, refer to: The Semantic Web (http://www.scientificamerican.com/article.cfm?articleID=00048144-10D2-1C70-84A9809EC588EF21&catID=2), Semantic Web Road Map (http://www.w3.org/DesignIssues/Semantic.html), The Semantic Web: An Introduction (http://infomesh.net/2001/swintro/), and The Semantic Web In Breadth (http://logicerror.com/semanticWeb-long).

Globus Toolkit is a reference implementation of Grid concepts and is considered as de facto standard for today's Grid computing. It employs a 'bag of services' approach. Users can select the set of tools that they need for their specific requirements during their application development. In this approach, the 'bag' can also be extended with additional tools. The toolkit includes resource management services such as resource discovery (using LDAP based catalogues), allocation, and monitoring. The toolkit also implements the Grid Security Infrastructure (GSI), which describes authentication techniques in wide area networks. More information on Globus and its services can be found at http://www.globus.org/.

DAIS. The most complete and solid proposal for *Database Access and Integration Services* (DAIS) on the Grid is described in [7]. The proposal is independent of any Grid implementation and of any data model or database access language and includes the following services: *Database discovery, database statements, delivery system, basic* and *distributed transaction interfaces, database metadata, virtual databases, selective replication* and *management services.*

Spitfire (http://edg-wp2.web.cern.ch/edg-wp2/spitfire/) provides a uniform way to access relational databases through standard Grid protocols and published Grid interfaces. It defines a set of operations to interact with the database. Query results can be returned in different formats, including XML.

Replica Manager and GridFTP. *GridFTP* protocol [24] extends the standard FTP to include a superset of features currently offered by various Grid storage systems. It includes features like GSI, third-party control of data transfer, parallel or striped data transfer and support for reliable and re-startable data transfer. The *replica management component* [24] is responsible for managing the replication of data sets. Its services include creating new copies of (collection of) files, registering these copies in a Replica Catalogue, and allowing the querying of the catalogue to find all existing copies of a data set.

METUFlow₂ [13] is specifically designed for dynamically adapting the business processes to changes in its environment. A workflow process is defined as a collection of blocks, tasks and sub-processes. Its *component server repository* contains Workflow Process Definition and Instance Monitoring tools. *Definitions Library* stores workflow definitions. History Manager handles the database that stores the information about workflow process instances.

WebWork [28] is a Web-based implementation of the **METEOR₂** workflow enactment system [29], which provides the command, communication and control for participating tasks in a workflow. Its main components are workflow schedulers, task managers, (application) tasks, and a run-time monitor. *Task managers* are used to control the execution of tasks. They communicate with *workflow schedulers* to establish global control and to facilitate recovery and monitoring. *Run-time monitor* is used to administer the system.

BEA WebLogic Process Integrator (http://e-docs.bea.com/wlintegration/v2_0/ processintegrator/index.htm) is a J2EE standards-based workflow engine supporting workflow definition and execution, data administration (managing the people involved in a workflow, rerouting tasks when needed, etc.), and workflow monitoring. It runs on BEA WebLogic Server, and supports both application- and human-interaction. In a workflow, organizations are defined first, followed by roles for each organization, and users for each role.

WfMC Reference Model. In order to facilitate the interoperation among different components of a workflow system, the Workflow Management Coalition (WfMC) defined a reference model for workflow management systems (http://www.wfmc.org /standards/docs/Ref_Model_10_years_on_Hollingsworth.pdf). The model is composed of five key interfaces: *Interface 1* supports the exchange of process definition data between BPR tools, workflow systems and process definition repositories. *Interface 2* facilitates client application integration with different workflow systems. *Interface 3* provides a common framework for 3rd parties to integrate other industry applications & services. Finally, *Interface 5* allows consistent audit and administration of workflow cases across systems.

BPEL4WS, WS-Coordination and WS-Transaction. The Business Process Execution Language for Web Services (BPEL4WS) specification defines a notation for specifying business process behavior based on Web Services. Together with two further complimentary specifications, the WS-Coordination and WS-Transaction it presents efforts to standardize business process workflow and execution to increase transaction reliability and synchronization.

BPEL4WS allows specifying business processes and how they relate to Web services. This includes specifying how a business process makes use of Web services to achieve its goal, as well as specifying Web services that are provided by a business process.

The WS-Coordination and WS-Transaction specifications complement BPEL4WS by providing a Web Services-based approach for improving the dependability of automated, long running business transactions, in an extensible and interoperable way. WS-Coordination describes an extensible framework for providing protocols that coordinate the actions of distributed applications. The framework enables existing transaction processing, workflow, and other systems for coordination to hide their proprietary protocols and to operate in a heterogeneous environment. The WS-Transaction specification describes coordination types that are used with the extensible coordination framework described in the WS-Coordination specification.

The specifications described above address directly the major problems of collaborative networks where different heterogeneous and autonomous business domains need to be jointly involved in the provision of common business processes. These specifications are not yet standardized. Furthermore, there are some other specifications, regarding the same field of the Web services, but supporting distributed business processes. The adoption of one of the considered specifications as standards by standardization bodies, as well as the maturation of the enabling tools and their implementations, will definitely bring a significant value to enabling collaboration between different domains.

ODMG Standard. The Object Data Management Group (http://www.odmg.org/) defines the *ODMG Standard* for modeling of persistent objects [30]. The *Data Model* component of the standard defines type specification and implementation. The *Object Definition Language* (ODL) is used to define the schema and operations of an object store. The *Object Query Language* (OQL) is an object manipulation language similar to SQL with extensions for object-oriented concepts. The *Object Interchange Format* (OIF) is used to dump the current state of an object store to a file and to exchange objects between object stores. ODMG also defines bindings for different programming languages, including Java, C++ and Smalltalk.

WebDAV Distributed Authoring and Versioning Protocol defines a set of extensions to HTTP (http://www.webdav.org/). Its objective is to reach interoperability by allowing users to publish documents in the Web and to co-author published documents in-place. It focuses on *overwrite prevention* to maintain the document consistency; *properties* of published documents (i.e. metadata) in the form of name-value pairs, and facilities for manipulating metadata and for inter-linking documents through hypertext links; and *name space management.*

The **Dublin Core Metadata Standard** contains an element set for describing a wide range of on-line resources. The standard is mainly developed for describing document-like objects, and contains elements for *document metadata*. However, the standard can also be applied to other sources if their metadata resembles a typical document metadata. The standard comprises fifteen elements, grouped into three: content-related elements, elements related to intellectual property; elements related to a particular instantiation of a document (http://dublincore.org/).

XML. The Extensible Markup Language (XML) is a World Wide Web Consortium (W3C) Recommendation for marking up data that cannot be marked up using the simple set of document presentation elements defined in the HyperText Markup Language (HTML). Whilst designed initially for the display of documentation distributed via the World Wide Web (WWW), XML is now widely accepted as a generalized method for interchanging information between computer programs over the Internet. XML is being defined in stages in a number of W3C Recommendations that the interested author could find at the W3C web site (http://www.w3c.org).

EDI (Electronic Data Interchange) is related with the use of general electronic transfer of business data from one independent computer system to another, using standard format as defined by the ANSI X12 standard (http://www.x12.org/international/Entrypoint.htm) or by the UN/EDIFACT (United Nations/Electronic Data Interchange for Administration, Commerce and Transport) (http://www.x12.org/international/edif.htm) standards. Many large enterprises and government organizations have invested greatly in traditional EDI systems over the years, however, there are traditional barriers to entry for EDI, such as large cost and trading volume requirements and proprietary software.

WSDL. The Web Services Description Language (WSDL) is an XML format for describing web services and how to access them. It specifies the location of the service and the operations (or methods) the service exposes. Once a service provider has developed a Web service, he can publish its description and a link to it in a UDDI repository so that potential users can find it. When someone thinks they want to use the service, they request the WSDL file in order to find out the location of the service, the function calls and how to access them. Then, they use this information in the WSDL file to form a SOAP (Simple Object Access Protocol) request to the service provider's computer. See http://www.w3c.org for the WDSL specifications.

WSIL. The Web Service Inspection Language provides an XML format for assisting the inspection of a site for available services and a set of rules for how inspection related information should be made available for consumption. A WS-Inspection document provides means for aggregating references to pre-existing service description documents which have been authored in any number of formats.

WSIL addresses directly one of the main problems of collaborative networks, i.e. finding a required service. Different, autonomous business domains must be jointly involved to provide upper level services. The finding of a partner providing the right service was reduced to the usage of a centralized registry, as a UDDI registry, until now. The WS-Inspection-Technology opens new possibilities to the service provider to advertise services as well as to the service requester to find the desired service. The very important thing is, WSIL does not exclude or restrict the already existing solutions, but extends them. WSIL is a specification proposed by IBM and Microsoft. Although WSIL is still a proprietary specification, both IBM and Microsoft have announced their intentions of submitting the WSIL specification to standardization bodies, probably the World Wide Web Consortium (W3C).

SOAP. Simple Object Access Protocol (SOAP) is an XML based protocol to let applications exchange information over HTTP. In the past applications used to communicate using Remote Procedure Calls (RPC) between objects like DCOM and CORBA, but HTTP was not designed for this. RPC represents a compatibility and security problem; firewalls and proxy servers normally block this kind of traffic. A better way to communicate between applications is over HTTP, because HTTP is supported by all Internet browsers and servers. SOAP was created to accomplish this. SOAP provides a way to communicate between applications running on different operating systems, with different technologies and programming languages. SOAP recommendations documents are available at http://www.w3c.org.

.NET Framework. .NET initiative was announced by Microsoft in the middle 2000 aiming at providing an infrastructure for building XML web services transparent to developers and users. .NET Framework consists of three main parts: the Common Languange Runtime (CLR) that is built on top of the operating system services and is responsible for actually executing the application, the Framework Class Library that provides a unified, object oriented, hierarchical, and extensible set of class libraries, or APIs that the developers can use from the languages they are familiar with, and a component-based version of Microsoft Active Server Pages ASP.NET that provides a Web application model for building Web applications. More information can be found at http://www.microsoft.com/net/.

J2EE (Java 2 Platform, Enterprise Edition) is designed for the development, deployment, and management of multi-tier server-centric enterprise applications. It is the result of an on-going industry collaboration led by Sun Microsystems. The J2EE architecture defines a *client tier,* a *middle tier* (consisting of one or more sub-tiers), and a backend tier providing services of existing information systems. The client tier supports a variety of client types, both outside and inside of corporate firewalls. The middle tier supports client services through Web containers in the *Web tier* and supports business logic component services through Enterprise JavaBeansTM (EJBTM) containers in the *EJB tier.* The *enterprise information system (EIS) tier* supports access to existing information systems by means of standard APIs. In addition, the J2EE specification defines a number of standard services for use by J2EE components. More information can be found at: http://java.sun.com/j2ee/.

Public Key Infrastructure (PKI). The term Public Key Infrastructure (PKI) is referred to the set of hardware, software, people, policies and procedures needed to create, manage, store, distribute, and revoke Public Key Certificates (PKCs) based on public-key cryptography. Digital Certificates are the cornerstone for any PKI, and a standardized Certificate Format is the starting point for achieving interoperability in large-scale PKI systems. Today a number of standards organizations (NIST, IETF, ETSI) have proposed common frameworks for digital certificate interoperability. Most notable is ITU-T X.509 [31] Digital Certificate Format on which the majority of PKI products are based. More information can be found at: http://www.pkiforum.org/.

Extensible Access Control Markup Language (XACML) is an OASIS (http://www.oasis-open.org) standard that describes both a policy language and an access control decision request/response language (both written in XML). The policy language is used to describe general access control requirements, and has standard extension points for defining new functions, data types, combining logic, etc. The request/response language lets you form a query to ask whether or not a given action should be allowed, and interpret the result. The response always includes an answer about whether the request should be allowed using one of four values: Permit, Deny, Indeterminate (an error occurred or some required value was missing, so a decision cannot be made) or Not Applicable (the request can't be answered by this service).

Security Assertion Markup Language (SAML) is an XML-based security framework for exchanging authentication and authorization information between systems, application servers, and XML exchange frameworks like SOAP and ebXML. SAML allows users to carry their credentials with them as they access partner Web sites and Web services, further enabling users to chain together multiple Web services while retaining "single sign-on" authentication. SAML is an ongoing work performed by OASIS Security Services Technical Committee (TC) (http://www.oasis-open.org/committees/security/#documents)

Security in a Web Services World: A Proposed Architecture and Roadmap. IBM and Microsoft propose a comprehensive Web service security model that supports, integrates and unifies several popular security models, mechanisms, and technologies (including both symmetric and public key technologies) in a way that enables a variety of systems to securely interoperate in a platform- and language-neutral manner. This model subsumes and expands upon the ideas expressed in similar specifications previously proposed by IBM and Microsoft (namely the SOAP-Security, WS-Security and WS-License specifications). More information can be found at http://msdn.microsoft.com.

The **XML Key Management (XKMS)** is a working draft specification that defines protocols for distributing and registering public keys, suitable for use in conjunction with the proposed standard for XML Signature developed by the World Wide Web Consortium (W3C) and the Internet Engineering Task Force (IETF) and an anticipated companion standard for XML encryption. The XML Key Management Specification (XKMS) comprises two parts -- the XML Key Information Service Specification (X-KISS) and the XML Key Registration Service Specification (X-KRSS). The draft specification can be found at: http://www.w3.org/TR/2003/WD-xkms2-20030418/.

XML Digital Signatures (XMLDSIG) is a specification of the use of the XML syntax to represent a signature (XML Signature). XML Signatures provide integrity, message authentication, and/or signer authentication services for data of any type, whether located within the XML that includes the signature or elsewhere. The specification was produced by the IETF/W3C XML Signature Working Group (http://www.w3.org/Signature/).

XML Encryption (XMLENC) is being developed by XML Encryption Working Group (http://www.w3.org/Encryption/2001/). It as an XML syntax used to represent the (1) encrypted content and (2) information that enables an intended recipient to decrypt it.

Web Services Security (WS-Security) specification (http://www-106.ibm.com/developerworks/webservices/library/ws-secure/) describes enhancements to SOAP messaging to provide quality of protection through message integrity, message confidentiality, and single message authentication. These mechanisms can be used to accommodate a wide variety of security models and encryption technologies. WS-Security also provides a general-purpose mechanism for associating security tokens with messages. Additionally, WS-Security describes how to encode binary security tokens and includes extensibility mechanisms that can be used to further describe the characteristics of the credentials that are included with a message.

RosetaNet. RosettaNet is a self-funded, not for profit private consortium of the leading companies of Information Technology (IT), Electronic Components (EC), Semiconductor Manufacturing (SM), Telecommunications and Logistics. The mission of RosettaNet is the development and deployment of open electronic commerce standards that align the business processes between partners in high tech supply chain. The main aim is to the means of an interface that companies should apply to their legacy systems in order to participate in a wide supply chain eBusiness process. RosettaNet standards documentation can be found at: http://www.rosettanet.org.

ebXML. ebXML was started in 1999 as an initiative of OASIS and the United Nations/ECE agency CEFACT. The goal of ebXML was to create an infrastructure for a single global electronic market. The ebXML architecture includes the formal modelling of business processes, trading agreements, and message components. It includes aspects related to the sharing of component definitions that can form the basis for the better integration of data management features. It also defines messaging protocols applicable at the applications level. More information can be found at http://www.ebxml.org.

Open Applications Group Integration Specification (OAGIS). Open Applications Group Integration Specification (OAGIS) [32] developed by Open Applications Group (OAG) is a set of specifications that define the business object interoperability between enterprise business applications. It aims at supporting horizontal business transactions in inter organizational environment rather than vertical IT integration within a company. Today, OAGIS supports financial transactions, ERP to ERP interoperation, Supply Chain interoperation, etc.

FIPA. The Foundation for Intelligent Physical Agents (FIPA) has produced, and is continuing to evolve, an architecture and an associated set of specifications for distributed, communicating, software agents. The emphasis is on the practical commercial and industrial uses of agent systems. The aim is to bring together the latest advances in agent research with industry best practice in software, networks and business systems. FIPA specifications can be found at: http://www.fipa.org.

5. CONCLUSIONS

This chapter provided an overview of emerging technologies and standards that may serve as the enablers for the development of the required support infrastructure for VOs. In order to study the technologies and standards, and to identify their possible usage in the VO support environment, a high-level classification structure is defined. This structure divided the areas covered by the study into three categories:

o The main problem areas that need to be supported for a properly functioning VO infrastructure
o The focus areas of current research and development efforts, and a snapshot and classification of representative examples of today's technologies and standards
o Brief descriptions of these technologies and standards

The structure is also used to provide the mappings between these three areas. As shown in Figure 8, a number of focus areas of the current research and development efforts can provide the required support for a number of the problem areas. Figure 8 also shows that for each focus area, there are already some example technologies or standards, either existing or emerging (and being at their early stages).

As presented in this chapter, there are a number of classes of enabling technologies and standards, where each class in turn contains a number of example technologies and standards. Considering that the examples named in this chapter only represent a selection of the technologies and standards at the time, it is clear that developers of supporting tools/infrastructure for VOs face with a complex problem of choosing from a wide spectrum of enablers, which require a survey of available tools and a study/evaluation of their applicability to the application under consideration. As also mentioned earlier, choosing solutions depends on the specific needs and circumstances of each application, therefore is specific per application. We hope that this chapter provides an overview of existing and emerging technologies and standards at an adequate level of detail, and serves as the starting point for the task of choosing solutions that best fit to the application.

6. REFERENCES

1. H. Afsarmanesh, V. Mařík, L. M. Camarinha-Matos. Challenges of Collaborative Networks in Europe. In L. M. Camarinha-Matos, H. Afsarmanesh, editors, Collaborative Networked Organizations – A research agenda for emerging business models, chapter 3.3. Kluwer Academic Publishers, 2004.
2. L. M. Camarinha-Matos, and H. Afsarmanesh, 1999, Infrastructures for Virtual Enterprises - Networking Industrial Enterprises (Kluwer Academic Publishers, Boston).
3. IDEAS Consortium WP3. A Gap Analysis. Required Activities in Research, Technology and Standardization to close the RTS Gap. Roadmaps and Recommendations on RTS activities. 30 May 2003. Available at http://www.ideas-roadmap.net
4. I. Foster, C. Kesselman, and S. Tuecke. The anatomy of the grid: Enabling scalable virtual organizations. International Journal of Supercomputer Applications, 15(3):200-222, 2001
5. I. Foster, C. Kesselman, J. Nick, and S. Tuecke. The physiology of the grid: An open grid services architecture for distributed systems integration. Technical report, Global Grid Forum - Open Grid Service Infrastructure Working Group, 2002.
6. M. T. Ozsu and P. Valduriez. Principles of Distributed Database Systems. Prentice-Hall, 1999.
7. N. W. Paton, M. P. Atkinson, V. Dialani, D. Pearson, T. Storey, and P. Watson. Database access and integration services on the grid. Technical Report UKeS-2002-03, National e-Science Centre, 2002.
8. A. Sheth and J. Larson. Federated database systems for managing distributed, heterogeneous, and autonomous databases. ACM Computing Surveys, 22(3): 183-236, 1990.
9. C. Garita, H. Afsarmanesh, and L. O. Hertzberger. The prodnet federated information management approach for virtual enterprise support. Journal of Intelligent Manufacturing, 12:151-170, 2001.
10. O. A. Bukhres and A. Elmagarmid, editors. Object-Oriented Multidatabase Systems - A Solution for Advanced Applications. Prentice Hall, 1996.
11. C. Bruce Schneier. Applied Cryptography Second Edition: Protocols, Algorithms and Source Code in C. John Wiley & Sons, Inc. ISBN 0-471-12845-7.
12. V. Kashyap and A. Sheth. Information Brokering Accross Heterogeneous Digital Data - A Metadata-Based Approach. Kluwer Academic Publishers, 2000

13. P. Koksal, I. Cingil, and A. Dogac. A Component-Based Workflow System with Dynamic Modifications. In Proceedings of Next Generation Information Technologies and Systems (NGITS'99), pages 238-255,1999.
14. D. Hollingsworth. The Workflow Reference Model. Technical Report. TC00-1003. The Workflow Management Coalition, 1994.
15. Institute of Electrical and Electronics Engineers. *IEEE Standard Computer Dictionary: A Compilation of IEEE Standard Computer Glossaries.* New York, NY: 1990.
16. IDEAS Consortium. Description of Work. 13 May 2002.
17. E. Jardim-Golcalves, A. Steiger-Garcao. A framework for adoption of Standards for Data Exchange. 7th ISPE Int. Conf. on CE: Research and Applic.- CE'2000, pp.333-342, Technomic, ISBN 1-58716-033-1
18. D. Chen, G. Doumeingts. "Basic Concepts and Approaches to develop interoperability of enterprise applications". In Processes and Foundations For Virtual Organisations, pp. 323-330. Kluwer Academic Publishers. ISBN 1-4020-7638-X.
19. ISO 14258, 1999, Industrial Automation Systems – Concepts and Rules for Enterprise Models, ISO TC184/SC5/WG1, 1999-April-14 version.
20. IDEAS Consortium WP1. State of the Art, Part C – Architectures and Platforms State of the Art. 29 May 2003. Available at http://www.ideas-roadmap.net
21. ISO TC184/SC4, IS - ISO 10303, Parti - Overview and Fundamentals Principles, 1994
22. ISO CD 18629-1, 2001, Industrial automation systems and integration, Process Specification Language (PSL), Part 1: Overview and Basic Principles, JW8/ISO 184/SC4/SC5.
23. S. P. Hidalgo, R. M. Gasca, L. M. Navas. Report on security, encryption and authentication. TeleCARE (A Multi-Agent Tele-Supervision System for Elderly Care) Project Deliverable D6.1. 2002.
24. B. Allcock, J. Bester, J. Bresnahan, A. L. Chervenak, I. Foster, C. Kesselman, S. Meder, V. Nefedova, D. Quesnel, and Steven Tuecke. Data management and transfer in high-performance computational grid environments. Parallel Computing Journal, 28(5):749-771, 2002.
25. H. Afsarmanesh, M. Wiedijk, L.O. Hertzberger, F.J. Negreiros Gomes, A. Provedel, R.C. Martins, and E.O.T. Salles. Cooperation of CIM expert systems supported by Peer. Journal of Studies in Informatics and Control, 5(2):157-169, 1996.
26. J. C. Lavariega and S. D. Urban. Donaji: A semantic architecture for multi-database systems. In Proceedings of the Workshop in Intelligent Information Integration, pages 39-54, 1998.
27. L. M. Haas, P. M. Schwarz, P. Kodali, E. Kotlar, J. E. Rice, , and W. C. Swope. DiscoveryLink: A system for integrated access to life sciences data sources. IBM Systems Journal, 40(2):489-511, 2001.
28. J. A. Miller, D. Palaniswami, A. P. Sheth, K. J. Kochut, and H. Singh. WebWork: METEOR$_2$'s Web-Based Workflow Management System. Journal of Intelligent Information Systems, 10(2):185-215, 1998.
29. A. Sheth, D. Worah, K. Kochut, J. Miller, K. Zheng, D. Palaniswami, and S. Das. The METEOR Workflow Management System and its use in Prototyping Healthcare Applications. In Proceedings of the Towards An Electronic Patient Record (TEPR'97) Conference, pages 267-278, 1997.
30. R. G. G. Cattell, D. K. Barry, M. Berler, J. Eastman, D. Jordan, C. Russell, O. Schadow, T. Stanienda, and F. Velez, editors. The Object Data Standard - ODMG 3.0. Morgan Kaufmann, 2000.
31. ITU-T X.509 Recommendation, "Information Technology – Open Systems Interconnection – The Directory Public Key and Attribute Certificate Frame-works", June 2000
32. OAG, 2001. OAGIS: Open Applications Group Integration Specification, Open Application Group, Incorporated, Release 7.2.1, Doc. No. 20011031, 2001.
33. M. N. Huhns, M. P. Singh. Ontologies for Agents. IEEE Internet Computing, 1(6): 81-83, 1997.
34. V. Guevara-Masis, O. Unal, E. C. Kaletas, H. Afsarmanesh, and L. O. Hertzberger. Using Ontologies for Collaborative Information Management: Some Challenges & Ideas. To appear in Proceedings of the Third Biennial International Conference on Advances in Information Systems (ADVIS 2004), 2004.
35. E. C. Kaletas, H. Afsarmanesh, and L. O. Hertzberger. A Collaborative Experimentation Environment for Biosciences. To appear in the International Journal of Networking and Virtual Organizations (IJNVO).
36. U. Dayal, M. Hsu, and R. Ladin. Business Process Coordination: State of the Art, Trends, and Open Issues. In Proceedings of the 27th VLDB Conference, 2001.
37. M. Bernauer, G. Kramler, G. Kappel, and W. Retschitzegger. Specification of Interorganizational Workflows - A Comparison of Approaches. In Proceeding of the 7th World Multiconference on Systemics, Cybernetics and Informatics (SCI 2003), 2003.

SECURITY FRAMEWORKS FOR VIRTUAL ORGANIZATIONS

Jarosław Magiera, Adam Pawlak
Silesian University of Technology, Gliwice, Poland
{magiera, pawlak}@ciel.pl

This chapter addresses security framework in virtual organisations. It identifies essential sources of threats to VOs security and presents technologies such as: confidentiality and integrity of data for secure communication, authentication, authorisation and access control to resources, to assure this security. The need for appropriate management of security measures deployed in a particular VO has been stressed. Security instruments developed and demonstrated by the IST projects E-COLLEG, EXTERNAL, PRODNET, and TeleCAREe follow. Finally, open R&D questions, related to VOs security framework, are addressed.

1. INTRODUCTION

The concept of security is inseparable from network-based information systems. It has a particular significance for virtual organizations whose activities either strongly or entirely depend on the network access. The safety level of the VO member organisations and their communication influences security of the entire virtual organization. Diversity of approaches to security issues in different virtual organizations is due to a variety of forms of their activities. VO member organizations are often built upon diverse network infrastructures and on diverse platforms (Voster, 2003). Furthermore, they use different strategies (NIST, 1998) to assure their own security.

Granting access to a member organization's resources to another member organization within the framework of the VO imposes changes on the organization security system. Since the whole VO is as secure as its weakest member organization is, each VO member organization becomes equally responsible not only for its own security, but also for security of common resources. Finding a simple, yet complete definition of the security framework is a real challenge, considering the fact that VO is based on a geographically dispersed information infrastructure, and additionally commonly accessible networks, like the Internet, are used for internal communication within the VO.

The security framework is a set of methods, tools and guidelines that a VO is expected to deploy in order to protect its resources, e.g. data being processed, information on the organisation and its users (system configuration, passwords, etc.), services offered, as well as, the whole infrastructure with its components (computers, network elements, wiring, etc.). An additional requirement is to assure the possibility to efficiently manage elements of the security framework. This includes: design, deployment and execution of the VO own security strategy.

In the following section, main sources of danger to VOs are identified. Further on, we point to security technologies that can provide remedy for the identified threats. Security measures developed and demonstrated by IST projects E-COLLEG (www.ecolleg.org), EXTERNAL (research.dnv.com/external/), PRODNET (www.uninova.pt/~prodnet), and TeleCARE (www.uninova.pt/~telecare) follow. We present in more detail the architecture and its security components that where implemented in the advanced collaborative infrastructure, developed by the E-Colleg project. In conclusions, we point to some open R&D questions related to the VOs security frameworks.

2. THREATS TO VOs SECURITY

There are different sources and types of potential threats to VOs security.

- Threats caused by an activity aimed at altering the present state of a system. What we mean is any attempt to break the protection in order to illegally use resources, any interference in the processed data, resulting in the data loss.
- Threats caused by activities not aimed at altering the present state of a system. This group includes eavesdropping and interception attempts which lead to loss of secrecy of the information being processed.
- Threats resulting from various accidents and errors, as well as malfunction of the system.

The first two groups assume the purposeful action aimed at unauthorised access to protected resources and their alteration. A number of techniques are being employed these days to break the protection system (Lockhart,2004) (Peikari and Chuvakin,2004). The most commonly used techniques are masquerading, eavesdropping, modification of transmitted information, password hacking by force or by a dictionary attack, analysis of traffic in the network, denial of service, code elements modification aimed at gaining access to resources (Burnett,2004), making use of bugs and errors in the security system (McNab,2004), social engineering and Trojan horses (Grimes,2001). The third group mentioned, apart from system errors contains natural threats such as hardware damage, supply failure, fire, flood, etc.

Some of these threats may be eliminated or minimized by a physical protection of the essential system elements. Such basic precautions as room access monitoring, fire protection, emergency power supply, equipment redundancy, backups, should be taken to protect the system. These measures not only protect, but also enable quick restoration of the system.

It is much more difficult, however, to eliminate or minimize the effects of purposeful action taken by a third party to break the system security. This is due to a wide range of attack techniques that already exist and new ones that are being created, like: viruses or hacking methods.

Apart from a few cases, e.g., denial of service attack or viruses, aggressors try to conceal their trails. Thus, the effects may be unnoticed for a long time.

3. ELEMENTS OF SECURITY FRAMEWORK

The rising importance of security measures has forced manufacturers to empower operating systems in mechanisms that increase protection of resources they manage. All OSs (Windows, Unix, Linux, etc) have tools that allow configuration of the system reducing danger of potential attacks. However, even the best configured OS is not able to eliminate all risks. Threats identified in previous Section require additional, more sophisticated methods and protection tools, like: firewall systems, antivirus scanners, Virtual Private Network (VPN), Intrusion Detection Systems (IDS). These precautions are especially important in case of geographically dispersed systems, as the VOs are.

This calls for a multi-layer security system (Figure 1) with the first layer being responsible for minimisation of attack possibilities. The next layer should detect a successful attack and generate proper alarms, while the third one, ought to remove immediately effects of the attack. Unfortunately, not all security systems are designed following this scheme.

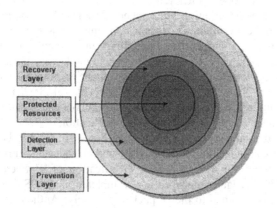

Figure 1 - Multi-layer security model

Dispersed locations of VO member organisations require broadcasting of information not only via local nets but also through the Internet that is commonly regarded as not being safe. A number of potential aggressors and spots they may attack from, increases. Thus, a secure VO should offer a wide range of services enabling effective realization of the security policy.

In this chapter we address the following main techniques for assuring security of virtual organisations:
- Communication security with confidentiality and integrity of information being preserved,
- Authentication of the actor participating in the operation, whether it is a human being or any other available resource, like host or programme,
- Authorization and access control to resources managed through assignment and verification of actor's privileges, and

- Security management elements - security policy formation and enforcing its rules through imposing of proper behaviour. Monitoring of the system operation and detecting hazard situations with alarm generation.

3.1 Secure communication – data confidentiality and integrity

VO member organizations are usually located at different geographical places. To facilitate information exchange, communication channels have to be established. However, the majority of these channels is beyond protected LANs and is constructed on the basis of common access networks such as the Internet. This gives rise to potential threats. There is a wide range of attack techniques, which aim at breaking confidentiality and integrity of the transmitted information. The most commonly used communication protocol TCP/IP does not have any built-in mechanisms, securing the transmitted information. Confidentiality and integrity assurance need to be shifted to upper layers of the ISO/OSI model. Simultaneous securing of both, confidentiality and integrity, is not always required. In some cases, securing of integrity alone is sufficient.

Security of the information exchanged through the virtual communication channel between the VO member organisations may be assured using cryptographic methods. Additionally, mechanisms signalling any attempt at interference in the transmitted data contents are used. . This model is used to secure safe communication by means of such solutions, as IPSec protocol (Scott et al.,1998), Virtual Private Network (VPN) (Scott et al.,1998), SSL protocol (wp.netscape.com/eng/ss13), and TSL protocol (Dierks and Allen, 1999). Protection mechanisms can be directly embedded in the application.

Since 1992 the Internet Engineering Task Force (IETF) has been working on a new protocol to broaden the functionality and introduce security to the already existing IP protocol. In 1995 the first specification of **IP Security (IPSec)** was presented which was later improved and completed. The IPSec protocol defines a new set of headers attached to the IP packets., namely: Authentication Header (AH) and Encapsulation Security Payload (ESP). This protocol can operate in a transport mode or a tunnel mode. They differ from each other in the way the data from higher level protocols is packaged. The IPSec protocol is complemented with the Internet Key Exchange (IKE) (Harkins and Carrel, 1998) negotiating IPSec parameters which are indispensable for the connection to be established.

One vital task of the **Virtual Private Network** is to enable such an application of the public computer network like the Internet, as if it were private. This can be achieved by means of ciphering methods and integrity securing methods. The Virtual Private Network attempts at combining advantages of public networks (low costs, accessibility) with those of private ones (security). Actually, every Virtual Private Network on the Internet operates on the same basis. The data integrity is ensured through cryptographic hash functions and confidentiality through encryption. The result is packed in new packets.

Once the destination is reached, the packet is properly unpacked. Its contents are decrypted and data integrity is checked. Virtual Private Network is designed based on various protocols, like Point to Point Tunnelling Protocol (PPTP), Layer 2

Tunnel Protocol (L2TP) and IPSec. IPSec operating in the tunnel mode is the most frequently used solution.

Secure Socket Layer (SSL) was developed in 1993 by Netscape Company in order to secure data integrity and to authenticate servers in the WWW network. It can also authenticate clients using the servers. Like most network protocols, it was modified several times. The most popular version now is SSLv3. Since 1996 Internet Engineering Task Force has been carrying out standardization work on to a new protocol. In 1999 **Transport Layer Security (TSL)** appeared, based on SSLv3 protocol. TSL and SSL enable authentication of both servers and clients, enciphering of the data between terminal modes and protection of data integrity. A client can be reconnected with the server previously used without renewed authentication and negotiating session keys, on the condition that the reconnection takes place shortly after the previous connection ended.

3.2 Authentication

Authentication is a process in which the user identity and the identity of a system element which, either is an information source, or requester of access to resources, should be recognized and verified. With the majority of the present systems, identity has to be verified prior to gaining access to private resources. Successful authentication is a base for other computer provided services such as authorization, access control and communication protection.

In the local environment, responsibility for authentication most frequently lies with the operating system. A user introduces his login name, thus identifying himself, and confirms his identity using a password.

In the VO distributed environment, member organisations can act on behalf of one another. This brings about necessity for repeated authentication through login name and password which is not favourable, particularly if the data transmitted via public network are unprotected. Authentication may concern one or both parties participating in the information. If both parties are authenticated then we call it a mutual authentication. However, using the public key, certificates and the private key technologies enables another approach to the authentication issue.

Central repositories, where credentials of the system elements are stored, enable the parties participating in the authentication process to refer to them. In IPSec in VPN and SSL/TSL protocols used for communication protection, the system elements between which the data are transmitted undergo authentication. In SSL/TSL protocols authentication is done during handshake, which is the initial and the most vital protocol phase. In Virtual Private Network based on IPSec protocol the Internet Key Exchange protocol is used to authenticate the virtual safe channel – attached elements of the system.

The above mentioned examples describe the cases when it is necessary to confirm the identity of the two system elements between which the data are exchanged. For the distributed environment with numerous components such solutions as: KryptoKnight (Molova et al., 1997), SPX (Alagappan and Tardo, 1991), or Kerberos (web.mit.edu/kerberos/www) can be used. **KryptoKnight** is responsible for authentication and key distributing for the units exchanging information in the network environment. It was designed to operate with minimum hardware requirements and without big system resources. It was possible to resign from 'hard' ciphering methods. Instead of one-way hash function and Machine Authentication Code (MAC) were used. It has been developed by both Yorktown Research Laboratories and IBM Zurich.

SPX as an authentication service is meant to be used in the open network environment. It makes use of both public and confidential key technologies. Global principal identities, unambiguously identifying users and servers in the system, are applied in the authentication process. SPX has a hierarchically organized structure of Certification Authorities whose task is to issue public key certificates for a group of logically connected users and servers. The generated certificates together with other information about a user or a server are stored in Certificate Distribution Centre databases (CDC). Each SPX domain should contain at least one CDC server. Both parties undergoing authentication based on the exchanged data and the data received from proper CDC can end the process successfully.

Kerberos has been defined by the Athena project realized by Massachusetts Institute of Technology, USA. It is applied in large systems with many servers and workstations where users who are not permanently ascribed to the same computer use a great number of distributed resources. In Kerberos, the confidential key technology is used. The user-server communication is enciphered. Resource access is available with limited validity tickets. The client-server communication continues until the ticket validity expires. Every announcement sent between the system elements is enciphered using private keys. Private keys of clients and servers, as well as temporarily generated session keys are applied.

3.2.1 Biometric-based systems

One of more frequently used authenticating methods for confirmation of a person's identity, are biometric techniques. Growing request for exact techniques of identity verification has caused that biometric systems are presently one of the most fast developing domains. Besides, increase in interest in such authenticating methods has reduced greatly accustoming costs. Biometrics-based methods are used for two basic purposes, i.e. to verify or to identify a human being on the basis of his/her biometric data. These data measure the individual's unique physical or behavioral characteristics. Generally, biometric measures are divided into two basic groups: physical and behavioral. Physical techniques identify or verify an individual on the basis of unique characteristics of the human body such as fingerprints, hand or palm geometry, as well as retina, iris, or facial characteristics. Behavioral techniques include signing features, keystroke pattern, voice, gait, etc.

A biometrics identification and verification process relies on the comparison of the analysed and processed characteristics collected by a biometric device to store individual's template. An ideal biometric technique should be characterized by several attributes: uniqueness; resistance to impact of environmental conditions; stability of measured characteristics in the long term; ease of access to measured characteristics; effective, efficient and compact biometric device enabling reliable and easy electronic capture of characteristics measure; fast and efficient algorithms for processing of measured data and comparing them with the stored templates; user acceptance.

As mentioned before, biometric systems can provide both identification and verification processes. Identification is more difficult of the two because a system must search a database of enrolled users to find a match (a one-to-many search). In a verification process measured characteristic is compared with a single template stored locally (e.g. smartcard). Presently known and applicable biometric techniques differ in many parameters (Table1). It means necessity for fitting a proper biometric method for individual demands, environmental conditions, and other application-specific parameters. Two terms placed in Table 1 require explanation. False Acceptance Rate (FAR) signifies that a non-registered user gains access to a biometrically protected system. This figure must be sufficiently low to present a real deterrent. False Rejection Rate (FRR) means that a registered user does not gain access to a biometrically protected system after one attempt.

Table 1 - Comparison of biometrics (Liu and Silverman, 2001)

Characteristic	Fingerprints	Hand Geometry	Retina	Iris	Face	Signature	Voice
Ease of Use	High	High	Low	Medium	Medium	High	High
Error incidence	Dryness, dirt, age	Hand injury, age	Glasses	Poor Lighting	Lighting, age, glasses, hair	Changing signatures	Noise, colds, weather
Accuracy	High	High	Very High	Very High	High	High	High
Cost	Low	Medium	High	High	Low	Low	Low
User acceptance	Medium	Medium	Medium	Medium	Medium	Medium	High
Required security level	High	Medium	High	Very High	Medium	Medium	Medium
Long-term stability	High	Medium	High	High	Medium	Medium	Medium
FRR	3-7%	<5%	<3%	< 3%	10-20%	<7%	10-20%
FAR	0.02 – 0.1%	<2%	<0.001%	< 0.01%	0.1-20%	<2%	2-5%
Template size (Bytes)	128-1000	9	96	512	88-1024	1500	<10000

One of the interesting uses of biometrics involves combining biometrics with smart cards and public-key infrastructure (PKI). It eliminates a major problem with biometrics, namely, the problem of the way in which the individual's template should be stored. The template stored in a centralized database is exposed to attack. Storing the template on a smart card enhances individual privacy and increases protection against a potential attack.

3.2.2 Smart cards

A small piece of plastic with a built-in microprocessor, EEPROM, ROM, RAM, and often an encryption coprocessor, has made a career recently (Figure 2). Physical and electrical characteristics of smart cards are based on the international standards ISO7810 and ISO7816. Furthermore, several standards and their extensions (e.g. ETSI GSM, EMV) were established to meet the specific needs of the industry (e.g. telecommunications, finance). Currently available and commonly used smart cards consist of 32 KB ROM, 32 KB EEPROM, 1-4 KB RAM and 8 or 16 bit microprocessor with an external clock of 1-5 MHz. Development of new generation architectures causes that smart cards' typical values are continuously rising.

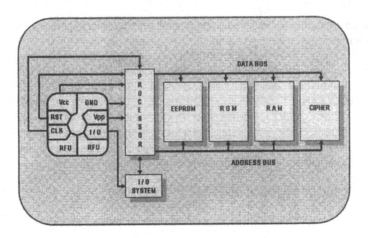

Figure 2 –Typical smart card architecture.

The smart card operating system is kept in the ROM while the EEPROM is responsible for storage application data and operating system extensions. The RAM is used for carrying out operations. The communication between a smart card and a device that accepts this card is supported by the I/O System. Data can be transmitted from 9.6 to 111 kbits/sec depending on a smart card architecture. The encryption coprocessor supporting encryption/decryption computations completes the smart card architecture. It increases the smart card and communication security level. Recent smart cards with new card operating systems enable application developers to create and download on-card application code on their own. JavaCard, Multos, as well as Windows for Smart Card are the examples. Java Card technology has become an open standard and reached dominance on the market through the last years.

3.3 Authorization and Access Control

These are the processes inseparably connected with the information system resources application. Authorization aims at determining and confirming the user's rights to use the resources, whereas the access control verifies the rights and finally decides about granting access. Authorization and access control are possible only after the unit requesting the information system resources access has been authenticated. Introducing satisfactory authorization and access control mechanisms is a challenge. While the increasing popularity of distributed technologies has significantly developed authentication methods, authorization and access control are still lagging behind. Additional complication arises from the fact that with distributed technologies resource access request can only be realized within delegation through mediators acting on behalf of the requesting party.

The **Access Control List (ACL)** is commonly applied in authorisation and access control processes. This solution was taken from operating systems, ACL connects an object, to which resource access is controlled, with a subject and access rights of pair list. ACL used for authorization and access control is suitable in centralized information systems of the client-sever type. ACL are implemented as databases in which each object possesses a list of subjects with rights. A problem with ACL application may be caused by the scale of the information system. ACL databases replication on different distributed servers may cause problems with the content updating and synchronization.

In the new approach to authorization and access control using authorization certificates, are considered. These are documents with a digital signature containing assertions on the object in question. Certificates may concern user identity, features and conditions of resource usage. They are complemented with components enabling distribution and verification of the certificates and with mechanisms which will properly join the information contained in the certificates and decide about allocation of the resource requested. The Akenti system is a case in point (www.itg.lb1.gov/security/Akenti).

3.4 Security management

The aim of every organization is realization of a specific task. It is necessary, however, to foresee situations when a number of factors may appear, hindering the organisation's activity. With organisations that are particularly dependent on information systems, it is vital that systems are well secured. However, application of various forms of protection does not guarantee a proper level of the system safety. The accepted solutions have to fit the profile of the institution activity. Security measures being expensive, potential threats and precautions should be well analysed considering the damages the institution risks if not protected. Taking into account new challenges, as well as dynamically changing environment, security management becomes a must. Security management is a continuous process in ever changing environment with new threats appearing and fast technology progress.

Security policy and the mechanisms used to realize it should be considered in 3 aspects: organizational, legal and technical. A number of rules have been worked out with reference to information security management. One essential document is composed of five parts ISO/International Electrotechnical Commission (IEC) Technical Report 13335 being a basis for national standards in some countries. There are other documents indirectly connected with security management issues, like ISO/ICE BS 17799-2:1999, ISO/IEC 15408.

Security management objective and task is to reach and maintain the assumed security level of the information system. The objective is reached if organisation's security policy is carried out. The following measures should be undertaken:

- Foreseeing potential threats and estimating the risk of their occurrence as well as their effects;
- Determining and implementing of indispensable optimal security measures;
- Monitoring of the system operation;
- Detecting cases of security rules infringement and reacting to such cases;
- Running proper training courses.

As mentioned earlier, security management is especially important in dynamically changing environments. New threats, alteration in the organizational structure of institutions, as well as changes in information system configuration, make security management a continuous process. It is, therefore, necessary to analyze the risk of losing the proper safety level. The analysis should compromise the value of protected resources, costs of security measures, potential effects. The result should enable selection of the adequate solution keeping the balance between the expenditure and an obtained level of security. To reach and maintain the assured safety level, the staff members should all cooperate as it is people who are usually the weakest link in the security system. At every structural level of the institution the staff should be properly trained to gain awareness of security significance, and be motivated and disciplined as to their behaviour. Even the best designed security systems are not capable to completely eliminate the risk of unforeseeable events affecting the information system. Thus, special emergency procedures are needed. ISO/IEC 17799:2000 "Code of Practice" for information security management gives guidelines useful while making plans for emergency.

4. SELECTED APPROACHES

This chapter shortly presents approaches towards security in four IST projects, namely: E-COLLEG, EXTERNAL, PRODNET, and TeleCARE. These projects address various safety aspects, considering mainly VO creation and operation phases. Although security was an important issue in all these projects they deploy various approaches to meet their security requirements and minimize potential threats.

Tool Registration and Management System (TRMS) that has been developed by the IST E-COLLEG project is intended for engineers working in distributed environments (Figure 3). TRMS constitutes an environment that enables agile management and invocation of tools which are distributed in the Internet space. TRMS is accessible through a user friendly GUI that allows management of tools, users and their privileges. A simple workflow editor helps an engineer create distributed workflows (Kostienko et al., 2003), (Fras et al., 2003).

The TRMS-based security framework (Magiera et al., 2003) presents an interesting alternative to VPN. Experiences of E-COLLEG industrial partners show that in many industrial scenarios VPN cannot be deployed. In companies with a very restrictive security policy and protected by sophisticated systems of firewalls establishment of a VPN communication channel requires reconfiguration of the existing security system and modification of their security policy. If these changes are to be held for a short time only, then the required modifications are usually rejected by security managers as inefficient and risky.

TRMS employs 80 or 8080 ports that are usually used by WWW servers. If these ports are not available, then E-COLLEG ANTS (Advanced Network Transport Services) (Schattkowsky et al., 2004) are used to transfer data to/from the protected network. ANTS use the fact that most of the existing firewall systems allow establishment of connections that are initiated from the interior of the protected network.

TRMS also allows transfer of data through the Proxy Server. TRMS requires neither changes in configuration of the existing firewalls nor installation of additional components. One can use the system upon installation of the Client program. Management of keys has been simplified. A client has a pair of his own keys only (public and private) that are stored in a password protected file, as well as, the public key of the GTLS server. Since in the process of authentication the identity of a user is to be confirmed, and not the one of the machine that he works on, the user can login to the system from any computer with the Client application installed.

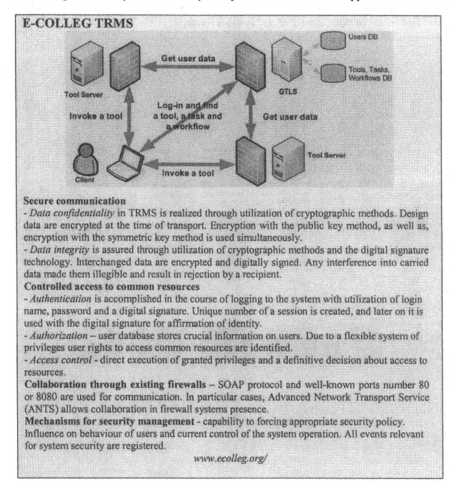

E-COLLEG TRMS

Secure communication
- *Data confidentiality* in TRMS is realized through utilization of cryptographic methods. Design data are encrypted at the time of transport. Encryption with the public key method, as well as, encryption with the symmetric key method is used simultaneously.
- *Data integrity* is assured through utilization of cryptographic methods and the digital signature technology. Interchanged data are encrypted and digitally signed. Any interference into carried data made them illegible and result in rejection by a recipient.
Controlled access to common resources
- *Authentication* is accomplished in the course of logging to the system with utilization of login name, password and a digital signature. Unique number of a session is created, and later on it is used with the digital signature for affirmation of identity.
- *Authorization* – user database stores crucial information on users. Due to a flexible system of privileges user rights to access common resources are identified.
- *Access control* - direct execution of granted privileges and a definitive decision about access to resources.
Collaboration through existing firewalls – SOAP protocol and well-known ports number 80 or 8080 are used for communication. In particular cases, Advanced Network Transport Service (ANTS) allows collaboration in firewall systems presence.
Mechanisms for security management - capability to forcing appropriate security policy. Influence on behaviour of users and current control of the system operation. All events relevant for system security are registered.

www.ecolleg.org/

Figure 3 - The E-COLLEG TRMS-based security framework.

The objective of the **EXTERNAL project** is to support establishment of extended enterprises (EE) that are characterized by a dynamic and limited in time cooperation of business partners. EXTERNAL solutions support effective cooperation through a dedicated methodology, infrastructure and tools, as well as business solutions for EE modeling, analysis, engineering and operation.

The client-server architecture was used with an Internet browser as a client interface. The HTTP/HTTPS protocol and XML are deployed as the data exchange formats. Secure transmission is guaranteed by the SSL protocol. Authentication and authorization of users are indispensable. Authentication is done through login with a password. A manner of assignment of resource access privileges to and their scope are determined by EXTERNAL tools, eg. Metis or XCHIPS. The infrastructure allows grouping of users with the same privileges and requirements. Management of data concerning users and their privileges is possible through an administrative service. The data that are stored on the server side can be ciphered however it is assumed that DBs have sufficient proprietary protection mechanisms. On the client side, ciphering of the stored data is also possible, as Windows 2000 is the recommended OS.

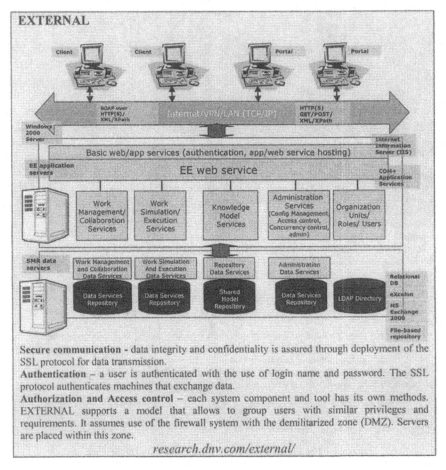

Figure 4 – Security issues in EXTERNAL.

The intelligent infrastructure developed by the EXTERNAL project assumes use of the firewall system with the demilitarized zone (DMZ) with servers that are placed in this zone (Figure 4). Application of the domain controller and login to the domain would allow one-off user authentication by a login process. In this case, a user would be authorized individually by system components, e.g. DBs, using their specific authorization methods. Since the situation where all system elements (from the servers side) are in one local network may be difficult in realization, it is foreseen that a user can be authenticated a number of times (External Project, 2002).

A configurable framework with new technological solutions supporting tele-supervision and tele-assistance for the elderly community, was the main objective of the **TeleCARE project** (Camarinha-Matos and Afsarmanesh, 2002) The security system has been designed in such a way that all its components are entirely independent from each other and from other elements of the architecture. This allows to add/remove particular components depending on chosen security measures. Very sensitive data which are handled must be kept secret and integral. Furthermore, diversity of actors (elderly, care workers, health workers, elderly relatives, etc) that use the TeleCARE infrastructure[1] calls for very solid authentication and authorization, as well as data access control. A range of assigned privileges should be adequate to the actor's role. In the TeleCARE project smart cards storing digital certificates necessary to authenticate the user to the VPN are used (Figure 5). A secure communication channel is created by VPN. VPN is built based on the IPSec protocol that is extended by ISAKMP or IKE protocols which negotiate connection parameters, as well as authenticate both sides of the communication channel. TeleCARE resources are protected through a firewall system and a system which detects intruders.

> **TeleCARE**
>
> The TeleCARE project requires advanced system of firewalls in order to protect its resources.
> **Secure communication.** *Data confidentiality* and *integrity* are assured through deployment of Virtual Private Network. Further more, VPN ensures: *replay attack protection, traffic analysis protection* and *IP address routing.*
> **Authentication.** User authentication is realised using the smard card technology, namely Java Card. Also biometric techniques can be deployed for user authentication.
> **Intrusion Detection System.** Intruder Detection Systems (IDS) are deployed. These might be either, Network IDS or Host IDS.

Figure 5 – Security issues in TeleCARE.

An open platform that employs new emerging standards and advanced technologies in communication, information management, and distributed decision making has been the objective of the project "Production Planning and Management in an Extended Enterprise" (**PRODNET**). The developed platform which is mainly directed to SMEs supports entrepreneurs in their business relations, assuring required security measures, like: data confidentiality and integrity, authentication, availability of services, non-repudiation and auditing. The majority of these measures are implemented in the Security Module (PCI component) (Osório et al., 1999) of the PRODNET architecture[1]. The PCI component assures among others: secure communication, also with legacy systems, and secure access from a Web client. Cryptographic methods are used in order to assure secure communication. A secure communication channel is established with the simultaneous use of symmetric and public key encryptions. The digital signature technology assures data integrity and user authentication (Figure 6).

---

[1]This architecture is shortly presented in chapter 2.1 "ICT infrastructures for VO".

PRODNET

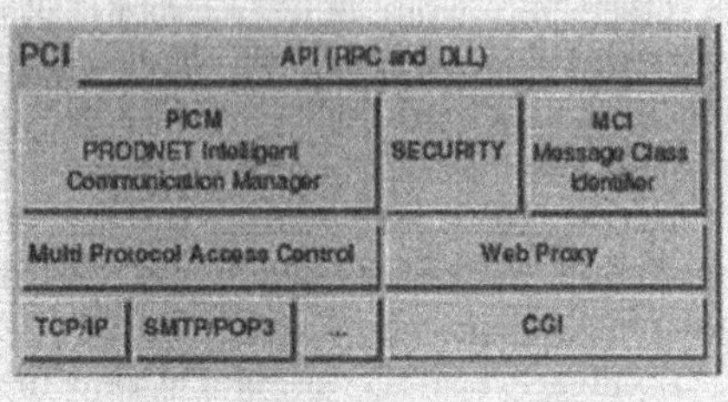

The PRODNET Communication Infrastructure (PCI) offers enterprises a communication medium supporting the most important security requirements.
Secure communication is assured by the Security Module, component of the PCI architecture.
Data confidentiality is achieved through utilization of cryptographic techniques. The encryption with the public key method, as well as encryption with the symmetric key method are used simultaneously.
Data integrity is guaranteed through the digital signature technology. A generated digital signature enables receiver to verify integrity of the received message.
Authentication is also based on the digital signature technology. In this way the receiver can confirm authenticity of the sender. Certificates essential for authentication and secure communication are managed by the PRODNET infrastructure.
PRODNET Web Proxy. Anyone can access to PRODNET information from a standard Web client. The connection is done through the Web proxy. First, Web proxy authenticates the user and depending on the credentials decides about user's access level. Next, a virtual channel between user's browser and the PRODNET node is established.

Figure 6 – Security issues in PRODNET.

The above presented security frameworks were developed for different domains (engineering, health care, production planning and management, etc.) and for different groups of users. However, they are all entirely dependent on the network infrastructure and focus on security solutions that need to be adequate to threats stemming from the operation over the Internet.

Application of diverse measures for reaching similar objectives, like: secure communication (E-COLLEG TRMS and PRODNET – encryption; TeleCARE – VPN; EXTERNAL - SSL) or authentication (E-COLLEG TRMS, and PRODNET – digital signature; TeleCARE – smartcards; EXTERNAL – login name and password) shows that designers have various solutions at their disposal. The final choice depends on project specificity and on existing infrastructure.

5. CONCLUSIONS

Securing Virtual Organizations is a complex endeavor that has three dimensions: technical, organizational, and a legal one. Although, in this chapter we concentrate on technical issues, the remaining organizational and legal[2] ones are equally

[2] The legal aspects that complement the presented security frameworks are presented in chapter 3.1 „Legal and Contractual Framework for the VO".

important for a consistent, robust and secure infrastructure for the Virtual Organization. Organizational and legal issues are relevant for VO member organization privacy. Here policies for definition of information flows in the organization which involve VO customers and the legal solutions adopted are central. Of course, privacy relies also on information security.

Assurance of security is not a single act, but rather it is a process, as apart from already existing sources of threats, new dangers are constantly appearing that need to be correctly recognized and neutralized. In the second section, the main sources of potential threats have been recognized, and in the following sections techniques for elimination of these threats have been addressed. The choice of the most adequate security framework for a particular Virtual Organization depends to some extent, on the operation domain of the VO. This choice is also influenced by the fact that VO member organizations have their own information systems and are not always able to deploy particular new techniques without interfering with their existing solution. In E-Colleg for example, the project industrial partners were not able to accept VPN and SSL to secure communication with external partners. Instead, E-Colleg own technology ANTS needed to be developed and deployed.

Section four contains solutions to security requirements in four projects. They illustrate that with different methods one may achieve required security level and that the VO operation specificity determines resources that must be especially well protected.

Although the security issue draws lots of attention, both in VO related research and generally in IT, there are still challenges that must be addressed in the near future in order to stimulate further proliferation of collaborative networks and based on them VOs. The identified open issues are:

- improved harmonisation between security and collaboration technologies,
- credible assessment of a security level in VO,
- seamless coordination among diverse security applications being deployed,
- more balanced development of new security-relevant applications.

Inter-organizational collaboration over the firewall systems is the security issue that still remains a challenge. Here, two technological efforts appear as orthogonal. On the one hand, each organization aims at the strongest possible protection of its own resources, on the other hand, the same organization would often like to enter a close collaboration. There are no good general solutions available now for this case, although E-Colleg demonstrates here an interesting contribution.

Assessment of a security framework through creation of a universal and possibly complete system for measuring security level through, e.g. benchmarking would help with designing more secure VOs. There exist tools that test sensitivity of a VO towards a particular attack (e.g., port scanners, pass breakers), though no complex assessment is feasible as it comprises a multitude of different factors.

With many diverse applications being deployed within the security framework, their inappropriate configuration might cause potential threats to the VO security. An interesting challenging solution would be introduction of a security coordination module that will supervise all security applications deployed in the VO. It would constitute an intermediate layer between the VO infrastructure and the applications and the only place, where all parameters essential for security will be defined.

This short survey allows for a conclusion that a large number of techniques and technologies are currently available for securing operation of Virtual Organizations. However, it must also be observed that development of new methods and tools intended for at particular security elements is unbalanced in terms of innovation and suitability for a particular type of VO. Methods securing communication (like, new AES ciphering algorithms, quantum cryptography) or new authentication techniques (smartcards, biometrics) are being developed much faster than say techniques for access control to resources.

6. REFERENCES

1. Alagappan K., Tardo J., SPX Guide Prototype Public-Key Authentication Service, Digital Equipment Corp., May 1991.
2. Burnett M., Hacking the Code ASP.NET Web Application Security, Syngress, 2004.
3. Camarinha-Matos L. M., Afsarmanesh H., Design of a virtual community infrastructure for elderly care. In Collaborative Business Ecosystems and Virtual Enterprises, Kluwer Academic Publishers, ISBN 1-4020-7020-9, May 2002.
4. Dierks T., Allen C., The TLS Protocol Version 1.0, 1999, RFC-2246.
5. External Project, EXTERNAL WP2 – D7- Final "Extended Enterprise Infrastructure version 2', http://research.dnv.com/external/deliverables.html
6. Fraś P., Kostienko T., Pawlak A., Szlęzak M., Magiera J., Witczyński M., Development of TRMS/GTLS – Global Tool Lookup Service, E-Colleg Workshop on Challenges in Collaborative Engineering (CCE'03), Poznań, Poland, April 2003.
7. Grimes R., Malicious Mobile Code, Virus Protection for Windows, O'Reilly, 2001.
8. Harkins D., Carrel D., The Internet Key Exchange (IKE), 1998, RFC-2409.
9. Kostienko T., Mueller W., Pawlak A., Schattkowsky T., Advanced Infrastructure for Collaborative Engineering in Electronic Design Automation, 10th ISPE Int. Conf. on Concurrent Engineering: Research and Applications - The vision for the future generation, (CE2003), Madeira Island, Portugal, 26-31.07.2003.
10. Liu S., Silverman M., A Practical Guide to Biometric Security Technology, IEEE Computer Society, IT Pro - Security, Jan-Feb, 2001.
11. Lockhart A., Network Security Hacks, 100 Industrial-Strength Tips & Tools, O'Reilly, 2004.
12. Magiera J., Kostienko T., Szlęzak M., Fraś P., Security Issues in Tool Registration and Management System (TRMS), E-Colleg Workshop on Challenges in Collaborative Engineering (CCE'03), Poznań, Poland, April 2003.
13. Molova R., Tsudik G., Herreweghen E., Zatti S., KryptoKnight Authentication and Key Distribution System. http://www.zurich.ibm.com/security/publications/1997/jty97.ps.gz
14. McNab C., Network Security Assessment, Know Your Network, O'Reilly, 2004.
15. NIST Special Publication 800-18, Guide for Developing Security Plans for Information Technology Systems, 1998 http://csrc.nist.gov/publications/nistpubs/800-18/Planguide.PDF
16. Osório A. L., Antunes C., Barata M. M., The PRODNET communication infrastructure, In *Infrastructures for Virtual Enterprises*, L. M. Camarinha-Matos, H. Afsarmanesh (Eds.), Kluwer Academic Publishers, 1999.
17. Peikari C., Chuvakin A., Security Warrior, O'Reilly, 2004.
18. Schattkowsky T., Mueller W., Pawlak A., Workflow Management Middleware for Secure Distance-Spanning Collaborative Engineering. In L. Fischer (ed.) *The Workflow Handbook 2004*, WfMC, Lighthouse Point, FL, USA, 2004.
19. Scott C., Wolfe P., Erwin M. Virtual Private Networks, O'Reilly & Associates, Inc., 1998.
20. VOSTER Project, Public Deliverable D4.4 "ICT support infrastructures and interoperability for VOs", Jan 2003.

INTERIOR FACILITIES

Karsten Menzel

Dresden University of Technology, Germany, Karsten.Menzel@cib.bau.tu-dresden.de

New organizational and management patterns such as Virtual Organizations (VO) require newly designed, integrated infrastructure systems. Information and communication technology (ICT) should be integrated into the built environment. ICT-components, presentation devices, lighting systems, and furniture need to be understood as one system, instead of being add-ons. This chapter explains the importance of integrated, flexible Building-Furniture-ICT-Systems (BFI) for the performance of VOs. On the example of typical work environments - a single office, a team space, and an integrated lab – it is explained how such a modular system can be introduced incrementally.

A methodology is developed describing the interdependencies between VO-functionalities on the one hand and ICT, immobile and mobile facilities on the other hand. Consequentially, a formalized synthesis strategy for integrated BFI-systems is developed. This strategy is based on evaluation criteria accumulating performance indicators of BFI-components.

1. VO-LIFE CYCLE PHASES AND VO-FUNCTIONS

The design, construction, and implementation of integrated BFI-systems aim at an optimal support of VO-functions. However, the different VO-functions require different levels of ICT-support (see [1]). Therefore, in Table 1 VO functions are classified into three groups.

Table 1: Characterization of VO-functions

Non-Formalized VO Functions and Trust Building	Formalized VO Functions with Interactive Team Work	Formalized VO Functions
VO-functions belonging to creation phase		
VO-Planning		Manage Resource Network
Contract Negotiation		Enterprise Catalogues
		Marketplace / Cluster
VO-functions belonging to operation phase		
Special Domain Functions	Distributed B.P. Planning	
	Distributed Logistics Mgmt	Performance Assessment
	B.P. Modelling/Simulation	
VO-functions belonging to dissolution phase		
	Lifecycle Support	Liability Definition
		Performance History

LEGEND: B.P. ... business process

1.1 Different ICT-needs and impact to interior systems

Non-formalized and trust building processes need different ICT-support than formalized VO-functions or interactive team work. For each of the categories depicted in Table 1 one can define different levels of ICT-needs.

Non-formalized VO-functions and trust building
This group of VO-functions is characterized through:
- The need for <u>intensive, spontaneous, and integrated</u> usage of communication and presentation devices, where the usage of communication devices is dominating.
- The necessity of video-supported communication. Trust-building needs a "face-to-face" communication.
- In some cases (planning, specialized domain functions) information and application sharing is needed to support brain storming and immediate documentation of work results.
- Meetings of teams and individuals are scheduled in a spontaneous way. Therefore the layout of spaces must be easily re-configurable.

Formalized VO-functions with need for interactive team work
This group of VO-functions is characterized by:
- Integrated usage of tools and devices for:
    - o   information sharing and communication,
    - o   interactive presentation
    - o   team-oriented modification.
- Audio communication and voting mechanisms are absolutely necessary. Video support might improve the quality of interaction but is not absolutely required.
- Formalization allows organizing <u>planned and scheduled</u> team meetings. However, individual workers must be able to <u>easily set-up and arrange meetings</u> with remotely working colleagues. Team areas and special labs must be available at a short distance from the home base of VO-team members.

Formalized VO-functions
This group of VO-functions is characterized by:
- Access to shared information and
- Little or no need for audio and video-supported interaction and communication. In case meetings with remote workers are necessary, these meetings can be scheduled in advance. Presentation material can be prepared before the meeting.

1.2 Flexible, modular Home Base in distributed management scenarios

Each work environment - the (Home) Base of the VO-members - must enable them in the best possible way to contribute to the common VO-goals by participating in different distributed work scenarios. Therefore, BFI-systems need to be (see [5]):
- modular and thus adaptable to different VO-scenarios,
- incrementally extendable to allow flexible management of ICT-investments,
- ergonomically designed to support optimal usage of ICT-components.

2. TYPES OF VO-WORK ENVIRONMENTS

This section specifies different types of VO-work environments. By re-arranging the layout and adding further components it is possible to incrementally extend the functionality of VO-work environments. Each type addresses specific scenarios: the single workspace supports quick and inexpensive establishment of VO-workplaces, the team-area focuses on the support of co-located workers, and the integrated lab can be used as hub of distributed teams.

2.1 Single Workspaces

The traditional home base of VO-members is most often a basic office facility. However, easy access to information and communication technology, less cabling, and ergonomic furniture is not always available. The "cubical" might be one low cost alternative to temporarily install an individual work environment supporting the usage of desktop communication systems in a silent place having project-centred storage space but also the ability for creating a personalized work environment (see also [9])

Figure 1: "Cubical" at the Intelligent Workplace CMU, Pittsburgh, PA

2.2 Team Areas

The second type of VO-work environments focuses on the support of co-located VO team members and considers primarily the local organization. Additionally, it allows the integration of VO-members working remotely. By attending electronically supported meetings and by using embedded ICT-infrastructure VO-members of locally distributed organizations can virtually meet with each other. It needs moderate additional investments to establish team areas.

Figure 2: Team Area at the Intelligent Workplace CMU, Pittsburgh, PA

2.3 Integrated Lab

The third type of VO-work environments focuses on supporting collaboration scenarios of distributed teams. Integrated Labs are used as hubs for VO-teams. Therefore, they shall be operated by leading VO-partners.

Integrated Labs combine sophisticated systems and components allowing to remotely access to equipment (e.g. machines, cameras, voice control, blinds) and specialized facilities for the management of multi-point, multi-modal virtual meetings. It is possible to build an Integrated Lab by extending a modular designed team area with additional system components (see also [10])

Figure 3: Scene-Lab at Braunschweig University

3. FROM SINGLE COMPONENTS TO BFI-SYSTEMS

Facilities and interior systems shall support VO-scenarios instead of dominating them. In order to achieve ergonomic work and to support flexible working scenarios the integration of certain building elements (e.g. shading or darkening devices, supply networks [air-conditioning, power, computing]) with interior systems (e.g. flexible walls, lighting systems, furniture, presentation systems), and with information and communication systems (videoconferencing components, computers) is absolutely necessary (see also [3]).

To better express the strong need for modular design and flexible integration of ICT-elements into built artefacts and furniture the term *Building-Furniture- and ICT-Systems* (short *BFI-systems*) is introduced.

A BFI-system allows accessing multiple components, or elements through one single interface.

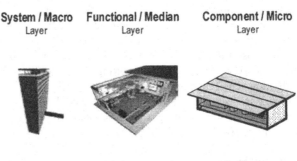

System / Macro Layer	Functional / Median Layer	Component / Micro Layer
BUILT ARTEFACTS	ZONES (Rooms, Floors)	SYSTEMS & COMPONENTS
Load Bearing Structure	Furniture Systems	Tables, Chairs
Wall Systems, Facade	Presentation Systems	Projectors, Smart Boards
Networks (all types)	Video-Conferencing Systems	Cameras, Microphones
Lighting Systems	Artificial Lighting Systems	Lamps, Task Lights

Figure 4: Classification of BFI-System Layers

3.1 Modular and Layer-Oriented Structure

BFI-systems are classified into three different layers described below. The layer-oriented structure is introduced in order to reduce the complexity when specifying a certain type of a VO-work environment.

COMPONENT or MICRO LAYER

Elements of this layer support a *dedicated activity* of an individual user (one specific role within the VO or one specific person responsible for that role); e.g. they support video-communication, or slide presentation and annotation.

FUNCTIONAL or MEDIAN LAYER

Elements of this layer deliver *main, general functionalities* to "the user" (the Virtual Organization, or the team in general); e.g. they support presentation, communication, or IT-supported team-scenarios.

SYSTEM or MACRO LAYER

BFI-Systems belonging to the macro layer *integrate* different BFI-systems of lower layers into one bigger system *using synergy effects* and finally supporting *more efficient performance* of VO-work scenarios.

3.2 Component or Micro Layer

Table 2 illustrates the proposed requirements or specifications for the above defined VO-work environment types. Each line of the table specifies the relationship between one specific BFI-system component and each of the three VO-work environment types. It is not intended to specify or describe all possible BFI-elements of the Component Layer rather than defining a framework and specifying examples that might help organizations to define their individual requirements in a structured and compatible way.

Table 2: VO-work environment types and relation to BFI-system layers and related elements

BFI-Classification			VO-Work Environment		
Macro Layer	**Functional Layer**	**Component Layer**	*Single Space*	*Team Area*	*Integr. Lab*
ZON: Zones	ZON: Presentation	ZON: Prs: Beamer		Required	Required
		ZON: Prs: Smartboard		Required	
		ZON: Prs: Document Camera			Required
	ZON: Video Conf.	ZON: Vic: Headset: mic./earphones	Suggested		
		ZON: Vic: Integrated video/audio	Suggested	Suggested	
		ZON: Vic: Room microphone		Required	Required
		ZON: Vic: Loudspeaker	Suggested		
		ZON: Vic: Cam. with auto focus	Suggested		
		ZON: Vic: Cam. w. stored positions			
		ZON: Vic: Cam. with remote control			Required
	ZON: Furniture	ZON: Fur: Integrated cabling		Suggested	Required
		ZON: Fur: Reconfigurable tables		Suggested	Required
		ZON: Fur: Flexible chairs	Suggested	Suggested	Required
		ZON: Fur: Roomware		Suggested	Required
LIG: Lighting	LIG: Artificial L.	LIG: Art: Task light	Suggested		
		LIG: Art: Dimming	Suggested	Suggested	Required
		LIG: Art: Indirect	Suggested	Suggested	Required
	LIG: Natural L.	LIG: Nat: External shading	Suggested	Suggested	Required
		LIG: Nat: Blinds w. remote control		Suggested	Required
NET: Network	NET: Wireless LAN		Suggested	Required	Required
	NET: Under floor cabling		Suggested	Required	Required
CCU: Central control unit				Required	Required

LEGEND: Suggested   Required

In chapter 5 *'Synthesis'* the VO-work environment types are evaluated against the several VO-functions. Both tables will allow especially SMEs to strategically plan and decide about the continuous development of their BFI infrastructure systems.

3.2.1 ROOMWARE: Example for Micro Layer

The concept of 'Roomware' was originally developed at the German 'Fraunhofer Institut für Integrierte Publikations- und Informationssysteme' (IPSI). It describes a certain type of ubiquitous computing - the integration of information and communication technologies with interior systems such as walls, tables, or chairs.
The first generation of roomware components was developed by the 'AMBIENTE – research group' within the i-LAND project under the leadership of Norbert Streitz in 1997/1998 (see also [8]). The 'Future Office Dynamics' consortium developed under the guidance of IPSI in co-operation with the 'Wilkhahn' company and the designer 'WIEGE' the second generation of roomware components.

CommChair ®

The CommChair with its integrated TFT-Display and the sensitive surface supports both, individual work and integrated team scenarios. Integrated wireless network components support easy integration into existing networks.

ConnecTable ®
The ConnecTable also supports individual and team work scenarios. Integrated sensors determine the distance between two tables. Within a certain limit the supporting software integrates the displays into one common workspace. The position of the display is ergonomically adaptable to individual working situations (standing, sitting).

Figure 5: CommChair

InteracTable ®
The InteracTable supports informal collaboration scenarios. A flat, interactive plasma display (PDP) is integrated into the table. Gesture and pen-based pattern-recognition is supported by the software tool and allows easy creation, annotation, modification, and manipulation of any type of 'information objects.'

Figure 6 : ConnecTable

DynaWall ®
The DynaWall is simply a combination of multiple touch-sensitive screens which are interlinked by special software. The common workspace is 4,50 m * 1,10 m

Figure 7 : InteracTable

Since 2001 all of the roomware-components depicted above are commercially available products.

3.3 Functional or Median Layer

BFI-Systems belonging to the *'Functional Layer'* combine different BFI-elements of the *'Component or Micro Layer'* with complementing functionalities into one integrated system supporting main, general VO-functionalities (see Figure 8).

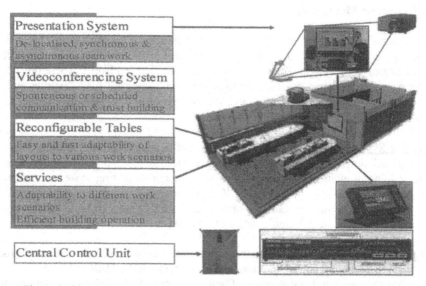

Figure 8: Integrating complementing support functions to system functionalities

Presentation Systems (Prs):
By projecting or receiving/scanning content these systems support *de-localisation* and *asynchronisation* – two of the main characteristics of VOs. They contribute to improved *co-operation and interaction* of groups working on different locations. Beamers, smart boards, and document cameras must be installed in a way that these devices can be used in combination with several sources and software types for presentations and interactive work (A) of VO-team members in one location, (B) of teams with remote audience, and (C) of teams with remote audience additionally supported by a video conferencing system.

Videoconferencing Systems (Vic):
These systems allow to exchange video/audio streams. In most cases data exchange and application sharing is supported as well. However, the pure availability of Vic-systems does not automatically guarantee an intensive, high quality interaction among VO-team members. The excellent technical performance of the Vic-system can be influenced negatively through missing or misfunctioning interior systems.
- Natural and artificial lighting systems as well as shading devices influence the performance of video components.

- Glazing influences not only the natural lighting but also the natural heat gain in wintertime and the over-heating in summer time.
- Geometry, material selection, flooring and curtains influence acoustics and thus the performance of audio devices.

Furniture Systems (Fur):
These systems shall support ergonomic work as well as easy and fast reconfiguration of space layout and usage scenarios of rooms (see also [7]).

3.4 System or Macro Layer

Components of this layer belong to the main elements[1] of the built artefact (e.g. the building) itself or they are strongly connected with them. There are little opportunities for changing these elements with moderate efforts. Therefore, they need to be designed in a careful way to address multi-purpose functionalities and to have enough extension capabilities over the whole of life of the built artefact (see also [5], and [6]).

Lighting Systems (LIG): support direct, indirect or task lighting. Shading devices, glazing and other types of natural lighting devices support or might even replace natural lighting elements. In this way, a well designed lighting system contributes not only to improved performance of ICT-systems (e.g. video-conferencing) but it also contributes to more sustainable operation of the VO-infrastructure and healthier working conditions of VO-employees (see also [4]).

Central Control Units (CCU): integrate from one single point with one single user interface the remote-control functions of BFI-systems of the *Median Layer*.
Thus, on the one hand the number of remote control devices decreases and on the other hand efficiency increases by reducing learning efforts for the usage of control devices. Additionally, the main control unit can be connected to the Internet and thus all devices can be remotely controlled through a web interface by VO-team members.

Networks (NET): The installation of W-LAN and under floor cabling supports easy accessibility of the different media such as electrical power and computer networks.

4. SPECIFICATION OF VO-WORK ENVIRONMENTS

Key features of VOs are better supported or even enabled through the modular design, and layout of BFI-Systems and their integration into the built artefacts. The following sections specify the different VO-work environment types.

The specification is done in four parts. The first part describes *Key Facets* and presents one typical illustration. The second part describes the functionality of the VO-work environment type. The third part characterizes specifics of selected BFI-

---

[1] Main elements:= load-bearing elements and enclosure

elements and systems. The fourth part is a graph, evaluating the importance of each BFI-component which is required or which is suggested for a specific VO-work environment type. Additionally, the rating of each BFI-component for the other VO-work environment types is shown. This allows the reader to decide, how (s)he can incrementally further develop a specific VO-work environment type.

The definition and evaluation criteria are based on surveys and questionnaires taken from the EU-cluster project VOSTER and merged with findings from the authors own work at Braunschweig University of Technology as well as at the Center for Building Performance and Diagnostics at Carnegie Mellon University, Pittsburg/PA.

4.1 Single Workspaces

Key Facets:

Furniture:
Flexible (ergonomic) chairs
Videoconferencing:
Integrated video / audio
Network:
Under floor cabling, wireless LAN
Lighting:
Task lights

Figure 9: Single workspaces

Single workspaces are introduced to allow the individual VO-member to quickly configure and inexpensively establish his temporary home base for one specific project. Single workspaces consist of basic components. However, they must address all requirements of VO-functions: ad-hoc interaction scenarios, trust building, formalized work scenarios with- or without interactive team work.

Within the interviews of the VOSTER-project ergonomic chairs (and tables) were evaluated as the most important feature supporting individual work. Furthermore, users requested that audio devices shall support two modes, private work with headsets as well as a public mode using loudspeakers in order to allow visitors to participate in audio and/or video conferences.

Individual VO-members must be able to connect different hardware devices easily and comfortably. Therefore, users described under floor cabling and wireless LAN as further key facets. Finally, task lights enable users to better adjust lighting to different working situations (e.g. reading, video conference, computer work).

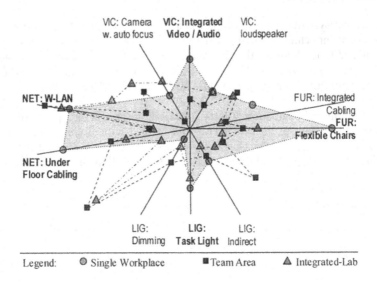

Figure 10: Graphical evaluation of BFI-systems

4.2 Team Areas

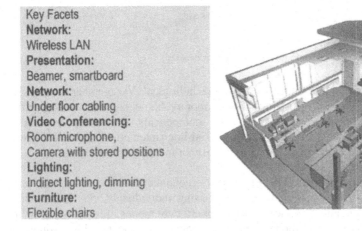

Key Facets
Network:
Wireless LAN
Presentation:
Beamer, smartboard
Network:
Under floor cabling
Video Conferencing:
Room microphone,
Camera with stored positions
Lighting:
Indirect lighting, dimming
Furniture:
Flexible chairs

Figure 11: Team areas

Team areas support interactive meetings of co-located VO-team members by simultaneously enabling the integration of remote co-workers.

One major pre-requisite for such scenarios is the flexible accessibility of computer networks through W-LAN. Team work additionally requires reduced cable work but sufficient and appropriate power supply for all hardware devices. Consequentially, W-LAN and under floor cabling are evaluated as key facets.

Additionally, there is a clear request for separated, high quality audio functionality expressed through the high ranking of room microphones and the decreased ranking of integrated audio/video capabilities. Furthermore, users requested easy usage of video conferencing services by defining camera with stored positions and sophisticated lighting devices as key facets. The importance of flexible (ergonomic) chairs decreases, because it is estimated that team areas are used for a limited time.

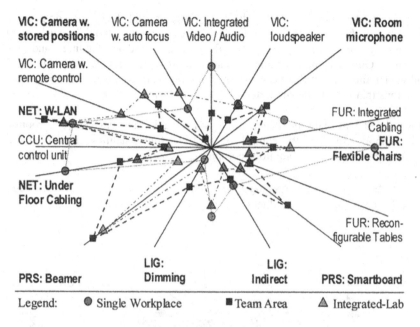

Figure 12: Graphical evaluation of BFI-systems

4.3 Integrated Lab

Figure 13: Single workspaces

Integrated Labs are required to serve as hub for the distributed VO-team members. When evaluating interview responses, it was discovered that many researchers and experts from industry follow a one-sided specification of flexibility and 'virtuality,' by over-estimating the de-localisation aspect. However, VO-customers deal with one (virtual) organization. Therefore, it needs one (physical) place – the hub – where VO-members can meet and interact with their customers.

The aggregated ratings of the different interior and facilities components of *Integrated Labs* illustrate either the lack of evaluation criteria for such complex systems or the request of users for flexible and modular facilities and interior systems. Only beamer, document camera, and wireless LAN achieved high individual ratings. Furthermore, users were not able to clearly specify the VO-functions that need to be supported by *Integrated Labs*.

However, the availability of integrated control units and devices (e.g. roomware) will support user-friendly control of multiple functionalities. It will definitely contribute to improved, ubiquitous computing scenarios.

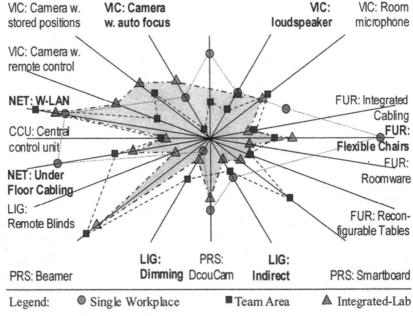

Figure 14: Graphical evaluation of I&M facilities: INTEGRATED LABS

5. SYNTHESIS

Considerable progress has been made in terms of design and development of single BFI-components, such as smartboards, videoconferencing units, or lighting systems. However, most of them are discovered as 'single pieces' instead of modules of an integrated system. However, the functionality of each component must address the need of specific *VO-functions* as well as of *VO-environment types* in order to avoid inappropriate, cost-intensive system design and configuration (see Table 3).

Furthermore, a sustainable implantation strategy of VO-work environments shall consider as early as possible systems and components of the *Macro Layer* because these elements are interconnected with main building elements. Therefore, it is not easy to add or modify such systems over the life-cycle of a built artefact (see [5]/[3]) Consequently, the category *'extendable to'* is introduced in Table 3 containing different types of lighting & presentation components, as well as network elements.

Table 3: VO-Workspaces, BFI-components and supported VO-functions

BFI-Component (C.) / VO-function	VO Planning	Manage Resource Network	Enterprise Catalogues	Marketplace / Cluster	Contract Negotiation	Distributed b.p. planning	Distributed Logistic Mgmt.	Performance Assessment	B.P. Modelling/Simulation	Special Domain Functions	Liability Definition	Lifecycle Support	Performance History	Others
C. required for all types of VO-Workspaces														
NET: Wlan: Wireless LAN	■	■	■	■		■	■	■	■		■	■		■
NET: Cab: Under floor cabling	■	■	■	■		■	■	■	■		■	■		■
ZON: Fur: Flexible chairs	■	■	■	■		■	■	■	■		■	■		■
ZON: Vic: Loudspeaker	■	■	■	■		■	■	■			■			
ZON: Vic: Camera with auto focus	▨	▨				■	■					▨		
C. supporting communication in formalized work scenarios											Single Workspaces			
LIG: Art: Task light		▨	▨	▨				■			▨		▨	
ZON: Vic: Headset mic. earphones		▨						■						
C. supporting improved communication scenarios					Single Workspace extendable to Team Area									
LIG: Art: Dimming	▨	▨				■	■		■			■		
LIG: Art: Indirect	▨	▨				■	■		■			■		
LIG: Nat: External shading	▨	▨				■	■	■	■			■		
C. supporting intensive interaction between teams					Team Areas extendable to Integrated Labs									
ZON: Vic: Room microphone	■				■		■		■			■		
ZON: Prs: Beamer	■				■		■		■			■		
ZON: Prs: Smartboard	■				■		■		■			■		
ZON: Vic: Cam. w. stored positions	■				▨		■		■			■		
ZON: Fur: Integrated cabling	▨				■		■		■			■		
ZON: Fur: Reconfigurable tables	▨				■		■		■			■		
LIG: Nat: Blinds w. remote control	▨				■		■		■					
C. supporting intensive, spontaneous team-work in non-formalized scenarios										Integrated Lab				
Prs: Document Camera	■				■					■				
Vic: Cam. with remote control	■				■					■				
Fur: Roomware	■				■					■				
CCU: Central Control Unit	■				■					■				

Legend : B.P. business process ■ required ▨ suggested

Finally one can conclude that because of the given characteristics an incremental extension of Team Areas towards Integrated Labs can be managed in an easier way than the extension of *Single Workspaces*.

6. CONCLUSIONS

Process re-organization and new forms of business organization need flexible infrastructure systems. Virtual organizations need other configurations of the built-environment and its facilities than traditional organizations, such as open office spaces, team areas, office-hotels, etc. (see also [2]). Quick, easy, and inexpensive reconfiguration of VO-environments consisting of ICT-infrastructure, furniture, lighting systems, moveable wall systems, etc. should be supported in a much better way.

Figure 15 illustrates the path how modular design and flexible, intelligent integration of interior systems will lead to BFI-functions that enable VO-scenarios and support more efficient work of Virtual Organizations.

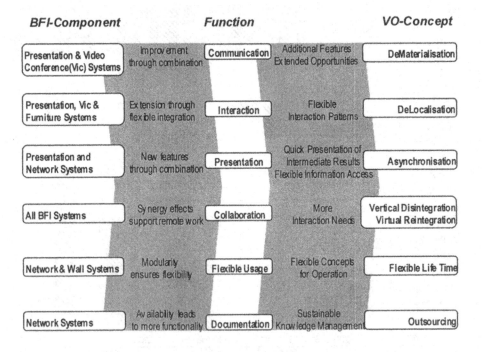

Figure 15: How BFI-systems enable VO-functions leading to VO-concepts

There are still a large number of system integration issues requiring further interdisciplinary research. Besides the 'technical' problems in the architectural and construction domain one major issue is to develop an improved understanding of collaborative processes. Each potential VO-member (individual or organisation) needs to understand and define in advance which VO-concepts (s)he intends to focus on. By reading Figure 15 from right to left one will get first decision support what BFI-systems or components might appropriately support a specific VO-scenario.

Even if VOs are characterized as dynamic, temporary forms of collaboration the individual team members need for this specific time period access to ergonomically designed VO work environments. VO work environments are one important enabler, supporting the individual VO-team member to contribute to the achievement of the common business goals within the restricted time frame and in best quality. Only easy, efficient usage of BFI-systems as well as adequate investment efforts will allow the majority of VO-members to concentrate on the core issues of VOs instead of being dominated by technical issues, BFI-system maintenance, re-configuration efforts, or financial problems.

Acknowledgements. The results included in this paper are partially developed in the context of the European IST VOSTER project. The author thanks the comments and contributions from his partners.

7. REFERENCES

[1] M. Apgar: *'The Alternative Workplace: Changing where and how people work':* Harvard Business Review: 1998.

[2] H. J. Bullinger, W.Bauer, S. Zinser: *'Zukunftsoffensive OFFICE 21':* vgs-verlagsgesellschaft Köln: 2000 (ISBN 3-8025-1442-4).

[3] K. Daniels: *,Technologie des ökologischen Bauens':* Birkhäuser Verlag: Basel, Boston, Berlin: 1995.

[4] V.Loftness, V. Hartkopf, A. Mahdavi, S. Lee, J. Shakvaram, K.J. Tu: *'The Relationship of Environmental Quality in Buildings to Productivity, Energy Effectiveness, Comfort, and Health – How much Proof do we need?':* Proceedings of *IFMA World Worklplace Conference,* Miami Beach (FL), 1995.

[5] V. Hartkopf, V. Loftness, P. Drake, Fred Dubin, P. Mill, G. Ziga: *'Designing the Office of the Future : The Japanese Approach to Tomorrow's Workplace':* John Wiley & Sons; (April 1993) ASIN: 0471595691.

[6] P. Jodidio: *'Sir Norman Foster':* Benedikt Taschen Verlag GmbH: Köln, 1997.

[7] N. Streitz, Th. Prante, C. Röcker, D. van Alphen, C. Magerkurth, R. Stenzel, D. A. Plewe: *'Ambient Displays and Mobile Devices for the Creation of Social Architectural Spaces: Supporting informal communication and social awareness in organizations':* In: K. O'Hara, M. Perry, E. Churchill, D. Russell (Ed.): Public and Situated Displays: Social and Interactional Aspects of Shared Display Technologies: Kluwer Publishers: 2003. pp. 387-409.

[8] N. Streitz, P. Tandler, C. Müller-Tomfelde, S. Konomi: *'Roomware: Towards the Next Generation of Human-Computer Interaction based on an Integrated Design of Real and Virtual Worlds':* In: J. Carroll (Ed.): Human-Computer Interaction in the New Millenium (553-578), Addison-Wesley, 2001.

[9]   The CBPD at Carnegie Mellon University: http://weld.arc.cmu.edu/cbpcd/

[10] *'Scene-Lab'* (technical specification): http://cib.bau.tu-dresden.de/~karsten/...
      ...Forschung/GTIBW/global/scenelab/scene_main_engl.html

| 3. | **IMPLEMENTATION ISSUES** |

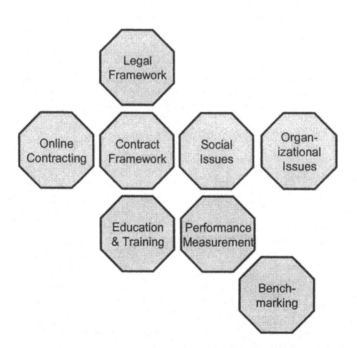

This page intentionally left blank

| 3.1 |

LEGAL AND CONTRACTUAL FRAMEWORK FOR THE VO

Mark Shelbourn, Tarek Hassan, Chris Carter

Department of Civil & Building Engineering, Loughborough University, Loughborough, LE11 3TU, UK.

m.a.shelbourn@lboro. ac. uk, t.hassan@lboro.ac. uk, c.d. carter@lboro.ac. uk

This chapter describes the legal and contractual considerations for organisations wishing to use ICT in their virtual organisation. The chapter describes a number of legal and contractual conditions, (mainly contracts), that must be met to enable legal and contractually valid transactions amongst the VO participants. These contracts and how to achieve them using software tools is described. These tools enable organisations to send electronic transactions in a secure and legally valid manner using technology that is readily available and easy to use. How this can be achieved is described. Bringing all this information together the chapter concludes with a small case study where a description of how these tools have been used in the VO environment is given.

1. INTRODUCTION

The digital communications revolution has enabled partners within the VO to increasingly use collaborative environments as a means of managing their communication. Collaborative environments employed by a VO could include: extranets, intranets, and groupware programs. Managers of the VO have sought to outsource technology requirements to innovative *"Application Service Provider"* (ASP) organisations, which set up and manage services on behalf of the VO, providing facilities and functionality for other members.

However, the use of collaborative environments has exposed unanswered legal and contractual questions, leading to concerns of trust and confidence associated with electronic transactions within the VO.

European studies (ALIVE, 2001, ALIVE 2001a & Shelbourn et al., 2002) have shown that there is little mention of a legally valid use of ICT within the VO environment. Where ICT clauses do exist, they are typically limited to specifying types of software or file exchange formats to be used in the VO, or simply state in broad and imprecise terms that *"data has to be valid, secure, well organised and properly managed"*.

To cover the application of ICT, the structure of a business contract could be amended to identify and define communications *"in electronic format"* instead of *"in writing"*. Official documents (correspondence, drawings, specifications, data) are formally submitted around the VO solely on paper. The use of ICT speeds up the transmission process, but often without legal validity. To fully realise the benefits of ICT, it must be applied in a way that supports the VO and its transactions and, more specifically, *"in a legally admissible manner"*.

2. LEGAL & CONTRACTUAL FRAMEWORK FOR THE VO

To enable the successful use of a legal and contractual framework by organisations in a VO, a number of contracts and agreements need to be in place. Figure 1 shows these. They are: a business contract; an ICT contract; an ASP contract (if required) and end user licences (if required).

The aim of this chapter of the book is to describe the legal and contractual issues associated with each of these contracts / agreements, concentrating on the ICT perspective. The proposed legal and contractual framework has been kept at a high level to fit any VO model with minimum customization.

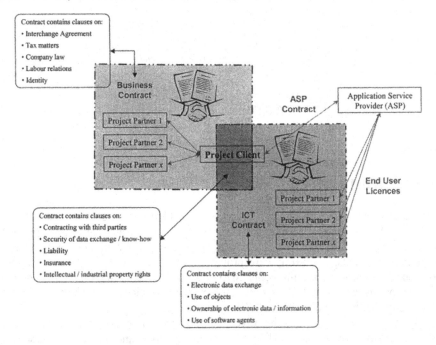

Figure 1 – A legal and contractual framework for the virtual organisations

2.2 The Business Contract

This contract is a traditional form of contract that covers specific issues related to the participation of businesses in a VO. Many of them are part of the *"company law"* issue. This primarily focuses on the consequences of shortcomings in the performance of contractual obligations of the VO. There are different outcomes for the breach of contractual obligations which are dependent on the legal identity issue of the VO. To bring a claim for liability against the VO will only be possible if the VO has a separate legal personality.

Having a legal personality is described in the *"identity"* issue of the business contract. This relates to the question of how and to which extent a VO can be identified. The legal personality means that the VO may be considered as a legal entity which could be sued if necessary. One of the major characteristics of the VO is the fact that it is a cooperation between legally independent enterprises, but it is perceived by third parties as one entity. Consequently many current legal systems will perceive the VO as a formula that has no nationality and no legal personality.

If the members of the VO do wish to give the VO a legal personality, they will have to comply with the national rules of a particular country regulating the setting up, structuring and working of a recognised company type. As soon as the members of the VO choose to do so the issue of identification will disappear and the VO will be seen as a company identifiable by the law of the country in which it has been incorporated. If the VO is perceived as having a legal personality the interchange agreement (the agreement between the members of the VO which provides the necessary provisions on how to pool the risks, liabilities or other financial obligations such as tax, etc.) will be replaced with the articles of association of the legal person. These articles of association can or will be governed by some type of company law deciding which issues need to be addressed in which way.

Without a legal personality, the VO does not legally exist and so cannot be identified as a legally independent entity. The significance of the interchange agreement changes dramatically when the VO is perceived as having no legal personality. In this case, the VO will be based on a contractual relationship between companies that want to stay legally independent. One option open for parties is to try to protect their interests and govern their relations through the use of contracts.

Other issues that need to be addressed in the business contract include tax matters and labour relations. In the tax matters issue the VO needs to consider this area if the business activity of the VO is mainly conducted over the Internet and so classified as eCommerce. This raises a number of questions / issues that the VO needs to be aware of. These include:

- The specific characteristics of eCommerce render both direct and indirect taxation cumbersome, eCommerce is global, while taxation is territorial;
- It is becoming increasingly difficult to identify the tax presence, i.e. where a company is based and consequently where taxes should be paid, where value is added or which country has the jurisdiction over global, multi-jurisdictional eCommerce;
- The classification of eCommerce is decisive as different rates currently apply to goods and services (Kommerskollegium, 2001);
- The speed of the transactions and the anonymity of the seller and buyer add to the complexity of the issue; and
- When no-tangible goods are transferred over the Internet (e.g. computer programs) it becomes very hard to control the amount of transactions that take place because there are no official contracts, order forms or invoices.

However, there exists the possibility that the VO would escape taxation through the difficulty of identification of the company. This is magnified by the fact that it may be difficult to trace the identity of the VO. Furthermore, if the VO has no legal personality, the VO itself cannot be taxed.

In the labour relations area, it should be defined clearly in the *"Interchange agreement"* exactly what is meant by labour relations. This issue is normally broken down into two areas: individual or private labour law, and collective labour law. More information on this issue and all issues described in this section can be found in (ALIVE, 2001a).

2.2 The ICT Contract

The ICT contract is a fairly new concept that has been developed by a group of like minded researchers in the eLEGAL (Specifying Legal Terms of Contract in ICT Environment (IST-1999-20570)) project (eLEGAL, 2002). This type of contract is made between the project client and the participants in the VO. Its main purpose is to define the use of any ICT in the VO, and can be separate, or part of the business contract. Clauses defined in an ICT contract often overlap with those of the business contract, examples include: contracting with third parties, security of data exchange and know-how, liability, insurance, and intellectual / industrial property rights, etc.. More specific clauses on electronic data exchange, the use of objects, ownership of electronic data / information, and the use of software agents, is included in the ICT contract.

Every company in the VO that uses ICT needs to guarantee that by transferring data online they do so in a secure manner, do not infringe privacy regulations or that the contracts concluded are valid and enforceable. The transfer of such data when carried out in a legally valid manner is often referred to as *"econfidence"*. Having specific clauses in the ICT contract that address electronic data exchange enable trust and confidence in electronic transactions to be reached by all parties within the VO.

One of the major uses of objects in the VO context, is the use of *"virtual sales agents"*. These are life-like characters promoting virtual sales on the Internet and can be used to search and procure products for a building, i.e. fire doors, windows etc. This type of agent technology is more than a user friendly interface, they are active, reactive, proactive and interactive. It is widespread opinion that this technology can generally provide advantages both for the seller and for the buyer, who can obtain specific and complex information and discuss issues related to the goods or service just as they could do in real life with a real shop-assistant (Wahlster, 2001). Another use for the agents is in the contract negotiation and execution stages. The agents are assigned parameters and criteria according to who they are allowed to contact, i.e. possible contractual parties – usually other agents – and to carry out transactions on behalf of the agent's owner. However, the legal status and the lawfulness of the agents actions still has to find a coherent framework in legislation and have not yet been adequately discussed by the legal doctrine.

The ownership of electronic data (including meta data) / information is an important issue that needs to be addressed in the ICT contract. Clauses should state who owns the information, who has access rights to the data / information to read, write, or delete data and information.

As part of the ICT contract clauses need to specify the medium and conditions of how electronic data / information is communicated around the VO. It is insufficient to describe the exchange as *"must be secure"*. The clauses must specifically identify protocols and software that is to be used to enable secure electronic data exchange within the VO.

2.2.1 Defining an ICT Contract Electronically

To enable the definition of an ICT contract (or any other legal contract) tools are available that enable this to be done over the Internet. A user can download a *"contract wizard"* which contains a clause library, contract editor, online negotiation of the contract using the Internet (Virtual Negotiation Room), and facilities to electronically sign the contract. The library is a collection of clauses to support the application of ICTs to business processes, including provisions for different types of project and the variations in national legal and regulatory frameworks across Europe. This library is the knowledge base of the wizard. A *"contract editor"* uses this knowledge base to electronically produce contracts – in this case an ICT contract – for different forms of VO or project based businesses. The various parties involved in the ICT contract can collaborate to agree the terms of the contract with the assistance of the *"virtual negotiation room"* (VNR). The VNR allows a user of the contract editor to download the latest version of the contract, edit it and return it to the VNR over the Internet in real or near real time. The contract can also be signed electronically using digital signature technology in the VNR.

It should be noted that these tools can be used to define any type of contract as long as the knowledge base is in place to support the type of contract needed.

More information on these types of tools can be found by visiting the eLEGAL project website at: http://cic.vtt.fi/projects/elegal/public.html where deliverables explain these tools in more detail and the software tools can be downloaded.

2.3 Clauses for the ICT and Business Contract

Many clauses overlap between the ICT and business contracts. These include: contracting with third parties, security of data exchange / know how, liability, insurance, and intellectual / industrial property rights. The descriptions of these overlaps are provided in this section.

If the VO has a legal personality, i.e. is a company type, then the conditions to conclude contracts in accordance with *"company law"* need to be satisfied. If there is ambiguity about the legal personality of the VO then the complexity of the validity of contracts entered into by the VO increases.

However, if the VO has no legal personality it cannot conclude a contract with third parties. The VO will generally be recognised as a form of (temporary) partnership, and as such contracts with third parties can only be concluded between third parties and the joint members of the partnership, but not with the VO itself. However, it is possible that one partner, acting in the name and on behalf of the others, can enter into joint contractual obligations.

Enabling secure data exchange and know-how between the VO is of great importance if it is needed to be carried out electronically. If the VO wishes to keep its competitive advantage in a business area, but wishes to use technology to exchange information then they need to have methods and tools in place to enable this to happen. This section proposed state of the art add-on tools to facilitate exclusive electronic exchange of information within the VO. When a stakeholder involved in the VO connects to a web server on the Internet to exchange private information they need to be sure that the persons who are responsible for the server are indeed who they say they are. The method used to do this involves independent verification of the server's owner or manager. A *"Secure Server Certificate"* is issued to the manager of a web server by a *"Certification Authority"*. This authority is an independent third party which examines the web servers domain registration and other business documents to ensure that the servers managers are the valid owners of the domain, and that the organisation is properly licensed and chartered in its geographic area. A valid certificate means that the users can be **confident** that information is being sent to the right place.

A *"digital notary"* can be used to prove: who has made an electronic transaction (what); with whom it was made, and when it was made. In general questions may arise for a participant in the VO who views the content of a digital / electronic transaction: who is the author of the record, i.e. the originator?, and when was this record created or last modified? There are solutions to both of these questions. One solution is the concept of digital / electronic signatures. In principle, a digital / electronic signature is an asymmetric procedure involving a pair of corresponding keys. A *"private key"* is used for the creation of the digital / electronic signature. This key is kept secret. The other corresponding key (known as the *"public key")* is publicly available. The public key is used to verify the received digital / electronic signature. In order to prevent someone from publishing a public key under a false name, it is necessary for all parties to register themselves with a trusted authority, usually known as the certification authority(CA). Special algorithms are used for signing documents, and for verifying documents and signatures. These have the property that knowledge of the public key does not enable an attacker to deduce the users' corresponding private key. However, if either through careless or intent, someone else gains access to the users private key, this person will be able to forge the legitimate users signatures on documents.

Digital *"notary services"* have become increasingly important as more business is undertaken electronically. The simplest example of a digital notary service is one designed to validate the existence of a particular electronic document, such as a contract, at a given point in time. The notary service receives the document with the author's electronic signature attached. It verifies the signature and then returns a copy of the document, complete with the notary service's digital signature, including a guaranteed date and time at which the verification took place. Being equivalent to a *"digital postmark"* this will be authoritative in cases of conflicting claims regarding, for example, a contract.

In the *"liability"* clause the main area to consider is the consequences of shortcomings in the performance of the contractual obligations of the VO. Bringing a claim against the VO will only be possible if the VO has a legal personality. Bringing a claim against one, several, or all individual members of a VO is possible if the VO does not benefit from limited liability. The mere fact that a VO has a legal personality cannot prevent that claims are addressed directly towards the members.

If the VO has no legal personality at all it will be structured on a contractual basis, with claims only being able to be brought against the individual VO members. However, in the latter hypothesis, claimants will probably suffer some difficulties in determining the exact identity of the different VO members, because of the appearance of the VO as one organisation.

For the VO taking out liability *"insurance"* they must have a legal personality. If the VO has no legal personality then attention should be paid to the fact of the possible liability of each of the VO members is covered. This means that an insurance policy needs to cover the individual liability of each of the VO members as well as the joint liability of the VO members. The VO must also take account of the necessity of adequate first party insurance. This will protect the VO against the financial consequences of certain losses, irrespective of the fact whether claims in liability are brought against the VO.

The final clauses of joint relevance for the ICT and business contract to be described are the issues affecting the industrial / intellectual property rights of the VO. The concept of intellectual and industrial property rights refers to patents, copyright and neighbouring rights, trademarks and designs, domain names, protection of databases, plant variety rights, protection of biological inventions etc. These issues are of major importance to the VO, in fact they are crucial to the existence of the VO. If these issues cannot be dealt with appropriately, companies may quickly lose interest in creating a VO or becoming a member of it. On the other hand third parties may not be interested in licensing to a VO. A consequence of this non interest is that *"potential"* VO members lose their interest in participating in the VO. This could especially become troublesome with regard to projects of concurrent engineering in which IPR often plays a significant role.

2.4 The ASP Contract

As more and more organisations are realising the benefits of ICT for collaborative working in a VO, so the more sophisticated the ICT needs of the VO become. This has meant that not all VOs are able to provide the software tools and infrastructure needed by the VO. This has led to innovative technology organisations to realise the importance of ICT for the VO and other project based businesses, and providing them with a solution that enables them to outsource the ICT for the VO or project to a third party organisation. These organisations are called *"Application Service Providers"* (ASPs). They set up and manage services on behalf of clients, providing facilities and functionality for other project participants.

To enable this outsourcing to the ASP the project client has to make a contract with the ASP to provide the services to the VO or project based business. They do this by defining an ASP contract. This can be done using traditional paper based methods or electronically using the tools described within this chapter.

2.5 End-User Licences

End user licences are agreements between the ASP and the individual members of the VO. The licences enable the individual stakeholders within the VO to develop and negotiate the terms and conditions of how they are going to use the tools and services provided by the ASP. Once again this can be achieved using traditional paper based methods or electronically using the tools described within this chapter.

3. EXAMPLES OF THE LEGAL & CONTRACTUAL USE OF ICT IN THE VO

Figure 2 shows how the tools described within this chapter are being used by an Italian SME (GEODECO, a geo-technical engineering consultancy) to promote their Geotechnical services to other organisations within a small VO. GEODECO has implemented the tools and methods described to their collaboration platform (Merz and Mangini, 2002).

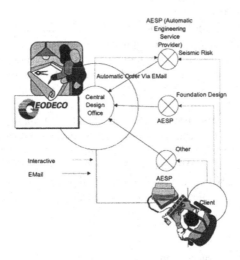

Figure 2 – Graphical representation of an SMEs use of the electronic tools for online contracting (Merz & Mangini, 2002)

A user inputs the coordinates of a site (by clicking on an interactive GIS map) where they want to build the structure, and the available information about the soil characteristics and the structure typology. The system provides, free of charge, the results of a simplified analysis useful to establish the real need for a more sophisticated analysis that will be performed off-line through human intervention by experts in the field using innovative methodologies. Traditionally, a standard contract adapted to the needs of the specific project would be sent to the client for signature. The client would then sign it and send it back to the Design Office at GEODECO. By means of the described tools, used in connection with GEODECO's collaboration platform (AESP Automatic Engineering Service Provider), it is possible for the two parties to negotiate and digitally sign every clause of a consulting contract. This will ensure that remote consulting activities do not differ from traditional *"contact-based"* consulting. Digital signatures on the relevant documents, also ensure the necessary tracking and consequent liability from the consultant's side. All contractual issues are finalised using the tools described in section 2.2.1, in an extremely short time, which is crucial for services which may be required at very short notice. A graphical representation of this is shown in Figure 2.

4. FUTURE DEVELOPMENTS FOR LEGAL AND CONTRACTUAL ISSUES FOR VOs

The acceptance of the legal accountability of electronic transactions is an area where all stakeholders of the VO have to be in agreement. Having transactions that a user has trust and confidence in the use of ICT for electronic transactions will be a real benefit to the business. This can in turn lead to increased quality and profitability of the finished product. Assessing and fully addressing the IPR, security, privacy, and ownership implications of electronic data will have to be defined in contractual aspects of the project.

The development of comprehensive online smart contract configuration tools to enable the editing of contracts from the negotiation to the final process of digitally signing the contract will play a major part in addressing the IPR, security, etc issues. These tools should also provide support for assigning and defining contractual liabilities, including the liabilities of the partners in relation to the accessibility of electronic data as part of these contract definition tools.

Virtual identity management is the next progression to allow document validation, in such a way that it is possible to guarantee the author identity of a document. This ensures that no changes have been carried out to the original when they should not have been. The identification and clarification of the benefits of addressing the legal and contractual aspects of using the digital signature and notary technology in any country is also a big challenge for future research.

Digital rights management (DRM) systems that restrict the use of digital files in order to protect the interests of copyright holders are also needed. DRM technologies should be developed to control file access (number of views, length of views), altering, sharing, copying, printing, and saving. These technologies may be developed to be contained within the operating system, program software, or in the actual hardware of a device.

Trust models need to be used to assign different levels of trust to different stakeholders within the project dependent upon the nature of the transaction taking place between the stakeholders using the ICT. Transaction monitors should be used to monitor the flow of electronic information and documentation to ensure that they meet the pre-defined levels of legal validity, e.g. it conforms to the terms of the clauses set out in the ICT contract, the level of security, e.g. the level of digital signature required, and the amount of trust from the party that has sent the information.

5. SUMMARY

The role of ICT in the VO is a crucial one, in fact the VO cannot operate if the ICT is not present. There are many issues that the VO needs to address to enable the ICT to be used in the correct manner. These include the legal and contractual aspects. This chapter has described a framework (of contracts and agreements) that needs to be in place to enable the legal and contractually valid use of ICT in the VO or project based businesses. Within these contracts and agreements many different clauses need to be included to enable the contract to be suitable from many business as well as ICT contracts. These clauses have been described in the chapter and many effects of their non-inclusion have also been discussed.

Many organisations who participate in the VO do not have legal representatives employed by them, particularly SMEs. One method of overcoming this problem has been to use software tools and the Internet to define, negotiate and sign contracts electronically. How this can be achieved, and examples of its use have all been described within this chapter.

A number of new research areas have been identified. These include the development of complete legal infrastructure that incorporates virtual identity management, transaction monitors and trust models as new research areas to compliment the ones already identified and described in this chapter.

6. ACKNOWLEDGEMENT

The authors wish to acknowledge the European Commission for their support, and our gratitude and appreciation to all the partner organisations from the eLEGAL, ICCI, ALIVE and VOSTER projects for their contributions to this chapter.

7. REFERENCES

1. ALIVE, (2001) *"Deliverable D01: Virtual Organisation reference lifecycle processes and associated legal issues"*, ALIVE: Advanced Legal Issues in Virtual Enterprises, IST-2000-25459, available from http://www.vive-ig.net/projects/alive/ under the download area, pp.51-53. (last visited 26.11.2003);
2. ALIVE, (2001a) *"Deliverable D03: Virtual Enterprise Legal Issue Taxonomy"*, ALIVE: Advanced Legal Issues in Virtual Enterprises, IST-2000-25459, available from http://www.vive-ig.net/projects/alive/ under the download area, pp.51-53. (last visited 26.11.2003);
3. eLEGAL, (2002), *"Deliverable D31: Specification of ICT support tools"*. eLEGAL: Specifying Legal Terms of Contract in ICT Environment, IST-1999-20570, available from http://cic.vtt.fi/projects/elegal/public.html under the results section; (last visited 10.11.2003);
4. Kommerskollegium (2001) Swedish National Board of Trade, *e-Commerce: implications for Existing Trade Policy,* Rapport, 2001:2. Available from http://www.kommers.se/publications.asp#10 last visited 20th November 2003;
5. Merz, M & Mangini, M (2002), *"eContractng and remote engineering consulting services".* Proceedings of the eLEGAL 2002 European Conference on Legal Aspects of ICT Application in Project-Based Business, 3-4th October 2002, Loughborough University, UK. Proceedings available under the EVENTS section at: http://cic.vtt.fi/projects/elegal/public.html (last visited 7.11.2003);
6. Shelbourn, M., Hassan, T., Carter, C. & Baldwin, A. (2002), *"A review of the of the legal and contractual issues for the use of ICT in construction".* Proceedings of the eLEGAL 2002 European Conference on Legal Aspects of ICT Application in Project-Based Business, 3-4th October 2002, Loughborough University, UK. Proceedings available under the EVENTS section at: http://cic.vtt.fi/projects/elegal/public.html (last visited 7.11.2003);
7. Wahlster, W. 2001, *"Virtual Sales Agents for Electronic Commerce"*, Proceedings of 9th ECCAI Advanced Course ACAI-01, Czech Technical University in Prague, Czech Republic, July 2-13, 2001; (for a free online version see at http://www.dfki.de/~wahlster/acai2001/ last visited 21st October 2003).

PERFORMANCE MEASUREMENT

Volker Stich[1], Martin Weidemann[1],
Andreas Sennheiser[2], Knut Glaubitt[1], Matthias Schnetzler[2]

[1]*Research Institute for Operations Management (FIR) at the
Technical University of Aachen (RWTH), Pontdriesch 14/16,
D-52062 Aachen, Germany
wei@fir.rwth-aachen.de*

[2]*Center of Enterprise Sciences (BWI) of the Swiss Federal Institute of
Technology (ETH) Zürich, Zürichbergstrasse 18, CH-8028 Zürich,
Switzerland
Andreas.Sennheiser@ethz.ch*

*Performance Measurement has become an important management support for
any kind of organisation in recent years. Companies use performance
indicators not only to measure their own performance, but also the
performance of their business partners. So far, new forms of collaborative
organisations have not been considered in the performance measurement
systems and benchmarking initiatives. Therefore, performance measurement of
VO is a young emerging research area. On one hand, the performance
indicators of traditional organisational forms can also be applied for VOs, but
they miss the advantages, which VOs offer to enrich business opportunities of
nowadays companies. Hence, new performance measurement systems need to
be developed, which consider e.g. enhanced capabilities of organisations. On
the other hand, the comparison of performances of goal oriented networks and
traditional forms of organisation in benchmarking studies can help promoting
the concepts of VO, if the performance measurements are well chosen. This
chapter describes the traditional benchmarking approach. It discusses its
restrictions and suggests an alternative benchmarking approach, which is
more suitable for today's need of flexible adaptation of organisations towards
market requirements. Furthermore, it discusses issues in setting up
performance measurement systems.*

1. INTRODUCTION

Achieving business excellence is a major objective of companies participating in
virtual organisations (VO) and goal oriented networks. Measuring the performance
of the network and participants of a network is an important building block towards
this goal. In the late 1970's Xerox began to compare its operational performance
with other companies: the idea of benchmarking was born [1], The comparison with
the best in class enables a company to position itself in the field of competitors, to

identify improvement potentials and best practices, and, in the end, to improve its performance [2, 3].

The concept of VOs is still not taking up in Europe. One reason might be that it is difficult to prove the advantages of VO in contrast to more traditional organisational forms. Benchmarking could be a way to compare the performances of these organisational forms, if suitable performance measurement systems are chosen.

Usually, performance is measured and assessed using so-called performance indicators (PIs) or performance metrics [4, 5]. While PIs measuring the internal operations of an enterprise have been available for decades, the measurement of the performance of networks and on the network level is quite new [6].

Within the IST-programme some projects have elaborated and used performance measurement systems for different purposes. The NIMCube project (IST-1999-11926) has developed a metrics system to measure the effectiveness and efficiency of knowledge intensive processes in early phases of the value chain, whereas PRODCHAIN (IST-2000-61205) has performed benchmarking studies to improve the logistics performance of production networks. Other projects, like CO-OPERATE (IST-1999-12259) have elaborated measurement systems (e.g. for manufacturing planning and control between partners of a supply chain), as a side effect, since these projects had other research priorities. Within these projects, the use of performance indicators has always been welcomed by the industrial project partners as useful and ensured active participation of industry. Still, in each case performance measurement systems needed to be developed which considered the specific focuses of these projects.

Nevertheless, as a survey shows, until now only approximately one third of enterprises use PIs for performance comparisons internally or against other companies [7]. The following reasons are obstacles explaining this result:

- Companies do not feel that their business is comparable to other companies and networks, especially to companies and networks of other branches.

- Companies do not feel that the performance indicators used in benchmarking initiatives reflect their business goals.

- There is a large number of PIs available; this makes a selection of appropriate PIs difficult [8]. Moreover, often "measurement systems have measured too many things and the wrong things" as Holmberg argues [9, p. 852]. This may lead to inefficiencies.

Therefore, there is the need for an approach towards a goal-oriented application of PIs and a systematic development of new benchmarking approaches, which only takes companies or networks with similar characteristics into account. Such approaches would help network managers to understand how performance can be measured and compared with companies or networks, which operate under similar conditions in similar markets.

In the following, the classical benchmarking approach will be explained and major obstacles highlighted. Then a possible solution for a more open benchmarking approach will be presented, which can help to overcome these obstacles. Finally, issues of PI decompositions will be discussed, which should be considered for VOs in benchmarking.

2. BENCHMARKING

Benchmarking can be considered a specific management tool for improving performance in goal driven organisations that is based on the classical concept of performance comparison [10, p. 407]. By comparing the performance of one's own method, process, product or service against companies that consistently distinguish themselves in that category of performance, performance gaps (differences in performance) are revealed and analysed [11, p.5]. Based on this analysis, best-practices are identified and adapted to one's own organisation, leading to sustainable superior competitiveness. Best practices can be defined as "the state of the art of how to perform a particular business process. They are the means by which leading organisations have achieved top performance" [12, p. 254]. According to Camp [1, p.12] the overall objective of benchmarking is "...the search for those best practices that lead to superior performance".

This section briefly describes how to conduct a benchmarking study following the generic benchmarking process model of Xerox [1]. According to Luczak [2, p. 11] (see also [13, p. 8]) the basic work steps of the various benchmarking methodologies do not differ significantly from each other. Differences exist mainly in a more or less detailed elaboration of specific work steps depending on the author or company requirements. Thus, it is acceptable to concentrate on only one benchmarking model for explaining the basic work steps of the benchmarking process.

The benchmarking process represents a continuous improvement process (plan-do-check-act cycle or Deming cycle) in which the 4 phases (plan, do, check and act) are reiterated. This emphasis's the long-term orientation of the benchmarking concept. Benchmarking is a continuous, systematic improvement process, in which best-practices must be continuously evaluated, identified, and adapted for the purpose of gaining long-term superior competitiveness. In addition to the 4 phases, Camp introduced a 5th phase, which he called maturity. "Maturity is achieved when best practices are incorporated in all business processes and the benchmarking approach is institutionalised" [14, p. 5].

Achieving business excellence or a high degree of maturity is also the goal for initiating VOs. Therefore, VOs should compare their performance with other organisational forms in order to prove the superiority of VO concepts. The only question, which has not been answered, yet, is: What is the superior performance of a VO and, moreover, how to express these in performance indicators?!

Until now, benchmarking partners are selected out of companies and networks out of the same branch, which is preventing the transfer of best practices from other branches. Also it blocks the spreading of VO concepts and practices, especially since the underlying performance measurement systems have been design for traditional forms of organisations.

3. ANONYMOUS BENCHMARKING

After the benchmarking hype during the 90's many companies have become disillusioned about benchmarking. Although they invested significant amount of time and money in benchmarking studies the results often did not meet expectations as significant competitive advantages could not be obtained. One reason for this is that conducting benchmarking studies effectively and efficiently is a difficult task. Especially small and medium sized companies often lack the substantial resources and knowledge required for conducting benchmarking studies successfully in a methodological right way.

One remedy for overcoming the large time and resource demands of "classical" benchmarking is anonymous performance benchmarking [15, p. 20], also called disguised benchmarking [16, p. 202]. Although it is often referred to benchmarking, this type of performance comparison is different from the "classical" benchmarking process described in the previous sections. Usually, anonymous performance benchmarking studies focus solely on performance indicators that are collected from benchmarking partners through a clearinghouse (e.g., independent consulting firm). The clearinghouse then computes performance averages and other statistical values [15, p. 20] [16, p. 202]. The term "anonymous" indicates that each benchmarking partner receives only anonymous statistical values and does not reveal his identity to other benchmarking partners. A detailed analysis of performance gaps, and identification and implementation of best-practices, (e.g., phases do, check and act of the benchmarking process) is not performed. Therefore, an anonymous performance benchmarking study can be conducted with relatively low effort and, consequently, low costs. A further advantage of the anonymous benchmarking is that the concept (for example, the performance indicator definitions and the data collection) has already been worked out and implemented by professionals who, as a rule, are members of specialised institutions such as PMG (Performance Measurement Group). This also ensures a higher level of objectivity towards the investigation object. The overall objective of this type of study is to rate the performance of each company against other comparable companies.

But what is a comparable company, organisation or network? Companies, organisations and networks are different. Therefore, if not comparing companies and networks of the same branch, then the question arises on how to compare and what determines comparability.

In general, companies and networks are characterised by their logistics determinants, which define market/customer requirements. The diversity of logistic determinants in different companies is a corollary of the various market challenges. Since the logistics measures and the set up of a company are chosen to mastering the challenges the company faces, the key processes a company has to excel in to respond to the market can be identified. This connection of determinant values and key processes shall be explained with the following simplified example of benchmarking traditional production companies (Figure 1).

The example in Figure 1 illustrates, how a single determinant – in this case the production environment (Make-to-Stock (MTS) vs. Make-to-Order (MTO)) – can lead to totally different key processes although the market requirements are similar e.g. the influence of the determinant on the design solution of a company changes. Consequently, different sets of performance indicators are needed to actively monitor the performance of the key processes. This fact in mind gave birth to the idea of a two-step clustering, where first a subset of determinants is evaluated, namely those who affect the interpretation of the others significantly.

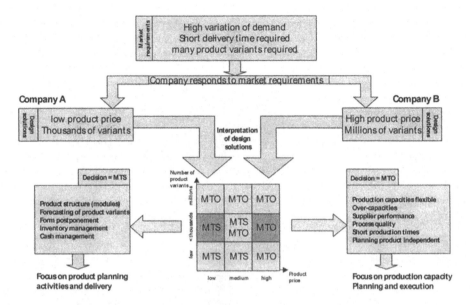

Figure 1: Deriving key processes from determinants.

The first set of determinants focuses on the general comparability of the organisations. To detect candidates cluster analysis should be performed with the data resulting from a determinant survey. The obtained clusters need to be analysed concerning their determinant structure. Best Practices for these structures can then be allocated depending on the benchmarking results of the collected PIs. The set of PIs chosen for the benchmarking highly depends on the cluster and its typical organisational goals!

In this sense, anonymous performance benchmarking can be considered an integral part of the planning phase of the "classical" benchmarking process loop as shown in figure 2. After the benchmarking object has been defined in step 1, anonymous performance benchmarking is used to continuously monitor the organisation's performance over time. If any significant performance gaps are revealed, a comprehensive benchmarking study is triggered in order to identify the root causes and to implement best-practices to close the performance gaps. This approach ensures that the 4-phases (plan, do, check and act) of the benchmarking process loop are only reiterated if there is a call for action. There is no need to execute all phases of the classical benchmarking process, which reduces cost.

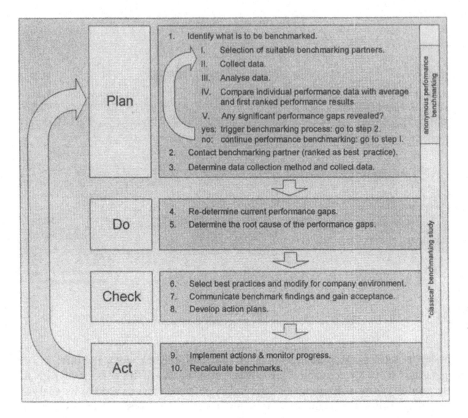

Figure 2: Benchmarking process with anonymous performance benchmarking loop

At first glance, step 4, in which current performance gaps are re-determined, seems to be dispensable, as significant performance gaps have already been identified through anonymous performance benchmarking. However, performance gaps that were determined with anonymous performance benchmarking, must be strictly distinguished from those determined in step 4. The performance gaps identified with anonymous performance benchmarking are usually based on average values of performance indicators related to specific groups, depending on its determinants. Furthermore, companies usually have no influence over which performance indicators are used by the clearinghouse. Thus, with anonymous performance benchmarking, a selection of performance indicators according to the special needs and circumstances of the participating companies does not take place [15, p. 22]. Therefore, performance gaps obtained from anonymous performance benchmarking can identify areas that require improvement, but usually cannot be considered suitable for detailed, subsequent analysis. In step 4, the previously identified critical areas are measured and investigated more thoroughly with specific benchmarking partners (including site visits, site investigations, etc.). The performance gaps that have been determined in this way provide the basis for a subsequent in-depth analysis of the root causes of the performance gaps (i. e., step 5).

The main advantages of this modified benchmarking approach for VO are summarised in the following:

- In contrast to "classical" benchmarking, anonymous performance benchmarking implies so-called "killing" factors, which indicate whether it is useful to undergo a best-practice study. Thus, instead of continuously reiterating the 4 phases (plan, do, check and act) of the benchmarking loop, as suggested in literature [13, p. 10] [10, p. 12] [17, p. 11] [16, p. 202], comparison only takes place with organisations, which follow similar goals.
- World-class, or best-in-class, companies usually are not interested in a comparison with small benchmarking partners. Therefore, anonymous performance benchmarking studies, which are conducted through a clearinghouse, may enable VOs to compare their performance to world-class companies and to demonstrate its advantages [17, p. 204].
- Since anonymous performance benchmarking studies are carried out on a regular basis, it is possible to compare one's performance with extensive performance indicator databases, over an extended period of time [15, p. 22]. This allows companies to easily recognize State-of-the-Art developments, etc.

In principle, the methodology is applicable to any kind of performance measurement systems using PIs. It addresses primarily network managers and network controllers, but also business developers and controllers. Therefore, it would be feasible to apply this methodology also to VO, if the appropriate PIs are selected.

4. PERFORMANCE INDICATORS AND THE IMPORTANCE OF PROCESS MODELS

Besides finding the right benchmarking partner, the right performance indicators (PI) must be chosen for the benchmarking. Since many performance measurement systems consisting of PIs exist, several approaches were consolidated (especially [18] and SCOR [19]) in the PRODCHAIN project (IST-2000-61205). In general, the selection of PIs should always depend on the high-level goals of the organisation, decomposed to an operational level.

In general, PIs are not independent from each other. In the following, PIs having impact on a specific PI are named "driver PIs", while those PIs a specific PI impacts are called "outcome PIs" (see Figure 3). Two types of interdependencies can be distinguished: decompositions and influences.

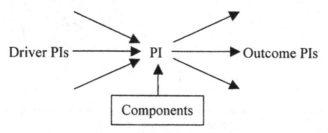

Figure 3: Performance indicators, components, drivers and outcomes

Decomposition (or PI hierarchy) is a hierarchical interdependency in a mathematical, quantitative sense. It shows which components the PI consists of. See Figure 3 as an example. These components can be other PIs of the PI set.

When decomposing the PI and building up the performance measurement system, models are needed as reference. On the one hand, these models give a clear definition of the processes to be measured and, therefore, ensure the comparability to other companies or networks. On the other hand, the process models help to operationalize the performance measurement systems on the lower levels and allow distinguishing different types of organisational forms. Furthermore, a decomposed process model also clarifies the influences among the decomposed PIs. Important for the decomposition is the linkage of performance indicators to the process model on the top levels (PI y) and on the lower or operational level (PI x). If this is done properly and if similar calculation rules are used, different types of organisation, which follow the same goals, become comparable on the top level although the process models and metrics systems might differ on lower levels.

In figure 4, a simple example out of a traditional organisation shall clarify these relations. It explains the decomposition of a PI and how the PI system can be calculated and linked to the decomposed process model of a traditional supply chain. The example is total supply chain management costs. It can be decomposed into inventory costs, order management costs, transportation costs etc. and calculated by summing these elements up.

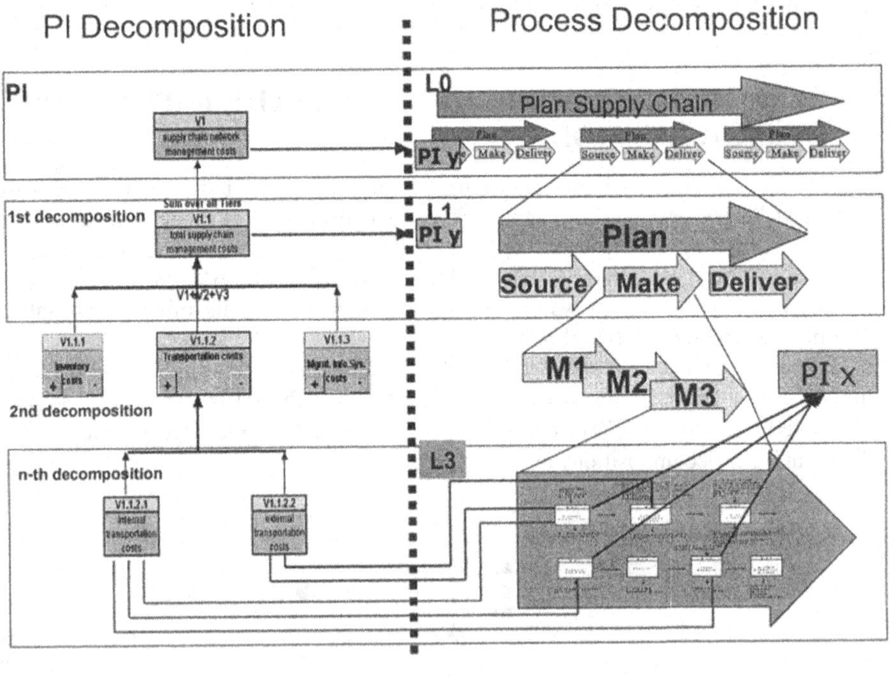

Figure 4: Decomposition of management costs and related process model taking a supply chain as an example (excerpt)

Impacts among the PIs are more implicit interdependencies (in a more qualitative sense). In principle, they result from logistics business logic ("logistics common sense") and represent cause-and-effect relationships. Improved sales forecast accuracy, for instance, may lead to a higher service level rate (positive impact); thus, sales forecast accuracy is a driver of service level rate. However, these PIs cannot be linked with each other in a mathematical sense – meaning that there is no obvious explicit formula. E.g., the service level rate cannot be decomposed into sales forecast accuracy. Furthermore, the impact can be positive or negative and usually depend from the specific business and logistics environment. Also, in an engineer-to-order environment, a shorter lead time does not necessarily lead to lower logistics cost since no stocks are held.

This simple example makes clear, how models can link low level PIs with high level goals. Thus, by following a similar approach, different types of companies and organisations become comparable as long as they follow similar goals. Benchmarking the high level PIs would show, which organisational forms have advantages under which conditions and environments. For VOs, it would be a strong tool to demonstrate its advantages, if suitable performance measurement systems are used.

5. CONCLUSION

The methodology described above enables managers aiming at improving performance to develop specific improvement strategies for different types of organisations with the help of performance measurement and benchmarking. It facilitates the understanding of how improvements of high-level objectives can be achieved by lower-level improvement measures and how PIs interact. This way, it supports decision making. The decomposition of the PRODCHAIN PI, as an example, demonstrates how a PI is calculated and which elements it consists of. A similar approach would be useful to be developed for VOs, integrating VO goals as described in this book.

VOs have to compete with the traditional organisational forms. For the final customer, it is regardless which organisational form supports the product creation, production or the service he wants. Therefore, similar high level goal oriented PIs have to be taken into account, when measuring the performance of organisations. So far, missing PI systems, which regard advantages of VOs, are major obstacles for the broader implementation of VOs, since a proven comparison to the traditional organisational forms in terms of improved performances of VOs is missing to convince the protectionists of the traditional organisational forms of organisation. The described alternative to the classical benchmarking can be a methodology to perform performance comparisons across different kind of organisations and to promote concepts of VO. In summary, the following three points need to be fulfilled, before benchmarking VOs:

1. The advantages and goals of VOs need to be investigated carefully.
2. Standardized reference models need to be developed through decomposition of high level processes supporting VO goals. Reference models are needed for transparency reasons and to ensure comparability of PI values.
3. Goal oriented PI systems need to be developed integrating VO goals. These PIs need to be linked to standardized reference models.

6. REFERENCES

[1]   Camp, R.C.: Benchmarking. Milwaukee: Quality Press: 1989

[2]   Luczak, H.; Weber J.; Wiendahl H.P. (Hrsg.): Logistik-Benchmarking. 2. Auflage, Springer Verlag, Berlin , Heidelberg 2004

[3]   Freytag, P.V.; Hollensen, S.: The Process of Benchmarking, Benchlearning and Benchaction. In: The TQM Magazine, Vol. 13, No. 1, pp. 25-33 (2001)

[4]   Chow, G.; Heaver, T.D.; Henriksson L.E.: Logistics Performance: Definition and Measurement. In: International Journal of Physical Distribution & Logistics Management, Vol. 24 No. 1, pp. 17-28 (1994)

[5]   Gunasekaran, A; Patel, C.; Tirtiroglu, E.: Performance Measures and Metrics in a Supply Chain Environment. In: International Journal of Operations & Production Management, Vol. 21, No. 1/2, pp. 71-87(2001)

[6]   Hieber, R.: Supply Chain Management. Zürich: vdf, 2002

[7]   Nienhaus, J.; Schnetzler, M.; Sennheiser, A. et al: Trends im Supply Chain Management. Zürich: BWIETH Zürich, 2003 (English edition in preparation)

[8]   Beamon, B.B.: Measuring Supply Chain Performance. In: International Journal of Operations & Production Management, Vol. 19, No. 3, pp. 275-292 (1999)

[9]   Holmberg, S.: A Systems Perspective on Supply Chain Measurements. In: International Journal of Physical Distribution & Logistics Management, Vol. 30 No. 10, pp. 847-868 (2000)

[10]   Fong S. W.; Cheng, E. W.; Ho, D. C. K.: Benchmarking: a general reading for management practioners. In: management decision, Vol. 36, No. 6, pp. 407-418 (1998)

[11]   Watson G.H.: The benchmarking workbook: Adapting best practices for performance improvement. Productivity Press, Cambridge, Massachusetts 1992

[12]   Van Landeghem, R.; Persoons, K.: Benchmarking of logistical operations based on causal model. In: international journal of operations and production management, Vol. 21, No. ½, pp. 254-266 (2001)

[13]   Horvath P.; Herter, R.: Benchmarking – Vergleich mit den Besten. In: Controlling, Vol 4, No 1, pp. 4-11 (1992)

[14]   Camp R. C.: Learning from the best leads to superior performance. In: journal for business strategy, Vol. 12, No. 3, pp. 3-6 (1992)

[15]   Ester B.: Benchmarks für die Ersatzteillogistik. Erich Schmidt Verlag GmbH & Co., Berlin 1997

[16]   Töpfer A.: Benchmarking. In: WiSt, No 4, pp. 202-205 (1997)

[17]   Spendolini, M. J.: The benchmarking book. Amacom American Management Association, New York, Boston 1992

[18]   Schönsleben, Paul: Integral Logistics Management. 2nd ed. Boca Raton (etc.): St. Lucie, 2003

[19]   Supply Chain Operations Reference-model (SCOR) 5.0, Supply Chain Council, www.supply-chain.org

SOCIO-ORGANIZATIONAL ISSUES

Yacine Rezgui and Ian Wilson
Informatics Research Institute, University of Salford, Salford, UK.
y.rezgui@salford.ac.uk and i.e.wilson@salford.ac.uk

Wendy Olphert and Leela Damodaran
Information, Technology and Society Research Group, Department of Information Science,
Loughborough University, UK.
c.w.olphert@lboro.ac.uk and L.Damodaran@lboro.ac.uk

Whilst virtual organizations are enabled via existing and emerging technologies, they remain principally human constructs. The authors argue that the success of the VO throughout its lifecycle, from creation to dissolution, relies on its capability to create and sustain value. In this context, the human capital of the VO, and more generally, its 'intangible assets' play a determinant role. Thus the socio-organizational 'equation' consists of a combination of technology, culture, and organization, in which issues including trust, confidentiality, knowledge sharing, etc., must be blended successfully toward the shared VO purpose. This chapter explores the social and organizational aspects of virtual organizations and highlights important issues that need addressing in order to negotiate the necessary transition from a traditional to a knowledge driven organization that can engage effectively in knowledge driven alliances characterized by virtual business modes.

1. INTRODUCTION

Organizations are currently facing important and unprecedented challenges in an ever dynamic, constantly changing, and complex environment. Several factors, including the pace of technological innovation and the globalization of the economy, have forced business and industry to adapt to new challenges triggered by an ever sophisticated society characterized by an increasing demand for customized and high quality services and products in various segments of industry. New business models have emerged where value added alliances, and virtual business modes and operations empowered by latest advancement in information and communication technologies (ICT), are becoming key ingredients to success.

Moreover, ICT has had major implications on organizations and their business processes. Consequently, active and constant changes in business as well as political and social environment are putting an increasing pressure on organizations to respond to environmental alterations and adapt to them. Companies need to predict and monitor these transformations and implement them as efficiently as possible to their own business environment and culture. Virtual business modes emerge as a result of a desire to improve market position, gain competitive advantages and of course, the will to create value. Companies deploy and participate in virtual partnerships in order to effectively detect market demand, develop new products and services, identify new opportunities, improve the quality of their work, and lastly find possibilities to lower organizational costs.

In a wish to maintain and expand the competitive edge, so essential in today's business environment, companies worldwide are refocusing strategies to deliver new and existing products and services with maximum value to the customer at the lowest price. All these strategies are based on effectively connecting and participating in an organizational cluster to identify what is relevant to the particular corporation at a specific time. The uncertainties of the business are growing and new game plans are being drawn every day by organizations concerned with their profitability. The future has only two predictable features – 'change and resistance to change' and the very survival of the companies will depend upon their ability not only to adapt to but also master these challenges [16].

This chapter will first explore the concept of intangible assets and the role of corporate intellectual capital within it. It will then introduce the key parameters of the socio-organizational equation. These are traditionally overlooked by organizations. The authors argue that proper consideration should be given to these aspects if today's organizations are to survive in an increasingly competitive business environment. The following section explores the human capital dimension of an organization and the need for proper learning and training strategies to sustain their capability building and value creation. Finally, the chapter introduces the requirement for migration strategies where several barriers, including resistance to change, need addressing in order to negotiate the necessary transition from a traditional to a knowledge driven organization that can engage effectively in knowledge driven alliances characterized by virtual business modes.

2. INTANGIBLES IN THE VIRTUAL ORGANIZATION

The knowledge economy generated by the Internet, mass computer reach, and as a result, an increasingly demanding and sophisticated society, are posing complex problems to all stakeholders in charge in one form or another of the provision of the goods, products and services to all categories of citizens and populations. These complex developments are requiring essential attributes, skills and knowledge from organizations in order to adapt in this ever-competitive environment. In many instances organizations feel simply incompetent to address, on their own, their customers' expectations to deliver the right products and services. New business models are required, supported by new organizational structures, capabilities and values where individuals take a central position. Moreover, an organization's intangible assets are now recognized as one of the key ingredients to value and capability creation, which, in turn, are essential to sustain a level of competitiveness that would ensure growth and survival. An organization's intangible assets include its intellectual capital. However, while most organizations tend to concentrate on their physical goods and infrastructures, they tend to systematically overlook their intellectual capital and more generally the intangible assets (business processes, human and intellectual capital, customer and supply chain relationship, research and development, patents, brands, etc.) that exist within them and that are essential in order to engage into any virtual collaboration and cooperation mode. This section will explore the strategic importance of knowledge in the virtual organization and its nurturing through communities of practice.

2.1 Knowledge in the Virtual Organization

It is widely acknowledged that one of the key sustainable advantages that a traditional firm as well as a virtual organization can have comes from what it collectively knows, how efficiently it uses what it knows, and how readily it acquires and uses new knowledge [5]. While the first generation of knowledge management research has concentrated on knowledge sharing, current research has moved to the issue of knowledge creation based on existing knowledge and how this can be used to meet the strategic vision and goals of the virtual organization. Furthermore, knowledge management is a framework for designing a traditional as well as a virtual organization's goals, structures, and processes so that it can use what it knows collectively through its members to learn and create value for its customers and community [4].

Traditional as well as virtual organizations are beginning to comprehend that knowledge and its inter-organizational management, as well as individual and organizational capability building, are becoming crucial factors for gaining and sustaining competitive advantages [19], and as an after-effect, connections and partnerships with other organizations in order to trade knowledge have become of significant importance. Venkatraman et al. [23] have defined a virtual corporation as 'a strategic approach that is singularly focused on creating, nurturing, and deploying key intellectual and knowledge assets while outsourcing tangible, physical assets in a complex network of relationships'. The ability to recognize and alter knowledge to gain maximum results within a partnership or a network is vital as effective knowledge management institutes and maintains networkability. Klueber et al. [8] have understood this process of knowledge management as threefold:

- Knowledge of business partners, their processes and systems.
- Knowledge of how to set up and configure these relationships to allow rapid identification and qualification of potential partners.
- Knowledge enables an increase in efficiency due to the effects of experience in linking processes and systems.

It is now widely acknowledged that it is essential for virtual organizations to combine the right capabilities to leverage their knowledge if they are to compete successfully in future markets. The knowledge base of the virtual organization needs to be efficiently managed to ensure creation of new knowledge, its distribution and ready accessibility to all members.

2.2 Communities of Practice

Several studies and research, including [21] have reported knowledge sharing related success stories where group of employees following their own initiative got together to solve business-related problems. The success of these individually-led initiatives leading to some sort of virtual organic structures, that did not rely on or even involve senior management staff or directive, have gradually attracted interest from both the research community and corporate senior management staff within and outside these organizations. These organic virtual structures, termed and known as "Communities of Practice" relate more generally to groups of individuals within or across organizational boundaries that share a common concern, a set of problems, or a passion about a topic, and who deepen their understanding and knowledge of this area by interacting using face-to-face or virtual means (synchronous and asynchronous) on a continuous basis [24].

The gaining popularity of Communities of Practice have been reinforced by the quest for innovation and value creation as it is widely recognized that these only happen when empowered individuals are well connected using a variety of means and communication mediums both inside and outside the organization.

3. THE PARAMETERS OF THE SOCIO-ORGANIZATIONAL EQUATION

Organizations are essentially "social arrangements for achieving controlled performance in pursuit of collective goals" [8]. Whatever the goals of the organization (service provision, design, construction, manufacture etc.), the arrangements necessary for achieving controlled performance will involve the organization and manipulation of certain constant elements. At a basic level of description, Leavitt [12] states that organizations consist of four main elements – people (staff), technology (systems), tasks (skills) and structure. Other organization theorists, such as [18] have identified further elements of the organization which they have incorporated into what is known as the "seven S" model - adding strategy, style and shared values to the four elements described by Leavitt [12]. These elements are all inter-related (as indicated in the diagram below), so that changes to any one element will have knock-on effects on the others, like an equation which must be balanced. Furthermore the elements must all operate in harmony together for the organization to operate effectively.

The creation of effective virtual organizations will require consideration of the same combination of elements as for the design of 'traditional' organizations. Technological, cultural, and organizational factors, (including issues such as trust, confidentiality, knowledge sharing, etc.) must be blended successfully in order to achieve the shared objectives of the VO. However, managing and controlling the different elements so that they operate in harmony poses particular management problems for virtual organizations which cross the boundaries of more than one 'real' organization. Evidence suggests, for example, that in such circumstances management teams can find their control declining. Departments that are in a 'grey area' between two firms are generally agreed to be the most difficult to control because of the influence of 'outside' information, although such departments may otherwise be regarded as vanguards of change and examples of innovation and good practice [7].

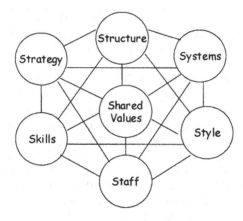

Figure 1 – The "Seven S" Model of Organizations [17]

3.1 Technology

Technology is the cornerstone of the virtual organization, by enabling people to work collaboratively although separated by space or by time. Technology not only supports the tasks which individuals and organizations need to perform, but enables knowledge and information to be easily shared regardless of organizational boundaries. New technologies are constantly emerging which offer potential benefits to organizations for improved efficiency and effectiveness, enhanced competitivity, delivery of new products and services. Introduction of new technologies is one of the main drivers for organizational change. However from the "Seven S" model shown above, it is clear that technology or systems are only one element of the organizational landscape, and that the introduction of new technology will undoubtedly impact on all other aspects of the organization. For example, new technologies can enable new ways of working; for the organization to benefit from these, new skills and/or new staff may be required, together with changes in structure and procedures. Research consistently shows that the introduction of new technology is unlikely to result in the anticipated organizational and economic benefits unless the impact on other elements of the organization is identified and the required changes are proactively managed (e.g. [15]). Socio-technical systems theory [6] highlights the importance of designing social and organizational systems in parallel with technical systems, in order to achieve optimization of both.

3.2 Culture

While new technology may be one of the key drivers for organizational change, organizational culture can be regarded as one of the key potential barriers. The willingness of staff to accept and capitalize on new ways of working, including participating in virtual organizations will depend in part upon the prevailing organizational culture. The culture of an organization (shared values, in the "Seven S" model above) represents the "glue" which holds an organization together. A strong, i.e. clear and widely shared, organizational culture is now widely claimed to be critical to organizational success (e.g. [18]). The culture of an organization can be defined as "the collection of relatively uniform and enduring values, beliefs, customs, traditions and practices that are shared by an organization's members, learned by new recruits, and transmitted from one generation of employees to the next." [8]. Organizational cultures derive from basic assumptions and values held by key individuals in the organization (e.g. the founder, the CEO, the senior management team) which shape organizational objectives, structures, and processes, and which are promoted and shared both directly and indirectly through a range of mechanisms. While the virtual organization may be a "temporary" structure, its human resources may be drawn from a range of other organizations, each with their own (possibly conflicting) cultures. The lack of a shared culture may create difficulties for the effective operation of a virtual organization. This is partly due to reduced opportunities for interaction between employees, particularly face-to-face interaction, which provide opportunities for new employees or members of the virtual organization to learn about e.g. company values, history, and folklore. Asynchronous communications, which are typical of the virtual organization, mitigate against the development of a sense of community, although the use of synchronous electronic meeting spaces may help to develop a community with a sense of shared culture [13].

4.   THE INGREDIENTS FOR SUCCESSFUL MIGRATION TOWARDS VALUE NETWORKS

Virtual working and the concept of value networks rely on cooperation between dispersed stakeholders working towards a common purpose. In order to efficiently meet this purpose there is a strong requirement for the goals of the (virtual) enterprise to be shared and embraced collectively. As noted by Lipnack and Stamps [12] "Virtual team success or failure begins with the relationships among people and goals." Whilst network organizing is enabled via new technologies, organizations remain principally human constructs. There is a need for the people within the networks to embrace change (see section 5 below), and adopt a new culture, the sustainable adoption of which continues to be a main concern [17]. Three key aspects can be recognized as ingredients for successful migration from traditional organizational forms to value networks: knowledge sharing (already addressed in the previous sections), trust and confidence, and continuous learning.

4.1 Building Trust and Confidence

As argued in [3,9], trust takes on added importance in the context of a virtual organization because it acts as a substitute to two important factors: the first is endogenous, the hierarchical control associated with traditional organizations, and the second is exogenous, the legal framework needed to regulate the formation, operation, and dissolution of the virtual organization. Technology has the potential to overcome the trust barrier that exists in the virtual organization. There is, however, still a lack of integrating infrastructure guaranteeing a global interoperability [17]; trust and confidence in the technology therefore, can only be achieved when suitable and dependable 'working' infrastructures have been implemented, tested, and validated in a real-world context.

Trust in technology is only one small dimension of the needs of the value network however, and the fact that we are using new tools to accomplish tasks does not change the fact that we rely on people to engender trust. Indeed people work together because they trust one another and successful virtual teams pay special attention to building trust [14] throughout their lifecycle. Research (e.g. [22]) indicates that people generally tend to trust people rather than companies and that trust ultimately emerges where communicated information is reliable, people stand by their promises, and outcomes equal or exceed expectations. This suggests another important factor for engendering trust, the one of ethics. It is important that all members of a virtual organization have clear policies in place within their native corporation about business ethics, which must exist as a set of formal or informal norms, and also as a demonstrated propensity to behave ethically [9].

Business understanding is another important factor in any cooperation within a virtual organization. The concept of identity or business mission that exists in traditional organizations is not easy to implement in a virtual cooperation setting. It is important that a shared vision sustains the formation of a virtual organization and clear definitions of role members, tasks, responsibilities and expectations within the virtual team are defined.

4.1 Education and Training Dimension

To achieve successful exploitation of advanced ICT to enable virtual organization requires not only the implementation of innovative technologies but also new working practices, and organizational structures and cultures. The potential benefits of such innovation can only be realized through individuals at all levels learning and developing a considerable array of new capabilities. Furthermore, innovation increases through the creation of a continuous learning culture, in which users share knowledge. One way in which a true culture of learning and continuous training can be developed is through the employment of a learning and training strategy. Further details on the issue of education and training can be found in [20] where an iterative strategy has been described which includes the following phases:

- Awareness raising.
- Core business process analysis.
- Current skills analysis and mapping.
- Define/review ICT strategy.
- Identify skill gap.
- Identify/review new/existing roles and responsibilities.
- Plan and organize user-centered education and training.
- Measure and evaluate progress.

5. THE IMPERATIVE FOR CHANGE

Many organizations find themselves in an almost constant state of change, as they strive to respond to the pressures of the increasingly global, competitive environment in which they exist. Drivers for change include:

- strategic and commercial considerations such as the need to lower costs, improve efficiency, introduce new products and services; such drivers will entail organizational changes including implementing new ways of working, new contractual models, supply chain partnerships, etc.
- mergers and acquisitions which involve the bringing together, rationalization and harmonization of two or more organizations;
- the availability of new technologies;
- legislation.

The virtual organization is a temporary enterprise, combining members who may be temporarily incorporated into the VO from a variety of other organizations. As such, the creation and operation of the VO will be regarded as a change within those organizations who are contributing their resources to it. As a temporary enterprise, its members are likely to experience a time-compressed version of the organizational lifecycle – set-up, operation, and winding down. Each of these different phases in the VO's existence is, in turn, likely to involve changes in staffing, tasks, objectives and resources. Recognition of the nature and scale of the changes involved in creating and operating a virtual organization, and effective management of those changes, is central to the success of the enterprise.

Despite the frequency of change, evidence shows that many change projects are unsuccessful [11]. Section 3 above highlights the fact that the many different facets of an organization are interrelated, so that change to any one aspect of the organization will have knock-on effects on other aspects. One of the main reasons for the lack of success of change projects is the failure by management to take a strategic approach to change management and to identify the full impact of changes so these can all be managed. However, another problem can be resistance to change amongst employees in the organization. At the individual level, organizational change raises concerns e.g. about security, status, skills and job content, and therefore a key element of any change management programme must be an effective communication strategy to provide information about the rationale, process and consequences of the change and, where possible, to allay employees' concerns. Resistance to change is most likely when change is imposed on individuals. In this situation individuals frequently perceive neither the need nor desirability for the proposed change. This means that they have little or no motivation to invest in learning the required new skills or to change their established ways of operating. In such circumstances the change is unlikely to generate the positive benefits sought by those driving the changes – unless or until at least some of those who will be affected are in favor of the change.

5.1 Engaging Stakeholders

There is extensive evidence in the academic and business literature to show that for a planned change to be successful, it is crucial that those who will be affected by it (the stakeholders) are engaged in the planning of that change (e.g. [1]). Note that this does not mean that all stakeholders have to be involved in every aspect of the change programme, but it is essential to identify key stakeholder inputs (requirements, concerns etc.) and address these if the change is to be effective. There are also significant benefits to be gained from enabling stakeholders to actively participate in a change project, compared to simply communicating to, or seeking information from, stakeholders. Through investing time and effort in the change process, stakeholders begin to identify with and to develop personal goals for the planned change. The engagement process also gives early warning of potential difficulties, which often enables solutions to be found before significant adverse impact occurs.

In order to engage stakeholders and to understand the nature of their 'stake' in a change project, it will be necessary to establish who the stakeholders are, what roles they hold in relation to the change (in particular their relative power and influence), how they are likely to accept the change (this will be influenced e.g. by their current concerns and their expectations about how the change will affect them), and what requirements they have in relation to the change.

5.2 Change Strategies

There are four main types of change strategy, which can be summarized on a 2 x 2 matrix as shown in the figure below. The strategies differ depending both on the nature of the change (whether it is a 'big bang' – where stakeholders stop using the old system one-day and switch to a fully new system the next, or whether it is incremental, with stakeholders progressively making the change over a period of months), and in terms of the end result which is sought (i.e. whether the change involves a major transformation of the organization or parts of the organization, or whether it involves a smaller realignment). The greater the scale of change at one time (i.e. when there is both a 'big bang' approach to a major transformation), the more difficult it is for stakeholders to adapt . However, there is no "right" way – management must choose the one most appropriate for the organization, bearing in mind the organizational culture and context. Each of the different strategies has different advantages and disadvantages, and different implications for the likely time and resource requirements for the change programme. For example a 'big bang' approach provides an integrated, centrally managed way of ensuring the implementation takes place. Sometimes this is the only way to make a change, for example the recent change to the Euro currency in many European countries. An incremental approach is usually chosen where avoidance of risk to business is a top priority. A common example is introducing a new computer and letting people work on both the old and new machines together until they are totally familiar with the new one. However the disadvantage of this strategy is that staff are doing the same job twice and there is a tendency for staff to retain the existing social system during this period (which may make it difficult, for example, to operate new work structures effectively. It is of course possible to use a combination of strategies during the course of a programme.

		End Result	
		Transformation	*Realignment*
Nature	*Incremental*	Evolution	Adaptation
	Big Bang	Revolution	Reconstruction

Figure 2 – Types of change

While the transition from 'traditional' organizations towards 'virtual' organizations may be accomplished in a limited or partial way by the creation of virtual projects, when organizational boundaries are being crossed the nature of the changes required internally may be quite large. Issues of confidentiality and security will be paramount, ensuring that systems are put into place, which enables the virtual work to take place and information and knowledge to be exchanged, but protecting and preserving the confidentiality of other organizational knowledge. It will be necessary to create management and leadership structures that apply to the virtual organization, although these may not be in harmony with existing structures within the 'real' organizations. Similarly, communications processes will need to be established, and working styles, roles and rewards may need to be moderated for the virtual organization to work effectively. When a virtual organization temporarily incorporates some members from another enterprise, it should be recognized that changes that benefit the members of the virtual organization may cause resistance or discontent amongst other members of the 'home' organizations who are not part of the VO and this will need careful management.

Senior management must therefore adopt a strategic approach to change management, taking into consideration not only at the 'virtual' organization but also at the parts of the 'real' organization that are likely to be affected and ensuring that the impact of the change is managed in both.

6. CONCLUSION

This chapter presented an overview of the key socio-organizational issues that must be addressed for the effective implementation of virtual organizations. Whilst the virtual organization is enabled via existing and emerging technologies, organizations remain principally human constructs where the management of knowledge and the creation of value networks rely on human capital and 'intangibles'. Thus the socio-organizational 'equation' consists of a combination of technology, culture, and organization, in which issues including trust, confidentiality, knowledge sharing, etc., must be blended successfully toward the shared virtual organization purpose. The migration path to successful networking is grounded in human and cultural elements that engage all stakeholders in a manner that is supported by continuous learning. Migration towards any new way of organizing and working is an exercise in change, which requires new mechanisms to enable participation and communication.

The research highlights some essential factors that should be developed by modern organizations, including the will and ability to:

a. Increase individual and organizational capabilities.
b. Develop a culture of individual led initiative and collaboration.
c. Exploit at best current developments, existing solutions, and advances in ICT.
d. Review and improve business processes and general organizational procedure on a continuous basis.
e. Implement learning and training strategy aimed at all staff.

Finally, the authors would like to end this chapter by arguing the case for the need to develop a business oriented social and organizational roadmap, aimed not only at senior management but all categories of staff of an organization. Such a roadmap would aid in paving the way to knowledge-driven alliances where intangible assets are given proper and full consideration.

4. REFERENCES

[1] Bennis, W., Benne, K., and Chin, R., (eds.) (1985) The Planning of Change, 4th Edn. Holt, Rinehart & Winston: New York.
[2] Camarinha-Matos, L., and Afsarmanesh, H. (eds.) (1999) Infrastructures for Virtual Enterprises: Networking Industrial Enterprises, IFIP TC5 WG5.3 / PRODNET Working Conference on Infrastructures for Virtual Enterprises (PRO-VE'99), Porto, October 1999. Kluwer Academic Publishers: Boston.
[3] Camarinha-Matos, L., and Afsarmanesh, H. (eds.) (2004) Collaborative Networked Organizations: A Research Agenda for Emerging Business Models, Kluwer Academic Publishers. ISBN: 1402078234.
[4] Choo, C.W. (1999). The FIS Knowledge Management Institute, session presentations. Faculty of Information Studies, University of Toronto, http://www.choo.fis.utoronto.ca
[5] Davenport, T.H. and Prusak, L. (1998). Working Knowledge: How Organizations Manage what they Know. Boston: Harvard and Business School Press.
[6] Emery, F.E. and Trist, E.L. (1960) "Socio-Technical Systems". In: Management Sciences Models and Techniques, Vol. 2. London.
[7] Harrington, J. (1991) Organizational Structure and Information Technology. Prentice Hall, UK.
[8] Huczynski, A. and Buchanan, D. (2001) Organizational Behaviour: An Introductory Text, 4th Edn. Prentice Hall, UK.
[9] Kasper-Fuehrer, E.C and Ashkanasy, N.M. (2001) Communicating Trustworthiness and Building Trust in Interorganizational Virtual Organizations, Journal of Management 27, pp 235-254.
[10] Klueber, R., Alt, R., and Osterle, H.: Implementing Virtual Organising in Business Networks: A Method of Inter-Business Networking, in Malholtra, Y. (2000) Knowledge Management and Virtual Organisations. Idea Group Publishing.
[11] Kotter, J. (1996) Leading Change. Harvard Business School Press: Boston.
[12] Leavitt, H. (1965) "Applied organizational change in industry: structural, technological and humanistic approaches", Handbook of Organizations, James March (ed.) Rand McNally.
[13] Liegle, J.O. & Bodnovich, T.A. (1997). Information Technology in Virtual Organisations: A Needs Assessment from the Perspective of Human Resource Management. In: Proc. AIS 97, Indianapolis, Indiana, Aug 15-17 1997.
[14] Lipnack, J., and Stamps, J. (2000) Virtual Teams: People Working Across Boundaries with Technology, 2nd edn. Wiley & Sons: New York.

[15] Lyytinen D & Hirschheim R : "Information Systems Failures : A Survey and Classification of the Empirical Literature" : Oxford Surveys in Information Technologies: vol 4 : 1987

[16] Mamutty, C. (1998) The Power of Learning Organisation. Indian Management, Sept. 1998, pp. 37-40.

[17] Moniz, A. B., and Urze, P. (1999) Socio-organizational Requirements for a VE, in [2], pp.77-94.

[18] Peters, T. and Waterman, R.H. (1982) In Search of Excellence. Harper & Row, New York.

[19] Preiss, K., Goldman, S.L., and Nagel, R.N. (1996) Cooperate to Compete. Building Agile Business Relationships. Van Nostrand Reinhold: New : New York.

[20] Rezgui, Y., Damodaran, L., Olphert, W., and Wilson, I.E., (2003) ICCI Action plan on training in construction. Deliverable D32, EU Project IST-2001-33022 (ICCI) (http://cic.vtt.fi/projects/icci/public.html)

[21] Saint-Onge, H. and Wallace, D. (2002). Leveraging Communities of Practice for Strategic Advantage. Butterworth Heinemann.

[22] Swan, W., Cooper, R., McDermott, P., and Wood, G., (2002) Trust in Construction: Achieving Cultural Change. Centre for Construction Innovation, www.ccinw.com

[23] Venkatraman, N., and Henderson, C. (1998) The Architecture of virtual organising: leveraging three independent vectors. Discussion Paper, Systems Research Centre, Boston University, School of Management.

[24] Wenger, E., McDermott, R., Snyder, W.M. (2002). Cultivating Communities of Practice: A Guide to Managing Knowledge. Cambridge, MA: Harvard Business School Press.

4.

CASE STUDIES

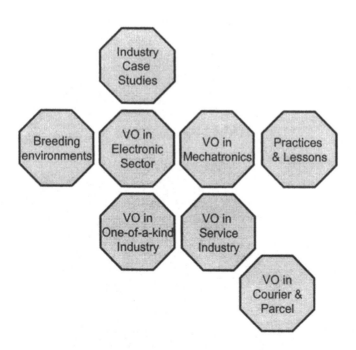

This page intentionally left blank

SURVEY OF INDUSTRY CASE STUDIES

Roberto Santoro, Andrea Bifulco

European Society of Concurrent Enterprising Network /ESoCE-NET,Italy,
rsantoro@esoce.net
CE Consulting /CEC, Italy, abifulco@ceconsulting.it

This chapter details the results of a case study carried out by the VOSTER project Consortium, aimed at identifying current and advanced socio-organisational practices for using, implementing and exploiting existing or emerging ICTs in the Virtual Organisation (VO) context. The industrial case survey has resulted in the identification of some emerging VO practices, which have shown, to some extent, successful application in truly industrial environments. Even though they suffer the limitation of being the very first implementation of innovative concepts, resulting in some weak points to be addressed for improvement by future research, the achieved maturity level is deemed adequate to provide some advantage from their utilisation in the establishment of future Virtual Organisations.

1. INTRODUCTION

This chapter details the results of a case study carried out by the VOSTER project Consortium, aimed at identifying current and advanced socio-organizational practices for using, implementing and exploiting existing/emerging ICTs in the Virtual Organization (VO) context. Within VOSTER, a large number of VO cases were considered, including actual business implementations of the VO paradigm, as well as pilot demonstrations of the latest research results in the field within the industrial environment.

To cover the broad spectrum of industrial networking and cooperation activities entailed by the VO general concept, the scope of the information base for the study included all VO topologies, from Peer-to-Peer Virtual Enterprises to Supply-chain networks and Main contractor driven Consortia, whilst also considering Source Networks, as examples of breeding environments for dynamic, efficient and agile creation of Virtual Enterprises responding to specific business opportunities. Furthermore, in order to capture the differences and commonalities of VO practices' implementation issues across varying industrial contexts, the survey was not restricted to specific industrial sectors.

An overview of the business cases considered within the study is given in the following section, along with more detailed information regarding a few specific cases, it being impossible, within the limits of this book, to present the totality of the information collected. The choice of cases was made by privileging, where possible, the publication of actual VO implementation in real business contexts, as opposed to pilot demonstrations executed within the framework of research projects, in order to give the reader a more tangible impression of real Virtual Organizations currently.

The VOSTER study attempted to distinguish, from the collected information, those practices specific to the innovative VO paradigm and underpinning its practical realization, with the intention of identifying the most successful industrial implementations of VO concepts and methodologies in terms of effective and efficient application in industrial environments. The extracted practices were also analyzed with regard to issues of their success, transportability and implementation effort, with the aim of determining their potential for successful reuse in other business cases within equivalent or different, industry sectors. As the focus of this study is the identification of innovative practices from the first testing of new methodologies in recent research efforts, the maturity level of the practices identified is generally incomplete. Conversely, a number of additional VO implementation issues were identified on the base of the experience gained in operative industrial environments.

The emerging VO practices were then organized according to a classification of the main different application areas:

- *VO Constitution,* focusing on partners' search and selection, and start-up and dissolution issues;
- *Business Model & Organization,* including the definition of roles within the VO along with their relationships with the VO partner legacy organizational structures, VO business models, strategic planning, enterprise engineering and related issues;
- *Legal framework,* addressing the establishment and negotiation of VO contractual issues, VO legal identity, VO internal/external liabilities and regulations, as well as VO collaboration principles such as benefit/profit share, IPR and property of the results;
- *VO Management,* regarding the definition and execution of the VO management processes as well as the VO product, process and organisation information utilized for managing set-up and operation;
- *ICT infrastructure,* including the utilization of specific ICT architecture and applications for enabling cooperation among the VO partners, the management of evolving network technology, the use of standards and related issues.

The Emerging Practices section of the chapter introduces an overview of the state of VO practices in the main areas of application, along with a description of the most innovative and promising ones for auspicious future broad use.

2. VIRTUAL ORGANIZATION BUSINESS CASES

This section provides some descriptive information about industrial clustering and cooperation cases structured as Virtual Organizations. Examples of both Source Networks / Breeding Environments and Virtual Enterprises (VE) [1] belonging to the different topologies defined in the previous chapters provide an overview of the actual implementation of VO concepts and methodologies within different industrial sectors.

2.1 Source Networks / VO Breeding Environments

Source Networks are clusters of companies established to form a stable breeding environment for the dynamic generation of temporary Virtual Enterprises driven by specific business opportunities. The rationale for such a networking approach results mainly from the necessity of achieving efficiency in the processes underpinning the VE creation and dissolution phases, and of providing a centralised and standardised support to the actual operation phases.

Selected examples of operative Source Networks established in different industrial sectors are described below.

2.1.1 Virtual Factory (Virtuelle Fabrik)

The Virtual factory case (VF) is the linking together of real companies for the purpose of entering new markets or realizing concrete projects that for the individual companies would not be possible in a profitable manner [7-8].

- With an order orientation, the core competencies of the network partners are utilized efficiently and flexibly.
- At present, there are 37 companies in the network, employing a total of 3,000 employees.
- In the entire value-added chain, the VF offers total solutions and services for assemblies and sophisticated components and replacement parts.
- Through Intranet communication, all partner companies can post projects and seek possible cooperation partners.

The legal form of organization of the VF as well as its structural organization is the association, or society. The management of the association is the responsibility of an elected Executive Committee, which is made up of five members (representatives of partner companies) and headed by a chairman, the president. A general meeting is held once a year, while six conferences for the mutual exchange of experience take place annually. All partner companies take part in the conferences for purposes of mutual exchange of information and experience. In addition, there are six working parties composed of representatives of the partner companies. Each company in the network is supposed to be represented in at least one working party. The working parties meet monthly.

The association serves as a resource pool from which partnerships can be formed to fulfill a customer request or to take advantage of a market opportunity. These partnerships end, when the particular project has been executed.

The virtual company concept provides for various roles in the formation of project-based partnerships as well as a behaviour code and standardised business processes that are stated as so-called ground rules of cooperation. All member companies are familiar with and accept the ground rules, which makes it possible for project-based partnerships to form rapidly.

Customer benefits: For customers, the purchasing of individual goods and services from various suppliers is a problem, because coordination demands a great deal of effort. The virtual factory takes over interface management for the customer and offers goods and services from one source, for the virtual company puts together the value-added cabin.

Partner benefits: For the partner companies, the VF is first of all an acquisition instrument through which the companies can acquire new customers and orders. It serves as a marketing platform and offers the possibility to build up a net of relationships. Second, the VF is a - diversification instrument, for it opens up new markets and extended business areas, and more comprehensive orders can result. Third, the VF is an arena for learning that helps companies to identify and strengthen core competencies and that allows mutual exchange of experience. Partner companies gain access to market information and can acquire training in communication and cooperation.

A monographic chapter of this book (chapter 4.6) is dedicated to an extensive description of this Breeding Environment.

2.1.2 Net "A " - Finnish Source Network/ Breeding Environment

"Net A" consists of 17 high tech enterprises in the Varkaus region in the eastern part of Finland. The main focus areas are automation and instrumentation technology, electronics, precision mechanics and software. In addition they offer design, training and consultancy in the field. Together they form a network or breeding environment enabling turnkey deliveries as a large company, whilst benefiting from the flexibility efficiency of the small partner companies [9-10].

"Net A" was established in 1992 after a very turbulent period in the region, which has a strong background in pulp and paper manufacturing and manufacturing of energy production machinery. A considerable amount of SMEs supported the activities. During the recession in the late 1980s and early 1990s the large industries in the area underwent a major restructuring process. Three large American companies (Honeywell, Foster & Wheeler and CEC) became owners of most of the manufacturing capacity in the area; only the paper production remained as Finnish owned. To answer the threats the SMEs in the area, which earlier had supported the manufacturing industry, decided to collaborate and join their efforts to survive during this turbulent era.

In ten years the number of employees in the member companies has grown threefold, and from local service providers the companies have also become international and can offer services world-wide. The collaboration is based on common agreements, whilst maintaining flexibility, in which the member companies have learned to collaborate in the network and market each other's capacity. They can also benefit from acquiring common services as a "large" company.

2.1.3 Hungarian Fashion Cluster

At the end of 2002 many players of the Hungarian textile and clothing industry decided to co-ordinate their market and economic activities and to establish the Fashion Cluster in order to counteract the dumping of cheap but low quality clothes from the Far East. Manufacturers, service providers and designers entered the cluster, whose activity is supported by several institutions of branch unions, regional development and science and venture capital associations.

The declared objectives of the cluster were:
- The cluster should be a grouping of reliable companies, providing higher than average quality.
- The cluster should pool firms that can together trust each other, focusing on the co-operation in merit.
- The cluster serves the members' joint and individual business enrichment by joint market presence, joint tenders, and exchange of information and experience helping each other, technological and capacity support, and other useful means.

The Fashion Cluster is a co-operative network of equal, high quality, reliable enterprises that also wishes to promote this image outwards. The services provided by the cluster include:
- Fashion Cluster portal (www.divatklaszter.hu) – open to each cluster member, it serves as an information portal and a business communication channel for members. It also has a marketplace where members can buy and sell their products and service.
- Cluster office – a modern office with sophisticated ICT infrastructure that can be used by cluster members for business purposes.
- Information service – informing interested parties about the functioning of the cluster and its events, it also addresses cluster members by informing them about calls for proposals, etc.
- Organisation of professional events and conferences.

In order to help their members develop according to market needs, the cluster elaborated the system of supporting modules. These modules are:
- Training – organising different training courses as required by cluster members.
- European Union – providing information about the EU and the changes it will bring about for the textile and clothing industry. It also helps members build European relationships by searching for potential partners, organising visits abroad, building partnerships and preparing proposals for European calls.
- Innovation – the cluster promotes technology transfer.
- Technology — the cluster helps its members acquire new machinery.
- Organisational development – the cluster advises on organisational problems, management issues, etc.
- Human resource management – including services such as recruitment, performance measuring, motivation schemes, etc.
- Workflow management – consultancy services, the spread of good practices, etc.
- ICT – the cluster offers solutions for ICT problems including network development, maintenance, etc., focusing on viable solutions for SMEs.
- Financing – the cluster helps get funds, acquire credit, etc.
- Quality management.
- Marketing and PR.

2.1.4 Pannon Automotive Cluster

The Pannon Automotive Cluster was among the first Hungarian clusters to be established. It is located in the West Pannon Region of Hungary, a region which attracted many automotive SMEs (aspiring to become suppliers) to settle down because of the proximity of various multinational companies (Opel, Suzuki, Audi). These SMEs soon realised that rivalry did not lead to success. Without co-operation, the majority of these SMEs could not hope for supplier status.

The primary objective of the cluster was to enable its members to become efficient suppliers of large integrator companies. Therefore, Pannon Automotive Cluster aims at:
- Fostering the creation of co-operative networks of enterprises;
- Accelerating the establishment of new supplier links;
- Supporting investment projects to improve competitiveness;
- Encouraging innovation;
- Encouraging foreign automotive ventures to settle down in the region.

After the foundation of the cluster, a large number of automotive industry SMEs joined, and to date the cluster has 62 members, mostly SMEs. Membership is open to every company/institution with an interest in the automotive industry.

The cluster provides the following services:
- Assistance in project foundation;
- Provision of information;
- Communication services;
- Company audit;
- Consultancy;
- Training;
- Organization of events,
- Workshops and conferences;
- Marketing and PR activities;
- Stimulation of e-business.

The cluster has achieved a variety of results including:
- PANAC web portal (www.panac.hu): The portal offers on-line registration (for potential members, visitors, interested parties etc.), on-line data management; it publishes automotive and business news as well as information on new projects, funding opportunities; it has professional fora (public, member and closed group fora); it offers an electronic newsletter service. The most frequently visited part of the portal is the database, where companies can browse the available data and information on their potential partners. This database enables members to choose the most appropriate partner for a specific project or action or even for long-term co-operation.
- Establishment of international co-operation network: it has generated business forums, business meetings and EU projects.
- Organization of a project generation workshop.
- Company audits: One of the basic services of the cluster is the company audit. This audit enables the gathering of all data and information necessary for the on-line database, and estimation of the level of supplier readiness of the company.
- Elaboration of a modular training course on supply chains.

- Organization of supplier development programs (all together 57 days with the participation of 680 people).
- Collection of best practices.
- Training courses (all together 28 courses in 2002).
- Benchmarking club: Several key indicators have been identified to which members can benchmark their performance. This benchmarking club has positively contributed to the spread of the inter-company learning culture.
- Demonstration effect: By concentrating needs, cluster members prove their capability to co-operate effectively with integrator companies.

2.2 Peer-to-Peer VEs

This section presents relevant business cases belonging to the Peer-to-Peer VO topology, characterised by an equal level partnering among partners sharing risks and profit, eventually coordinated by a third party – the Business Integrator. Peculiar to this VO topology, is the VIVE (Virtual Vertical Enterprises) methodology [2-3], which was developed by CE Consulting with the support of a number of dedicated research projects carried out under the fourth and fifth EC Framework programme (VIVE, BIDSAVER, ALIVE, ACTIVE, PROVE-SME). The VIVE concept enables the integration of products and services of SMEs selected according to specific project characteristics, and allows large customers to interface with their vertical Value Networks for the provision of entire Subsystems, as they were an unique big supplier, whilst taking advantage of SMEs' flexibility, effectiveness and efficiency.

The VIVE initiative addresses the issue of stimulating the co-operation between SMEs through the constitution of Virtual Enterprises based on:

- A new entity, the "Business Integrator", facilitating the constitution of new VEs by providing consolidated business relation schemes and a new level of services supporting SMEs;
- ICT infrastructure and co-operative work environment definition, allowing SMEs to integrate their business processes, and including a solution to enable full VE operation with reference to technical, logistic, administrative and management aspects.

2.2.1 KUBA Virtual Enterprise

The main objective for the KUBA VE [4] is to commercialize a flat active antenna for receiving satellite television signals. The product is a natural evolution of the parabola kits, which are currently widely adopted all over the world. The KUBA antenna will provide better electrical performance, minimized dimensions and a competitive price with respect to parabolas.

Companies from three European countries acting with the following four roles form the KUBA VE team:

- Business Integrator – assuming overall responsibility for liaison between the parties ;
- Mechanical Designer – supporting design role;
- Developer – in charge of analysing the technological needs of the potential partners in agreement to identified partners' available technologies and to

the actual business opportunities, identifying the technical solutions provided by its products;

- Producer – capable of analysing the needs of the market and the effective business opportunities, industrialising, producing, marketing and selling the identified and selected products.

The KUBA VE team produced the final antenna specifications, matching the market requirements (automatic electrical steering between satellite beams, ease of installation) with the available technology and processes. A working antenna breadboard, suitable for addressing the manufacturing and engineering phase is available. A final VE business plan was also agreed, in order to proceed with a search for additional funding for the start-up phase.

The benefits experienced in this VE constitution and first operation were compared with conventional business practices in industrial cooperation of the same typology. The implementation of the methodology indicated the following benefits:

- Reduction of the financial investment of the partner most exposed of 50%;
- Reduction of the overall investment level by 20%;
- Reduction of cooperation set-up time by 50%;
- Reduction of the overall time to market by 25% with respect to similar projects;
- Consistency of project development costs with forecasts;
- Increase of partners' revenues by at least 25% (projections for coming years).

2.2.2 The SCOP VE

The SCOP (Small COgeneration Plants) VE [4] aims to deliver Combined Heat and Power (CHP) production plants (of small size – from 1 to 6MW) to the market. CHP plants optimize the utilization of energy sources (diesel, gas, bio-gas, and so on) by delivering heat obtained from the engine refrigerating circuit (otherwise dispersed to the environment in other applications) to users. Users can be private houses (which save the heating costs and do not emit combustion gases into the atmosphere) as well as utilities of an industrial plant (in this respect, the heat can be used in the specific process, e.g. in paper mills, etc.). Co-generation systems allow for dramatically reducing the costs related to energy transmission (electricity transmission losses and investment for enhancing the transmission grid), and also the environmental impact of the grid.

The SCOP VE team is formed by four Italian organizations (Ulstein Italia, STC Colenco Engineering, COTECO, and CE Consulting). The first three companies used to co-operate on occasional basis, but not in the frame of CHP plants. Their motivation to join the VE project was to establish a strategic alliance in order to better seize the business opportunities in the small co-generation sector. These organizations performed the following four roles:

- Business Integrator – in charge of coordinating current projects and discovering additional business opportunities;
- Engine Supplier – in charge of supplying the endothermic engines (to be fed with fuel gas) and relevant alternators;

- System Engineer – in charge of design and procuring recovery system constituted by heat exchangers for the use of the heat contained in the cooling water, the lubricant oil and the exhausts; and
- Control Engineer – in charge of designing the control system of the plant.

The design phase for the supply of a CHP plant was completed and delivery to site started. Co-operation between the Business Integrator and the other three partners is supported by the availability of common product and activities models. Additional exploitation channels (co-operation with foreign partners) are also in place.

The benefits experienced in the VE establishment, in comparison with the initial co-operation targets, included:

- Formalization of partners' roles inside the VE;
- Reduction of financial exposure of the leading enterprise by 25%;
- Formalization of extra-costs allocation mechanism;
- Reduction of lead time, which is now consistent with market requirements but which can be improved by 10%;
- Optimization of the project cash flow, with the consequent increase of about 25% of the project operating margin;
- Reduction of cooperation set-up time by 50%;
- Increase of partners' revenues by at least 20%, due to improved exploitation channels.

2.2.3 CTS (Commercial to Space) VE

The CTS (Commercial To Space) VE [4] aims at designing and delivering Attitude Control and Electrical Power subsystems to the space market, obtained by evolving/qualifying commercial components (commercial Off-The-Shelves) in order to keep the cost of commercial space missions low. CTS subsystems are intended to target the requirements of so-called 'nanosatellites', able to carry space missions for science, technology demonstrations and applications such as remote sensing, telecommunications and meteorology.

The CTS VE is composed of CE Consulting, plus three SMEs performing the following roles:

IMT is acting as System Leader with the main following functions:

- Business Integrator – responsible for VE management and co-ordination;
- System Leader – responsible for Project Technical Management, System Architecture Definition, Development of the CTS Validation Process, CTS Functional Selection, Validation Operative Procedure Transfer, and System Integration and Validation;

"Eurosolare" is responsible for designing, selecting and validating the CTS components based on photovoltaic technology (i.e. for power generation and distribution sub-systems and solar sensors)

"Alta Industries" is responsible for designing, selecting and validating the CTS components of its own competency (i.e. magnetic and electronic components).

The design and characterisation phase for Attitude Control and Electrical Power subsystems to be used in Nanosatellites is complete, and the sub-systems and unit specifications are consolidated and available for the elements development. Co-operation among the three partners and the Business Integrator is supported by the availability of common product and activities models. Additional exploitation channels are also in place. The benefits experienced, compared with initial co-operation targets and with established benchmark, included:

- Reduction of the overall investment level by 15%;
- Reduction of cooperation set-up time by 50%;
- Reduction of the overall time to market by 25% with respect to established benchmark;
- Consistency of project development costs with forecasts, with deviations lower than 5%;
- Increase of partners' revenues by at least 30% (projections for coming years).

2.3 Supply chain topology Virtual Organizations

This section presents some relevant industrial pilot cases addressed at the implementation of enhanced Supply-chains organised as VO. By taking advantage of current ICT tools, traditional Supply Chains are evolving to Value Chain/Networks, in which complementary skills and competencies are valorized by more pervasive interactions, which go well beyond hierarchical vertical supply relationships. Therefore the emphasis is on both effectiveness and efficiency of the supply-chain.

2.3.1 Mechanical Supply chain VE

The Supply Chain VE is addressing the production phase optimisation process through the exploitation of the VE methodology and ICT infrastructure support. The class of product object of this VE are engineering systems for power transmission in the agricultural machines sector and industrial environment.

In this case the "customer" is a Large Enterprise (LE) needing to optimise its international supply-chain: the identified solution is to transform it in a VE. The LE is of course directly involved in the VE partnership.

After the identification of the VE partners, the main aspects addressed were:

- Communication analysis requirements among the enterprises (in terms of speed, clarity, technical data exchange, etc.);
- Analysis of the impact on the company organisation (and on the way of working): the learning curve;
- Comparison study between the new ways of operating within the VE with respect to the traditional;
- Integration with the enterprise management solution currently adopted at the SME sites. This integration has to ensure a high level of interoperability between the actual SME's ICT and the new one;
- To ensure seamless connection of the proposed ICT tools, developing new interfaces and data-exchange functionality, where necessary.

A specific characteristic of this VE is the involvement of SMEs from Eastern Europe, so that specific attention is paid to the assessment of readiness to technology and to co-operation concepts.

The Supply Chain VE is an international Partnership, composed of companies from Italy, Slovakia and Slovenia, interested in the development of new methodologies and computer based information and communication technologies aimed to accelerate the exchange of information between enterprises and suppliers.

2.3.2 PRODCHAIN SME network cases

The following three cases refer to pilot applications, which have been carried out within the PRODCHAIN project, aimed at the development of enhanced Supply Chains solutions.

Television set manufacture – this pilot VE model is a supply-chain. The leading company is producing one of the core elements of a modern TV set, the control chip. Due to little competition in Europe, this company dominates this VE and has created its own network by enhancing co-operation with selected companies.

The partners selected for this VE are strategic partners. Co-operation already existed for several years on the basis of usual business relationships. Once the VE operates efficiently, more business partners shall join the network. Therefore this first VE is functioning as a test bed.

The objective of the VE is to increase efficiency along the supply chain due to the exchange of reliable data and to collaborative planning. Furthermore, since strategic partners have been chosen for this VE, streamlining the different objectives of the partners shall strengthen the business relationship.

Manufacture of packaging machines – this pilot VE is also a supply-chain. The core company is a packaging machines manufacturer, and the VE has been created to identify the best supply chain from case to case. Within these supply chains the objectives change from case to case: time might be the most critical issue in one case, whereas in the next case cost might be much more important. Therefore, the leading company has created this VE to enhance the co-operation along the supply chain to ensure fulfillment of the order's main objective.

The partners selected for this VE are from one supply chain, in which co-operation already existed for several years. Changing a partner is not an issue, since this long-term co-operation is very trustful already.

The objective of the VE is having means to make short-term decisions on how a single order shall be processed through the supply chain in order to meet the customer's main objective.

Engineering network – this VE pilot case is an engineering network, which also operates along a supply-chain. Its products are customized equipment for production lines.

The partners selected for this VE have worked together for a long time. The analysis phase has shown that as yet there is hardly any ICT in use between these partners. A decreased time-to-market with the help of ICT is the main objective of this network.

2.4 Star topology Virtual Organizations

This section describes some business cases regarding Virtual Enterprises characterised by a star topology, namely co-operation networks led by a main contractor.

2.4.1 Pulp Mill manufacturing

This VE operates in pulp mill manufacturing, and the VE model consists of a main contractor driven temporary consortium. The lead company has created its own network gradually, partly by outsourcing some activities, partly by enhancing co-operation with selected companies [11].

There are different partners and different relationships in the network depending on the level of co-operation between the partners. Strategic partners are used to perform critical parts of the project, and for some activities there are alternative subcontractors / suppliers. In addition, there are occasional partners.

The VE is a temporal consortium created from a network for a specific customer request. The core of the VE may participate already in the Sales phase to create the bid for the customer. As there is a customer order the VE is created from the network, the composition depending for example on the scope of the product. For one-of-kind product deliveries the following phases are typical: planning of the delivery project, design of the product, purchases, manufacturing, transport, installation, start-up.

The objective of the VE is the delivery of the product to the customer in good quality, in due time and to cost. Each partner in the VE has its own objectives; it may be included in many VEs/networks at the same time and the objectives of the different VEs may cause conflicts (for example in the case of insufficient resources). In the same way the objectives of the different partners may be in contradiction with each other.

2.4.2 The ICIV Pilot cases

The ICIV project [5-6] was developed over a period of four years, from 1998 to 2001, and was funded by the Italian Ministry of Research, ENEA (an Italian major research organisation) and the European Commission. The objective of the project was to provide support, in areas of low economic development, to networks of SMEs in the effort of integrating their participant enterprises. The basic paradigm adopted, for the level of integration pursued, was that of reaching levels of co-operation, among network members, to make them operate as if they were all departments of one larger, virtual enterprise; hence, much of the work has been devoted to the development of an appropriate VE Model.

The model proposed in ICIV foresees a hub and spoke architecture, where the hub is covered by two subjects: the "Virtual Enterprise Manager" and the "Technical Service Center" (both to be meant as enterprises). Around the hub, the SMEs are grouped with equal rights and duties, but different functions. The grouped SMEs should be complementary over the product/service life cycle, but also SMEs of the same kind (competitors) should be involved in the effort to increase the productive capability and then achieve higher control of the market.

With this approach, problems of both horizontal and vertical integration had to be coped with. Horizontal integration was tackled with a set of rules as to how the VE workload is to be split among members of the same nature, i.e. enterprises who provide the same product/service. Basically, the splitting criterion praises the level of involvement of each member in the VE (members that contribute the most take the most out of the VE procurement).

Quite a different approach was followed for vertical integration. Here the solution was pursued in the adoption of the appropriate technological tools, with emphasis among these on Concurrent Engineering tools. In fact much reliance was placed on the capability of these tools to improve the co-operation between complementary members (such as, for instance, designer and manufacturer) and to provide solutions to problems, which typically arise at the interfaces between members that complement each other, in the supply chain.

Some of these tools have been requisitioned on the market, such as a Design for Manufacturing and Assembly, a simulator of manufacturing processes, a fast prototyping machine, a PDM endowed with a virtual prototyping feature, etc. Other tools developed within ICIV include a Design for Environment (applicable to processes as opposed to products), a Design for Size (a tool which helps in reducing the size and encumbrance of what is being designed), etc.

A focal problem that emerged was that of the acquisition, maintenance and utilization of the tools of a VE, which typically are used by all, or many, members. The solution of the Technical Service Center proved providential here. In the model proposed within ICIV, this special member is in charge of the acquisition and (optionally) development of these tools, as well as the maintenance and making the tools available to other members. The other VE members pay for these services, thus contributing to the investment made.

Only technically skilled enterprises should cover the role of the Technical Service Center, however the required skills are many and therefore difficult to find in just one enterprise. A result of this limitation is the further solution of resorting to a network of Technical Service Centers, in order to provide the whole technical assistance that each VE requires. Within this approach one technically skilled enterprise acts as the Technical Service Center for a particular VE, but if it needs a service it is unable to provide, it resorts to the appropriate Technical Service Center of another VE.

Within ICIV, all the above has been tested with seven different networks of SMEs and with five technically skilled SMEs acting as Technical Services Centers. All the enterprises involved are Italian and operate in areas of lower economic development. The enterprises involved as Technical Service Centers, due to the prototyping nature of the whole ICIV initiative, were Research Consortia (i.e. groups of SMEs devoted to research activities as their main mission); as such they were well endowed with technical skills.

Some of the key lessons learned from the ICIV initiative include:
- The involved SMEs showed significant enthusiasm in participating to the research;
- The time and financial resources needed to establish a VE proved to be larger than expected within the project;
- Concurrent engineering tools are difficult to introduce as normal technical endowment; it takes a special effort to promote their usage and to build up the right skills in the SME workers, but once achieved, the SMEs are enthusiastic about those tools;

- The "Quality Function Deployment" is the tool/methodology which has collected the highest level of agreement;
- A wide program of learning is required, possibly as e-learning, due to the difficulties of gathering together, in the same time and place, workers of different SMEs.

3. VO EMERGING PRACTICES

VO emerging practices are intended as the most promising industrial implementation of VO concepts and methodologies, which showed effective and efficient application in industrial environments, and possibly eligible to be reused successfully in other business cases.

The identification of socio-organisational practices for using, implementing and exploiting existing/emerging ICTs in the VO context, was carried out through the analysis of the information collected for a number of VO Business Cases such as those above. The practices identified were organised according to a classification of the main VO application areas and were qualified for their success, transportability and implementation effort. The main VO application areas are:

- VO Constitution (Partner Search)
- Business Model & Organisation
- Legal framework
- VO Mangement
- ICT infrastructure

This section introduces an overview of the state of practices in the main areas of application, along with a description of some promising innovative ones. As noted in the introduction, the maturity level of the practices identified is generally incomplete, however, a number of additional VO implementation issues were identified on the base of the experience gained in operative industrial environments.

3.1 VO partners' search

Partner search is usually carried out among traditional business partners, for whom trust is not an issue and co-operative mechanisms have already been implemented in the past. For Supply-chain and Hub & Spoke VO topologies, structured qualification mechanisms are commonly used, leading to company clusters of 'qualified suppliers'. Co-operation with new partners on a project (especially in Peer-to-peer VOs) usually faces several barriers (human, technical, methodological) that result in poor efficiency with high integration time and costs. Early clusters organised as VO Source Networks were established to facilitate the formation and start-up of VOs. The companies belonging to the cluster can then co-operate in customer projects that none of the partners could undertake alone, by combining complementary as well as competing competencies for different design and manufacturing functions. Clusters are defined by their:

- *Affiliation rules*: the contractual framework ruling the affiliation of a company to the cluster, specifying the duties, liabilities and benefits of a company joining the cluster;

- **Composition**: the criteria establishing the cluster composition in terms of members' typology, member number, etc.;
- **Management**: the cluster management structure and management processes;
- **ICT infrastructure and services**: the ICT infrastructure supporting the operation of the cluster and the services available to members;
- **Marketing & Business Opportunity Identification**: the marketing approaches of the cluster itself, and its mechanisms for identifying a business opportunity and sorting out the potential partners of the constituent VE.

Clusters of companies (mainly SMEs) have been established at a regional/ sectoral level, with different extent of integration, ranging from quite loose associations up to cases characterised by a unified Marketing structure (e.g. the Virtuelle Fabrik case). Despite the success of some business cases, the actual practices have not yet been consolidated and formalised in a way to be generalised, depending themselves on the particular context in which they were adopted.

3.2 VO Business model & Organization

This practice application area addresses the different issues of definition of roles within the VO along with their relationships with the VO partner legacy organisational structures, VO business models, strategic planning, enterprise engineering and the like.

The establishment VE of Supply-chain or Star-like topology, usually leads to the creation of a new entity with specified roles and responsibilities allocated to the participating companies, where the VO hierarchical cross-company organisation and the business processes at the companies' interfaces are specified in detail. The organisation mechanism enabling the integration of different partners consists of an inter-company 'Project Team' or 'Co-ordination Office', sorted by the VE participating companies.

Very first attempts of Industrial co-operation for specific business opportunities according to the Peer-to-Peer VE paradigm have been established, which include the role of a Business Integrator or Coach. This practice is described in further detail below.

3.2.1 The Business Integrator as catalyst for the VE set up

The VE paradigm proposed by the VIVE methodology has been aimed at providing an effective solution to the issues of constituting and operating peer-to-peer Virtual Enterprises: when a business opportunity arises, which cannot be exploited individually by SME, a grouping approach becomes necessary, to be deployed rapidly and with minor legal constraints.

The methodology builds upon an innovative management concept, based on a new entity, the 'Business Integrator', in charge of co-ordinating the VE's activities and relationships during its whole life cycle, from business idea, to operation, and closure of co-operation.

The Business Integrator needs to be capable of:

- Identifying and structuring market opportunities;
- Searching, qualifying and aggregating suitable industrial partners;
- Supporting the constitution of the VE, and;
- Selecting and adapting ICT commercial solutions, suitable to respond to the specific needs of the venture.

In particular, as the Business Integrator is a peer-level third party enabling the establishment of new co-operations, its catalyst function is considered to be an innovative practice for creating VEs, as opposed to the traditional way in which peer-to-peer associations are usually established. As an industrial actor identifies a market opportunity and a need for co-operating partners, he contacts a Business Integrator, which can act as a trusted catalyst for aggregating partners in a peer-to-peer relationship.

The practice aims to promote peer-to-peer VE creation in an efficient and effective manner. In terms of the practice implementation effort, as the Business Integrator is itself a partner of the constituting VE, it shares its costs and benefits as any other partner. Therefore the industrial partner who identified the business opportunity does not need to invest further to receive the Business Integrator services.

3.3 VO legal framework

This practice area addresses the establishment and negotiation of VO contractual issues, VO legal identity, VO internal/external liabilities, and regulations, as well as VO collaboration principles such as benefit/profit share, IPR and property of the results.

Classical Consortium establishment or Contractor-Supplier contractual relationships usually rule industrial co-operation. Within these contexts, Companies make use of Contractual templates, which have to be tailored, and instantiated for the specific collaboration.

Very early VE cases were established with no new legal entity (one of the member acting as the external contractual interface with the client), by implementing a Frame Cpontractual Agreement among the different parties. Nevertheless, at the state-of-the-art, comprehensive legal solutions for accommodating all the contractual and legal issues of the dynamic VE co-operation scheme, are still lacking.

3.3.1 VE Frame Contractual Agreement development

As a business opportunity has been identified along with the potential VE partners, the Business Integrator signs with each of them a "Letter of Intent", where the single industrial Partner confers to the constituting VE the rights of commercially developing the identified product/service. After that initial commitment, the business opportunity qualification is carried out and, if successful, all the VE partners, including the Business Integrator, sign a Frame Contractual Agreement regulating internal/external liabilities of the VE, prescribing VE management structure and mechanisms and allocating mutual responsibilities.

The Agreement does not imply the constitution of a new legal entity. A number of 'legal templates' are utilised by the Business Integrator for producing the contracting documentation. This practice fulfils the necessity of creating a common commitment among the potential partners of a VE, whilst protecting the business idea, during the first phase of the VE creation. The legal templates, which will progressively be refined to take into account regulation evolution and lessons learned by their utilisation, allow for a fast and legally correct development of the complete VE legal framework.

The practice utilisation has allowed the constitution of the KuBA VE via the signing of the Frame Contractual Agreement, in a considerably short time.

The legal templates, having a character of generality to be applicable to different business opportunity typologies, still need some effort to be instantiated into Contractual Documents. There is the expectation of further developing the legal templates (maybe differentiating them for different VO typologies) in order to decrease the development time and effort for the finalisation of VE Frame Contractual Agreements.

The practice could be implemented in a timeframe of a few weeks. By using the available legal templates the practice implementation can be achieved with limited costs, even avoiding legal advice. The practice is intended to be implemented and managed by the VE business integrator, which includes or acquires the services of legal consultants.

3.4 VO Management

This practice area addresses the definition and execution of the VO management processes as well as the VO product, process and organisation information utilised for managing set-up and operation.

In the VO, project management principles based on product and process breakdown structures are usually used, both in the creation and operation phases. The very first cases of concurrent development of the Organisation structure along with the product/process development (product/process/organisation business breakdown structure) are observed in the case study survey. Advanced practices are mainly addressed at solving the necessity of implementing effectively and in very short time the shared management processes of fast changing business and developing common understanding among the VO partners.

3.4.1 Value System Designer (VSD) Methodology

The Value System Designer (VSD) tool and methodology is used to design, visualise, and improve New Business / Co-development processes in a dynamic environment, to create a common understanding, to define the processes' boundaries, and to define the roles of the involved business units and participants.

The steps that are followed are:

- Identification of Core Processes to be studied;
- Identification of Process Objectives;
- The Detailed Design of the core Processes is performed;
- Identification of process' weak points;
- Suggestion for process' weak point removal are made;

- Process' transformations are implemented based on the evaluation and approval of the improvement suggestions.

After these steps a scheme of continuous improvement efforts is entered.

The practice was successfully used in designing the process of Professional Services that are provided in cooperation with a business partner. The evaluation results indicated that the VSD approach highly supports the following topics related to the company's New Business / Co-development process:

- Imprinting and visualising all the business activities,
- Monitoring and improving its process on a continuous basis,
- Reducing the required time to implement such a process.

The main problems identified in this practice are related to Human factors, as people prove reluctant to participate in implementing the practice. Human familiarisation with the approach requires between three and five sessions depending on the culture of the company, country and individual. In addition, commitment from top management in implementing the changes should be ensured at the beginning of the practice implementation. The practice could be implemented within a couple of months for a new complex process.

3.5 VO ICT Infrastructure

This practice application area addresses the utilisation of specific ICT architecture and applications for enabling co-operation among the VO partners, the management of evolving network technology, the use of standards, and related issues.

The implementation and configuration of a VO support infrastructure still requires considerable engineering effort, an obstacle to dynamic VOs. Even the most advanced infrastructures coming out of leading R&D projects require complex configuration and customisation processes hardly manageable by SMEs. The lack of interoperability between different commercial systems is still a substantial barrier to the deployment of the VO paradigm.

There is nevertheless an extensive use of Intranet services, with interaction among enterprises mostly limited to data transfer, e-mail and teleconferencing for communication; whilst videoconferencing applications are not widely diffused. The use of CSCW systems for data sharing and workflow management is constantly growing.

3.5.1 VO common ICT infrastructure

This practice consists in developing a VE ICT infrastructure by utilising a:

- pre-defined co-operation centred ICT platform,
- with customisable partner roles and shared processes,
- instantiated by an integrator in the VE constitution phase.

Within this approach provision for including third party service providers are foreseen. The common ICT platform, when utilised in Source Network for supporting specific VE creation and operation phases, could benefit from the utilization of source network databases, already including relevant data of the network companies.

The single company IT systems shall focus on core business data and processes. The application integration with the common platform will be enforced by common business semantics. The practice has been developed and tested in an industrial environment within a few relevant research projects (e.g. OSMOS for the Construction Industry [12-14]). Despite the promising results achieved in those technical feasibility cases however, the practice is still far from being a mature methodology.

The optimization of implementation efforts has to be further addressed, along with the interoperability issues regarding the integration of companies' legacy systems to the common platform.

4. THE ENVISAGED FUTURE SCENARIO

The scenario resulting from an integrated view of the identified emerging practices in the Virtual Organization domain has been summarized in the following vision:

"Source Network of Companies or VE Breeding Environments with formalized participation rules and mechanisms for dynamic VE constitution on specific business opportunities, will provide the base for deploying the Virtual Enterprise paradigm on a large scale.

These breeding environments will embed the third party role, i.e. the Business Integrator, deemed necessary for building trust among potential partners and for carrying out efficiently and effectively the VE dynamic integration process, which is its "core" business. Source Network Companies will then concentrate on their core activities.

Legal Templates will include commonly agreed cooperation principles and rules (risk and profit sharing, internal external liabilities, IPR issues) to be instantiated during the contractual framework actual development of new Virtual Enterprises

Advanced distributed management processes will be addressed to both the Source Network itself as well as to the generating Virtual Enterprises.

Each new Virtual Enterprise ICT infrastructure, to support all VE life-cycle phases up to dissolution, will be instantiated by the Source Network integrator in the VE constitution phase, utilising a pre-defined co-operation centred ICT platform with customisable partner roles and shared processes. "

5. CONCLUSIONS

The industrial case survey carried out by the VOSTER consortium has resulted in the identification of some emerging VO practices, which have shown, to some extent, successful application in truly industrial environments. Even though they suffer the limitation of being the very first implementation of innovative concepts, resulting in some weak points to be addressed for improvement by future research, the achieved maturity level is deemed adequate to provide some advantage from their utilisation in the establishment of future Virtual Organisations. Further applications will also decisively contribute to the practice refinement and improvement, towards the realisation of the identified vision.

The following chapters of this section are dedicated to a further investigation of the specificities of the current and envisaged applications of the VO paradigm in different industrial sectors, as well as to an extensive description of a relevant Source Network case.

6. REFERENCES

[1] Camarinha-Matos, Afsarmanesh; Elements of a base VE infrastructure; J. Computers in Industry, Vol. 51, Issue 2, Jun 2003, pp. 139-163.

[2] R Santoro, M. Conte "The BIDSAVER project, a step forward in the Business to Business relationships between Business Integrators and Enterprises", ISBN 0-9519759-9-4, Proceedings of ICE 2000 Conference pp 29-34, June 2000.

[3] R Santoro, M. Conte, L. Spotorno "The dynamic Constitution and Management of Virtual Enterprises", Proceedings of IFIP PRO-VE 2002 Conference pp 545-552, May 2002..

[4] R Santoro, M. Conte "Evaluation of benefits and advantages of the Virtual Enterprise approach adoption for Actual Business Cases", ISBN 0-85358-113-4, Proceedings of ICE 2002 Conference pp 19-26, June 2002

[5] R Tononi, G. Amorosi, G Federici "SMEs, Research Consortia and Concurrent Engineering – the basic ingredients of the Virtual Enterprise being experimented by ENEA in southern Italy" , ISBN 0-9519759-9-4, Proceedings of ICE 2000 Conference pp 1-11, June 2000.

[6] R Tononi, G. Amorosi "Experience gained applying Concurrent Engineering Tools to Networks of SMEs" , ISBN 0-85358-113-4, Proceedings of ICE 2002 Conference pp 47-54, June 2002.

[7] Plüss, A. und Huber, Ch. (2002): Virtual Organizations – State of the art and development of the Virtual Factory, Proceedings of the 2nd Nat. Meeting of IPLnet, 10/11th of Sept. 2002, Saas Fee Switzerland.

[8] Plüss, A. (2002): Virtual Factory Northwest and Central Switzerland – practical experience of a virtual organization. 8th International Conference on Concurrent Enterprising; Virtual Professional Networking, Communities of Practice, 17-19 June, Rom

[9] Ollus M, Ranta J, Ylä-Anttila P: Network Revolution; How to manage networking enterprises (in Finnish),Taloustieto, Helsinki 1999, ISBN 951-628-282-2

[10] Salkari I, Kalliokoski P, Poikkimäki J, 2002. eBusiness Readiness of SMEs Key Results of a Regional Study in Finnish Metal Industry Networks. Proceedings of eBusiness & eWork 2002 Conference, Prague.

[11] Karvonen, I. Management of one-of-a-kind manufacturing projects in a distributed environment. VTT Research notes 2044, 2000.

[12] Rezgui, Y., Zarli, A. Information and Communication Technology Advances in the European Construction Industry, Special Issue of the Journal of Information Technology in Construction, Vol. 6 (2001), ISSN 1400-6529.

[13] Ian Wilson, Yacine Rezgui, Toward the digital construction virtual enterprise, ECIS 2002, European Conference on Information Systems, Gdansk, 6-8 June 2002.

[14] Yacine Rezgui, Marc Bourdeau, Abdul Samad Kazi, Alain Zarli, An open specification and framework for the construction dynamic virtual organisations: the OSMOS project, e.2001 – eBusiness and eWork 2001, (Venice, Italy, 17-19 October 2001).

VIRTUAL ORGANIZATIONS IN THE ELECTRONICS SECTOR

Maciej Witczyński, Adam Pawlak

Silesian University of Technology, Gliwice, Poland
{witczynski, pawlak}@ciel.pl

This chapter identifies different types of virtual organizations that are emerging in the electronics sector. Examples of VOs are introduced that represent different forms of network-based functionality. A vision on electronic engineering VOs based on new ICT infrastructures developed within European R&D projects is shortly depicted. It is believed that new technologies of engineering collaboration supported by these infrastructures will enable new concurrent engineering design methodologies, adequate for complexities of currently designed Systems-on-Chip.

1. INTRODUCTION

Virtual Organizations and Virtual Enterprises (Camarinha-Matos and Afsarmanesh, 1999) constitute a noticeable trend in the electronics sector of industry. They present different types of network-based functionality. Following other branches of ICT-based industries there are VOs, like: information brokers or virtual libraries which process and deliver highly specialized information to professionals. They often manage e-commerce on-line trading centers of IP (Intellectual Property) electronic components. There are also VOs more specific to electronics domain, like virtual consortia of e-commerce electronics companies. They support co-operation of traditional companies by introducing specific standards necessary for collaborative engineering in electronics. They also operate as information brokers and enable creation of electronic components exchange centers.

It is however VOs deployment in organization of complex System-on-Chip (SoC) design and manufacturing that constitutes a real challenge. Since SoC design comprises a number of dispersed organizations arranged in value-added chains, VOs suiting a particular new system design would be a beneficial new solution. Realization of this vision requires most of all new advanced infrastructures that would allow agile establishment of new VOs suiting purposes of new SoC designs.

Some initiatives connected with European R&D projects (Pawlak, 2003) that invent and create prototype infrastructures for VOs in electronics need to be referred in this chapter as well. VOs based on these collaborative infrastructures designed for electronics industry contribute to future models of engineering collaboration (Nottingham, 2003) on distributed SoC designs. System design methodologies will be even more closely related to the Intellectual Property (IP) components reuse paradigm. This paradigm should be easily adoptable in VOs with geographically distributed design teams.

The following sections of the chapter are devoted to a description of different VO types. The subsections contain some examples from electronics industry. In the fifth section, examples of R&D projects, working on ICT infrastructures relevant to electronic engineering VOs are shown, and a vision for future research agenda in this domain is outlined.

2. e-COMMERCE ELECTRONIC ENGINEERING VOs

e-Commerce electronic engineering virtual organizations aim at improved business performance through the adoption of new e-commerce and Internet-based collaboration technologies. Deployment of new collaboration technologies and services gives many advantages to the VO members, like: reduced costs, faster time to market, or improved design capability. With these new technologies they can more efficiently collaborate with each other in order to react promptly to emerging new business opportunities. VOs invest resources, expertise and time to support their member organizations in enhancing their business performance. This is feasible with networks that are secure, reliable, available and interoperable. We can cite the examples of such organizations: RosettaNet, Silicon Integration Initiative Inc., and Virtual Socket Interface Alliance. However, similar consortia, such as: CommerceNet (www.commerce.net) and PartNet (www.part.net) do not focus on electronics.

2.1 Rosetta Net

RosettaNet (www.rosettanet.org) is a non-profit consortium of more than 500 of the world's leading Information Technology (IT), Electronic Components (EC), Semiconductor Manufacturing (SM) and Solution Provider (SP) companies working to create, implement and promote open e-business process standards. It creates a new way of communication between partners in a supply chain which enables reliable real-time information, efficient e-business, dynamic trading-partner relationships, and new business opportunities. Companies which follow the RosettaNet standards report reduced costs and increased productivity.

Vision and Mission
RosettaNet drives collaborative development and rapid deployment of Internet-based e-business standards, creating a common language and open e-business processes. These standards are vital to the evolution of the global, high-technology trading networks (RosettaNet, 2003).

Human-to-human business exchange is successful and efficient only if business partners agree upon the process from the most basic level. RosettaNet standards are based on the basic observation that people produce and hear sound, use a common alphabet to create words, apply grammatical rules to words to make ialogue, use dialogue, to form business processes, and conduct business through an instrument such as the telephone. In electronic business exchange, HTML/XML functions are used as the alphabet, and e-commerce applications serve as the instrument by means of which e-business processes are transmitted. Standards are needed as an underlying agreement on the words, grammar and dialog that constitute e-business processes.   RosettaNet dictionaries provide the words, the RosettaNet

Implementation Framework (RNIF) acts as the grammar and RosettaNet Partner Interface Processes® (PIPs®) form the dialog (Figure 1).

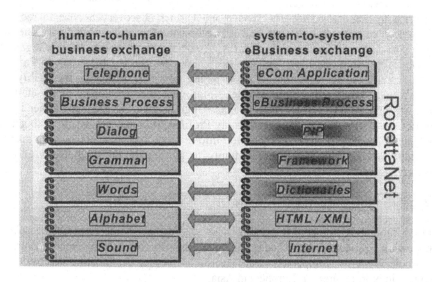

Figure 1 - RosettaNet role in electronics business (www.rosettanet.org).

VO topology, Business Model and Activities

The structure of the RosettaNet organization has a star topology. Member companies centre around RosettaNet's global Executive Board which includes the RosettaNet chief executive officer and equal representation from each industry (IT, EC, SM, and SP) global Supply Chain Boards. Global Executive Board provides direction for the global organization and oversees issues that apply to different industry supply chains. RosettaNet Partners guarantee financial support and resources to be involved in the development, approval, adoption and implementation of RosettaNet standards. RosettaNet Partners are members of the EC, IT, SM or SP trading networks. Supply chain companies, such as manufacturers, distributors, resellers and end users, provide subject matter expertise and human resources for RosettaNet project teams, and later implement RosettaNet standards in their own companies. Solution providers supply the products and services that facilitate the implementation of RosettaNet standards. Non-profit standards bodies, trade associations and government agencies work to enlarge the support base and constituency of RosettaNet by increasing its exposure. Since 2002 RosettaNet has been a subsidiary of the Uniform Code Council, Inc. (UCC). By forming a common architectural environment, the two organizations drive joint development of B2B standards supporting multiple industries, thereby increasing the speed and number of implementations across user communities, while attracting other similar industry sectors (RosettaNet, 2002).

System architecture proposed by the VO

Members of the RosettaNet consortium have access to a broad range of opportunities, tools and services. Benefits are incremental, increasing with the level of membership, from Associate Partner via Partner to Premier Partner. Joining RosettaNet as an Associate Partner ensures access to the Web site and regional seminars, forums, and implementation support and services. Associate Partners may subscribe to Standards Delivery Service and Partner Discovery Service to receive notification of new and updated standards and business profiles, making it easier to stay up-to-date and find trading partners. Associate Partners can publish regional profile information and may help start-up a new Council. By upgrading to Partner status, companies have access to provisioning services, including the ability to retrieve and view Connectivity Profiles, improving interoperability of RosettaNet standards and trading partner requirements. Upgrading to the Premier Partner level affords the ability to publish Connectivity Profiles, enabling consistent, automated exchange of trading partner configuration information. Premier Partners have access to additional services and the opportunity to participate in RosettaNet's Global Industry Councils.

2.2 Silicon Integration Initiative Inc

Silicon Integration Initiative Inc. (Si2) (www.si2.org) was founded in 1988 as CAD Framework Initiative, Inc. Today Si2 represents semiconductor manufacturers, electronic systems companies, and Electronic Design Automation (EDA) tool vendors in North America, Europe and Asia.

Vision and Mission
Si2 is an organization of industry-leading electronics companies focused on improving productivity and reducing costs in design and manufacturing of integrated systems on silicon. Si2 provides to member organizations with dedicated support services which facilitate industry adoption of standards and new collaborative technologies. Si2 provides leading companies with a unique collaboration forum that monitors emerging trends and priorities, as well as explores supplier-partner relationships and investigates open technologies.

VO topology, Business Model and Activities
Si2 is a network organization acting in a star topology. This virtual organization includes many companies from silicon industry, and is coordinated by one project leader, who has administrative and financial power. Membership in Si2 is open to any company or subsidiary associated with SoC (System-on-Chip) design or development including ASIC, EDA, semiconductor and systems. Si2 members form councils (e.g. Design Technology Council – DTC), coalitions (e.g. Open Access Coalition – OAC), and working groups which deal with different specific projects (e.g. Open Library Architecture - OLA, Universal Data Model – UDM, Electronic Component Information Exchange - ECIX) (Figure 2).

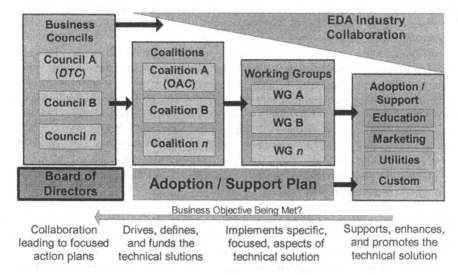

Figure 2 - Si2 Operation Model (www.si2.org).

System architecture proposed by Si2
The projects mentioned above, like OLA or ECIX have already been finished with success. They have proposed collaborative architectures for electronics companies that can be adopted in VO. Certain standards and collaborative tools useful for SoC design and development were created and accepted by semiconductor companies which are members of the organization. Si2 further works towards its goals within new projects and activities, like OAC. Open Access Coalition progresses its work towards the OpenAccess standard that will bring a full-featured EDA database to supports distant access and manipulation of data. New companies can join and use worked out solutions to improve productivity and reduce costs.

2.3 Virtual Socket Interface Alliance

The Virtual Socket Interface Alliance (VSIA) (www.vsia.org) was formed in 1996 with the aim of establishing a set of standards for SoC (System-on-Chip) design based on IP (Intellectual Property) components. The most critical element of the reuse paradigm is mix and match of IP components from multiple sources.

Vision and Mission
The Alliance vision is to accelerate SoC development by specifying open standards that facilitate the mix and match of Virtual Components (including software and hardware IPs) from multiple sources.

VO topology, Business Model and Activities
The VSI Alliance has been structured as an open organization, encouraging the membership and active participation of representatives from all segments of the SoC industry, including systems, semiconductor, IP and EDA companies. Currently there are about 70 VSIA member companies. The organization topology combines two

types of VO topologies. It works in the manner of consortium/star topology but also in a peer-to-peer relation. It is managed by a Board of up to 10 members which oversee the work of the working groups called "Pillars".

VSIA specifies open interface standards, which will allow Virtual Components (VC) to fit quickly into "Virtual Sockets", at both the functional and physical levels. This will allow VC providers to develop products and maintain a uniform set of IP deliverables, rather than have to support numerous sets of deliverables required for the many unique customer design flows. The VSIA specifications identify information required to enable VC integration onto SoC. While some of this information comes in the form of documentation, much of it comes as executable models or machine-readable design descriptions. The goal of the VSIA is to specify a complete interface that provides a practical, reliable link between the VC provider and the VC integrator (www.vsia.org).

System architecture proposed by VSIA
VSIA used to partition the technical problems into specific focus areas, which were then addressed in parallel by separate Development Working Groups (DWGs). DWGs meetings were conducted both face-to-face and by teleconference. Till the restructuring of VSIA, there had been following DWGs in VSIA: Analogue/Mixed-Signal, Implementation-Verification, IP Protection, Manufacturing Related Test, On-Chip Buses, System-Level Design, Virtual Component Transfer and Verification. To be the organization that addresses current and emerging SoC and IP issues through strategic, standards-based commercial and technical solutions VSIA had to restructure its administration and staff and move from many different working groups (DWGs, Adoption Groups, Advisory Committees, etc.) to a "Pillar" approach. The Pillars are new working groups that address both technical and commercial issues and are supported with legal and marketing support - all within the Pillar. Each Pillar has a base of representation from at least four large companies who are committed to the Pillar issues. Any company of any size who wants to work with the group will be encouraged to participate but the Pillar will not be created without the large companies. The reason for this approach is to assure that the work created reflects industry needs and will therefore be more likely to be adopted. The Pillars will be created when there is sufficient industry interest to work together to solve issues. Initially, the VSIA created the Quality IP Pillar (former Quality IP DWG), the IP Protection Pillar (former IP Protection DWG) and the R&D Pillar (former Signal Integrity, Analog/Mixed Signal, Verification-Implementation, Platform-Based Design and Hardware-dependent-Software DWGs) (VSIA).

3. VIRTUAL LIBRARIES FOR ELECTRONICS ENGINEERS

Virtual libraries (VLs) are catalogues located on the Internet. These catalogues list interesting Internet resources related to a specific subject. VLs also give access to search engines that look through the sites linked with the VLs. Information found with the help of the VL is very up-to-date since links collected are systematically verified. Examples of VLs include: WWW Virtual Library (http://vlib.org), EEVL - the Internet Guide to Engineering, Mathematics, and Computing former known as

Edinburgh Engineering Virtual Library (http://www.eevl.ac.uk), IEEE Xplore (http://ieeexplore.ieee.org).

Although there are parts of these catalogues dedicated to electronics domain, in general they are designed for broader audience. Web catalogues are usually led by a free confederation of volunteers, who compile pages of key links for particular areas in which they are experts. Virtual libraries are a kind of virtual organizations as they integrate volunteers, who create their content but also because individual indexes exist often on many servers around the world. Nevertheless there is always a central catalogue linking them. Hence they also act in the star topology as well. Some virtual libraries are university initiative (e.g. EEVL) supported by other parties and universities. In general they are non-for-profit organizations, so searching in the library is free for all users.

Table 1

Key Features of *WWW Virtual Library* (http://vlib.org)
• Led by a free confederation of volunteers
• Free access
• Registration for those to be listed
• Catalogues of various engineering information with links to many sites
• Search engines
• Individual indexes exist on many different servers around the World
• All server administrators are responsible for the content of their own pages, as long as they follow rules decided by the association

Electronic engineering sub-catalogues can be found in two of the above mentioned libraries – i.e. WWW Virtual Library, IEEE Xplore. Sometimes in electronics circles the term: "Virtual libraries" can be associated with internet catalogues of electronic systems or IP components. Although such catalogues are present on the Internet, they do not rather use a name "virtual library". Internet catalogues of electronic and IP components are usually kept by electronics information brokers who connect them with on-line trading services.

The PROCAT-GEN (PROduct CATalogues for Global Engineering Networking) *(www.procat-gen.org/)* (C-Lab, GEN) project elaborated the technology for product catalogues. It constitutes an application of SGML, network and multi-media technology that develops more attractive online catalogues with a much richer content, and a multi-media use for faster and easier information access.

4. INFORMATION BROKERS AND ENGINEERING NETWORKS

Information brokers (Fikes, 1995) play an important role in electronic system design, as they provide relevant, up-to-date information on electronic IP components. The components are catalogued in databases that are kept and managed by brokers. Often brokers enrich information they serve by providing links to producers' and other sites, where more information is available. The IP-related information that is gathered and exposed by brokers carries important engineering knowledge that is a key element in a SoC design process. In addition, IP brokers provide news, research, marketing and trading services, as well as IP design tools.

Similar to information brokers are Engineering Networks (ENs) which are virtual commercial organizations. They also focus their activities on providing information and services to engineers. However, they unify industrial engineering companies and present their offers on the web, unlike information brokers who mainly serve information collected from different sources. ENs provide the engineering community with subject classified information and links to various technology companies. This type of VO serving for electronics professionals has star-topology as well. Usually they are coordinated by one leading company, and other companies are in a partnership relation. All together they form information centers often with additional services, like e-commerce negotiation and trading, professional forums, and design.

The examples of engineering networks and information brokers are:

- ChipCenter & QuestLink (www.chipcenter.com),
- Virtual Component Exchange - VCX (www.thevcx.com),
- Canadian Engineering Network (www.stealthstuff.com/CEN/),
- Electronics & Engineering Network (www.eenet.com),
- EETimes Network (www.eet.com),
- Thomas Regional (www.thomasregional.com/), and
- Design Net (www-cdr.stanford.edu/SHARE/DesignNet.html).

Design & Reuse is one organization of this type. It is especially concentrated on brokerage in electronic engineering. Since it presents most of the features characteristic of this VO type, it deserves special attention and will be described in more detail below.

4.1 Design & Reuse

Design & Reuse (D&R) (www.design-reuse.com) was founded in 1997 as a web portal for added-value information in the field of electronic virtual components, i.e. IP (Intellectual Property) components and SoC (System-on-Chip).

Vision and Mission
The mission of D&R is to deliver state-of-the-art technology for publicizing, managing, and exchanging of IP /SoC design data. D&R acts as an eCommerce centre that stimulates the IP business through reuse of IP components. It collects market IP requests and makes dialog forums between potential suppliers and customers, thus creating an innovative e-commerce negotiation process. At the beginning of 2004, D&R has reached over 17000 registered users. The D&R IP Catalogue allows access to a documentation of over 1750 cores from 190 vendors of ASIC (Application Specific Integrated Circuit) and PLD (Programmable Logic Device) technologies.

VO topology, Business Model and Activities
D&R creates around itself a kind of a virtual organization which incorporates members of a global SoC supply chain. Registered partners can use resources

delivered by D&R and purchase more sophisticated tools developed by D&R with partners' feedback.

Originally, D&R was the worldwide leader as the web and B2B portal in the IP/SoC field. Currently, it plays the role of an IP-trading centre with IPs organized in catalogues. Also tools and services for SoC validation and IP Exchange have been offered on this portal. At the moment, D&R concentrates on providing intranet IP/SoC resource catalogues. Such a service includes both the management of information update in cooperation with the suppliers and the intranet catalogue installation. Thus, D&R delivers to the market a comprehensive intranet IP supply chain and IP based SoC design data management infrastructure. As an intranet e-software provider D&R has put on the market the two first e-management software in this field, namely: IP Manager Series for creating intranet catalogues and intranet IP exchange completed by e-Design Manager ™ which bridges these tools to the designer site by automated import of IP releases before exchange. These tools are written in Java and based on XML encapsulation (Dziri, 2002).

Table 2

Key Features of Design & Reuse – an example of an information broker
• Commerce company
• Free access but registration required
• Yellow pages
• Search engines
• Trading with engineering tools and services
• Catalogued IP components information
• IP trading centre

In general, information brokers supply on-line access to value added engineering information (IP components, standard components data catalogues, and validation). An IP can be searched for with the use of an ordinary www browser and other dedicated tools. This is a very useful technology, required by new design methodologies based on reuse and an easy on-line access to IP components (Ghanmi et al, 2002).

4.2 Global Engineering Networking Initiative

Similar in concept (i.e., re-use paradigm, IP search engines and design tools available on line) was Global Engineering Networking (GEN) Initiative (www.c-lab.de/gen/). The GEN Initiative started in 1995 with the mission to provide a global electronic market place for engineers. The purpose of the association which comprised both industry and university partners was promotion of global engineering networking. One of the GEN objectives was to improve the quality of engineering work by ensuring exact and efficient searches according to standard engineering classifications and keywords.

The GEN concept (Radeke, 1999) was supported by the idea of a public collaborative network with intelligent nodes and services for large-scale distribution and control of engineering knowledge. Due to the new collaborative network paradigm, organizations should become capable of faster changes enabling smart design and production. Particularly SMEs were supposed to benefit from such infrastructure because co-operation was based on engineering objects independent of the size of organizations. In general, GEN Initiative dealt with business-to-business electronic commerce in engineering and addressed the following aspects: electronic communication between dispersed individuals and teams involved in distributed engineering processes, intelligent access to engineering information in electronic networks, electronic publishing of engineering information. GEN Initiative comprised in fact many complementary projects, e.g. GENIAL, PROCAT-GEN, BRAIN, and B2B-ECOM (C-Lab, GEN).

5. TOWARDS VOs FOR SoC DESIGN

A virtual organization that facilitates collaboration on a new SoC (System-on-Chip) design is still a challenge. Except for the GEN project a number of R&D projects have worked on proper collaborative infrastructures that contribute to the concept of Global Engineering Network in the electronics sector. The examples of the projects are: VILAB (www.ite.waw.pl/vilab/) and E-COLLEG (www.ecolleg.org).

MOSCITO is an Internet-based multi-agent system (Schneider, 2002) that results from the VILAB project. It proves useful for distributed electronic system design within a virtual enterprise. The system provides among others:

- Encapsulation of design tools;
- Communication between tools for data exchange to support distributed, Internet-based work; and
- Uniform user GUI for tool configuration, control of the workflow and the visualization of result data.

The E-Colleg consortium (www.ecolleg.org) has developed an Advanced Collaborative Infrastructure (ACI). ACI is designed to secure data exchange and distance spanning engineering collaboration during the design of complex electronic systems. ACI is based on core services and a complimentary transport service, which enable secure firewall crossing and communication between the components.

The ACI core components are implemented as Web Services that are interconnected using the Simple Object Access Protocol (SOAP). The SOAP messages between the components are transported using Advanced Network Transport Services. In a general case, all ACI components are on separate machines connected to the Internet. Thus, they need to communicate through insecure media and all data have to be encrypted and digitally signed by a sender. Using this infrastructure distributed teams of designers coming from different enterprises can co-operate in common projects (Kostienko, 2003).

Both systems MOSCITO and E-Colleg ACI constitute innovative infrastructures designed for collaboration of electronics engineers. They seem to be promising solutions for future developments of virtual organizations or virtual enterprises working in the electronics sector, as well as for the global electronic engineering networks (Radeke, 1999).

6. CONCLUSIONS

It is expected that engineering collaboration within the framework of virtual organizations will improve design methodologies of complex electronic systems. With the VO technology it should be possible to create consortia of partners dedicated to design and development of new sophisticated SoCs. These consortia may comprise not only system design houses and IC manufacturers but also design SMEs can be included in an agile way. This will create efficient temporary partner relationship that is well supported within VOs. The basic time frame for such design and manufacturing VOs will be spanned over the SoC development period.

In this vision new design methodologies using network-based reuse of IP components are central. True network-based engineering is however still a challenge, as more adequate ICT infrastructures are required. Development of these infrastructures apart from technological requirements, like: security and availability of high-bandwidth, needs to adopt many new standards. In the paper, we have identified main organizations and initiatives that aim at changing a paradigm in electronic engineering by enabling distributed collaborative B2B processes through development of new standards and technologies. Examples of virtual organizations that operate as electronic engineering specific e-commerce VOs, information brokers, engineering networks, and virtual libraries have been given in this chapter.

7. REFERENCES

1. Bauer M., *et all..*, ,,Advanced Infrastructure for Pan-European Collaborative Engieering". In Stanford-Smith B; Chiozza E: *E-work and E-commerce, Novel solutions and practices for the global networked economy,* pp. 644-650. IOS Press / Ohmsha, Berlin, 2001.
2. Camarinha-Matos L. M., Afsarmanesh H. "The Virtual Enterprise Concept" in "Infrastructures for Virtual Enterprises – Networking industrial enterprises", Kluwer Academic Publishers, Sept 1999.
3. C-Lab, GEN – Global Engineering Networking Initiative, http://www.c-lab.de/gen/
4. Design & Reuse, http://www.design-reuse.com
5. Dziri A. *et all.* "E-Design Based on the Reuse Paradigm", Proc. DATE'02 - Design, Automation and Test in Europe, March, 2002, Paris, France.
6. Fikes R., Engelmore R., Farquhar A., Pratt W., Network-based Information Brokers, Knowledge Systems Laboratory, KSL-95-13, Stanford University, January 1995.
7. Ghanmi L. et all. (2002) "E-Design Based on the Reuse Paradigm", 2002 Design, Automation and Test in Europe (DATE), March, 2002, Paris, France.
8. Kostienko T., Mueller W., Pawlak A., Schattkowsky T., "An Advanced Infrastructure for Collaborative Engineering in Electronic Design Automation". Proc. 10th ISPE Int. Conf. on Concurrent Engineering: Research and Applications - The vision for the future generation, (CE2003), Madeira Island, Portugal, 26-31.07.2003.
9. Nottingham P., Collaboration as a Competitive Weapon, E-Colleg Workshop on Challenges in Collaborative Engineering (CCE'03), 15th-16th, April 2003, Poznań, Poland.
10. Pawlak A., "Overview of 5th FP projects and activities in the domain of collaborative engineering", Proc. E-Colleg Workshop on Challenges in Collaborative Engineering, 15-16.04.2003, Poznań.
11. Radeke E., Korzonnek J. "Distributed Information Management in Virtual Engineering Enterprises by GEN", RIDE-VE99 Int. Conf. on Research Issues on Data Engineering - Virtual Enterprises, Sydney, 23-24.03.1999.
12. RosettaNet Annual Summary Report 2002/2003.

13. Schneider A., Ivask E., Miklos P., Raik J., Diener K.H., Ubar R., Cibáková T., Gramatová E., „Internet-based Collaborative Test Generation with MOSCITO", Proc. DATE'2002, Paris.

14. Si2, Silicon Integration Initiative Inc., http://www.si2.org

15. VSIA, Virtual Socket Interface Alliance, http://www.vsia.org

| 4.3 | # VIRTUAL ORGANIZATIONS IN ONE-OF-A-KIND INDUSTRY |

Iris Karvonen

VTT Industrial Systems,Finland,   Iris.Karvonen@vtt.fi

The knowledge and resource requirements of one-of-a-kind industry call for the creation of cooperation networks and VOs. The paper describes the characteristics of VOs in one-of-a-kind manufacturing based on industrial cases in recent research projects. The inter-organizational distribution and mutual dependencies of the activities as well as the complexity of one-of-a-kind products requires efficient information management and VO coordination. Lately, the product lifecycle view has become very important for one-of-a-kind manufacturers.

1. INTRODUCTION

Distributed manufacturing has been the practise in one-of-a-kind industry already before the concepts of networking and Virtual Organizations (VO) have been launched. With the development of business environment and ICT technology networking has become a strategic issue requiring the consideration of core competencies and development of preparedness for VO creation and operation.

This paper summarizes the experience of VOs in one-of-a-kind industry based mainly on cases of VO research cluster VOSTER (IST-2001-32031). First one-of-a-kind products and their lifecycle are described (chapter 2). Reasons for networking and observations of typical network/ VO types are described in chapter 3. VO management structures, relationships and an information viewpoint are considered in chapter 4. Chapter 5 gives the conclusions.

2. ONE-OF-A-KIND MANUFACTURING

2.1 One-of-a-kind products

One-of-a-kind (OKP) manufacturing denotes an industrial field where each product is unique. Typically the products are complex and large systems, like industrial plants, large machines or buildings. The recent VO research projects have included cases like power plants, pulp mills, ships, telecommunication networks, production lines and food production machines (Globeman21, Karvonen, 2000, Globemen, IMS GLOBEMEN, 2003).

The products are manufactured only to order. For the customer they are often infrequent and extensive investments, and the success of the delivery may have a significant effect to the customer's business. Also for the manufacturer the number of orders / products is limited. As each delivery is a finite assignment with a specified deadline the manufacturing is often organised and followed in projects. Because of this terms "project industry" or "project business" are also used for this industry sector.

The "one-of-a-kind" feature causes that each product must be engineered and manufactured more or less individually. To do this there are basically two approaches:

1. Tailored systems
   These are in principle designed and manufactured from scratch according to specific customer requirements. In practise this is seldom possible due to costs and schedules, and most often tailored systems or parts of them are based on previous implementations and existing components. An advantage of tailored systems is that the customer needs can be followed in detail. Correspondingly, the high resources required and uncertainties in the implementation cause a disadvantage of high risk to the product quality, schedule and costs.
2. Configurable systems
   These are based on existing modules or components of which the most applicable ones are selected, possibly modified according to process parameters, raw material etc, and integrated to a working system. The advantage of modularization is a decrease of required resources and time and re-use of qualified components and subsystems thus decreasing also the risk of failure.

In practise these two approaches are overlapping and may be present also in the same delivery. Re-use and modification of previous tailored solutions is necessarily not so far from configurable systems. In addition it is not always cost-effective to modularize all the components of a large complex system.

2.2 One-of-a-kind product lifecycle

As each one-of-a-kind product is an individual or an instance of a more generic product family, the concept of product lifecycle is important. The generic lifecycle of GERA (GERAM, 1999) is applicable (Figure 1).

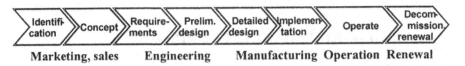

Figure 1. Lifecycle of one-of-a-kind product

A more restricted and concrete example from a previous industrial pulp mill - case (Globeman21) is presented in Figure 2 (Karvonen, 2000). The manufacturing phase with a limited time frame and a specific goal complies with the definition of a project: "a temporary endeavor undertaken to create a unique product or service" (PMBOK Guide, 1996). Figure 2 shows the delivery subphases which affect each other by producing information, control orders, physical material or equipment. The process is not just a simple procedure where phases follow each other. To shorten the total lead time the activities are performed concurrently. As this requires using default values in design it often causes a need for iteration (changes to defaults).

The manufacturing project of Figure 2 incorporates two types of inter-dependent processes: the project execution process (product delivery) and the project management process. Project management includes project planning, monitoring the progress and setting up actions both proactively and reactively to keep the project on track. The actions may consist of starting up activities, rescheduling, adding resources etc.

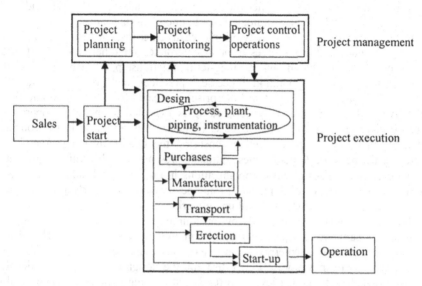

Figure 2. One-of-a-kind manufacturing project (pulp mill example, Karvonen, 2000).

3. ORGANIZATIONAL NETWORKING IN ONE-OF-A-KIND INDUSTRY

3.1 Reasons and modes for networking

The resource and knowledge requirements of one-of-a-kind industry are affected by the following features:
-   Because of the scale and complexity of one-of-a-kind products a high amount and different kinds of resources, competences and knowledge are needed for engineering and manufacturing. For an industrial plant delivery this includes different kinds of *product* and *manufacturing* knowledge: process behaviour, equipment, mechanical structures, electrification, instrumentation, automation, manufacturing, shipping, installation, testing; *project planning and management* capabilities, knowing the local *(customer)* environment and potential *partners* and suppliers.
-   Variation in the product scope and configuration also leads to the variation of the resource, competence and knowledge needs in different projects.

- The temporary nature of deliveries and unstable demand also create unstability in the demand of resources and knowledge.
- The nature of one-of-a-kind products often requires "on-site" activities and the inclusion of local resources.

Thus no one company alone is able to hold all the needed resources and competences and collaboration is needed. The distribution of work to several companies has been the practise in one-of-a-kind industry already before the terms "networking" and "virtual enterprises / organizations" have evolved. With the emergence and development of networking concepts and supporting IT and tools networking has now become a strategic issue to one-of-a-kind industry.

In the current concept of networking each enterprise focuses on its core competence and uses the resources of other enterprises for other tasks. Most often the co-operation is based on a long-term relationship, which enables the development of the collaboration processes, practices and tools. In case of a customer request a VO/ VE (Virtual Enterprise) is created from the network to fulfil the delivery. The preparation by networking is expected to make the operations more efficient both in proportion to costs (resource utilisation, scale of economy) and time (fast VO set-up) as well as ensuring the quality by the pre-validation offered by the network. Other business rationale presented are flexibility, agility etc.

The current practises of virtual organizations in one-of-a-kind industry are based mainly on a historical development. From the network manager's point of view there are basically two modes to build up networks:

- *Divergent,* creating a network by outsourcing functions. For example, the design department is separated from the manufacturing enterprise. The idea is that the new design enterprise could serve also other customers and thus the resources were in a more efficient use and the design enterprise could develop its knowledge at a higher level. Currently outsourcing is quite a visible trend in the companies even if it is not always the best long-term solution.
- *Convergent,* creating a network by reinforcing co-operation with selected enterprises, consultants, subcontractors or suppliers. The procurement of a critical or knowledge-intensive part requires trusting the supplier. The trust is mainly based on earlier experience. Over the time the suppliers performing best have been given more responsibility and they have earned a partner role in the network.

Different modes of network creation may co-exist. Usually building the co-operation relationship, methods and tools is easier for the outsourced functions than for the initially external companies. The creation of the network is not a one-off task but it requires long-term development. It can be considered as an investment or preparation for future needs, which is reimbursed by faster and more efficient operations as there is a customer request, by the possibility to offer the customer more extended products or to reach new markets.

The development of ICT has further contributed to the organizational distribution of operations. It also enables integrated operations independent of location which is very useful for this industry field where products often need to be installed at the customer site (in different locations of the world). The advanced communication has also further created interest for extending the co-operation relationships to new organizations. However, the expectations of dynamics to be achieved have not always sufficiently taken into account the need for trust.

3.2 Product and contractor -centric networks

If a customer makes a decision about the investment in a new industrial plant / machine it does not purchase the product from a network or a VO. Instead it approaches a company (future VO manager), which it considers to be trustworthy enough to take the responsibility of either the product delivery as a whole or of a subsystem (in this case the customer itself will manage the whole). In one-of-a-kind industry thus companies able to manage "the whole" are needed. This requires knowing the potential partners (the network), understanding of the customer requirements and sufficient product knowledge. In addition VO management requires specific capabilities for project management in an inter-organizational environment and within different cultures.

In the industrial cases of research projects Globeman21 (Karvonen, 2000) and Globemen (IMS GLOBEMEN 2003) the delivery to the customer was most often managed by the "product owner" or Original Equipment Manufacturer (OEM), i.e. the company taking care of the development of the product or of a core part of it. These companies operate within the whole product lifecycle from Marketing and Sales to Operation Support and Renewal. Thus the networks built in one-of-a-kind industry are often product-centric, built around a certain OEM and a product or a product family.

In one-of-a-kind industry there are also companies specialised in the management of large investment projects in a specific sector without having an own product. In addition to project management capabilities these companies have sound knowledge of the sector and often outstanding engineering resources. In fact they can operate in different VOs in different roles; managing the VO or acting as an engineering partner. In addition to OEMs these "project companies" may thus operate as one-of-a-kind product VO managers.

Similar observations come also from other studies. In CE-NET community (Concurrent Engineering – Network of Excellence) research on Virtual Enterprises performed in the past decade has been reviewed (Katzy & Löh, 2003). In this study three distinct types of virtual enterprises are distinguished. One of them, led by a hub firm in a central role, is called "lead-contractor network". It is mentioned to appear e.g. in construction industry. Buildings are also one-of-a-kind products. The distinction to plant or equipment manufacturing is, that in construction the lead contractors seldom have a branded product which is often the case for the OEMs.

Correspondingly a summary of case studies in Germany calls a VE with one leading enterprise a "General Virtual Contractor" (Hausner et al., 2003), with examples in the construction industry and large equipment manufacturing (OKP), but also in automotive and telecommunication industry.

In ThinkCreative –project challenges of collaborative networks in Europe have been analyzed. In the study three basic types of VOs were identified. VOs in one-of-a-kind industry typically correspond to the type "A" of long-term partnership with one dominant partner which owns the core knowledge, trademark, logo etc. and plays a decisive role in defining the cooperation rules (Afsarmanesh et al. 2004).

VOs aiming at complex and large products are often built in a hierarchic manner: a VO is consisted of sub-VOs, which again have the responsibility of a specific module of the product. Accordingly, the networks can be seen as built of sub-networks, which may be managed by a System supplier. Both the network and the VO can thus be seen as a system of systems.

3.3 Networks in the product lifecycle

Currently one-of-a-kind manufacturers are very interested to increase and stabilize their business by offering (as a product extension) services to the customer in the operation phase. To do this OEMs/ contractors need to search partners to support in different phases of the product lifecycle.

Figure 3 illustrates the different networks and temporary consortia, virtual enterprises (VE) in the product lifecycle as identified in Globemen-project (Karvonen et al., 2002). For complex products collaboration is needed already in sales to pre-qualify a tender and to create a tender. In the delivery phase often a hierarchic VE built of several subVEs for different tasks is created. In the operation (service) phase there may be several different service tasks performed by different consortia. As the Sales, Delivery and Service (Operation support) networks all require knowledge about the product and its manufacturing, the networks are partly overlapping. In addition specific knowledge of sales / delivery / operation is needed in each phase. In case of a strong product-centric network the same company (for example OEM) may operate as the network manager for all these networks.

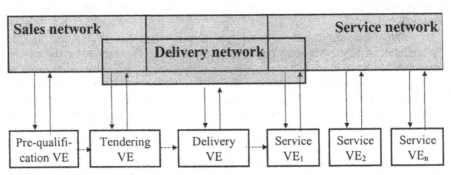

Figure 3. Networks and virtual enterprises in product lifecycle phases in one-of-a-kind manufacturing.

The overlapping of the networks of different product phases supports the knowledge accumulation and sharing in the product life cycle by removing organizational barriers. The Service network manager is operating in close link to the customer and able to follow the product operation. This special position enables the accumulation of the operational experience of the customer. The knowledge may be used for both product development and engineering. In addition it allows the identification of customer needs for modernization or improvement and may thus contribute to new sales opportunities.

4. VO MANAGEMENT IN ONE-OF-A-KIND INDUSTRY

4.1 Structures and relationships

In one-of-a-kind industry products are high value investments. It is very important for the customer to start the plant and to receive payback in the planned schedule. To achieve the objectives efficient VO management is needed. The allowed costs and time as well as the required quality are restrictions within which the project must perform as a whole.

As described in the example of Figure 2 the different phases, activities and partners are dependent on each other by:

- input –output –relationships: creating information, material, structures or control orders for each other. These relationships often create temporal dependencies of one task being workable only after another.
- potentially using the same resources for different tasks. This may cause temporal, exclusionary conditions.

In a system of dependencies the distributed activities do not reach the common goal by themselves. *Coordination* is needed to allocate the objectives to subphases, activities or product elements and to monitor and control their performance. Project management methodologies, like managing the project through *work breakdown structure (WBS)* (PMBOK, 1999) are often used.

In a VO the delivery project activities are distributed in different organizations. Also the management or coordination of a VO is distributed in two respects:

- The activities and partners to be controlled are distributed.
- The management of the VO itself is partly distributed: the subtasks have their own management function.

To achieve the project objectives also integrative project management is needed.

Monitoring of all the numerous activities, product parts and organizational units at the lowest level regarding costs, time and quality would be too heavy for the VO manager. That's why management hierarchies are often used. An example of a VO structure from a pulp mill case (Globeman21, Karvonen, 2000) is presented in Figure 4. The higher levels set subgoals (for example due dates) to the lower levels, which plan and manage their activities in the given limits. If the conditions are not suitable for the lower level they must be re-discussed or another partner taking the task must be found. The idea is that each level interacts with the nearest level up and down and the project management at the highest level does not usually need to care about the lowest levels.

The management structure in Figure 4 represents a hierarchic "star topology" or "hub and spoke" topology presented in section 1.4. of this book (Löh & Zhang, 2004) as one of three VO topologies. The topology aims to represent the partner interactions in a VO (information & material flows & governance relationships). What must be noticed is, that at least in one-of-a-kind industry the management structure does not present all the interactions and relationships in the VO. Even if the management is hierarchically vertical, there may be horizontal relationships between the partners. Identifying the needed interactions and dependencies is not always easy.

In Globemen–project the different structures and relationships in a VO were analysed in case of a paper mill project (Figure 5, Zwegers et al., 2003). The objective was to combine the structures described by WBS, Organizational Breakdown Structure, Project Network Diagram (PERT chart) and Bill of Material in a multi-enterprise environment and to define the relationships among the partners in a VO. The services used for this are called extended relationship management (XRM). Even though the details of the figure are not recognizable here it gives an impression how complex these relationships may be.

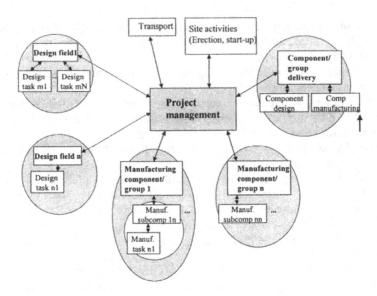

Figure 4. Example of VO management hierarchy.

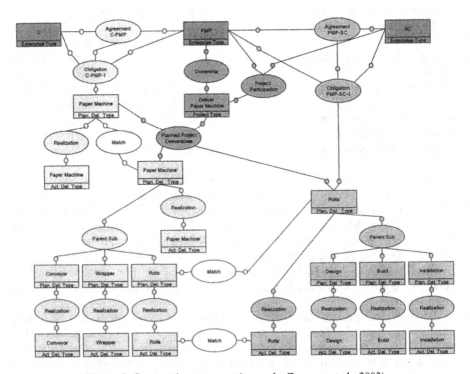

Figure 5. Cooperation structure (example, Zwegers et al., 2003)

There is not only one possible solution for manufacturing a one-of-a-kind product by a VO. Product modularization has an effect on how it may be manufactured. The project structure may also be built according to grouping of activities (design, manufacturing,...). In addition, a combination of product and activity structure may be used as in Figure 4. The manufacturing project structure should be appropriate to the network (and vice versa); otherwise new capabilities need to be developed. The activities should fit to the partners' capabilities and resources and excessive distribution of one partner to several distinct activities should be avoided. A proper partner to take over the responsibility of each activity should be found. As a conclusion, defining the VO structure is dependent on the product structure and the network, i.e. the potential partners and their knowledge. And thus correspondingly, the needs of the VOs create requirements for the network creation and development.

4.2 N-to-n relationships

Typically in one-of-a-kind industry each participant may operate in several networks and VOs. The same enterprise may even have the role of partner in one network/VO and the role of manager in another network/VO. The partners are independent companies with their own objectives. They make the decisions themselves and also are responsible for them. It is not assured that they always behave as the network/VO management would expect.

Management of a network means preparing the conditions and knowledge adequate for an efficient VO creation and operation in case of a customer request. In this task each company aims to build a proper network around itself, in-one-of-a-kind industry often a product-centric network. If the managers of different networks require different operating procedures or tools from their partners, a company participating in several networks may run into difficulties.

Correspondingly a company may operate at the same time in several VOs the interests of which may cause conflicts. This may become from simultaneous, too high need of resources. As the partners are independent enterprises the management of a VO has no authority to dictate them. This makes a difference to intra-company project management. Minimizing the conflicts requires proactive co-ordination and adjustment of the partner prospects with the requirements of the VO is needed.

4.3 Viewpoint of a partner operating in network(s)

The research and development of one-of-kind manufacturing processes and tools has most often the viewpoint of the Network/ VO manager. This is natural as the objective is to make the overall manufacturing system to work efficiently. However, this often leads to the assumption that sufficiently partners, which are able to perform as required, can always be found, and that all the partner companies are willing to adopt the processes and tools making the network operations effective.

There are some cases where the viewpoint for the development has been that of a network partner. In a Finnish national project risks of enterprise networking were analysed from the partner point of view to support their decision making (Karvonen & Pulkkinen et al., 2002). In another project the horizontal collaboration of the network partners and common development of tools were in the focus (Salkari et al., 2002). To be robust, the network must enable the partners to maintain viability, which may be in contradiction with the short-term objectives of minimum costs and maximum flexibility.

4.4 Management of information in one-of-a-kind industry

Management of information is a critical part of managing one-of-a-kind deliveries. The development of information management support for VOs has been in the focus in most of the industrial cases in recent research projects.

Figure 6 gives an overview of different information types in one-of-a-kind product phases from marketing to operation (delivery is not detailed) (IMS/Globemen, 2002). The classification is two-dimensional: according to information content (what it is about) and information type (degree of generality).

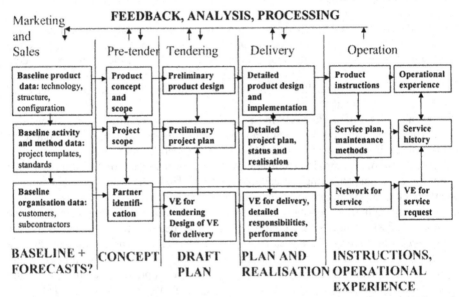

Figure 6.   Information types in one-of-a-kind product life cycle (IMS/Globemen 2002).

By content the information can be classified to:

- Product data (what): this includes product technology, design, drawings, configuration, structures, parts, materials etc.
- Project/ activity/ method data (how and when): this tells how the one-of-a-kind product is manufactured. The content may be potential project templates, project break down to activities, required cost and time, quality requirements etc.
- Organizational data (by/to whom) including different organizations, their role, knowledge or capacity, activity information, performance values, contact information etc.   In addition of organizations operating in the same network as partners or subcontractors information about customers and competitors is needed.

By generality the information may be classified to:

- Baseline data: This includes models and templates for the product, project or network/VE. As one-of-a-kind products are individual also the activities and organizations are different in different deliveries. The re-usable baseline templates are needed to make the creation of the individual product more efficient. The templates may be created by generalising the experience data.

- Forecasts, concepts, draft plans and plans are all different stages of planning and design. This data always includes a degree of uncertainty: it is evolving and open for changes from the sales to the end of delivery. The design drafts and plans are often created on the basis of the baseline templates.
- Realisation data and operational experience tell about what actually has been implemented, how the activities have been performed by the organizations and what kind of experience is gained from the operation. Thus this includes the final product descriptions, the cost and time reports of projects, the operational data of the product etc.

A normal direction of information flow is following the product lifecycle order: from sales to operation. Also in this direction there are deficiencies and failures in the current practises and inter-enterprise information exchange is needed both inside the phases and between them. Another challenge is to create also the "backward" flow: to generate generalised information about the realisation for the marketing, conceptual and delivery phases. An attempt to this direction is made by a power plant case in Globemen (Välikangas et al., 2003).

5. CONCLUSION

Inter-enterprise cooperation is necessary for one-of-a-kind industry because of extensive and varying resource requirements in customer deliveries. A VO must be designed and created separately for each customer order. To be effective, this requires development of a cooperation environment, procedures and tools: i.e. a network, from which the VO may be created fast. The preparation in the network can be seen as an investment, which is paid back with more efficient operations in the product delivery. This investment needs to be balanced according to the expected benefits.

In VOMAP project (IST 2002-38379, Roadmap Design for Collaborative Virtual Organizations in Dynamic Business Ecosystems) a roadmap has been created to identify the future research challenges in VOs (Camarinha-Matos et al., 2003). Most of the actions presented are important also for one-of-a-kind industry.

The main challenges in one-of-a-kind industry networks and VOs come from the management of complex systems in an unstable environment. The systems may appear as products, organizations and processes. The systems may include heterogeneous organizations which on one hand have interdependencies with each other but on the other hand have autonomous decision-making and potentially conflicting objectives. More understanding is needed about the long term benefits, risks and criteria of distributing operations. The benefits achieved by networking may be lost by the increase of management costs, quality problems and/ or delays in deliveries.

The viewpoint most often considered while analysing networks is the one of the network manager. In one-of-a-kind industry, where networks are typically product-centric, these are often formed around powerful companies. On the other hand the partners operating in the network are typically SMEs. Thus they are not equal either in power or capabilities and their development potential is largely dependent on the

network manager. These partner companies should also need guidelines and
decision support for participating in networks.

6. REFERENCES

1. Afsarmanesh, H., Marik, V., Camarinha-Matos, L., Challenges of Collaborative Networks in Europe.
   In Camarinha-Matos L., Afsarmanesh, H. (Ed.), Collaborative Networked Organizations: A
   research agenda for emerging business models, Kluwer Academic Publishers, Boston/ Dordrect/
   London, 2004, 77-90.
2. Camarinha-Matos, L., Afsarmanesh, H., Loeh, H., Sturm, F., Ollus, M., A strategic roadmap for
   advanced virtual organizations. In Camarinha-Matos L., Afsarmanesh, H. (Ed.), Collaborative
   Networked Organizations: A research agenda for emerging business models, Kluwer Academic
   Publishers, Boston/ Dordrect/ London, 2004.
3. GERAM - IFAC/IFIP Task Force on Architectures for Enterprise Integration, "GERAM: Generalised
   Enterprise Reference Architecture and Methodology, ISO15704:2000". (available on:
   http://www.cit.gu.edu.au/~bernus) 1999.
4. Hausner, U., Teichmann, K., Albers, S. & Hussla, I. Management of Virtual Enterprises: Results
   from Case Studies in Northern Germany. In Weber, F., Pawar, K. & Thoben, K.-D. (eds),
   Proceedings of the 9th International Conference on Concurrent Enterprising: "Enterprise
   Engineering in the Networked Economy", Espoo, Finland , University of Nottingham, 2003;. 337-
   342.
5. IMS-GLOBEMEN project. Deliverable D13, Guidelines for Sales and Services. http.//globemen.vtt.fi
   2002.
6. Karvonen, I.. Management of one-of-a-kind manufacturing projects in a distributed environment.
   VTT Research notes 2044, 2000.
7. Karvonen, I. & Jansson, K. & Ollus, M. & Hartel, I. & Burger, G. & Anastasiou, M. & Välikangas,
   P. & Mori, K. Inter-enterprise eCollaboration in Sales and Service of one-of-a-kind products. In:
   Stanford-Smith, B. & Chiozza, E. & Edin, M. (Ed.). Challenges and Achievements in E-business
   and E-work, IOS Press / Ohmsha, Berlin, Germany, 2002; 1388-1395.
8. Karvonen, I., Pulkkinen, U., Lehtinen, E., Virolainen, V.-M. and Holmalahti, A. Enterprise
   Networking – Risk Transfer or Risk Reduction? VTT Industrial Systems Review, VTT Industrial
   Systems, 2002; 65-70.
9. Katzy, B. & Löh, H. Virtual Enterprise Research State of the Art and Ways Forward. In Weber, F.,
   Pawar, K. & Thoben, K.-D. (eds), Proceedings of the 9th International Conference on Concurrent
   Enterprising: "Enterprise Engineering in the Networked Economy", Espoo, Finland , University of
   Nottingham, 2003; 343-353.
10. Löh, H. & Zhang, C. Reference models for Virtual organisations (this book), 2004.
11. PMBOK Guide. PMI Standards Committee. A guide to the project management body of knowledge.
    Upper Darby, PA, USA: Project Management Institute, 1996.
12. Salkari I, Kalliokoski P, Poikkimäki J. eBusiness Readiness of SMEs – Key Results of a Regional
    Study in Finnish Metal Industry Networks. In: Stanford-Smith, B. & Chiozza, E. & Edin, M.
    (Ed.). Challenges and Achievements in E-business and E-work, IOS Press / Ohmsha, Berlin,
    Germany, 2002; 972-979.
13. Välikangas, P., Puttonen, J. Knowledge Creation and Virtual Enterprises in Power Plant
    Construction, in Karvonen et al. Global Engineering and Manufacturing in Enterprise Networks
    (GLOBEMEN), VTT Symposium 224, 2003.
14. Zwegers. A., Wubben, H., Hartel, I., van den Berg, R.. Managing Relations in Networks of
    Enterprises, in Karvonen et al. Global Engineering and Manufacturing in Enterprise Networks
    (GLOBEMEN), VTT Symposium 224, 2003.

VIRTUAL ORGANISATIONS
IN THE SERVICE INDUSTRY

Kim Jansson

VTT, Finland, Kim.Jansson@vtt.fi

The provision and delivery of a product is not sufficient alone; in addition the customers expect value adding service around the product. The delivery of value adding services imposes a strong need to create networks and various forms of collaboration to deliver integrated product-services configurations.

This chapter describes the problems encountered in industrial services and explains how Virtual Organisations in the service business can help to tackle these problems. The highlight is a special case of VO, the Service Virtual Organisation whose characteristics are analysed in detail.

1. INTRODUCTION

The European engineering industry represents a quarter of the total European Union manufacturing output and in 2001, its total EU production value was € 1208 billion. In total the industry comprises some 140,000 companies employing about 7.5 million people. The European engineering industry is highly specialised and strong in niche markets. However, the industry now operates in a highly competitive market, with smaller profit margins and changes in both internal and external customer expectations. The provision and delivery of a product is not sufficient alone; in addition the customers are expecting value adding service around the product to an increasing degree. Enterprises are concentrating on their core competence, which is another noticeable trend. Thus, the delivery of value adding services imposes a strong need to create networks and various forms of collaboration to deliver integrated product-services configurations.

In an attempt to remain competitive and to strengthen its position in the world market, the engineering industry is undergoing a transition from being the product provider into being the provider of value added services.

2. INDUSTRIAL SERVICE OFFERINGS

Usually the services are traditional and closely related to the delivered products. Industrial companies often strive for knowledge-intensive services, which usually requires deep understanding of the customer processes. Figure 1 gives examples of industrial service offerings.

Industrial services are often regarded as merely after-sales services, not dealing with the entire life cycle of the products. When looking at the life-cycle as a whole, various service types can be grouped as follows (Kalliokoski et al. 2003):

- **Basic services;** spare parts, consumables, maintenance and repair, installation and start-up, removals and re-installation, local support.
- **Advanced services;** project engineering, troubleshooting, inspections, performance guarantees, refurbishment, renewals, financing.
- **Knowledge services;** process consultancy; training, (remote) operation, simulation, securing return on investment.

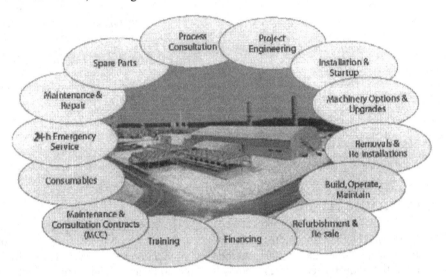

Figure 1. Industrial service offerings (Kalliokoski et al. 2003):

Through their service offerings and operations, the enterprises position themselves differently in relation to their customers. In (Kalliokoski et al. 2003) five different supplier positions or "roles" relative to the customer are identified (list below). The first two of these roles focus the supplier's activities on the customer's investment decision, with limited involvement in the remaining life cycle of the delivered product. The three others extend also to the operational phase.

- **Machinery supplier.** The focus of the business relation is on delivering a piece of machinery or equipment that fits the customer's technical specification.
- **System supplier.** The focus of the business is on delivery of a system, e.g. a production line, which is usually designed for a specific customer process and comprises a wider scope of supply than only one piece of equipment.
- **Maintenance partner.** The focus of the business expands to include also continued supplier involvement during the remaining life cycle of the delivery. This role adds contractual after-market elements, such as spares and consumables agreements, to the supplier-customer relationship.
- **Performance partner.** In this role, the supplier is closely involved in operating the customer's technical process by taking partial responsibility for the performance of the system, e.g. through availability warranties. This role requires the supplier to maintain at least a minimum of continuous on-site presence. The focus of the customer relationship is on securing effective operation of the unit or production line.

- **Value partner.** The supplier is directly involved in the customer's business, e.g. through operation and maintenance agreements, where the customer pays pre-determined price for the actual output of the system. Both parties focus on profitable daily operations, and the supplier is responsible for the day-to-day operation of the plant or line.

In addition to "generic" engineering and manufacturing competencies a "machinery supplier" must have a good understanding of the customer's purchasing process. A "system supplier" must add to this the ability to understand and interpret the customer's actual operations. The next step, "Maintenance partner" adds a new competency, professional maintenance management and work. As a "performance partner" the supplier often takes partial responsibility for the actual daily performance of the system. This adds the customer's process to the list of competencies. Finally, as a "value partner", the supplier is involved in the customer's value generation, e.g. in providing electricity at a given quality and price. This then adds the customer's business to the list of competencies. In all of these roles "competency" implies a level of knowledge and experience that puts the supplier on the same level as the customer and opens the way for productive communication between the partners.

3. REQUIREMENTS FOR SERVICE ORGANISATIONS

The different service provider roles listed above thus require several different competencies and knowledge. In addition, the nature of services causes also other challenges, especially for SMEs:

Remote customer location: Small and medium-sized enterprises (SMEs) manufacturing industrial products frequently focus on engineering, procurement, and construction, while neglecting after-sales activities. Most products require advanced after-sales activities that demand distinct skills, abilities and knowledge. Therefore, providing after-sales services is closely linked with the actual service capability of the producer. Since SMEs frequently have extremely limited human and financial resources, how to organize the delivery of after-sales services to the customer site is a major problem. Traditional service organisations are mostly sufficient within the local or regional market of the producer, i.e. a service technician travels to the customer. However, traditional service methods do not fulfil customer needs in distant markets. The cost of plant or machinery downtime does not allow for the travel time of a service technician, for example. In these circumstances, after-sales services require a new organisation to enable quick and reasonably priced service activities world-wide (Hartel et al. 2002)

Complex products: Industrial products are getting increasingly complex, containing various parts, systems and components, mechanical, electrical and electronic, software, different materials etc. Delivering service to these products demands a variety of professional skills. It is difficult to produce the service alone as a single enterprise. (Jansson et al. 2003)

Operational Feedback: In addition to solving acute problems and providing repair services, SMEs face other challenges as well. These include providing proactive maintenance as well as learning and accumulating operational experience from the delivered and running one-of-a-kind products. A common denominator among these challenges is the requirement to get operational feedback to the organisation delivering the product from the user organisation. When virtual organisations are involved, these requirements become even harder to fulfil. (IMS-Globemen project)

Measuring value: A starting point for any industrial service business is the understanding of value and how it is created in collaborative networked organisations. It forms the basis for costs, effort, profit and risk sharing among the business partners.

To fulfil the requirements the engineering industry is currently undergoing a transition from being the product provider to being the provider of customer value and product-related value-added services. This paradigm shift can be named as the "Framework of value transition". This framework covers the complete transition of the industry from "parts supplier" to "value provider"; in other words, all the elements that a company or group of companies needs to become an integrated product-service provider. There is a lack of understanding how product-service architectures should be designed and managed to develop customised industrial product-service configurations. Moreover it is poorly understood how these offerings should be designed and managed over the industrial product-service life cycle.

4. ORGANISATIONAL STRUCTURES IN INDUSTRIAL SERVICE

4.1 Virtual Enterprise Reference Architecture applied to Industrial Service

Because of the large variety of knowledge and skill requirements, industrial service provision to customers often requires the participation and collaboration of several enterprises. The organisational units in Industrial Service can be represented at three levels (adapted from Tølle et al. 2002, Globemen project):

Enterprises are the actual operators performing the industrial service functions. In addition, some of the enterprises may also have a management role.

Networks are composed of enterprises working together in long-term co-operation. A network is not performing the customer delivery but creating a preparation for that. In engineering, manufacturing and industrial service networks are usually managed by an enterprise that may take total product and total service responsibility for the customer. Often the networks are hierarchical; thus, a network may include several sub-networks.

Virtual Enterprises (VEs) or Virtual Organizations are temporary consortiums created from the network to fulfil a customer request. In Industrial Service VEs may be created for fulfilling different service requests: in after-sales for example for repair, preventive maintenance or renewal.

4.2. Service network formation in product-related service

For an industrial product, such as a ship, a power plant, large equipment, or a factory, the operational life-cycle phase is by far the longest phase in the life-cycle. The core competencies of every partner engaged in the construction and delivery of the product are no longer needed during the operational phase. The delivery VE can be dissolved and a Service Network developed to be prepared for required service tasks.

If there is only one industrial product producer in the network, then as a rule this producer will be responsible for network operation and customer contacts. The distinctive features of network partners are competencies, technical aids, available Information and Communication Technology (ICT), locations, and capacities. Typically the following types of companies can be recognized in a product-related service network:

- **The customer,** who usually is the end user of the product, may also act as a collaborative partner. The size of the customer company may range from small and medium-sized enterprises with one production location to large corporations with a number of globally distributed locations. The customer plant can be made up of machines or installations purchased from one or more producers. Efficient product operation support and information management over the lifecycle require the consideration and involvement of the customer in the product lifecycle service processes.

- **The project contractor,** the enterprise that takes total responsibility for the product on behalf of the customer in the delivery phase. The project contractor may be in the role of delivering its own product, usually as the main component or system in the delivery. Alternatively, the project contractor can specialise in managing project deliveries and provide the main concept design work. The project contractor may also have a managing role in the service during the product operation.

- **Companies with own products.** The companies normally deliver an industrial product and want to deliver service to their customers and generate additional revenue by arranging the product service during the operational phase of the product.
  - **Subcontractors,** suppliers and consultants operate in the networks of the project contractor for delivery or service. The subsuppliers again operate in the networks of the subcontractors, suppliers and consultants on a lower level. Thus, they may not be visible to the project contractor. However, they must be taken into account in integrating and developing the inter-enterprise processes.
  - **Subsidiary companies** of the enterprise may operate on a specific geographical area or in specific fields.

- **Service providers.** The companies are specialised in delivering industrial service often giving total service to a variety of products and brands. The provided service can extend from design and engineering services all the way to actual shop floor repair work.
  - **Local service providers** or partners operate in co-operation for delivering operation support and services. They may partly be the same as the subcontractors in the delivery and service. Alternatively, they may be specialised service partners located geographically close to the customer.
  - **Contract manufacturing companies.** The companies offer manufacturing capacity and specialised manufacturing skills as a service. Normally the companies do not have their own product development and own brands. Their competence lies in efficient manufacturing capability.

The type of a company is not always clear, large companies can have activities in several sectors and, for example, contract manufacturers have not always been regarded as service companies.

4.3 Service Virtual Enterprise (SVE)

In the context of the machinery industry, the SVE can be defined as "a short-term form of co-operation to fulfil services among legally independent one-of-a-kind producers, service companies, suppliers, or sub-contractors in a service network of long-term duration" (Hartel et al. 2002). The services aim to provide support to customers in the operation of their machines and installations, and to solve problems as quickly and as cost-effectively as possible.

As there is a customer request for service a service virtual enterprise is formed from selected network partners (Figure 2). Together, the network partners can deliver the specified service. The service is divided into different tasks. Each network partner in the SVE is responsible for performing a part of these tasks in accordance with its competencies and available technical aids and ICT. Occasionally, collaboration is necessary in order to perform a task, for example, when a local service provider repairs a machine by installing new spare parts but does not have the know-how to reset the machine controls after completion of the repairs. However, the service provider can perform the resetting under the direction of the industrial product producer. Here, the network partners depend upon modern ICT for co-ordination. Communication can be extremely efficient using video conferencing and application sharing, for example.

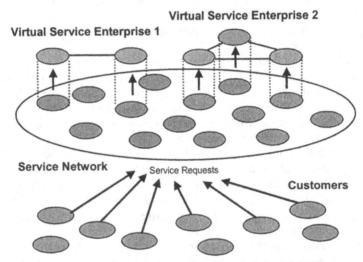

Figure 2. Model of the virtual service enterprise (Hartel et al. 2002).

SVEs contain various actors, such as project engineers and contractors, equipment suppliers, plant operators or local service providers. The business objectives and main business functions of these actors can be different to some degree. However, some business objectives are common irrespective of the actor's role in the network. One common and a major industrial objective is to deliver products that are leading in their respective field or branch of business. The objective further requires supporting the customers in identifying their potential in the utilisation and updating of technology and systems. Knowing how a machine or equipment has been used, and how the equipment has functioned in customer environments yields valuable information for the equipment provider. This information can be used in R&D for improving the equipment or designing its next generation.

Thus, for an industrial producer, it is at the same time important to provide quick remote service and short repair reaction time, and at the same time to collect feedback from the operational behaviour of the product. The realisation of these two objectives may lead to partially conflicting requirements and solutions.

4.4 Characteristics of a Service Virtual Enterprise

In addition to the deliverables and types of enterprises in the network, the following characteristics generally distinguish a service virtual enterprise from more traditional, product delivery, VEs:

Length of time required to build the SVE: the time required for design and implementation (roll-out) of the service virtual enterprise is very short; it can be measured in hours, not days. Proactive maintenance should nevertheless be planned carefully over time.

Lifetime of the SVE: the period between roll-out and termination of the service virtual enterprise is (hopefully) short for acute problems and repair services. In the case of proactive maintenance, the lifetime may be long.

Number of network partners that, depending on specific market opportunity, band together to form the various service virtual enterprises. To be able to have a global reach or large geographical coverage, the number is high.

Number of partners in the service virtual enterprise that generate the product service. Normally, this is small.

Information and communications technologies applications that are implemented during the lifetime of the service virtual enterprise. There is no time for implementation. All applications must be in place and standards agreed in the network.

Information and information flow needed in the SVE. The amount of information to repair a complex product can be considerable. The information flow is in both up- and downstream directions, and resides on different media. Sophisticated tools are required to manage it quickly, interactively, and reliably.

5. INDUSTRIAL CASE EXAMPLE OF A SERVICE VIRTUAL ENTERPRISE

This model, developed in the GLOBEMEN project (Hartel et al. 2003), is currently being implemented by Toyo Engineering Company, Japan together with an Indonesian customer.

Initial situation: A one-of-a-kind producer ("OKP1") develops and sells large chemical installations. It has a large network of suppliers and sub-contractors for the manufacture of these installations. There are 100 of these installations in operation by customers worldwide. In the past, OKP1 developed specific ICT for service , such as a remote plant monitoring system and a training simulation system to support after-sales services. However, OKP1 does not have its own team of service technicians. A customer ("C1") operates several installations in Asia, and has its own teams for inspection and maintenance. Another large one-of-a-kind producer ("OKP2"), which is not a direct competitor of OKP1 but works at the same level in the value chain, has a number of its own external service centres. OKP2 receives support from various service providers if there are capacity bottlenecks or if time is critical.

OKP1 would like to be more active in after-sales service in Asia in the future, and provide its customers with the ICT it has developed. However, without its own technicians, it is dependent upon collaboration.

Structure of the service network: The service network is made up of OKP1 with selected suppliers and sub-contractors, OKP2 with its service stations and service provider in Asia, and C1's service teams. As only OKP1 customers receive the after-sales services, OKP1 takes on the role of hosting provider (see Figure 3).

Enterprise configuration: If a customer requires maintenance on a reactor and replacement of spare parts of the supply pipes, a service virtual enterprise ("SVE1") could take the following configuration: a service technician from OKP2, who has reactor training, goes to the customer on-site. At the same time, a supplier delivers to the customer the pipes it has manufactured or drawn from inventory. During the repair procedures, the service technician receives required additional information from a developer at OKP1.

If, in another case, the installation is not producing the quantity or quality of product that the customer desires, the virtual enterprise might consist of a service technician from customer C1 and a specialist from OKP1 ("SVE2"). Here, the service technician would, for instance, optimise the installation on-site. He would require the results of a simulation trial that the OKP1 specialist would run using simulation software developed by OKP1, and he would receive the results via e-mail.

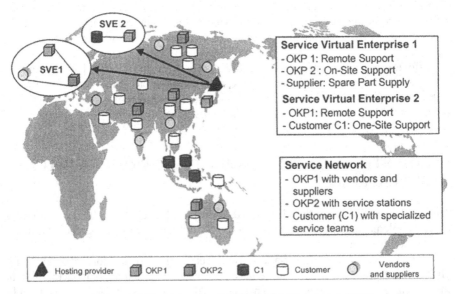

Figure 3. Industrial case – GLOBEMEN (Hartel et al. 2003).

Benefits: The form of co-operation described above would allow OKP1 to actively offer after-sales services. By implementing its various ICT, OKP1 can gather new experience and data on the operation of the installation. This information can be used profitably in new development of the installation. OKP2 and C1 benefit from collaboration with OKP1 because they will have better utilisation of their service capacities. In addition, technicians from C1 will benefit from the increased experience through service work at other companies. They can apply this expert knowledge within their own company.

6. RECOMMENDATIONS

Existing product-service strategies must be reviewed and redesigned. Companies must rethink their strategy on how to arrange after-sales services. Further work is needed to develop not only organisational models to implement virtual organisations in the service industry but also to develop methods supporting the delivery of integrated product-service configurations. There is a continuing lack of methods and tools for
- Design and innovation of products and services concurrently. New "service products" are needed.
- Delivering services through the combined utilisation of local personnel and the knowledge at the products supplier.
- Tools enabling the communication of product related information to the remote service provider and also enabling the accumulation of operational experience back to the product design.

7. CONCLUSION

The service virtual enterprise, explained in this paper, is a new way of organising co-operation with the objective to fulfil various after-sales services collaboratively. New markets are opening up for industrial service, and even small and medium-sized enterprises can enter into such networks with their specialised skills. The present contribution has introduced an initial model of what future collaboration might look like in after-sales services. It is a step towards being a value providing partner.

8. REFERENCES

1. Hartel I, Billinger S, Burger G , Kamio Y. Virtual organization of after-sales service in the one-of-a-kind industry. In: Camarinha-Matos L M (Ed.): Collaborative Business Ecosystems and Virtual Enterprises, pp. 405-420, Kluwer Academic Publishers, Boston (USA), 2002, 631 pages
2. Hartel, I., Burger, G., Kamio, Y., Zhou, M. A Reference Model for Collaborative Service, in Karvonen et al. Global Engineering and Manufacturing in Enterprise Networks (GLOBEMEN), pp. 135-149, VTT Symposium 224, 2003.
3. IMS-GLOBEMEN project, Deliverable D13, Guidelines for Sales and Services. http.//globemen.vtt.fi
4. Jansson K, Kalliokoski P, Hemilä J. Extended products in one-of-a-kind product delivery and service networks. Conference Proceeding of the eChallenges 2003 Conference, Bologna, Italy. 2003.
5. Jansson K, Karvonen I, Ollus M, Hartel I, Kamio Y. Service virtual organisations and information feedback in one-of-a-kind production. VTT Industrial Systems Review 2002 (2002), pp. 58 - 64 . VTT Industrial Systems (2002)

6.   Kalliokoski P, Andersson G, Salminen, Hemilä J. BestServ Feasibility study. Final report. Technology Industry in Finland 2003

7.   Karvonen I, Jansson K, Ollus M, Hartel I, Burger G, Anastasiou M, Välikangas P, Mori K. Inter-enterprise eCollaboration in Sales and Service of one-of-a-kind products. In: Stanford-Smith B, Chiozza E, Edin M (Ed.): Challenges and Achievements in E-business and E-work, pp. 1388-1395, IOS Press / Ohmsha, Berlin (D), 2002, 1636 pages

8.   Karvonen I. Management of one-of-a-kind manufacturing projects in a distributed environment. VTT Research Notes 2044, Espoo 2000

9.   Tølle M, Bernus P , Vesterager J. Reference models for virtual enterprises. In: Camarinha-Matos L M (Ed.): Collaborative Business Ecosystems and Virtual Enterprises, pp. 3-10, Kluwer Academic Publishers, Boston (USA), 2002, 631 pages

VIRTUELLEFABRIK.CH – A SOURCE NETWORK[1] FOR VE IN MECHATRONICS

4.5

Adrian Plüss and Charles Huber
Centre of Process Design [ZPA],
University of Applied Science, 5210 Windisch, Switzerland
a.pluess@fh-aargau.ch; ch.huber@fh-aargau.ch

This chapter will give a short description how the network was built up and has developed during the last 6 years. It will describe then the business model with concept and organization of the source network as also of the VF temporary organization for a specific customer demand. Then the VF temporary organization of a real business opportunity is shown in a more detailed manner with the internal order management system. At the end of the chapter an actual cluster project within of the source network will give some ideas about the source network development to the future.
Success factors of the source network as also of the VF temporary organization are mentioned at the end of the article.

1. INTRODUCTION

The virtual factory (VF) in the north-western part of Switzerland is linking together of real companies for the purpose of entering new markets or realizing concrete projects that for the individual companies would not be possible in a profitable manner (Katzy, B. et al., 1996; Schuh G. et al., 1996). Co-operation is not new to industry, but in the past, companies were operating in a business environment of relatively stable markets. In recent time the economic pressure increased considerably and forced companies to establish cooperative structures. At the same time customers demand more complex products, enhanced services and the achievement of perfect logistic quality (Wiendahl, H.P. et al., 2002). Important competitive advantage in the network is the selection of appropriate partners and the efficient use of information technology in order to optimise inter-company communication (Plüss & Huber, 2003).

---

[1] VO Breeding Environment

2. DEVELOPMENT OF THE VIRTUAL FACTORY

2.1 History
The VF Project was granted financial support by the Swiss CIM (Computer Integrated Manufacturing) Action Program (1997 to the end of 1998). In the starting phase, the project worked closely with the Institute for Technology Management (ITEM) at the University of St.Gallen. At the end of the two-year period, the network had developed its own dynamics to the extent that it was functioning independently and profitably. Since four years the network is a business network with no external financial support.

2.2 Products and services
Today the source network offers a broad spectrum of products and services and is therefore for customers more attractive than the individual SME (Plüss, A. & Huber, 2002). With its order orientation, the core competencies of the network partners are utilized efficiently and flexibly for a customer demand. At present, there are 37 companies in the network, employing a total of 3'000 employees. Their core competencies lie in the areas of design, engineering, mechanical processing, precision mechanics, sheet metal processing, metal working, surface treatments, heat treatments, fitting, welding techniques, plastics injection moulding, plastics working, electrical and electronic engineering. In the entire value chain, the VF offers total solutions and services for assemblies and sophisticated components and replacement parts. In future time the network want to offer more complex services.

3. DESCRIPTION OT THE SOURCE NETWORK

3.1 Relationship between Source network and VE temporary organization

Figure 1 describes the relationship between the Source network / Breeding environment of the Virtual Factory and the VE temporary organization of the Virtual Factory.

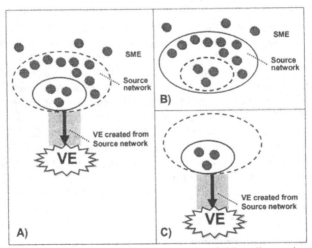

Figure 1 – Virtual Factory A) with the Source network / Breeding environment (B) and the VE temporary organization (C).

This chapter 3 concentrates now to the Source network (see Figure 1B) whereas the VE temporary organisation will be described in chapter 4 (see Figure 1C). Figure 1A shows the whole relationship as shown in the VOSTER Guidelines.

3.2 Structural organization of the Source network

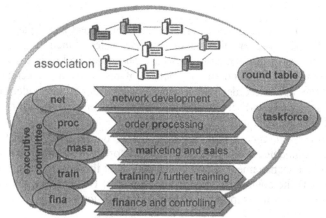

Figure 2 – Organization, working groups and processes in the Source network

The legal form of organization of the Source network as well as its structural organization is the association. The management of the association is the responsibility of an elected *Executive Committee,* which is made up of five members (representatives of partner companies) and headed by a chairman, the president. A general meeting is held once a year, while six conferences for the mutual exchange of experience take place annually. All partner companies take part in the conferences for purposes of mutual exchange of information and experience.

In addition, there are six working parties composed of representatives of the partner companies (see Figure 2). Each company in the network is supposed to be represented in at least one working party. The working parties meet monthly. At present there are six working parties responsible for the operational use of the network as also for the further development:

(1) Finances and Controlling
(2) Marketing and Sales
(3) Network Development and Member Acquisition, Infrastructure (IT)
(4) Training and Further Training
(5) Order Processing (optimization and further development of the process).
(6) Executive Committee

Working parties in turn can set up work groups to handle special topics. For instance, the working party on *Marketing and Sales* has a number of work groups that focus on preparation for trade fairs, roundtable meetings on sales, communication, and so on. Each member of the *Executive Committee* supports a working party. This ensures communication among the working parties and the Executive Committee.

3.3 Roles and rules

Within the Source network and the VE temporary organization the following roles can be distinguished

- The *order broker* acquires external orders for project-based partnerships within the VF. The broker also takes on the sales function and markets the competencies of the company network. The order broker is the entrepreneurial motivating force behind the formation of one or more concrete partnerships within the VF. The order broker can be an external broker under contract to the VF to sell goods and services for the VF, or any one of the partner companies in the VF can act as a broker.
- The *order manager* brings together the resources and competencies of the partner companies within the VF, signs for order processing, and is responsible for project management. During the course of the project lead time, the order manager is the contact person for the customer. He signs the sales contract with the customer and supply contracts with VF-internal partners and external suppliers.
- The *in- and outsourcing manager* is named by each member company to function as the interface between the VF and its own organization. This in- and outsourcing manager may submit and award contracts within the VF.
- The *network coach* is responsible for building and expanding the network. One of his most important tasks is relationship management among the network partners. He is also responsible acquiring new partners.
- The *auditor* monitors order processing in the VF as a neutral authority and ensures that the ground rules are upheld.

A web based intranet platform was set up to facilitate communication within the source network as also for the VE temporary organization for a customer demand. Through intranet communication, all partner companies can post projects and seek possible cooperation partners. One of the ground rules of the VF is that the partner companies must check the intranet platform at least once a day. This obligation was agreed upon so that projects can be processed as rapidly and efficiently as possible.

3.4 Levels working together in different Source networks

Figure 3 describes four different network levels of the source network cooperation: Level 1 describes the link from the company to the source network. With level 1 the partners are communicating to the market using individual company websites. Level 2 describes the network cooperation inside the source network. Inside the network different processes are supported such as order acquiring, order processing, knowledge management, training of the partner and acquiring of new partners. Level 3 describes the interface to the market, where all the services and competencies of the partners are shown and where the customer can interact with the VF. Level 4 presents the linking to the other network, one in the eastern part of Switzerland (Euregio-Bodensee) and one in the southern part of Germany (Baden-Würtemberg).

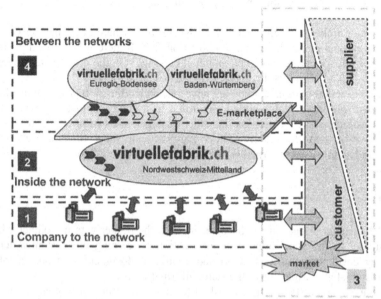

Figure 3 – Different levels working together in the source networks (Huber et al, 2002). For the description of the different levels refer to the text.

The three different VF have their own portal to the market, but may also be reached by the international portal called www.virtuelle-fabrik.com. Level 3 shows the interface from each partner communicating with the VF. Level 4 describes the interface to the market, where all the services and competencies of the partners are shown and where the customer can interact with the VF.

4. VE TEMPORARY ORGANIZATION

To handle the VE temporary organization rapidly for a customer demand a specific *internal order management system* was developed by the centre of process design. All partners are involved and handle the demand through process steps such as *demands, offers* and orders (Huber, Ch. et al., 2002).

If an external demand is posted using the web interface a broker has to be found within 24 hours. If no one takes the external demand within 24 ours, a so called cleaner (only in charge of the network for a certain time) is temporarily in charge to find actively the broker. The customer demand follows the steps explained in the chapters 4.1 to 4.3. Figure 4 shows the life cycle of the VE temporary organization built from the Source network

4.1 Demands

There are two different possibilities to put demands externally by a customer using the World Wide Web (1A) or internally by the network broker (1B) (see Figure 4). For example, a *customer* of one of the VF partner companies is looking for someone to manufacture a product for which a prototype has already been built.

(1) The order broker posts the demand on the *Intranet,* where every partner company can see it and respond, making competition fair. If there is a demand posted on the web, every partner receives an email message. On the other hand, going into the intranet a list shows the actual demand posted in the VF.

(2) Once interested partner companies have responded the partner that will play the greatest role in the value-added chain due to its core competency will take on *responsibility* for execution as the order manager. He can now put in additional information and documents. Other partners can show their interest in this demand and can see any further development with a newsletter.

4.2 Offers

(3) If the demand is taken into the offering box, the broker gets in contact with the customer to get some additional information concerning the customer demand. Every customer contact is noted and additional documents are posted into the web so that all partners have the same information level.

(4) Now every interested partner is asked to make an offer. At this stage the order manager, who is the responsible person for the customer gets in charge. He *selects* the partners he wants to work with, whereby economic efficiency stands in the foreground. Sometimes, targeted inquiries have to be made of potential partners, if the required competencies can not be configured.

(5)

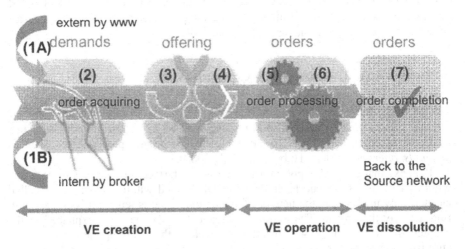

Figure 4 – Life cycle of the *VE temporary organization* built from the *Source network.* The different stages of order status for 1A to 7 are explained in the text.

4.3 Orders

(6) The result of this process is the *VE temporary organization* or *virtual company* that will provide the goods and services: one company provides the welding, a second the sheet metal parts and the order manager's company is responsible for the mechanical parts, assembly, and start-up of the product. The order manager is in charge to notice every status change in contact with the customer. The partners are informed by automatically generated mails. The partners use therefore a project room, where only the partners for this specific order are involved and no more all the partners of the VF.

(7) *Agreements* are drawn up regarding prices, quality, and delivery dates, just as for conventional orders. *Target agreements* accord with these criteria. The order manager takes on *project management.* He does not have a *managing function,* however, in relation to the employees in other partner companies. There, order processing proceeds as always. In cooperation with the other partner companies, contact will take place mainly with company spokesmen, but at times with executing employees as well, such as with staff in administrative operations planning & scheduling.

(8) Ending the order the order manager informs all the partners about the success of the order acquiring and order processing. The status of a finished project is also put into the intranet. It is important, that the knowledge is shared ending an order to give the experience to all the partners having continues improvement for the Source network.

The *internal order management system* is a very important instrument to guarantee transparency on the platform. Working with 37 partners together it is no more possible to communicate with email or fax because there is also one partner not informed. Therefore it is important for every partner to put important information directly in the platform Webcorp (Katzy, B & Ma, 2002). If no partner is found for the customer demand the demand is posted by the *order manager* into the *international portal VF2VF* (Plüss & Huber, 2003), where the 3 different network are linked together (see also Level 4 in Figure 3)

5. CLUSTER PROJECT WITH THE SOURCE NETWORK

In the year 2002 the question was raised up during the partner acquisition process, in what kind of branches the VF is mainly active and which partners are associated to the different branches. On the other hand the VF wants to handle not only components, but also market more and more complex projects and systems solutions. That was the reason, why in the year 2003 the partners accepted to a cluster project.

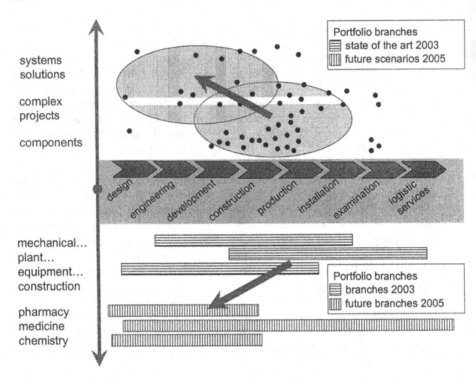

Figure 5 – Cluster projects of the Source network: On one hand the VF wants to handle more and more complex projects and systems solutions and on the other hand add new branches such as pharmacy, medicine and chemistry.

The goal was to define for each partner on one side the main field of market activities in terms of "type of market services" form *components* over *complex projects to systems solutions* and on the other side the branches (see Figure 5) a partner is active. Each partner gives then his actual state of the art report and his future activities he would like to develop.

Beside the partners view the Source network has his strategy in terms of services and branches its wants to develop. The gap between future and present activities (see arrows in Figure 5) will give a substantial impact to the *partner acquisition team* focussing by searching new partners.

6. CONCLUSIONS

The VF is a Source network of 37 companies that make available their core competencies for the production of joint orders building a rapidly a *VE temporary organisation.*
The volume of the orders realized during the last 4 years and the number of customer inquiries received confirm that there is a market demand for virtual companies.

Together the partners have in-depth, mutual know-how at their disposal forming a stable platform. This - as well as their joint market processing - is what distinguishes them from traditional *work alliances, consortiums,* or *general contractors.*

The enterprise culture of the partner companies is based on openness, readiness to share information, trust and honesty. Personal contact among representatives of the partner companies has proved to be indispensable. SME's are predestined to become partners because owners and general managers often become actively involved. This results in rapid decision-making.

The demands the VF places on management and employees should not be underestimated. Both are often unaccustomed to investing their efforts in higher level interests and accepting occasional competitors as partners in a network. It is not easy to recognize that there is a long-term benefit for oneself and one's own company in offering the customer not only individual company goods and services, but rather a *VF system solution.* Companies that would like to join a virtual company should be aware of the fact that network membership can have consequences similar to the effects of changes in company strategy and changes in enterprise culture. This means that time and human resources will be bound up with the establishment of the new orientation for a long period.

Success factors of the VF mentioned by the partners concern the concept, structure, market, strategy, innovation willingness, multiplication effect, partnership and the culture of communication.

The VF is an open, simple, densely woven *concept,* with rules and roles, which works. With the VF, the required professionalism can become visible.

The VF has a flexible *structure;* the customer deals with only one dedicated customer service representative for all problems and gains the services of the entire value- added chain.

Large-scale customers want to purchase complex goods and services that can be produced reasonably only by value-added chains. This is confirmed by the *market*'s perception and acceptance of virtual companies.

In the entire group of network partners, there is a large proportion of companies that follow *expansion strategies* and that want to develop the VF accordingly. This means that these partners are not merely seeking to optimize their capacity loads in recessive economic environments. Instead, it is also their goal to put the offensive potential of the VF to work in periods of economic upswing.

In terms of innovation willingness the companies in the network have to have enthusiasm for the "new," seek new developments, and be prepared to make the occasional investment even if the potential return is not immediately measurable.

There is a *multiplication effect* if the companies with their own established contacts are pooling their contacts so that new market opportunities can be targeted. Each member company profits from the networks of the others.

The *"chemistry"* among the partners is good, and their interests point towards the same goals, so they can achieve together what they set out to do. The value of *partnership* becomes particularly apparent when a company has a project and the others refuse to let the company down, even if they themselves are managing heavy loads. If the relationships are good, you help the partner out. Even those partners that are unable to provide that degree of engagement have to be brought into projects again and again.

The *face-to-face events* (conferences for the mutual exchange of experience) have to be held frequently enough that thoughts can be exchanged and the "worlds" brought into alignment, so that everyone speaks the same language and follows the same goals. The Executive Committee has the job of making transparent various ways of looking at things, for the network is not looking only to decide by the majority, but rather to examine varying possibilities as well. One of them could turn out to be a potential strength (Huber and Plüss, 2003).

Finally, the partner of the Virtual Factory have made the experience that pursuing a business opportunity with a virtual organisation works best, when players are prepared: in order to be able to quickly respond to market needs and to not having to invest too much time to build up necessary network competencies and processes for each new business opportunity the *source network* as a stable and trustful platform is the precondition for the execution of individual business opportunities.

7. REFERENCES

1. Wiendahl, H.P. and Lutz, S. (2002): Production in networks, Annals of the CIRP Vol 51, p. 1 – 13.
2. Huber, Ch., Plüss, A. und Schoch, R. (2002): Auftragsmanagement im virtuellen Netzwerk, new management Nr. 12, p.63-69, 2002
3. Katzy, B.; Schuh G, und Millarg K. (1996): Die virtuelle Fabrik – Produzieren im Netzwerk – neue Märkte erschliessen durch dynamische Netzwerke, in Technische Rundschau 43/1996, p 30-34
4. Plüss, A. and Huber, Ch. (2002): Virtual Organizations – State of the art and development of the Virtual Factory, Proceedings of the 2nd Nat. Meeting of IPLnet, 10/11th of Sept. 2002, Saas Fee Switzerland. www.iplnet.ch
5. Plüss, A. (2002): Virtual Factory Northwest and Central Switzerland – practical experience of a virtual organization. 8th International Conference on Concurrent Enterprising; Virtual Professional Networking, Communities of Practice, 17-19 June, Rom
6. Plüss, A. und Huber, Ch. (2003), Order acquiring and –processing in the Virtual Factory, in : Camarinha-Matos, L & Afsarmeanesh (eds), Proceedings and Foundations for Virtual Organizations, H. (2003), Kluwer Academic Publishers, p. 95-102.
7. Schuh G; Millarg K. und Göransson A, (1998): Virtuelle Fabrik, neue Marktchancen durch dynamische Netzwerke, Carl Huber Verlag, Munich, 1998
8. Katzy, B. & Ma, X., (2002): A Research Note on Virtual Project Management Systems, in: Pawar, K., Weber, F., Thoben, K. (eds), Proceedings of the 8th International Conference on Concurrent Enterprising ICE, 2002 Rome, Italy; University of Nottingham, p.517-520.
9. Huber, Ch. und Plüss A. (2003): Vertrauenskultur – Erfahrungen aus dem Produktionsnetzwerk Virtuelle Fabrik Nordwestschweiz/Mittelland; in Vernetzt planen und produzieren, TU Chemnitz, Sonderforschungsbereich 457, Tagungsband p.143 – 147.

4.6

VIRTUAL ORGANIZATIONS IN THE COURIER, EXPRESS AND PARCEL INDUSTRY

Holger Luczak, Volker Stich, Patrick Wader

Research Institute for Operations Management - FIR, Aachen, Germany
luczak@fir.rwth-aachen.de stich@fir.rwth-aachen.de, wader@fir.rwth-aachen.de

This chapter introduces characteristics of the courier, express and parcel industry. It states why this industry gives examples of virtual organizations. Players and structures are explained, planning and control processes as well as delivery services are discussed. Shortcomings of existing ICT are pointed out. The need for dynamic planning and control instruments for service delivery among many individual partners is derived.

The research project ParcelMan is then introduced. Research results regarding planning and control instruments are explained. Planning processes are assisted through a multi agent system. Process control is supported through software for mobile devices. Like that, virtual organizations of higher dynamics in the courier, express and parcel industry are enabled.

1. INTRODUCTION

The Courier, Express and Parcel industry (CEP) can be distinguished from the overall industry of road based logistical service providers by the predominant shipping form, which is smaller and lighter (compare a parcel or a document folder to a palette). In addition, the speed of transportation has a much higher importance in comparison to general freight forwarders (Glaser, 2000).

Even though recent years of little GDP gains in major European markets have slowed down the speed of growth, CEP markets continue to develop faster than other means of transportation (Puls, 2003). Smaller and faster shipments are increasingly dominant in future transportation markets (cp. Boeing, 2001).

This chapter points out virtual organizations in CEP markets as well as requirements and research results regarding enabling instruments.

2. THE COURIER, EXPRESS AND PARCEL INDUSTRY

2.1 Players and structures

Even though a strict definitional distinction between courier, express and parcel companies is possible in theory, market realities show vast overlaps between these pure forms. Players in the CEP market most often offer services that can be assigned to two or all sectors of CEP. However, other criteria are useful when evaluating CEP players.

Within Germany, around 80% of all external transports are carried out by companies with less than 20 employees, which corresponds to approx. 76,000 companies (Wäscher, 2003). Around 40,000 companies of these should be assigned to the CEP industry (Wäscher, 2001; Mathejczyk et al., 1999).

Further CEP specific data exist for the city of Hamburg, Germany. Figure 1 shows CEP company sizes with specific regard to full-time employees (Glaser, 2000):

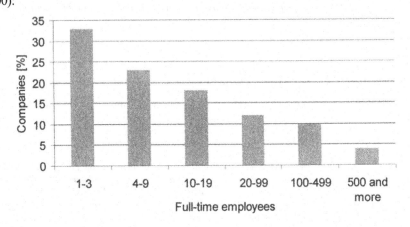

Figure 1 – CEP company sizes (Glaser, 2000)

A predominant SME structure becomes very evident. In Hamburg more than half of all CEP companies consist of ten or less employees, about a third of all CEP companies of only one to three employees.

Customers of CEP companies often only recognize brand names of big market players such as UPS or of the (former) national postal companies such as TPG/TNT, La Poste or Deutsche Post World Net/DHL. Often however, networks behind are made up of the identified SMEs that dominate the CEP market in sheer company numbers. Whereas that is accurate for most big players, this particularly holds true for all midsize networks.

The last decade showed a very high level of market changes with regard to bankruptcies, network reorganizations and mergers & acquisitions (cp. Klaus, 2003; Puls, 2003). Hence, companies act in changing networks, for changing brands and for a variety of partners. Additionally, a very large number of small and autonomous players characterize the CEP industry making it a prime example of virtual organizations (cp. Camarinha-Matos, 2002; Stich and Wader, 2002). A number of changing and legally independent partners act together to form a network of service creation towards a customer (cp. chapter 1).

2.2 Processes and services

Courier companies transport shipments in direct point-to-point relations without turnover points (hubs). Express or parcel companies, however, use at least a regional or national network of hubs and spokes (cp. to the star-topology in chapter 1; Zäpfel and Wasner, 2000). The direct (physical) contact with customers is usually carried out by distributed SMEs as contractors. Either drivers themselves make up independent enterprises (SMEs) or a number of drivers together form an SME by running a knot in the network. Figure 2 shows the typical hub and spoke setup.

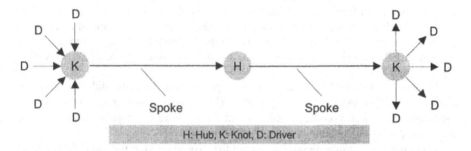

Figure 2 –Setup of express and parcel companies

These SMEs on the one hand collect shipments and feed them into the network. On the other hand, they also deliver shipments to customers and thus service the last mile of the delivery process.

Recently, often related to electronic commerce or other forms of distant trade, delivery companies have begun to include value added services (VAS) within the delivery process. Examples include delivering contracts and access data (PIN, TAN) for online brokerage, which need an identification or legitimation of the receiver, as well as exchanging broken electronic devices such as mobile phones or notebooks. In order to synchronize service delivery with customer reachability, small time windows have to be arranged with each customer during the planning process. Also, the qualifications of delivery drivers have to be included within the planning process: different VAS require specific qualifications that go beyond what is needed in the delivery of regular shipments such as packages. These restrictions, among many others, form a complex planning problem. Also, as customers that require services are demanding time window assignments in real time during an interaction with a service provider (e.g. phone call), the planning problem has to be solved dynamically.

The delivery within defined time windows, as well as VAS, require assisting instruments of high performance within the delivery process itself. A driver, for example, might need assistance when questions arise regarding steps of the service delivery or when simply finding a specific address. Also, the presence of time windows necessitates improved routing capabilities in order to keep promises to customers.

Hence, supporting instruments are required for planning as well as controlling service delivery.

2.3 Existing ICT

For planning and control purposes of service delivery CEP companies use proprietary solutions of relatively low performance (cp. Maruhn, 2003b). Parcel companies for example use scheduling aids for route planning. These do not, however, cover time windows for daily planning and do not take dynamic aspects into account.

As for controlling the last mile of distributing (as well as collecting) shipments, many CEP companies especially among the bigger players use mobile terminals. These mainly help to record the transfer of liability from the company to a customer or vice versa and often include identification technologies (scanners). These do not, however, include planning or control capabilities in the aforementioned areas. Data collected is mainly used to feed into track-and-trace-systems (cp. Cremer, 2003). Also, no CEP network is known that would use navigational systems network-wide (cp. Maruhn, 2003a).

Efforts to standardize data and data processing systems did not succeed. Therefore, ICT support is relatively limited (Manner-Romberg et al., 2001). This is especially true when it comes to SMEs that do not have the capabilities to develop proprietary solutions (Mathejczyk et al., 1999).

No dynamic planning method is known that would provide the required solutions to the introduced planning problem and that would adequately incorporate the autonomy and sheer amount of individual players within the addressed domain. Looking at instruments for controlling the service delivery process, a similar picture develops. No means or methods exist, that are based on existing infrastructures only and/or on open standards.

Daily planning activities, therefore, have to be carried out with very limited interaction of the involved players limiting the optimization of service delivery and the delivery of customer specific services, which otherwise would mark a form of mass customization (cp. chapter 1). In order to facilitate an optimized service delivery and enable VO of higher dynamics in the CEP industry, both planning as well as controlling instruments are needed to address these shortcomings.

3. RESULTS OF THE PARCELMAN PROJECT

3.1 Project players and setup

In an effort to address the challenges described above the research project "ParcelMan" has been set up. The project that started in October 2001 is made possible through research funds from the German Ministry of Education and Research (BMB+F) for thirty months. In order to sufficiently cover the wide scope of the project, various partners from different industry and research areas work together. The project is set up in different sub-projects to cover logistical and technological aspects as well as to include ergonomical studies that further aid delivery drivers. Therefore, partners of the project can be assigned to three different areas.

First, the CEP sector is present in the consortium through express/parcel companies as well as logistical research partners. Second, the technology focus is covered through partners with the needed specific hardware and/or software expertise as well as research capabilities. Third, there is a strong focus on employees working in delivery services/ergonomics through various research and transfer partners.

Key results of the project regarding planning and control of service delivery are described below.

3.2 Planning methodology for the delivery process

In order to model the described planning domain, the usage of multi agent theory is very well fit. Through various comparisons, the Gaia-methodology has been identified as a modeling aid (Wooldridge et al., 2000; Wader, 2004).

In order to fully utilize existing standards, FIPA (Foundation for Intelligent Physical Agents) standards have been applied wherever possible (FIPA, 2002). For implementation purposes the JADE platform (Java Agent DEvelopment Framework) has been identified as it is also based on FIPA and fulfills important requirements such as security support, platform support for mobile devices, graphical user interface assistance, etc. (Wader, 2004). The multi agent system has been fully implemented in JAVA.

The underlying planning methodology fully observes total autonomy of market players such as drivers and customers and totally integrates dynamic aspects such as customer appearances within the market (Wader, 2004). Market players in the model hold the required planning capabilities e.g. for route planning or for calculating transportation cost and time. The planning process combining the players is based on auctions that are implemented using the well established Contract Net Protocol (CNP, cp. Davis and Smith, 1983). Taken to the extreme, this planning methodology can enable true market interaction for each individual customer contact. Therefore, the goals and restrictions of relevant market players have been thoroughly included. Special emphasis has been given to real time interaction. Principles of the planning methodology can be adapted to applications in other domains where autonomous players interact in real time.

Figure 3 shows a fraction of the multi agent system implemented in JAVA and JADE observing a driver. It shows examples of a driver's behaviours and associated methods used when interacting with other agents within the CNP.

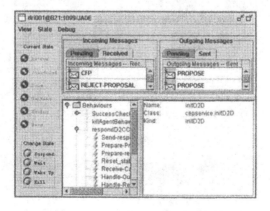

Figure 3 – Example of driver in multi agent system

The planning process results in a drop list (list of jobs) for each driver. This optimized list includes specific job data such as time window, planned arrival time, address, service type, etc. for each customer.

3.3 Supporting instruments in the delivery process

In order to assist companies in the actual delivery process, further instruments are required. The drop list mentioned above is the summary of all jobs a driver has to fulfill in a given day. Consequently, master processes have been developed for each type of job. To design these for regular shipments as well as for VAS, service engineering techniques have been applied (Gill, 2004). Lists of frequently asked questions (FAQs) for all steps within a particular service as well as general help functions have been developed.

For implementation purposes only readily available software techniques as well as widely applied hardware have been used. An integrated methodology for technology availability and assessment has been applied (Luczak et al., 2003). Companies can therefore use their existing infrastructures e.g. mobile phones or Smartphones. They are not required to invest in special devices.

Two technological scenarios have been implemented within the ParcelMan project, the first using a standard mobile phone, the second using a Smartphone. The later also represents a likely proxy for widely available technological standards within a few years including color display units, touch screens, etc. (see figure 4).

These technological implementations are being tested and optimized within ergonomical lab as well as field tests. Such, device quality in aiding drivers can be further improved.

Figure 4 – Examples of mobile support devices

4. CONCLUSIONS

The CEP industry shows key characteristics of virtual organizations. Various autonomous partners work together in changing networks. CEP brands most often act towards acquiring customers. Actual service delivery can be carried out by a high number of smaller companies.

New services emerge within the CEP market. These require planning methodologies of high performance to solve complex dynamic planning problems as well as aiding instruments for controlling service delivery. As many independent companies interact within the CEP domain, successful solutions have to be based on applicable standards and existing as well as widely used infrastructures. Within the ParcelMan project prototypic means and methods have been developed successfully to enable VO of higher dynamics within the CEP industry.

While the planning process described above is based on multi agent planning and communication representing relevant players and their interaction, the control process is not. Future research should further expand on multi agent interaction to also include controlling actual service delivery processes. This should include means that enable players of the delivery process to react in case of problems. Examples include dynamic route guiding systems or backup solutions based on market mechanisms that are fully integrated with the described planning structures. Like that, further improvements of service delivery can be accomplished. This would mark further steps towards virtual organizations that can be considered even more dynamic.

Acknowledgments

The project ParcelMan is made possible through research funds from the German Ministry of Education and Research (BMB+F) within the framework "Innovative job design – future of work". Project coaching is managed by a division of the German Aerospace Center (DLR-PT). Visit www.parcelman.de for details.

5. REFERENCES

1. Boeing. World Air Cargo Forecast 2000/2001 – International Express. Seattle: Press Release of The Boeing Company, 2001.
2. Camarinha-Matos, Luis M. Collaborative Business Ecosystems and Virtual Enterprises. Boston: Kluwer Publishers, 2002.
3. Cremer, Ludwig-Michael. Wie Sendungsverfolgung kundenorientierter wird. Logistik heute 25(2003)7-8: 24-25.
4. Davis R, Smith RG. Negotiation as a Metaphor for Distributed Problem Solving. Artificial Intelligence 20(1983)1: 63-109.
5. FIPA. The Foundation for Intelligent Physical Agents. www.fipa.org, 2002.
6. Gill, Christian. Architektur für das Service Engineering zur Entwicklung von technischen Dienstleistungen. Aachen: Dissertation RWTH Aachen, 2004 (forthcoming).
7. Glaser, Jürgen. Kurier-, Express-, Paketdienste und Stadtlogistik. Dissertation Technische Universität Hamburg-Harburg 2000. München: Huss-Verlag, 2000.

8. Klaus, Peter. Jammern hilft nicht weiter. KEP-Nachrichten-Sonderservice zur Ausgabe 10/2003, KEP-Nachrichten 9(2003)10.

9. Luczak H, Bleck S, Quadt A. Electronic business engineering – exploiting the potentials of a wireless world. International Journal of Internet and Enterprise Management 1 (2003)1: 31-52.

10. Manner-Romberg H, Müller B, Weber P. Demand for Communication – The increasing need for ways of efficient communication within the courier, express and postal markets. Proceedings of the 9th Conference on Postal and Delivery Economics, Sorrento, 2001.

11. Maruhn, Erwin. News „Mobile Board für Kurierdienste". KEP-Nachrichten 9(2003)18:3. (=2003b)

12. Maruhn, Erwin. News „Navigationsgerät im Fahrzeug eines Paketzustellers". KEP-Nachrichten 9(2003)28: 3. (=2003a)

13. Mathejczyk W, Uske H, Dorsch-Schweizer M. Kleinunternehmen im Transportgewerbe. Rundbrief Neue Selbständige in der Logistik o. J.(1999)2: 3-21.

14. Puls, Ulrich. Kein Land in Sicht. Logistik heute 25(2003)7-8: 20-21.

15. Stich V, Wader P. Supporting the Dynamic Structures of CEP Services. In Collaborative Business Ecosystems and Virtual Enterprises, Luis M. Camarinha-Matos, ed. Boston: Kluwer Publishers, 2002: 397-404.

16. Wader, Patrick. Konzeption einer agentenorientierten Planungsmethodik für die Leistungserbringung mit Zeitfensterrestriktionen bei Kurier-, Express- und Paketdiensten. Aachen: Dissertation RWTH Aachen, 2004 (forthcoming).

17. Wäscher, Dagmar. Portrait des Bundesverbands der Transportunternehmen. www.bvtev.de/portrait.-htm, 2003.

18. Wäscher, Dagmar. Wie viele Kleinunternehmen gibt es in der Transportbranche? Studie des Bundesverbands der Transportunternehmen. Dortmund, 2001.

19. Wooldridge M, Jennings NR, Kinny D. The Gaia Methodology for Agent-Oriented Analysis and Design. Autonomous Agents and Multi-Agent Systems 3(2000)3: 285-312.

20. Zäpfel G, Wasner M. Planung und Optimierung von virtuellen Hub-and-Spoke-Transportnetzwerken kooperativer Logistikdienstleister im Sammelgutverkehr. Zeitschrift für Betriebswirtschaft 67(2000) Ergänzungsheft 2: 243-259.

TOWARDS STRUCTURING THE RESEARCH ON VIRTUAL ORGANIZATIONS

5.

Martin Ollus
Technical Research Centre of Finland (VTT), martin.ollus@vtt.fi

One main aim of the work behind this book was to structure and consolidate the achievements in the area of virtual organisations. Four dimensions were used as a basis for the analysis: concepts, models, infrastructures and industrial practices. The consolidation of these areas is discussed in this book together with implementation issues, which are a prerequisite for successful use of virtual organisations. In this concluding remarks chapter, some of the findings in these areas are commented in the perspective of further development. It is claimed that the consolidation of concepts and approaches, which is presented in this book, can be a part of a sound basis for further development and consolidation of the area.

1. INTRODUCTION

This book is to a considerable extent based on results from the VOSTER project (http://voster.vtt.fi). One of the objectives of the project was to give an overall picture of the area of Virtual Organizations (VO) and to suggest directions for future research and activities. The need of such a consolidation was considered important, because a vast amount of development and research efforts had been devoted to activities, of which many had become isolated attempts. Common approaches were to a large extent lacking, which also could be seen in the variety of concepts and definitions appearing.

The content of this book shows that common concepts and approaches are evolving. The VOSTER project aimed at structuring and consolidating the achievements related to the formation, operation and disclosure of VO. Concrete activities were devoted to

- Consolidating VO related concepts and their relationships, VO types, characteristics and indicators into a reference model,
- Identifying and recommending useful approaches for VO modelling,
- Identifying relevant technologies and standards and assessing their potential for VO infrastructures and interoperability
- Identifying and promoting best practices for VO formation and operation with a particular focus on small and medium sized enterprises (SME).

Together the chapters of this book contain achievements in many of the mentioned respects. It can be seen that similar basic concepts are emerging. Also in the classification and structuring of methodologies and technologies commonalities are identified. In this concluding chapter some of the results are commented and future perspectives discussed.

2. BASIS FOR AN EMERGING FOUNDATION

In the field of networking, a variety of concepts and terms have been used. Part 1 of this book contains an approach to classify and systematize some of the basic needs for understanding, monitoring and controlling activities in virtual organisations. Despite of different terminology and approaches used previously, a distinction between the (long) lasting commitment to collaborate and the concrete collaboration in an actual virtual organisation can be done in most cases. The development of a vocabulary and definitions of terms rely on this distinction, which seems to become increasingly accepted in a sense that used models and approaches build on it. The work on a coherent terminology seems to support the convergence towards better understanding of terms and concepts. However, efforts are still needed before a widely accepted ontology and common understanding are achieved, because many concepts have been vaguely defined and the same terms may have been used in different meanings resulting in confusion in communication and understanding.

An analysis of both research projects and best practices shows that although modelling is mostly accepted as an important part of an enterprise project, many virtual organisations are still created and operated without any explicit use of modelling approaches. Few projects have modelled the business domain to provide detailed understanding of the set-up and business assumptions of the VO. Also the management aspects and the relationship between management approaches and the topology of the virtual organisations seem to have got little attention.

Future development in modelling would rely on an integration of models and modelling approaches from several different areas and for different uses (management and organisational models, product and production process models, information flow models, risk management models, etc.). To create an efficient management approach for virtual organisations, the interoperability between models and modelling tools needs to be supported. The consolidation of the concepts and modelling approaches, which is documented e.g. in this book, provides a starting point for a research agenda aiming at a sustainable foundation, which can be used for development, implementation and use of approaches for efficient utilisation of collaborative networks.

3. INTEROPERABILITY STILL A CHALLENGE

The rapid development in information and communication technologies (ICT) is a main driver behind the increase in networked collaboration. In addition to its support for networking and collaboration, the development pace of the ICT has, together with the lack of common frameworks and reference models, also created problems, especially related to interoperability. Many applications have been developed separately in isolation to fulfil the needs of specific small groups. A wider collaboration based on these achievements is very difficult and perhaps not motivated by the developers. Consequently, the creation of reference infrastructures for networked collaboration is still an urgent task.

Standardisation supports collaboration and provides the building blocks for collaboration. In a rapidly developing area, new solutions, which are more efficient than the previous ones, continuously appear. There exists a large amount of emerging technologies, which may form the basis for new standards. Some solutions may become de facto standards without official acceptance. Based on these technologies, services to be used for support of virtual organisations can be developed. Security is important for both users and providers of services. The measures to ensure security should be efficient enough, but on the other hand they should not be obstacles for collaboration and agility.

From the point of view of virtual organisations, the interoperability can be seen as efficient support of collaboration between networked organisations and people. Naturally, a prerequisite for this type of interoperability is interoperability between the services built on the horizontal ICT infrastructure, but also the functional interoperability between models and processes in the organisations is becoming increasingly important.

4. IMPLEMENTATION

A virtual organisation is not a legal entity and cannot easily be managed like a company or some other single organisation. Still it is assumed to behave in a similar organised way. These and other characteristics set challenges for successful implementation of the concept of virtual organisations. Especially, the legal aspects have recently received an increasing interest. A wide scope of legal issues appears in this context (e.g. partner agreements, liabilities, rights and intellectual property, etc.) and solutions still need to be developed.

Successful implementation of the VO concept also requires an assessment of the performance of the virtual organisations. The efficiency in fulfilling its task is a natural element of this assessment. Compared to traditional performance measurement the task is to extend the activity over organisational boarders. However, in relation to virtual organisations, an important task is also to assess the structure and the procedures in the created virtual organisations and to learn from previous experience. A future challenge seems to be the creation of mechanisms and services to support continuous improvement for creation, operation and disclosure of virtual organisations.

People are the main actors in virtual organisations. Their successful collaboration is supported by the socio- organizational environment they act in. A trust-building culture and intangible assets is considered to be some main requirements for this success. Training and education are important means to achieve such an environment. Future research and development seem to increasingly focus on the organisational environment.

5. EXISTING PRACTICES IN SEVERAL SECTORS

Collaboration between organisations for a specific mission is not a new idea. In many sectors collaboration between companies has been relatively common. However, the rapid development of the ICT has enabled fast and world-wide collaboration in real-time, which is required in the globalising world. The practical applications have usually been developed for specific purposes because of the lack of references. Despite of this trend, there are a few examples, where the approaches seem to partly follow the trends in the research field.

In Europe some networks, which have been formally established to act as a breeding environment, have been identified. The structure, the formality and the degree of deepness may vary, but some roles, like network manager or broker, are usually also identified. Some of these networks have already a history of over ten years. Analyses of their history, success factors and problems can give valuable information about the dynamics of networks and may also give hints for development needs. However, in many cases the existence of a support network is not explicitly recognised by the actors. Analyses show that also in these cases some kind of network exists in the background.

The overview of industrial practices in part 4 of this book presents examples of virtual organisations from a variety of industrial sectors. Both mass-production and one-of-a-kind manufacturing are included, so also the service sector. These cases give good examples of successful approaches, but they also define challenges and issues for further research and development. Based on the analyses of these and other examples, the VOSTER project has published a guidelines booklet, which is available on the project web-site (http://voster.vtt.fi). In this booklet experiences from some industrial practices are explained and guidelines for industrial application of networked collaboration are given.

New types of collaborative organisations, especially in other fields than manufacturing (e.g. in the public sector) will also give inspiration for further work. Also the increase of networking in innovative and knowledge intensive areas, like in product development, will require new approaches. As indicated above and in some of the chapters in this book, a solid foundation of theory together with related methodology and tools would be the basis for research agendas to support future collaborative networked organisations.

ANNEX – REFERENCE PROJECTS

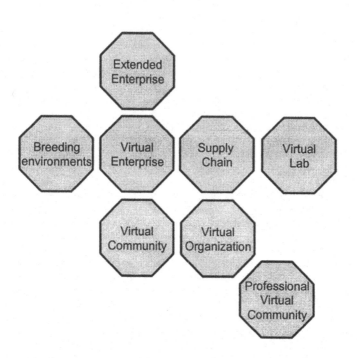

This page intentionally left blank

ALIVE: working group on Advanced Legal Issues in Virtual Enterprise

PROJECT SUMMARY

ALIVE was intended to foster cooperation among industry, legal and ICT professionals, with the aim to identify and classify the legal issues arising form the emergence of the Virtual Enterprise, to exchange information on ongoing relevant research and exploit co-operation opportunities on common themes. A further objective was to compare emerging issues and the existing legal and regulatory frameworks, in view to generating suggestions for future policy development and new RTD actions.

Program: FP5 IST (European Commission)   **Duration:** Jan 2001 – Dec 2002
Consortium: CEC Concurrent Engineering Consulting S.r.l., (I) [Project Coordination], Mazzeschi & Partners (I), Katholieke Universiteit Leuven, (B), CIRSFID (I), Ibermatica S.A. (E), Loughborough University (UK), Virtual Enterprise Architects BV (NL), IT Law Unit, Centre for Commercial Law Studies, Queen Mary, University of London (UK), Centre of International European and Economic Law (GR), J&A Garrigues, Andersen y Cía S.R.C. (E), Gruppo Formula S.p.A.(I), University of Lapland (FIN), University of Oslo (N) Fritze Paul Schmitt, Rechtsanwälte Notare (D), Kunz, Schima, Wallentin und Partner KSW (A) Schneider Electric (F) Delphi & Co (S)

TECHNICAL APPROACH

Due to the unique characteristics of the "virtual organisations" a range of legal issues are beginning to emerge which threaten to inhibit their growth and prosperity. The transition towards a global information society requires a new regulatory framework involving co-ordinated legislative initiatives and international negotiations. A rigorous approach was used in the project conduction, starting with the identification of a common taxonomy about legal issues in Virtual Enterprises (which can be also conveniently used as a basis to align the European research in the IST framework), then carrying out different studies on the issues recognised as having the right of priority, aimed of identifying key recommendations for their resolution:
(LI1) The nature and legal identity of the VE – (LI 2) Role of Actors/VE Architect - (LI3) ICT Law Issues for Virtual Enterprises (Electronic exchange of communications/ Electronic commerce of products and services) - (LI 4) Liability and Insurance - (LI5) Intellectual and Industrial Property rights – (LI 6) Consumer Protection & Contracting with 3rd Parties – (LI7) Control legislation/Competition law – (LI 8) Tax matters – (LI 9) The VE Interchange Agreement
To support and complement the ALIVE working group endeavor, as well as to activate an effective dissemination channel, a dedicated Interest Group was established, counting more than 200 members. Training packages were also developed for SMEs interested in learning more about the VE legal framework, and business and organisation models supported by the VE organisational reach.

MAIN RESULTS

The ALIVE project achieved the following major results:

Definition of **Contract Models/Legal Templates** for Virtual Enterprises, suitable for being re-deployed by users in different contexts.

o Letter Of Intent (LOI), addressing pre-contractual issues such as exclusive co-operation, non-competition, confidentiality, negotiation in good faith/fair dealing and costs. Once a VE Architect/Broker has identified a business opportunity and the competencies required to carry it out, he starts preliminary discussions with individual businesses which have the required competencies. As mutual interest increases, details begin to be discussed, the parties gain a sense of enthusiasm and urgency and might want to formalise their interest in writing. One mechanism that the VE Architect/Broker may use with each respective potential VE member is a letter of intent (LOI).

o Memorandum Of Understanding (MOU), as an alternative preliminary agreement aimed at creating a certain (regulatory) framework for potential partners who would like to create a VE. The negotiating parties may address some of the pre-contractual issues in a preliminary agreement signed between all such parties. This preliminary agreement – which should be distinguished from the final agreement setting up the VE – is being referred to as a "Memorandum of Understanding" to highlight the fact that the parties may decide that some parts of this document are not to be binding.

o VE Agreement Template, intended to provide a contractual framework for the VE, addressing the structural VE characteristics (such as objectives, operation and management, membership/ cation and termination of the VE), Intellectual property rights and confidentiality and Liability issues

Identification of **key recommendations** for future development of European Policies on Virtual Enterprises (ALIVE Roadmap). In particular, the roadmap consists of a detailed plan of integrated actions, having the objectives of providing guidelines for facilitating the implementation of the obtained key recommendations:

o Recognition at EU level of the VE's legal status
o Protection of customers & limitation of VE partners' liability
o Validation of the VE templates by the SMEs
o Creation of a specific insurance policy
o Creation of a specific ICT platform for VE.

Further information and downloadable documentation is available at the ALIVE web site: http://www.vive-ig.net/projects/alive/

SELECTED REFERENCES

1. Legal model contracts to support the creation and management of Virtual Enterprises – Results from the ALIVE Project (E.M Weitzenboeck, R Santoro, M. Conte), ISBN 0-85358-119-3, Proceedings of ICE 2003 Conference pp 359-366, June 2003.
2. Determining Applicable Law and Jurisdiction in contractual disputes regarding Virtual Enterprises (E.M Weitzenboeck), ISBN 0-85358-113-4, Proceedings of ICE 2002 Conference pp 27-34, June 2002.

Contributor: R. Santoro – rsantoro@esoce.net

BAP: Business Architect Project

PROJECT SUMMARY

The project furthers understanding of the broker in a virtual organizations and develops a set of supporting methods and tools. The Title Business Architect conveys the special focus on the early stages of defining and designing the temporary cooperation of independent firms that jointly pursue a business opportunity with an entrepreneurial mindset.

Three main tasks were identified in a survey to be the most important priorities of Business Architects. real options calculation of the financial value that the business opportunity represents, configuration of the entrepreneurial (virtual) team that will engage in the virtual organization, and finally value system design, as organizational design of the virtual value chain to deliver products and services.

The project has developed methods and supporting tools for these three tasks and validated their use in cases.

Program: FP5 IST (European Commission) **Duration:** February 2000 –June 2002
Consortium: VEA (NL) [project coordinator], BayernInnovativ (D), Booth Allen Hamiltaon (NL), DLR (D), ESADE Barcelona (E), ETIS (B). HollandVenture (NL), InMediasP (D),Intracom (GR), Philipps (NL), Rotterdam School of Management (NL), Unilever (NL), Wellington (D), University Bw Munich (D).

TECHNICAL APPROACH

It is generally acknowledged that firms today face a dynamic environment, changing at an increasingly rapid pace. Market opportunities in particular can arise and disappear again within a short period of time. However, the ability of traditional organizations to adapt to these changes remains limited.

The project undertook a process analysis of what brokers do when defining new projects in virtual organizations and how critical activities can be supported to increase the agility of virtual organizations. The overall thesis of the project is that entrepreneurial competencies, which are deeply embedded in the network, lead to higher agility and more business success of virtual organizations. Three important elements of the entrepreneurial competencies were identified and further development undertaken to support them:

First, create motivation amongst partners to join the endeavor and commit resources to it, means that te business architect needs to make the potential outcome of each virtual project concrete and visible. This means that the business opportunity has to be identified, markets and market volumes need be specified, and last not least financial expectation need be made explicit. Most traditional costing techniques proved to be too tedious for the necessary rapid decision making, or too rigid to cope with uncertainty and change. Therefore a strategic real options approach has been chosen that allows identifying, describing, and financially quantifying business opportunities. It has been adapted for virtual for virtual organizations and supported with a software tool to gather necessary information and calculate financials.

Second, attracting and retaining the right people for virtual teams, has proven a critical success factors for virtual projects. While most existing selection tools are based on professional skills, the here chosen approach is based on the psychological disposition of the individual to cooperate in the complexity of technology mediated virtual settings with the involvement of multiple cultures and multiple professions. A web based assessment instrument has been developed to specifically address issues of virtual organizations.

Third, the business architect has to quickly organize for delivery in the virtual team. The project has chosen a technique based on process oriented change management, which however accounts for the specifics of virtual settings, which mainly result from the inter-organizational design of process, such as in/outsourcing decisions on entire business processes, confidentiality of process knowledge that is not shared outside the member firm, and interface definitions.

MAIN RESULTS & RELATIONS TO VO CONCEPTS
The most significant results of the Business Architect Project include:

VSD – Value System Designer, a methodology for inter-organizational process design, which is optimized for fast implementation of process in a virtual project.

ROC – Real Option Calculator, a methodology and web based tool to rapidly collect information and expert opinions for strategic decision making about business opportunities and its financial calculation.

SELECTED REFERENCES

1. Dissel, M. C. (2003), Uncertainty and Managerial Decisions for New Technology Based Ventures, Dissertation at the University Bw Munich
2. Katzy, B. R., Dissel, M. C. (2001), Earnings vs. Innovation; Measuring Architectural Competencies, in: Society, I. E. M. (ed.), Proceedings of the Engineering Management (IEMC), Change Management & the New Industrial Revolution, Albany, NY: IEEE
3. Katzy, B. R., Dissel, M. C., Blum, M. (2001), Measuring Value - Creating Value; A Solution for Process Innovation in High-tech Company Networks, in: Proceedings of the e-Business e-Work Conference, Venice
4. Katzy, B. R., Dissel, M. C., Blindow, F. S. (2003), Dynamic Capabilities for Entrepreneurial Venturing; the Siemens ICE Case, in: Zedtwitz, M. v., Haour, G., Khalil, T., Lefebvre, L. (eds.), Management of Technology: Growth through Business, Innovation and Entrepreneurship, Oxford: Pergamon Press
5. Penrose, E. T. (1959), The Theory of the Growth of the Firm, Oxford: Basil Blackwell.
6. Teece, D. J., Pisano, G. P., Shuen, A. (1997), Dynamic Capabilities and Strategic Management, Strategic Management Journal, 18 (7), 509-533

Contributor: Bernhard Katzy – Prof. Katzy@CeTIM.org

BIDSAVER: Business Integrator Dynamic Support Agents for Virtual Enterprise

PROJECT SUMMARY

The BIDSAVER Project aims at facilitating the constitution and the management of Virtual Enterprises and supporting their dynamic and evolving configurations, driven by competitiveness-oriented criteria. In the BIDSAVER envisaged scenario, characterised by the full interoperability VE's processes and by high dynamics of the Virtual Venture, the Business Integrator needs to be provided with Business and Data models, capable of:

- providing the adequate structure for all the data to be handled in the Virtual Enterprise scenario, from product, process and organisation point of views;
- representing the Virtual Enterprise in its operational process and evolving configuration and requirements
- providing the basis for formalising legal agreements for co-operation and for implementing changes in the VE process and organisational structure throughout the enterprise life cycle
- supporting the search for partners according to specific characteristics required to fit individual roles in the joint venturing to respond to a business opportunity

Program: FP5 IST (European Commission)   **Duration:** Jan 2001 – June 2002
Consortium: Concurrent Engineering Consulting S.r.l., (I) [Project Coordination], Studio Legale Mazzeschi, Novelli, Porcari, (I),   DEMOCENTER (I),   Speed Tecnologie (I), Heletel (GR), Elsag (I), Soditech, (F), Teleinformatica e Sistemi (I), Telespazio (I), Comer S.p.A.(I), Livarna Vuzenica ltd (SL), Intercom (SK)

TECHNICAL APPROACH

The definition of the Data and Business models has been achieved starting from the Virtual Enterprise general phasing and methodology as defined in the VIVE Project (Esprit Project # 26584), and was also enriched by the contribution obtained by other initiatives and IST projects like ACTIVE, ALIVE, PROVE-SME.

The ICT strategy pursued by BIDSAVER exploited the availability of ICT solutions covering specific areas of generalised requirements, to be customised and integrated according to VE models. The ICT architecture was designed to:

- interface legacy, purchased and internally developed applications, regardless of their technologies
- be compatible with both the Microsoft (COM+) and Enterprise Java Beans (Java/CORBA) component platforms
- include a number of value-added services (flow control, transformation, message definition, message warehousing)
- support both the publish/ subscribe and request/reply styles of application interaction, as well as reliable and/or guaranteed message delivery
- be centrally managed and administered

In addition to this, the ICT infrastructure was structured according to the concept of servicing to multiple VEs, in order to support the operation of several initiatives from different industrial sectors with a regional centre of servicing, and it is based on a methodology which is independent from the specific set of tools adopted.

MAIN RESULTS

The major project results can be summarised as follows:

An **innovative methodology** for VE's constitution, set up, management and optimised partners' search, enforcing concurrency among VE Organisation dynamic constitution and VE product and processes development (product/process/ organisation Business Breakdown Structure management module)

A **legal framework,** including all the contractual templates, reflecting the BIDSAVER dynamic business model scenario.

An **ICT infrastructure prototype** and concept demonstrator, which represents the Information System available to the business Integrator to manage dynamically the VE.

The Information system is composed of three integrated management modules:
- a Business Breakdown Structure (BBS) management module, allowing the management of evolution of VE through a model (BBS) that accommodates cross mapping of product physical/functional items, tasks and associated resources/risks/timing, and responsible entities/organisations with associated contractual elements. The BBS model is targeted to provide the Business Integrator with the full data structure, integrating the Product Breakdown Structure, Work Breakdown Structure and the Organisational Breakdown Structure.
- an information capturing agent (ICA), responsible for the actual search on the web of potential partners (to be dynamically organised in the Virtual Enterprise according to best fit criteria) and for providing updated information on co-operation opportunities
- a Business Information Integration Module (BIIM), integrating operational functions, that leverage on e-Commerce and Internet technology, and on pre-selected commercial solutions to be configured according to VE requirements.

This chosen architecture allows for achieving a significant independence of selected commercial solutions, which might in time go below leading edge performances and be substituted through emerging technologies.

SELECTED REFERENCES
1. BIDSAVER: The dynamic Constitution and Management of Virtual Enterprises (R Santoro, M. Conte, L. Spotorno), Proceedings of IFIP PRO-VE 2002 Conference pp 545-552, May 2002.
2. Evaluation of benefits and advantages of the Virtual Enterprise approach adoption for Actual Business Cases (R Santoro, M. Conte), ISBN 0-85358-113-4, Proceedings of ICE 2002 Conference pp 19-26, June 2002.
3. The BIDSAVER project, a step forward in the Business to Business relationships between Business Integrators and Enterprises (R Santoro, M. Conte), ISBN 0-9519759-9-4, Proceedings of ICE 2000 Conference pp 29-34, June 2000.

Contributor: M. Conte – mconte@esoce.net

CE-NET II: Concurrent Enterprising Network of Excellence

PROJECT SUMMARY

CE-NET the "Concurrent Enterprising NETwork of excellence" was established in 1997 within the European Commission Esprit Programme, and evolved to a second phase on January 2001 within the IST programme. Its major aim is to develop a well co-ordinated and effective support infrastructure throughout Europe in order to share and exchange the latest developments in the CE domain. CE-Net objectives:

- Promote the concept of Concurrent Enterprising as the implementation of Concurrent Engineering in the Extended Enterprise to a world wide constituency
- Initiate the analysis of current trends and to provide a strategic vision on CE in Europe (long term focus)
- Act as a catalyst for implementation of CE by industry
- ·Collect, categorise and present knowledge on CE to a wide industrial and academic community
- Provide a forum for developing focused initiatives in the CE domain such as special interest groups or groups for international collaboration, for industry and academia

Program: FP5 IST (European Commission)   **Duration:** Jan 2001 – Jun 2004
Consortium: UoN University of Nottingham (UK) [Project Coordination], ADEPA Agence de la Productique (F), BIBA Bremen Institute of Industrial Technology & Applied Work Science, Universität Bremen (D) CEC Concurrent Engineering Consulting (I) CeTIM Center for Technology & Innovation Management (D) University of Cranfield (UK) DTU Technical University of Denmark (DK), ESoCE: European Society of Concurrent Engineering (F) PUB Polytehnica University of Bucharest (Romania), TUT Tampere University of Technology (FIN) UT: University of Twente (NL), VTT Electronics (FIN)

TECHNICAL APPROACH

CE-NET has developed structured and qualified WWW repositories made available for pulling 'distilled' information about CE projects, tools, methods, industrial cases, and organisations. Selected information are pushed by means of a project brochure, regular newsletters and customised messaging for reacting to specific information needs of individual organisations. Conferences and workshops bring together people for formal and informal networking in physical and virtual meetings. In particular CE-NET organise yearly ICE "International Concurrent Enterprising Conference", that is today established as the main European event on Concurrent Enterprising. Special interest groups encourage the nodes to work in dedicated groups on specific subjects. At the end of the EC funding period, the CE-NET community is intended to continue in pursuing its strategic objectives by evolving into a self-sustained Entity. The Knowledge Community ESoCE-Net (European Society of Concurrent Enterprising Network) has been identified as the legal entity instantiating this transition and represents the CE-Net evolution scheme towards the continuous development of the CE community.

MAIN RESULTS

CE-Net is currently made of 37 founding members from 13 European countries, whose composition represent a good balance between Industry, Academia and CE expertise, and associates some 380 members in 35 countries world-wide.

CE-NET develop and update a **CE Roadmap** aimed at monitoring the current business environment and trends, define CE research and development needs and providing a strategic vision for CE in Europe. The current version of the CE Roadmap includes the following major results:

- The CE-NET community established **2010 CE Vision** and the major challenges for CE in the five main areas of the CE domain (Business models & Organisation, Human Aspects , I/C Technology & Infrastructure, Product/service development, Policy and Regulations)
- The identification of **RTD priorities** deemed necessary for covering the gap existing from the current state of CE practices and the CE Vision, along with the evaluation of critical mass for carrying out such activities among the CE-Net community. The RTD areas identified by the roadmap are summarised as follows:
  1. Approaches for better meeting customer value (benefits)
  2. Plug and play approaches for networked organization
  3. Conceptual framework for shared business concepts across lifecycle phases
  4. Methods & technology for Business Scenario Experimentation and validation
  5. New collaboration approaches
  6. Innovative and better Product-Services to meet customer needs
  7. Seamless mobile working environment
  8. Design, deliver & manage concurrency during the Product/Service/Organisation (P-S-O) lifecycle
  9. Business & Management issues during the P-S-O lifecycle
  10. Management of inter-enterprise Knowledge in dynamic networked organizations

SELECTED REFERENCES

To know more about CE-net activities and for joining our Virtual Community please visit the following web sites: http://www.ce-net.org, http://www.esoce.net

Contributors: Prof. Kulwant Pawar – Kul.Pawar@Nottingham.ac.uk
                    Mr. Roberto Santoro – rsantoro@esoce.net

e-COGNOS: Methodology, tools and architectures for electronic consistent knowledge management across projects and between enterprises in the construction domain

PROJECT SUMMARY

The e-COGNOS project specified and developed an open model-based infrastructure and a set of tools that promote consistent knowledge management within collaborative environments in the Construction sector. The resulting prototype emerged from a comprehensive analysis of the business and information / knowledge management practices of the project end-users, and made use of a construction specific ontology that is used as a basis for specifying adaptive mechanisms that can organise documents according to their contents and interdependencies, while maintaining their overall consistency. The e-Cognos web-based infrastructure includes services which allow the creation, capture, indexing, retrieval and dissemination of knowledge. It also allows the integration of third-party services, including proprietary and legacy tools.

Program: IST (European Commission)   **Duration:** Jun 2001 - Oct 2003
Consortium: DERBi (F) [Administrative management], CSTB (F) [Technical coordinator], University of Salford (UK), YIT (FIN), Hochtief (D), Taylor Woodrow (UK)

TECHNICAL APPROACH

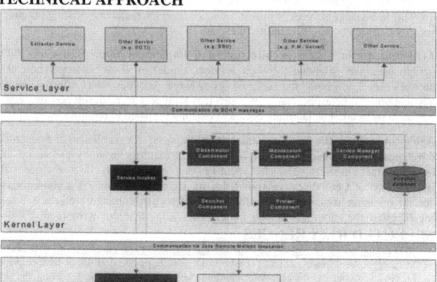

The e-Cognos consortium adopted a service-based approach for the design and development of the infrastructure, whereby the various knowledge management functionalities have been packaged as discrete services, each accessible via the e-Cognos API and brokered by the 'e-Cognos kernel'. The e-Cognos KM core services denotes the services offered as part of the E-Cognos platform. The various service managers define the API's for these services. The actual implementation of a service may be realised by e-Cognos, or by an external third party with the details of its implementation being of no concern as long as the API is adhered to (the service implementations need know nothing about each other and do not communicate directly with each other). Services may be registered with a public UDDI (Universal Discovery Description and Integration) registry and provide useful functionality to third parties without requiring any reference to the rest of the e-Cognos conceptual model. The e-Cognos manager and e-Cognos portal are the end user interfaces provided by the e-Cognos platform. These are delivered through a standard web browser as a web application.

MAIN RESULTS

The most significant results of e-COGNOS include:

Achievements in VE-related knowledge management. e-COGNOS introduced a 'service based' fully web enabled approach which packages internal knowledge management functionality and legacy external applications as e-COGNOS services. These services are accessible and usable by any partner organisation through a secure role based platform.

Achievements knowledge capture and dissemination. The e-COGNOS infrastructure developed several innovative techniques to capture knowledge. It allows the integration of and access to available information and (explicit or implicit) knowledge sources, while at the same time guaranteeing existing practices, security constraints, confidentiality rules, etc.

Achievements in system architecture and implementation. The e-COGNOS system uses and extended the web services model to allow interoperation at a network level of both the internal knowledge services and external legacy applications. Where necessary, web services wrappers were developed for legacy applications in order to facilitate access to existing knowledge repositories.

Achievements on the socio-organizational aspects. In parallel to the technical developments, an analysis was performed simultaneously to study the social and organizational impacts, and to identify the requirements for a successful implantation of a collaborative knowledge management system. As a consequence, special attention was devoted to the study of human computer interface issues, together with the cultural issues inherent in knowledge sharing environment.

SELECTED REFERENCES

1. Knowledge management for the construction industry: the e-cognos project, Wetherill, M., Rezgui, Y., Lima C., Zarli,, ITCON, Vol. 7 (2002), pp 183-193, ISSN 1400-6529.
2. Deploying knowledge management solutions for the construction sector using the web services model Matt Wetherill, Elaine Ferneley, Yacine Rezgui, , proceedings of the European eSM@RT 2002 Conference, Manchester, UK, 18-21 November 2002.

Contributor: Yacine Rezgui – y.rezgui@salford.ac.uk

E-COLLEG: Advanced Infrastructure for Pan-European Collaborative Engineering

PROJECT SUMMARY

The advanced collaborative infrastructure (ACI) for distance spanning, secure tool integration and management, as well as open interfaces for XML-based data exchange have been developed by the E-COLLEG project *(www.ecolleg.org).* ACI combines recent plug-and-play technologies and secure, peer-to-peer data transfer with XML-based tool integration. It has been tested with applications in the field of Electronic Design Automation (EDA). The infrastructure supports engineers in their Internet-based collaboration during the design of complex electronic systems.

Program FP5 IST **Duration:** Jan. 2000 –Dec. 2003
Consortium: Thales Optronique (F) [project coordinator], Siemens Business Services (D), Infineon Technologies (D), FTL Systems UK (UK) (until March 2003), Silesian University of Technology (PL), Institute of Electron Technology (PL), Paderborn University (D)

TECHNICAL APPROACH

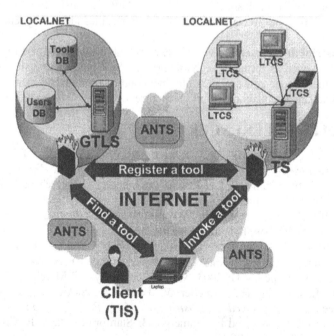

E-COLLEG ACI is based on three core services and a complementary transport service (ANTS) which enables secure firewall-crossing communication between the components. The Tool Invocation Service (TIS) is the interface used by clients to activate remote tools. TIS invokes the Global Tool Lookup Service (GTLS) to discover the appropriate tool for the requested task. The activation of the remote tool is done by the Local Tool Control Service (LTCS) via the Tool Server (TS). Together with the Advanced Network Transport Services (ANTS), the instances of these services form the E-COLLEG ACI infrastructure.

The E-COLLEG ACI core components GTLS, LTCS and TIS, as well as ANTS are implemented as Web Services that are interconnected using the Simple Object Access Protocol (SOAP). The SOAP messages between the components are transported using ANTS. In a general case, all ACI components are on separate machines connected to the Internet. Thus, they need to communicate through an insecure media and all data have to be encrypted and digitally signed by a sender.

MAIN RESULTS

Tool Registration and Management Services enable distance-spanning tool integration. Once registered, tools provide their service for distributed design teams. Advanced service discovery technologies connect to the most appropriate service with respect to optimal availability within the current configuration of the virtual engineering network.

ANTS - Advanced Network Transfer Services provide an abstract data transport mechanism through reliable Request/Response functionality that are mapped to actual transport mechanisms, i.e. SOAP/HTPP or just TCP. They enable collaboration over the firewalls and introduce an abstract addressing schema.

ACI industrial deployments - Various experiments which were performed by ITE and TOSA, as well as Infineon Technologies and SUT have given valuable results and recommendations concerning deployment and further development of the E-COLLEG advanced collaborative infrastructure.

SELECTED REFERENCES

1. Kostienko T., Mueller W., Pawlak A., Schattkowsky T., *Advanced Infrastructure for Collaborative Engineering in Electronic Design Automation,* 10th ISPE Int. Conf. on Concurrent Engineering: Research and Applications, Madeira Island, Portugal, 26-30.07.2003.
2. Proceedings of the E-Colleg Workshop on *Challenges in Collaborative Engineering,* Poznań, Poland, 15-16.04.2003.
3. Mueller W., Schattkowsky T., Eikerling H.J, Wegner J., *Dynamic Tool Integration in Heterogeneous Computer Networks,* Proc. Design Automation and Test in Europe DATE 2003, Munich, Germany, 3-7 March 2003.
4. Bauer M., Eikerling H.J., Mueller W., Pawlak A., Siekierska K., Soderberg D., Warzee X., *Advanced Infrastructure for Pan-European Collaborative Engineering,* E-work and E-commerce, B. Stanford-Smith & E. Chiozza (Eds.), IOS Press, 2001, pp. 686-692.

Contributor: Adam Pawlak, SUT – pawlak@ciel.pl

EKMF: European Knowledge Management Forum

PROJECT SUMMARY

The Project "European Knowledge Management Forum" (European KM Forum) developed and facilitated within the last three years a KM-platform for more than 40 European organisations having a common agenda: The build up of a pan-European web based Community on Knowledge Management.

The objective of the Knowledge Management Forum was to bring together the available critical mass of KM experts in Europe in order to share and exchange the latest developments in the KM domain and to develop visions for the future. EKMF aimed to establish and maintain a well co-ordinated and effective support infrastructure throughout Europe, enabling KM experts to co-ordinate their research activities and to network, both on formal and informal level. One of the major trends in companies applying KM is neither the focus on the individual nor the enterprise, but instead "...on some grouping of people who share common context, stories and passion, around a subject."[CIO 1999]. As this situation is to be scaled up to a Europe-wide situation, EKMF provided a means for individual organisations to find similarly oriented partners to build special interest groups in order to jointly discuss situations and seek for solutions without losing contact to other greater European view on KM, thus profiting from results achieved and experiences made in other European projects.

Program: IST (European Commission)   **Duration:** Jan 2001 – Dec 2003
Consortium: BIBA (D) [Admin. Project Management], Fraunhofer IAO (D) [Scient. Project Management], SIFT (UK) [Techn. Project Management], University of Nottingham (UK), IAT University of Stuttgart (D), Cezanne Software (I), Siemens ICN (D), BOC Information (A), KMI Open Univ. (UK), British Telecom (UK), Atos Origin (F), Ibermatica (S)

TECHNICAL APPROACH

EKMF developed with the KnowledgeBoard of an instrument capable of transparently structuring ongoing KM activities, and evoking energies between these activities in a comprehensive way to make European results on KM methods, instruments and tools available for European companies and research organisations.

The KnowledgeBoard at www.knowledgeboard.com

In the first project phase until August 2002 the work of the consortium was focusing on the set-up of the web based KnowledgeBoard and its first promotion among the European KM Community. As of September 2002 the sharing of knowledge and experiences came to the fore. In order to foster the build up of Special Interest Groups and to support the networking activities among the members of the platform, the EKMF consortium focused its further activities on special themes of interest. Within each month starting from October 2002, the project members focused their activities in online and offline workshops, discussion forums, surveys, keynote presentations and interviews on a dedicated theme. The results of a theme have been wrapped up and published in a dedicated synthesis report.

MAIN RESULTS

The most significant results of EKMF are:

- **Build up of a virtual community on KM with about 5700 registered members in December 2003. At the KnowledgeBoard, over 25 Special Interest Groups and geographical or language Zones evolved.**
- **Development of a new research approach that is potentially improving the integration of industry and academia and that should complement traditional long term research projects: The Interactive Flashlight Research.**
- **PhD students got the opportunity to share knowledge and experiences as well as to discuss insights on KM in three KM SummerSchools.**
- The KnowledgeBoard was bringing developer, researcher and user expertise together in order to achieve a common basis.
- The EKMF consortium stimulated and co-ordinated Special Interest Groups and international collaboration across countries, disciplines and organizations.
- Within this activities, EKMF increased the mutual awareness about existing KM methods and tools and To facilitate the access to these methods and tools and to support training and education initiatives.
- The KnowledgeBoard library provided information services to parties interested in KM and made it possible to collect, categorise and present KM knowledge.

SELECTED REFERENCES

1. Workshop Report from eBeW 2002: How can Europe Lead the Way in KM?. Weber, Frithjof: Available on-line at http://www.knowledgeboard.com/cgi-bin/item.cgi?id=94709.
2. Research in Evolving Domains: A Constructivist View and Practical Approach for Interaction between Industry and Academia. F. Weber, M. Wunram, P. Wolf. *In Proceedings of Echallenges Conference 2003*, Bologna, Italy, 2003.
3. KnowledgeBoard: www.knowledgeboard.com

Contributor: Dr. Patricia Wolf – Patricia.Wolf@iao.fhg.de

eLEGAL: Specifying Legal Terms of Contract in ICT Environment

PROJECT SUMMARY

ICT based information exchange in project based business such as construction and large-scale engineering has become common but is not properly covered by contractual practice. The full use of inter-enterprise ICT is hampered by poorly defined responsibilities, overlapping communication techniques and mistrust. The goal of eLEGAL was to define a framework for legal conditions and contracts regarding the use of ICT in project business.

Program: IST (European Commission)   **Duration:** Nov 2000 – Jan 2003
Consortium: Loughborough University (UK) [Project Coordinator], MASONS (UK), SEIB-ITC (D), OTT (D), GEODECO (It), VTT (FIN), ENeF (FIN), PONTON Consulting (D), Enprima Engineering Ltd. (FIN).

TECHNICAL APPROACH

The figure below shows the technical approach taken in the eLEGAL project.

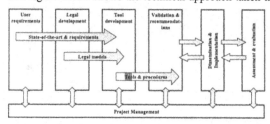

The aim of the project was to enable ICT-based communication to become a contractually valid practice in inter-enterprise collaboration. This was achieved by identifying the state-of-the art technologies, analysing the current and emerging contractual practice, legal conditions and emerging ICT. User requirements were then captured, describing the need for legal and contractual support for ICT based eWork in VOs. Contract clauses were collected and compiled for re-use. Contract configuration logic was explored enabling support tools for contract preparation to be developed. The tools were simulated and tested in a real industrial environment.

MAIN RESULTS

The eLEGAL contractual framework is shown in the figure. It consists of three different agreements / contracts. These are: End User Licences (EUL) – these agreements or EUL protect the software by obtaining users' acceptance of obligations regarding use and distribution.

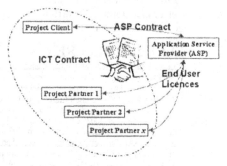

ASP Agreements – the use of project collaboration websites has resulted in the implementation of contracts between the service provider and the organisation that procured such a service for a project.

ICT Contracts – these enhance the operation of a project's ICT infrastructure by providing an agreement that specifies the provision and application of a project ICT environment, and is influenced by many factors – European & National legal & regulatory frameworks, and contractual practices that vary between countries. The eLEGAL contract editor can be used to edit a contract, using the ICT clauses to complete it. The eLEGAL contract wizard provides the basic contract clauses, drawing the appropriate options from the eLEGAL ICT clause library. The most significant results of the eLEGAL project are described in the figure below:

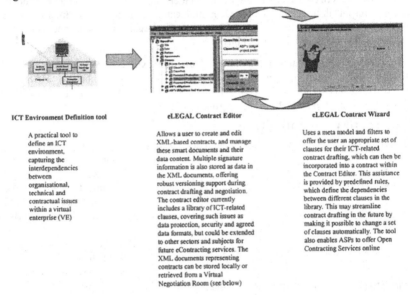

ICT Environment Definition tool	eLEGAL Contract Editor	eLEGAL Contract Wizard
A practical tool to define an ICT environment, capturing the interdependencies between organisational, technical and contractual issues within a virtual enterprise (VE)	Allows a user to create and edit XML-based contracts, and manage these smart documents and their data content. Multiple signature information is also stored as data in the XML documents, offering robust versioning support during contract drafting and negotiation. The contract editor currently includes a library of ICT-related clauses, covering such issues as data protection, security and agreed data formats, but could be extended to other sectors and subjects for future eContracting services. The XML documents representing contracts can be stored locally or retrieved from a Virtual Negotiation Room (see below)	Uses a meta model and filters to offer the user an appropriate set of clauses for their ICT-related contract drafting, which can then be incorporated into a contract within the Contract Editor. This assistance is provided by predefined rules, which define the dependencies between different clauses in the library. This may streamline contract drafting in the future by making it possible to change a set of clauses automatically. The tool also enables ASPs to offer Open Contracting Services online

Also included in the suite is the "Virtual Negotiation Room". This is a management tool that provides information on contract status, potentially encouraging the idea of ASPs offering legal support for e-contracting. The tool allows users to approve or confirm separate sections of contracts by digital signature. The 'Room' paves the way for bilateral and multilateral contract negotiations, where the contract is only in an electronic form. The different parties who want to form a contract are linked together via the Internet.

SELECTED REFERENCES

1. Legal Issues of Collaborative Electronic Working in Construction, C. Carter, E. White, T. Hassan, M. Shelbourn, and A. Baldwin, *Proceedings of the Institution of Civil Engineers, Civil Engineering,* Special Issue Two: Information Technology – The key to Collaboration, November 2002, pp 10-16.
2. The Impacts of Contractual Support for ICT on Working Practices, C.D. Carter, T.M. Hassan, A.N. Baldwin and M.A. Shelbourn, *Proceedings of the eBusiness and eWork Conference,* Prague, Czech Republic, October 2002: Challenges and Achievements in E-business and E-work, B. Stanford-Smith et al. (Eds.), IOS Press, Amsterdam, pp. 602-608, ISBN 1 58603 284 4.
3. The eLEGAL Project: Specifying Legal Terms of Contract in ICT Environment, C.D. Carter, T.M. Hassan, M. Merz and E. White, *International Journal of Information Technology in Construction,* Vol. 6, 2001, pp. 163-174, ISSN 1400-6529.

Contributors: Tarek Hassan – t.hassan@lboro.ac.uk

e-MMEDIATE: Electronic Managing of Product Manufacturing, Engineering, Design and Investment Applying Information Technology for SMEs

PROJECT SUMMARY

The e-MMEDIATE project developed a methodology for setting up and improving virtual enterprises (VE), especially consisting of small and medium sized enterprises (SME), including the selection, implementation and usage of supporting information technology (IT). The consortium consisted of four different VEs from four countries (Italy, Austria, Spain and Germany) whose member companies come from four different branches, namely fashion (Italy), tools (Austria), consumables (Spain), and automotive (Germany). The e-MMEDIATE project successfully demonstrated how the participating VEs could be improved by applying this common methodology in conjunction with supporting information technology (IT). Through the involvement of thirteen partners from different countries and branches and the thereby resulting best practice case studies, this methodology can be easily adopted to other SMEs and used as a general roadmap for enhancing virtual enterprises.

Program: IST (European Commission)   **Duration:** Apr 2002 – Nov 2003
Consortium: Profactor GmbH (A) [Technical coordinator], Consiglio Nazionale delle Ricerche – ITIA (I) [Financial coordinator], ITIA –LAB D&MC (I), Consorzio Centra Veneto Calzaturiero – CCV (I), MITICA srl – Mitica (I), Innovation network austria dienstleistungs-gmbh – INNA (A), Weba Werkzeugbau Betriebs GmbH – WEBA (A), Schöfer Werkzeugbau GesmbH – schöfer (A), ebner-tec GesmbH - ebner-tec (A), SchlumbergerSema sae – SEMA (E), Competitive Design Network - International S.A. – CDN (E), Investigation Total Ware – ITOWA (E), Manufactures de Plastics SOLA, S.A. – Sola (E), University of Stuttgart – IAT (D), Cirp GmbH Informationssysteme und Rapid Prototyping – Cirp (D), Leotech Rapid Prototyping und Werkzeugbau GmbH – Leotech (D), Josef Hofmann Modellbau – Hofmann (D), Modellbau Ralph Kurz – Kurz (D).

TECHNICAL APPROACH

In order to achieve a sustainable improvement for the participating SMEs as well as for the European community, the main challenge and focus of the project was the development of a commonly usable roadmap for VE enhancement. This approach covers all aspects of the entire product development cycle ranging from the negotiations of offers and demands, the clear definition of orders to the product creation and order fulfillment and finally the delivery of the product. It also takes into account the necessity of workflow optimization as well as the identification, selection and implementation of appropriate supporting IT-tools in the sense of eBusiness platforms for data, document, project management and order tracking in order to achieve an improvement of the overall performance of the VEs as a whole and also of course for each individual VE member.

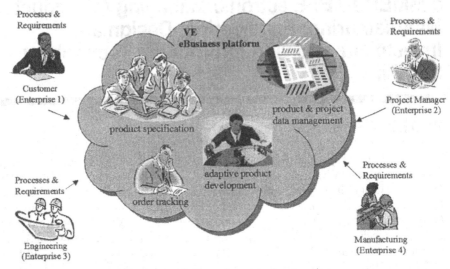

eBusiness platform for virtual enterprises

Based on these requirements and supporting IT-tools, eBusiness platforms (see figure above) have been set up to serve the VE members as a central data and project repository.

MAIN RESULTS

The most significant results of e-MMEDIATE include:

Roadmap for VE improvement: e-MMEDIATE introduced an easily adoptable methodology that can serve VEs (especially SMEs) as a general roadmap to guide them on their way of enhancing their cooperation capabilities and thus helps to improve the overall VE performance.

Best practice case studies: Based on the results of the four different VEs involved in the project, four best practice case studies are available. These studies describe by means of the different individual pre-requisites, requirements and implemented solutions of the project participants the accomplished activities of each VE in detail, including the evaluation of the achievements and first distinguishable improvements of the VE performances.

SELECTED REFERENCES

1. Das virtuelle Unternehmen - Koordination zwischen Markt und Hierarchie, Bullinger H.J., Brettreich-Teichmann, Fröschle H.P., *Office Management 43*, 1995, pp 18-22.
2. Final Dissemination Kit (Deliverable D8), e-MMEDIATE Project Consortium, 2003.
3. Management of Virtual Enterprises: A Case Study of German Rapid Prototyping SMEs, Wagner F., Eichert J., Schirra R., *Processes and foundations for virtual organizations*, 2004, pp 493-500.

Contributor: Jochen Eichert – eichert@iat.uni-stuttgart.de

EuroShoE: Development of the processes and implementation of management tools for the Extended User Oriented Shoe Enterprise

PROJECT SUMMARY

EuroShoE is a research project aimed at a dramatic renovation of the concept of the shoe as a product and of its production, based on the transformation of the first from a mass produced good to a mass customized one; this product evolution goes in parallel with a transformation of the footwear company into an extended and agile enterprise capable of handling the complexity that such a change in the nature of the product implies and of mastering the new challenges deriving from a direct involvement of the consumer in the design and manufacturing process of the shoe he is going to buy.

Program: Growth (European Commission)   **Duration:** Mar 2001 – Sept 2004
Consortium: ITIA - CNR (I) [Admin. and Techn. Management], BALLY (CH), Frau (I), Calana (E), Jefar (P), Lirel (P), LLOYD (D), ECCO (DK), FAGUS (D), Formificio Milanese (I), Centro Servizi Calzaturiero (I), CSM3D (UK), Graisoft (F), Massen (D), STRING (I), ATOM (I), Comelz (I), Molina & Bianchi (I), Torielli (I), PFI (D), Siemens (I), DELCAM (UK), AIB-Technische University München (D), Fondazione Don Carlo Gnocchi-Onlus (I), CIMRU -University of Galway (IRL), ICIMSI –SUPSI (CH) , Fraunhofer IAO, IBV (E), RPK- University of Karlsruhe (D), IFW – University of Hannover, Loughborough University (UK), PMAR- University of Genoa (I), Joseph Stephan Institute (SLO).

TECHNICAL APPROACH

In EuroShoE, a central role was the definition and the modeling of the mechanisms of an Extended Mass Customizing Enterprise - marketing, sales, logistic, production, administration, etc.- with a view to restructure the processes involved in the product life cycles - design, production, distribution, and dismissal. Here, the transformation from manufacturing of mass produced shoes to production of customized (customer oriented) ones, requires a thorough revision of the above mentioned processes. In connection to the new processes of the Extended User Oriented Shoe Enterprise (EuroShoE) appropriate (or new) IT-systems have to be established.

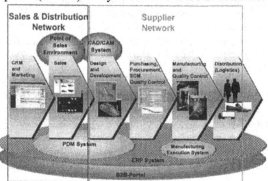

The process for mass customized shoes and the enabling IT system support within EuroShoE

The processes of the 'Extended Mass Customizing Enterprise' (see figure) are very dynamic. The main stream process is the internal process at the manufacturer side. Beside this the interfaces to external partners, suppliers and subcontractors (supplier network) as well as the interfaces to the market/customers (distribution network) are part of the processes. This includes also the workflow management, handling of distributed manufacturing processes, the offer making/order process management and the selection of subcontractors and suppliers. To manage these holistic processes appropriate and integrated IT systems are essential. The process builds the basis for the requirements regarding enabling IT for the process support of the extended enterprise offering mass customized products.

MAIN RESULTS
The most significant results of EuroShoE are:

- **A reference model of the business and operational processes (sale, design, procurement, production, distribution) of the Extended User Oriented Shoe Enterprise.**
- **A set software tools and procedures to select, configure, integrate ERP/PDM/CAD/CAM.**
- **A fully implemented integrated IT infrastructure (ERP/PDM/ CAD/CAM) for the Extended User Oriented Shoe Enterprise**
- A new generation of foot feature capturing devices and camera based foot scanners (NEXGEN, OPTISCAN, WEBSCAN).
- A knowledge based CAD/CAM software for the design of customised shoes
- A variety of new conception, versatile and multi purpose shoe machines and systems.
- A physical and virtual (web based) sale environment for the selection of customised shoes (Point of sales Environment - POSE).
- **An Integrated Pilot Plant in Italy, where all the developed processes, methods, tools and machines are implemented for the validation and demonstration of the Extended User Oriented Shoe Enterprise.**

SELECTED REFERENCES
1. Towards the Extended User Oriented Shoe Enterprise: Enabling IT for the process management of Mass Customization, H.-J. Bullinger; F. Wagner; M. Kürümlüoglu; A. Bröcker, *The Customer Centric Enterprise: Advances in Mass Customization and Personalization;* p. 451-464; ISBN 3-540-02492-1, Springer: New York / Berlin, 2003.
2. Mass Customisation in der Schuhindustrie: Der kundenindividuell gefertigte Schuh, D. Spath, M. Kürümlüoglu, R. Nøstdal, *Marktchance Individualisierung,* XVI, ISBN: 3-540-00594-3, Berlin [a.o.]: Springer, 2003.
3. Enabling IT for Mass Customization: The IT architecture to support an Extended Enterprise offering mass customized products; J: Warschat, M: Kürümlüoglu, R: Nøstdal, Proceedings of the *World Congress on Mass Customization and Personalization,* CD-ROM, Munich, 2003.
4. EuroShoE: www.euro-shoe.net

Contributor: Mehmet Kürümlüoğlu – Mehmet.Kueruemlueoglu@iao.fhg.de

EXTERNAL: Extended Enterprise Resources, Network, Architecture and Learning

PROJECT SUMMARY

EXTERNAL addressed the challenges met when forming and managing Extended Enterprises (EE). An EE or VO is characterized by dynamic, networked organizations and time-limited collaboration between business partners.

The main focus was on developing an EE methodology, a layered intelligent infrastructure, and business solutions for three use-cases. The project provided new ways of doing knowledge engineering, team collaboration, work management and model-based solutions. Two results have already been absorbed in the Computas products, and the AKM Intelligent Infrastructure is a continuation of the EXTERNAL Intelligent

Program: IST- 1999-10099   **Duration:** Jan 2000 – Jan 2003
Consortium: Det Norske Veritas (N) [Project coordinator], Computas (N), Zeus (GR.), Fraunhofer IPSI (D), SINTEF (N)

TECHNICAL APPROACH

EXTERNAL followed the Active Knowledge Modeling (AKM) approach, realizing the AKM technology, for achieving innovative model designed and driven solutions.

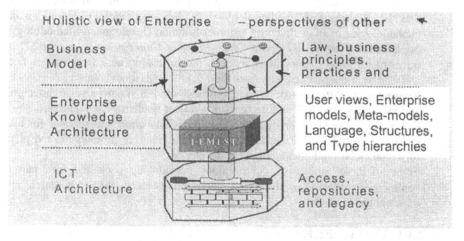

EA knowledge layers integrated, extended and adapted by Intelligent Infrastructure services

The EXTERNAL Intelligent Infrastructure and embedded services (work process tasks) have made it evident that new approaches will soon be provided for development of decoupled business operations, enterprise knowledge management, and ICT solution management developing, delivering and deploying AKM generated customer solutions, and model-driven software production. This will enable concurrent work execution, planning, and management across multiple lifecycles, automating knowledge and solution management.

MAIN RESULTS
The most significant innovative results of EXTERNAL include:

Implementing an Extended Enterprise (Networked Organization) based on new paradigms of the AKM (Active Knowledge Model) technology, exploiting meta-models for enterprise integration and convergence. Opening up new approaches to most areas of Systems Engineering and Industrial Computing.

Implementing Multiple Views of active objects enabling reflective views, recursive processes, repetitive tasks and replicable meta-models, exploiting the true nature of work process (situated) knowledge.

Implementing layered Process and Task Modeling, Task Management, and Work Execution and Monitoring. These process modeling languages and meta-models form the kernel for implementing intelligent infrastructure and services, and model designed and generated solutions with customers.

Applying Model Evolution and Management processes enabled by commercial solutions based on the same core concepts and common meta-models.

Developing Model Building and Management services with constructs to support semi-automatic Model and Meta-model development and management.

Implementing a four-layered Intelligent Infrastructure with open EE formation and operation capabilities for dynamic IT component inclusion, open knowledge representation, and work and model management.

Implementing an EE Engineering Methodology supported by and linked to the layered Enterprise Architecture integrated by Intelligent Infrastructure services. The EE Engineering methodology is a key methodology among many methodologies in an embracing Customer Solution Development Methodology.

Implementing real use cases for Proof-of-Concept and supported by infrastructure and methodology models, demonstrating new working practices and assessing the practical values of the EXTERNAL innovations.

Enterprise Architecture describing business models, knowledge architectures and technology and ICT architectures that reflect implemented solutions

Implementing services for dynamic Solution Generation and services for user environment and workplace design and generation were prototyped, and plans for commercial implementation were developed.

Some of these innovative contributions are already packaged into partner commercial offerings while other contributions need further research and development.

SELECTED REFERENCES

1. Model-Driven Business Operations. E. Dehli, F. Lillehagen and H. Smith-Meyer, ECSQ 2002, Springer LNCS Series, Springer-Verlag, Berlin, Heidelberg, N. Y.
2. Active Knowledge Models and Enterprise Knowledge Management. Frank Lillehagen and J. Krogstie, in Enterprise Inter- and intra-organizational integration, Kluwer Academic Publishers, Kosanke K. et al (ed.), 2002.
3. Computas 2003, Metis Enterprise: http://www.computas.com/metis/
4. AKM Intelligent Infrastructure: http://www.akmii.net
5. The Athena IP: http://www.athena-ip.org

Contributor: Frank Lillehagen, Computas – fli@computas.com

FETISH-ETF: Federated European Tourism Information System Harmonization – Engineering Task Force

PROJECT SUMMARY

The FETISH project designed and developed a horizontal infrastructure to support tourism services in a distributed and heterogeneous context of multiple service providers. Among the considered requirements, special attention was put on the harmonization of tourism service using the Internet. The concept of tourism Value Added Service, which is the result of a multi-level composition of tourism services, was introduced. Both creation / edition, execution and execution monitoring are supported, based on new extensions made to the WfMC (Wofkflow Management Coalition) standards. Another meaningful aspect was guaranteeing privacy constraints brought up by the information exchange and share needs.

Program: 5FP IST (European Commission)   **Duration:** Jan 2000 – Jun 2002
Consortium: T6 (I) [project coordinator], CNR-IASI (I) LEKS (I), FORTHnet (GR), Herzum Software (I), IBIT (E), ICEP (P), Sun MicroSystems (E), University of Amsterdam (NL), UNINOVA (P).

TECHNICAL APPROACH

FETISH followed a service-oriented approach for the design and development of its horizontal infrastructure. Each node within the FETISH infrastructure consists of a toolkit mainly composed by a Service Directory Infrastructure Module – FADA, a Service Catalogue Module – Serv-Cat, and a Process Management System – PROMAN. These nodes provide the needed framework to let each Tourism Service Provider to create a wrapper around its services and connect them, making possible their usage worldwide. All the nodes are also connected to a common FETISH Ontology.

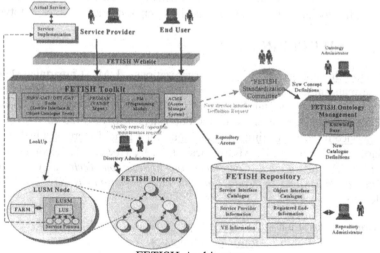

FETISH Architecture

Some important features of the developed infrastructure are:

- Support of Value Added Services – the base for the creation of VE,
- Information privacy guarantee,
- Configurable levels of information access and visibility rights,
- Distributed harmonized service infrastructure,
- Common tourism ontology

MAIN RESULTS

Key results of FETISH-ETF include:

Achievements in VE-related activity coordination. The FETISH-ETF project introduced the Value Added Service (VAS) concept, built up by the composition of lower level VASs or basic tourism services. These VASs provide a hierarchical structure of internet-based services, tourism services in this case, similar to tourism packages provided by travel agencies. (PROMAN prototype)

Achievements in Workflow specification. The FETISH-ETF project introduced extensions to the WfMC (Workflow Management Coalition) standards regarding two additional entities – Split and Join– used to produce more accurate activity graphs – the service coordination workflows, as well as to provide more flexibility in their execution (PROMAN prototype).

Achievements in integrated VE information management. The FETISH-ETF project produced a three tier Federated Information Management System (FIMS), able to store service interface information, as well as to provide search facilities (Serv-CAT prototype).

Achievements in Internet-based Service Infrastructures. The FETISH-ETF project also produced an innovative distributed architecture based on Jini, able to define service interfaces and create implementations in a wide network as internet, providing fast lookup functionalities, based on graph theories (FADA prototype).

SELECTED REFERENCES

1. Service federation in Virtual Organizations. L.M. Camarinha-Matos, H. Afsarmanesh, E. Kaletas, T. Cardoso, *Proceedings of PROLAMAT'01,* 6-9 Nov 2001, Budapest, Digital Enterprise Challenges (G.L. Kovács, P. Bertók, G. Haidegger, Ed.s), Kluwer Academic Publishers, ISBN 0-7923-7556-4.
2. A Service Interface Definitions Catalogue for Virtual Enterprises in Tourism. C. Garita, E. C. Kaletas, H. Afsarmanesh, L.O. Hertzberger, Proceedings of the *5th IEEE/IFIP International Conference on Information Technology for Balance Automation Systems in Production and Transportation - BASYS'2002,* Cancun, Mexico.

Contributors: J. Barata – jab@uninova.pt
                      T. Cardoso – tomfc@uninova.ppt

GENESIS: Global Enterprise Network Support for the Innovation Process

PROJECT SUMMARY

Shortening product life cycles and faster changing technology have led to an enormous need of process and change management methods for technology based firms, which work across and beyond organizational and national borders. It is possible to greatly benefit from development and co-development processes. Business units at Siemens and Intracom use an adapted process management methodology from the BAP project for their innovation process. In the Genesis Project the change performance is measured to provide an all-in-one solution for innovation managers.

Program: FP5 IST (European Commission) **Duration:** July 2000 – June 2002
Consortium: CeTIM (D) [project coordinator], Siemens (CH), Intracom (GR), Adepa (F).

TECHNICAL APPROACH

It is generally acknowledged that firms today face a dynamic environment, changing at an increasingly rapid pace. Virtual and networked organizations are equipped to cope with such dynamic situations better than traditional organizations, as they are designed to behave in an agile manner towards market opportunities.

However, information required to make adequate managerial decisions and make performance transparent is often not available. Existing ERP and MIS systems often do not support controlling and performance management for decisions under uncertainty and in situations of change, like the innovation process.

In Genesis, successful methods and tools from the logistics area have been adapted to conform to the latest thinking in strategic innovation management. The first version of an auditing approach has been developed. The approach has been evaluated in cases provided by Siemens and Intracom.

MAIN RESULTS & RELATIONS TO VO CONCEPTS

The most significant results of Genesis include:

Xtrend – the technology that was initiated in Genesis and later refined in the spin-off firm Xpert SA Switzerland is XTrend, a process-based performance measurement tool that uses a unique real-time data collection process. This data is ideally suited to provide managers with real-time information on for example productivity and performance figures and extrapolations to shape decisions and evaluate the impact of these decisions on future financial results.

Together with VSD, the process design methodology and tool resulting from the BAP project two distinct technologies have been integrated to form a comprehensive innovation engineering and innovation controlling approach.

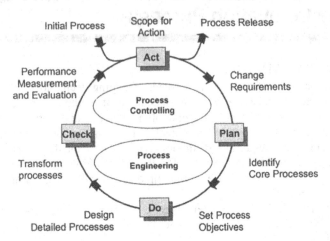

Genesis Process engineering and process innovation controlling approach

The results of the trials showed process productivity improvements in process engineering for new business development and product introduction of 57%.

The auditing tool Xtrend proved fruitful in the provision of ratio's that, when compared over time, can provide insights in the firms capability to deal with dynamic situations. These ratios have been found adequate and useful by the trial firms to enhance their decision making capabilities. By implementing the two technologies this newly created dynamic capability ratio saw an increase of 39%. This finding provides a solid basis for further exploration of such ratio's.

SELECTED REFERENCES

1. Dissel, M. C. (2003), Uncertainty and Managerial Decisions for New Technology Based Ventures, Dissertation at the University Bw Munich

2. Katzy, B. R., Dissel, M. C. (2001), Earnings vs. Innovation; Measuring Architectural Competencies, in: Society, I. E. M. (ed.), Proceedings of the Engineering Management (IEMC), Change Management & the New Industrial Revolution, Albany, NY: IEEE

3. Katzy, B. R., Dissel, M. C., Blum, M. (2001), Measuring Value - Creating Value; A Solution for Process Innovation in High-tech Company Networks, in: Proceedings of the e-Business e-Work Conference, Venice

4. Katzy, B. R., Dissel, M. C., Blindow, F. S. (2003), Dynamic Capabilities for Entrepreneurial Venturing; the Siemens ICE Case, in: Zedtwitz, M. v., Haour, G., Khalil, T., Lefebvre, L. (eds.), Management of Technology: Growth through Business, Innovation and Entrepreneurship, Oxford: Pergamon Press

Contributors: Bernhard Katzy – Prof.Katzy@CeTIM.org and
                    Marcel Dissel   – Marcel.Dissel@ CeTIM.org

GLOBEMEN: Global Engineering and Manufacturing in Enterprise Networks

PROJECT SUMMARY

The aim of GLOBEMEN was to support integration of business and engineering processes executed by a Virtual Manufacturing Enterprise (VME) in a global and multicultural environment. The focus of GLOBEMEN was on one-of-a-kind production, like manufacturing of process and power plants, infrastructure projects or production lines. GLOBEMEN pursued a holistic view to support networking in different life cycle phases of a one-of-a-kind product. To achieve this a reference architecture and methodology called VERAM was developed. VERAM was complemented with guidelines for the set up and management of networks and set up, operation/ management and dissolving of VEs. The research was based on industrial cases, in which also ICT tools were developed and demonstrated.

Program: ESPRIT FP5 IST (European Commission), IMS **Duration:** Jan 2000 – Mar 2003

Consortium: YIT Corporation [project coordinator], VTT (FIN), Fortum Engineering Ltd. (FIN), EPM Technology AS (N), Baan (NL), INTRACOM S.A. (GR), Technical Univ. of Denmark (DK), Bühler AG (CH), ETH – BWI (CH), Toyo Engineering Corporation (Japan), Mitsui Engineering & Shipbuilding Co. Ltd. (Japan), OMRON corporation (Japan), IBM Japan Ltd. (Japan), Hosei University (Japan), JSPMI (Japan), CRC-IMST (Australia), CSIRO (Australia), Griffith University (Australia).

TECHNICAL APPROACH

GLOBEMEN approached the one-of-a-kind manufacturing through the following business processes:

- Sales and Services
- Inter-enterprise Delivery Process Management
- Distributed Engineering

Sales included sales and marketing of one-of-a-kind products in a networked environment. Services focused on supporting the operation phase of one-of-a-kind products, with operation support, preventive and repairing maintenance and renewal or improvement. In the delivery process management the focus was in managing a distributed manufacturing project. Distributed engineering dealt mainly with the information exchange in a distributed environment.

For all business processes the requirements for supporting the operation in a networked environment were identified, tools, methods and guidelines were developed and selected functionalities were demonstrated in company-specific prototypes. The requirements and findings from the different business processes were drawn together ending up with VE guidelines and a reference architecture called VERAM.

MAIN RESULTS

Main results include:

- reference architecture & methodology VERAM based on ISO/DIS 15704 Generalised Enterprise Reference Architecture and Methodology (GERAM).
- guidelines for setting up and operating virtual enterprises
- demonstration of collaboration support tools and business benefits in lifecycle phases of one-of-a-kind procuct

The VERAM architectural framework aims to organise knowledge about the formation and operation of virtual enterprises. More specifically, it:
• supports the operation and set up of virtual enterprises
• organises generic knowledge about virtual enterprise formation and operation
• standardises and utilises those parts of the procedures, tools, and methods which are similar
• results in time and cost-effective virtual enterprise operation
• results in faster set-up of the virtual enterprise
• results in more efficient and effective virtual enterprises

VERAM components are presented in the figure below.

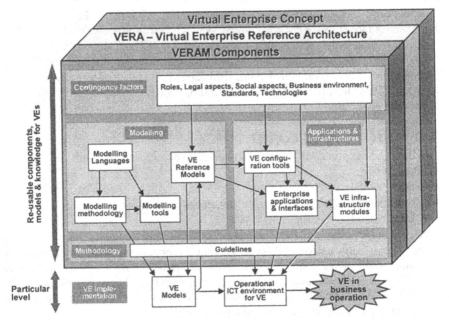

SELECTED REFERENCES

1. Global Engineering and Manufacturing in Enterprise Networks (GLOBEMEN). I. Karvonen, R. van den Berg, P. Bernus, Y. Fukuda, M. Hannus, I. Hartel and J. Vesterager. *In VTT Symposium 2003*, pp. 224 – 395. (http://globemen.vtt.fi)

Contributor: Martin Ollus – martin.ollus@vtt.fi

GNOSIS-VF: Towards The Virtual Factory Delivering Configuration, Scheduling and Monitoring Services Through a Web-Based Client-Server Architecture

PROJECT SUMMARY

The Virtual Factory is a virtual combination of factories that are connected as a virtual manufacturing process that can be designed and operated as a single entity. The idea of the Virtual Factory is to combine high reactivity and maximal efficiency through the optimal use of distributed manufacturing resources. The resources are assigned to a particular order on efficiency and availability consideration alone, without prejudice of their geographical or organisational location. The Gnosis –VF project has developed XML-based prototype tools to support the operation of the Virtual Factory.

Program: ESPRIT (European Commission), IMS **Duration:** Oct 1998 – Jun 2002
Consortium: ILOG (F) [project coordinator], Schroff (D), EMA (F), ADEPA (F) ABB Control (FIN), IAF (D), Delfoi (FIN), SCE (I), VTT (FIN) [technical coordinator], Democenter (I)

TECHNICAL APPROACH

Overall functional design

The general implementation architecture of the Virtual Factory management system is a web-based four-tiered client-server architecture with a presentation layer, an applications layer, a middleware services layer and a data sources layer.

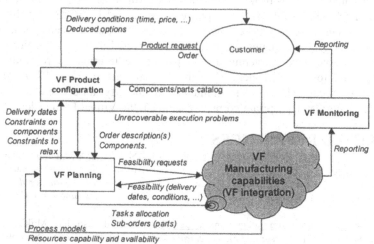

Functional architecture of the Virtual Factory management system

The integration within nodes in a Virtual Factory concerns mostly data access. The VF applications need to access several data sources with proprietary data models. This functionality was not a primary target of development in the project, since many state-of-the-art software tools are already commercially available. The integration between the nodes of a Virtual Factory concerns data exchange and distributed transactions, including remote data access. The transportation mechanism of the messaging depends on the specific virtual factory. Data exchange between sites based on messaging, is the simplest to implement and thus improving the prospect for easy adoption of the approach. The XML format for the messages is recommended.

MAIN RESULTS
VP Planner
The nodes in the Virtual Factory are autonomous: they manage their own internal resources according to their own strategy. As a consequence of the nodes autonomy, there is no common direction or co-ordinated global strategy and there can be no central planning that would be able to optimise the use of all elementary resources involved in the Virtual Factory, possibly as internal resources of a node. A functional module in charge of assigning tasks and deadlines to the individual nodes is therefore required at the Virtual Factory level., the *"VF Planner"*.

VF product configurator
A functional module is in charge of the configuration of the order, in interaction with the Customer and with the VF Planner, the *"VF product configurator"*. The VF product configurator proposes to the customer solutions that are based on the manufacturing capability of the VF network as described in the part or component catalogue provided by the nodes.

VF monitoring
Individual nodes deal with the tasks allocated to them as orders from the Virtual Factory. Each node is thus able to report e.g. expected delivery date, quality levels, delays, through its legacy system, with respect to the tasks allocated to it only. A functional module aggregates the information reported by the single nodes at the Virtual Factory level, extracting and preparing the information relevant for the customer and for the management of the Virtual Factory, the *"VF monitoring"* module. In particular, the VF monitor will identify unrecoverable execution problems and order appropriate corrective action at the Virtual Factory level.

SELECTED REFERENCES
1. Experiences from the development of an XML/XSLT-based integration server for a virtual enterprise type co-operation. Seilonen Ilkka, Nurmilaakso Juha-Miikka, Jakobsson Stefan, Kettunen Jari, Kuhakoski Kalle, *Proceedings of the 7th International Conference on Concurrent Enterprising (ICE 2001)*. Bremen, DE, 27 - 29 June 2001 (2001), 321 - 328
2. XML-based supply chain integration: a case study. Nurmilaakso Juha-Miikka, Kettunen Jari, Seilonen Ilkka, *Integrated Manufacturing Systems*, Vol. 13 (2002), 586 - 595

Contributor: Kim Jansson – kim.jansson@vtt.fi

iCSS: integrated Client- Server- System for a Virtual Enterprise in the Building Industry

PROJECT SUMMARY

The goal of iCSS was the development of an integrated client-server system encompassing all team members in an entire building construction project. This system enables seamless and co-ordinated co-operative work, and on-line as well as temporarily off-line information exchange over the Internet. A basic requirement was the establishment of an adequate information and communication system, so that smaller and medium-sized design companies can form a powerful virtual enterprise, enabling them to be in a competitive position with regard to large enterprises, such as leading design consultancies and contractor firms.

Program: BMBF (German Government)   **Duration:** 1 Jan 2000 - 31 Dec 2002
Consortium: Obermeyer Planen + Beraten (D) [Administrative management], Technische Universitat Dresden (D) [Scientific coordinator], Acerplan Planungsgesellschaft mbH (D), Schmitt Stumpf Frühauf und Partner (D), Thomas Liebich Consulting (D), Anwaltskanzlei Dr. Handschumacher & Merbecks (D), FIDES (D), Planungs- und Ingenieurbüro für Bauwesen (D).

TECHNICAL APPROACH

iCSS was developed as an open system to all persons involved in the building process. The underlying system framework is based on a shared building-model repository, which enables the seamless electronic exchange of any physical data of the building project. Furthermore the co-ordination of decentralised design team members is possible as well as conflict management, transparency of the work progress and distribution of responsibilities.

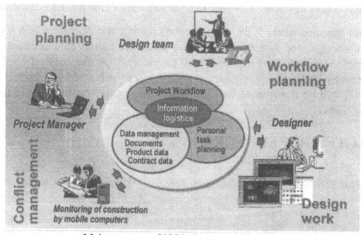

Main concept of iCSS, Roles and Servers

ICSS was implemented as software prototypes based on a multi-tier client server architecture comprising a product model server, a workflow management system, a contract model server and a project document server with corresponding clients.

MAIN RESULTS

The most significant results of iCSS include:

Coordination of the planning processes. The workflow management system developed for iCSS is of high relevance to the operational phase of the VO, since all individual tasks are scheduled in this system and linked to the appropriate project data. Dependencies as well as priorities are stored in the system and possible conflicts will be recognised prematurely and so reactions can be started earlier. The system is divided into two layers separating project specific tasks from company specific tasks, thus internal processes are invisible to other partners and privacy is guaranteed. Furthermore a notification service was integrated into the system to automatically exchange project information.

Conflict management. Planning processes in the building industry are very flexible. Novel or changed situations have to be adaptable by the workflow management system at any time. In case of a conflict it will be observed by the system and processes for the conflict solution will be integrated into the project schedule. iCSS has developed different modules for conflict management and integrated them into the workflow system, the notification service and CAD-System.

Product data management. Projects that are managed by iCSS are based in the IFC product data model (version IFC2x) and supported by a central product data server. This server fosters integrated, product model based work processes by supporting versioning control as well as the extraction of partial models. Thus a consistent data basis for all partners of the VO is provided.

Document management. A new developed document management system (DMS) has been integrated into the over-all iCSS architecture, capable to administrate and manage physical as well as meta data in a relational database. In addition the DMS supports the connection between documents and construction objects. Thus an intelligent access to documents via 3D representation of the model is possible.

Contract management. ICSS supports the creation and operation of a VO with a contract management system. Information about the parties to a contract and their tasks (including dates and payment) will be entered into the contract client, singed by the parties and stored in a contract model. Afterwards, relevant data (e.g. names and tasks) will be transmitted into the workflow management system of the virtual planning team.

SELECTED REFERENCES

1. iCSS – Ein integriertes Client-Server-System für das virtuelle Planungsteam, Juli R., Scherer R. J., *VDI-Tagung 11.-12. April 2002 / Bonn „Bauen mit Computern", VDI-Berichte 1668,* VDI Verlag, Düsseldorf, 2002.
2. Towards a Cross Project Workflow Integration for Multi Project Participation, Scherer R.J., Keller M.: *Proceedings of the 8th International Conference on Concurrent Enterprising (ICE),* Rom, 2002.
3. Modellbasierte Projektkoordination für das virtuelle Planungsteam, Keller M., Scherer R.J. *IKM 2003, Internationales Kolloquium über Anwendungen der Informatik und Mathematik in Architektur und Bauwesen,* Bauhaus-Universität Weimar

Contributor: M. Keller – martin.keller@cib.bau.tu-dresden.de

IDEAS: Interoperability Development for Enterprise Application and Software

PROJECT SUMMARY

The IDEAS project was a thematic network aiming at elaborating strategic roadmaps in the domain of enterprise application and software interoperability and to propose to the European Commission a structure and an organization to support the implementation of these roadmaps in the sixth Framework Programme. IDEAS distinguished three main research themes or domains that address interoperability issues, namely: Architecture and platform, Enterprise Modeling and Ontologies.

Program: IST (European Commission)   **Duration:** Jun 2002 – Jun 2003
Consortium: University of Bordeaux I (F) (Financial and administrative co-ordinator), Graisoft (F) (Technical and scientific co-ordinator), SAP (D), EADS-CCR (F), Baan (NL), INTRACOM (GR), Uninova Lisbon (P), Computas (N), CR-FIAT (I), Formula (I), IC Focus (UK), AIDIMA (E).

TECHNICAL APPROACH

In order to reach its objectives, IDEAS consortium elaborated a state of the art in each of the research domains of the Interoperability study: architecture & platform, enterprise modelling and ontology, to report on the available research efforts, technology and standards (RTS) to support interoperability. The consortium also collected user requirements to express short term desired situation with regard to interoperability.

The long term desired situation was expressed in the vision statements that were collected. The collected vision statements were analysed and harmonised into the IDEAS vision for interoperability statement that was also expressed from various perspectives. The consortium identified also opportunities for the European Industry for the 21st Century, as well as challenges, threats and risks that industry will have to tackle to meet the vision.

Following the consortium perform a gap analysis. The gaps have been identified on the basis of the state-of the Art analysis, User Requirements, Industrial Goal and Challenges and the IDEAS vision. Further, the knowledge base was extended by conducting three gap analysis workshops during which IDEAS members and domain experts were asked to contribute areas in which they see demand in terms of RTS.

The roadmap process that came after concerned with proposing actions to close the identified gaps, outlining the dependencies among the proposed steps and providing a time horizon and priorities concerning the need of the European industry to realise them.

IDEAS consortium felt the need for a reference framework to be used by the various task for interrelating the collected information from many perspectives as well as for facilitating comparison. IDEAS Interoperability Framework (IIF) was defined early in the project to serve this purpose.

MAIN RESULTS

The most significant results of IDEAS include:

State of the Art. IDEAS produced a State of the art comprising three parts: (i) he state of the art on Architectures and Platforms (ii) the state of the art on Enterprise Modelling and (iii) the state of the art on Ontology.

Requirements. The requirements document presents 57 generalized requirements that were derived by synthesizing the requirements specified through the analysis of real life scenarios and the discussions of IDEAS consortium. The document also presents the real life scenarios that were developed to derive IDEAS requirements. For each scenario, its analysis that lead to the requirements specification is also provided.

The Vision for 2010. This document presents the harmonized IDEAS Vision Statement and its instantiation into e-business, e-Government, Solution Provides, Technologist and Research views. The document also presents the collected individual vision statements from IDEAS partners, leading business companies of different categories, leading market research organizations and standardization bodies.

Goals and Challenges of the industry for the 21st century. This document describes the collected, synthesized and structures goals and industrial challenges of industry for the 21st century.

Gap analysis. IDEAS identified 36 gaps by comparing the state of the art with the desired situation expressed through the requirements, Vision and goal statements. A gap is measured as the missing pieces in research, technology and standardization to achieve a particular goal.

Roadmaps and Recommendations on RTS activities. The conducted roadmap process resulted in a five horizontal roadmaps in the domains of (i) enterprise modelling, (ii) enterprise modelling and ontology, (iii) enterprise modelling and ontology and architecture & platform, (iv) architecture & platform and ontology and (v) architecture & platform. In each of these roadmaps time horizon was assigned and a priority of each gap was identified.

IDEAS Interoperability Framework. IDEAS Interoperability Framework was developed in order to facilitate the interrelating the collected information from many perspectives as well as for facilitating comparison. It is based on the ECMA/NIST Toaster Model and ISO 19101 and 19119. It introduces two-dimensional views comprising Interoperability Aspects and Quality Attributes/Extra functional concerns.

SELECTED REFERENCES

All IDEAS results are publicly available at: http://www.ideas-roadmap.net

Contributor: Maria Anastasiou – mana@intracom.gr

ISTforCE: Intelligent Services and Tools for Concurrent Engineering

PROJECT SUMMARY

The major goal of the ISTforCE project was to provide an open, human-centred Web-based collaboration environment maintained by a service provider, which supports concurrent engineering while working on multiple projects simultaneously and offers easy access to specialised engineering services distributed over the Web on rental basis.

Program: IST (European Commission)   **Duration:** Feb 2000 – Apr 2002

Consortium: Obermeyer Planen + Beraten (D) [Administrative management], Technische Universitat Dresden (D) [Scientific coordinator], Cervenka Consulting (CZ), GEODECO Spa (I), Indra Sistemas S.A. (E), CSTB (F), FIDES (D), Aplicaciones de Ingeniería y Formación S.L. (E), AEC3 (UK), Institute of Structural and Earthquake Engineering and Construction IT (SL).

TECHNICAL APPROACH

The consortium has developed a novel human-centred Concurrent Engineering Service Platform (CESP) for multi-project participation that is like an autonomous lean CE system. The platform is capable of docking on servers of different virtual enterprises with a newly developed plugging-in technique, providing access to the electronic market place and supporting e-commerce as a business model. The user-relevant information like product and process data will be kept on the platform, whereas data storage itself will be outsourced.

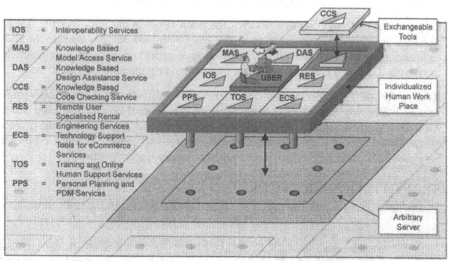

The ISTforCE Concurrent Engineering Service Platform (CESP)

The main innovation of ISTforCE is in the human-centred approach enabling the integration of multiple applications and services for multiple users and on multi-project basis - to support the work of each user across projects and team boundaries.

MAIN RESULTS

The most significant results of ISTforCE include:

Core Information Services (CIS): The functionality of the CIS support the creation and operation of a VO in several ways: (1) assure openness to multi-project, multi-services, so that any other service, can be plugged in and used simultaneously during the collaborative work, (2) CIS provide an infrastructure for identification and communication between people, companies and projects as well as available services that are accessible via ISTforCE platform, and (3) information stored in the core services should be available both through a graphical user interface (GUI) and through and application interface (API).

Personal Planning Service (PPS): Using the PPS coordinating efforts will be optimized and the communication between the project partners improved. The goal of the personal process planning service is to enable the control of multi project participation via interaction with distributed project management systems. Thus, different organizational topologies are supported and multiple alliances are possible.

Project Data Server (PDS): The PDS offers the ability to track the evolutions of the project model data, which is needed to keep a track of its subsequent versions, and to be able to retrieve any of them. Finally, the PDS is based on standards in terms of communication.

Model Access Service (MAS): The primary objectives of the MAS are, (1) to provide customizable and user-friendly capabilities for knowledge procurement and modification of the IFC project model data, and (2) to enable concurrent access to the information on all the projects a user may be working on at the same time. Thus multi level access to standardized project information is provided.

Engineering Ontology Service (EOS): The main target of the EOS was the design and software implementation of an engineering ontology for the domain of civil engineering, which has the primary purpose to support end-users in their practical work with IFC-based project model data in a natural (engineering language) way.

Remote Rental Engineering Services (RES): Five different RES, e.g. the Virtual Testing Laboratory Service, has been developed to support civil engineering tasks. All RES will be launched from the ISTforCE Platform and have access to the project model data. Users of RES will automatically charged by the Electronic Commerce Services (ECS), which offers different business models for accounting.

SELECTED REFERENCES

1. Intelligent Services and Tools for Concurrent Engineering - An Approach towards the Next Generation of Collaboration Platforms, Katranuschkov P., Scherer R.J., Turk Z. *Itcon, special issue,* 2001
2. A Personal Planning Approach for the Integration and Coordination of Multi Project Process Information, Keller, M., Scherer, R. J., Menzel, K., *5th European Conference on Product and Process Modelling,* Portoroz, Slovenia, 2002.
3. Integrated Model Access Service for human-centred engineering, Katranuschkov P. & Gehre A., *eSM@RT and CISEMIC 2002 conference,* Salford, UK (2002).

Contributor: M. Keller – martin.keller@cib.bau.tu-dresden.de

MASSYVE: Multi-agent Agile Manufacturing Scheduling Systems for Virtual Enterprises

PROJECT SUMMARY

The MASSYVE project aimed at developing an agile scheduling system for industrial virtual enterprises (VE), in low cost platforms, and considering its application to SMEs. Multi-agent systems and federated/distributed databases were the main technologies used. Furthermore, the project also developed training tools and methods to facilitate the use of the developed system by SMEs.

Program: INCO-DC (European Commission)   **Duration:** Oct 1997 – Dec 2000
Consortium: UNL - New University of Lisbon (P) [Technical coordinator], CSIN Lda (P), UvA - University of Amsterdam (NL), UFSC - Federal University of Santa Catarina (BR).

TECHNICAL APPROACH

Through the MASSYVE project's approach, both intra-organizational and inter-organizational schedules are generated and supervised via a cooperative and tightly coordinated information exchange among distributed and autonomous agents. At the inter-organizational level, each agent represents one VE member enterprise. In order to enhance the capabilities of the multi-agent scheduling system, each agent is provided with a FIMS (Federated Information Management System) layer through which it inter-operates with other agents. A federated database system is a multi-database system in which every node in the federation maintains its autonomy on the data and defines a set of export schemas that will be imported by other FIMS. FIMS supports the sharing and exchange of information among cooperating autonomous and heterogeneous agents without the centralization and data-redundancy. The figure below illustrates this approach. Consider an example case where a given agent (B) processes some information and generates some results (for example the product-X's actual end of the production date) that is needed to be accessed by another agent (A) who is the VE Coordinator. Then B sends a message to A (step 1), communicating that the data item on product-X's actual end of the production date is available in its local database. This control message sent from B to A informs A that this data item is available and can be accessed by A through its FIMS' *import schema*. Once this message is received at A (1), whenever it wishes A can retrieve this updated information. This access goes as follows: Agent_A queries this information from its own integrated schema in FIMS (2) requesting for the actual end of production date on product-X; an automatic access will occur from FIMS_A to FIMS_B (3) using the federated mechanisms that receives and returns this authorized information from B (4). This information returns to Agent_A for its internal processing (5). The essential concept exploited in that approach is that the *data* is not sent from one agent to the other via a high-level protocol, as in the traditional *push* strategy case, but rather through a *pull* strategy, via accessing to the respective agents' FIMS. This approach presents several advantages, such as i) the agents always access the necessary up-to-date data from its source, at the exact time they need it, and ii) data and control are separated from each other in multi-agent interaction.

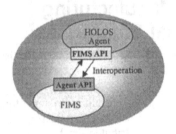

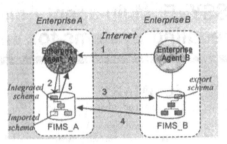

The MASSYVE agent   Exchange of data in a *pull* strategy

MAIN RESULTS
The most significant results of MASSYVE include:

Achievements in agile scheduling systems. Enhancing the definition of agile scheduling towards a VE meant the provision of conditions for enterprises to run under a truly on-line just-in-time system. This involved the design of new coordination methods, new scheduling functionalities, new approaches for information integration, and a high level negotiation protocol to support a more abstract communication with the planning / logistics levels, incorporating business-oriented functions and messages.

Achievements in integrated VE information management. A distributed / federated information management approach was developed, supporting essential VE requirements. The approach included a flexible export / import schema definition and a federated query mechanism.

Achievements in multi-agent systems. A multi-agent tool called MASSYVE KIT was developed to provide a small, easy, and interactive way for the fast development of multi-agent systems applications. This kit was essentially oriented to the education and training activities, although it can be used to develop multi-agent systems for other application domains, using either a socket or CORBA-based communication infrastructure.

Achievements in VE awareness in Brazil. An analysis of the ERP market in Brazil as well as the current enterprises' views, problems, needs and trends were carried out regarding the VE paradigm.

SELECTED REFERENCES
1. Multi-agent-based agile scheduling, R. Rabelo, L.M. Camarinha-Matos, H. Afsarmanesh, *Journal of Robotics and Autonomous Systems,* Vol. 27, N. 1-2, April 1999, Elsevier, pp. 15-28, ISSN 0921-8890, 1999.
2. Infrastructure developments for agile virtual enterprises, L.M. Camarinha-Matos, H. Afsarmanesh, R. Rabelo, in *International Journal of Computer Integrated Manufacturing,* V 16, N4-5, pp. 235-254, ISSN 0951-192X, 2003.
3. Applying federated databases to inter-organizational multi-agent scheduling, R. Rabelo, H. Afsarmanesh, L.M. Camarinha-Matos, in *Multi-Agent Systems in Production,* Ed. by P. Kopacek, Pergamon, ISBN 0 08 043657 9, 2000.

Contributors: R. J. Rabelo – rabelo@das.ufsc.br
                     L. M. Camarinha-Matos – cam@uninova.pt

NIMCube: New-use and Innovation Management and Measurement Methodology for R&D

PROJECT SUMMARY

Focus of this research project was the growing importance of knowledge and its management and measurement as one of the key factors for competitiveness of organisations in the globalisation process of today's economy.

The NIMCube research project was particularly working on a new perspective on the management and measurement of knowledge in organisations, aiming to reduce the so-called phenomena of "reinventing the wheel" which turned out to be a major opportunity for reduction of time and cost and also for increase of quality in the innovation process. Therefore, the main objective of NIMCube was to create a reference model for the evaluation of the quality and the use of knowledge to support the creation of a balance between the reuse of existing and the creation of new knowledge in knowledge intensive areas of today's organizations such as innovation processes and especially in research and development (R&D) and new product development (NPD).

Program: FP5 IST (European Commission) **Duration:** Jan 2000 – Jul 2002
Consortium: Fraunhofer IAO (D) [Admin. and Techn. Management], Cranfield University – Enterprise Integration (UK), Skandia Group (S), Eisenbeiss GmbH (A), Profactor Produktionsforschungs GmbH (A), Commtrain GmbH (CH), Edna Pasher Ph.D. & Ass. (IL), ECI Telecom Ltd.(IL).

TECHNICAL APPROACH

Based on an investigation of existing methods and tools and the analysis through expert interviews and practical requirements, a scorecard model regrouping the indicators into six facets was chosen for further development to handle the high level of complexity and to integrate quantitative as well as qualitative indicators in the methodology (Figure 1). In this scorecard model, the indicators of the innovation process from a knowledge oriented point of view were regrouped in the following facets: Reuse, Invention, Exploitation, Stakeholder's contribution, NPD Performance and Ecology.

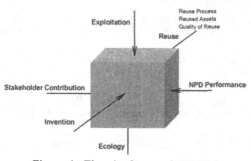

Figure 1: The six facets of NIMCube

In a next step, a modular methodology was built up through the development of a set of methods and tools supporting the process of evaluating the quality and use of knowledge. It mainly consisted of six components as well as a overarching methodology for linking the modules into a holistic change process. The six components that were developed are the following:

- **NIMLight**, an introducing questionnaire, aiming to relevance of the subject for the organization and the organizational focus,
- **NIMRate**, an assessment tool for the identification of improvement potentials in the six facets of the NIMCube scorecard model.
- **NIMStore**, a repository for potential reusable knowledge assets.
- **NIMMeasure**, a methodology for identification of appropriate indicators, measures and metrics in the six facets of the NIMCube scorecard model.
- **NIMSoft**, a software tool supporting NIMStore and NIMMeasure through a knowledge repository database, a hyperbolic navigation structure and an adaptive measurement system.
- **NIMBook**, a guidebook supporting the implementation of the NIMCube methodology.

This modularity enabled a high level of adaptability, the implementation by progressive stages and also the integration of only parts of the methodology in various reference cases.

MAIN RESULTS
The most significant results of the NIMCube research project are:

- The development of **a scorecard model**, regrouping the innovation process into six facets.
- **A reference model** consisting of modular methodology along the implementation process of the NIMCube toolset.
- **An innovative software tool** for storage, navigation and measurement of relevant knowledge assets in the innovation process.
- **A guidebook**, facilitating the implementation of the NIMCube methodology in organisations.
- **A set of reference** cases for cross organisational learning.

SELECTED REFERENCES
1. From Knowledge to Value: Unfolding the Innovation Cube – A Balanced Approach to New Product Development, R. Dvir; E. Pasher; N. Roth; ISBN 965-89454-0-9, Pasher, Israel 2002.
2. An integrated framework for New-Use and Innovation Management and Measurement, N. Roth; J. Prieto; R. Dvir; S. Evans, *Proceedings of Performance Measurement 2000 conference,* Cambridge, 2000.
3. Performance Measurement to Improve Knowledge Reuse and Invention in New Product Development, N. Roth, PhD Thesis, Cranfield University, Bedford, 2002.

Contributor: Sven Schimpf– Sven.Schimpf@iao.fhg.de

OSMOS: Open system for inter-enterprise information management in dynamic virtual enterprises

PROJECT SUMMARY

The OSMOS project specified and developed an open model-based infrastructure and a set of value-added Internet-based flexible services that support teamwork in the dynamic networks of the European construction industry. The resulting prototype emerged from a comprehensive analysis of the business processes and information management practices of the project industrial end-users, which facilitated the development of the OSMOS Generic Virtual Enterprise Process Model from which use cases were extrapolated to specify the technical requirements. The OSMOS web-based infrastructure includes services which allow the creation, capture, indexing, retrieval and dissemination of information. It also allows the integration of third-party services, including proprietary and legacy tools.

Program: FP5 IST (European Commission)   **Duration:** Jan 2000 – May 2002
Consortium: DERBi (F) [Administrative management], CSTB (F), JM (S), Granlund (FIN), University of Salford (UK) [Technical coordinator], VTT (FIN).

TECHNICAL APPROACH

OSMOS followed a service-based approach for the design and development of the infrastructure, whereby the various functionalities have been packaged as discrete services, each accessible via the OSMOS API. OSMOS platform federates services inside a common framework, and allows their use and collaboration. The OSMOS framework handles two categories of Services: Core Services and Third Party Services (TPS). Core Services were implemented as Java Objects and the TPS as Web-enabled applications.

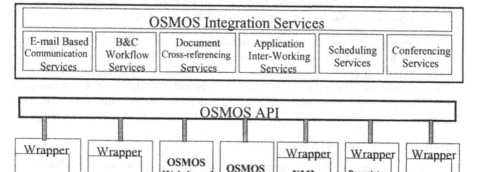

General view of the OSMOS Architecture

MAIN RESULTS

The most significant results of OSMOS include:

Achievements in VE-related activity coordination. OSMOS introduced three distinct roles needed to conduct VE-related activities: VE Service Provider, Third Party Service Providers, and VE Client. VE Service Provider offers its web-based VE service to clients (individuals and/or organisations) via the Internet. Third Party Service Providers offer their own applications and services to clients through the API of the platform provided by the VE Service Provider. This allows the clients to receive a complete VE management service customised to their specific project requirements.

Achievements in integrated VE information management. The OSMOS Information Management model allows the VE to integrate a set of repositories as information datawarehouses and make them accessible to the applications, end-users and OSMOS Services. The OSMOS Information Management Service provides added value to those repositories, by allowing those who take part in projects to locate, then view, all of the information held in a project; to specify relationships between information; to classify information; and to track and manage versioning of information, regardless of the physical location and technical structure of such objects or files.

Achievements in secure communications. The OSMOS infrastructure handles sensitive data via integrated security services providing: management of Actors, both Human and Entity, management and checking of Default Access Rights, management of Projects on the server and management of Project Roles.

Achievements in distributed process management. The OSMOS Generic Virtual Enterprise Process Model was developed from analysis of current business processes and information management practices in the construction VE. The model presents the complete set of processes that may need to be undertaken in providing the VE architecture, and in the creation, operation and dissolution of the VE.

Achievements on the socio-organizational aspects. OSMOS took an iterative testing and validation approach, which included the study of human and organisational impacts, business benefits of the solution, and identification of the requirements to handle BPR, change management and the need for training. A Business process report included recommendations towards the migration from current working methods to the digitally enabled solution proposed and developed.

SELECTED REFERENCES

1. OSMOS: Enabling the Construction Virtual Enterprise, Wilson, I.E., Harvey, S., Vankeisbelck, R., and Kazi, A.S., ITCON, Vol. 6 (2001), pp. 83-110, ISSN 1400-6529.
2. OSMOS Final Report, Rezgui, Y., and Wilson, I.E., (Eds) (2002). Available at http://cic.vtt.fi/projects/osmos/main.html

Contributor: Yacine Rezgui – y.rezgui@salford.ac.uk

PRODCHAIN: Development of a decision support methodology to improve logistics performance of production networks

PROJECT SUMMARY

One of the main objectives of the IST project PRODCHAIN (IST-2000-61205) is to develop a decision support technique and methodology to analyze and improve the logistic performance of globally acting production and logistics networks by guiding SME to successfully integration of business processes into production networks. This guidance takes place with the help of performance indicators.

Program: FP5 IST (European Commission) **Duration:** Mar 2002 – Aug 2004
Consortium: Forschungsinstitut für Rationalisierung (FIR) an der RWTH Aachen e.V. (D) [project coordinator], Micronas GmbH (D), Centre for Enterprise Sciences (BWI) of the Swiss Federal Institute of Technology (ETH Zuerich) (CH), SIG Pack International AG (CH), Possehl Electronic NL BV (NL), Arch Chemicals NV (B), ICON Gesellschaft fuer Supply-Chain-Management mbH (D), Sony Espana, S.A. (E), Aachener Demonstrationslabor für Integrierte Produktionstechnik GmbH (D), Consiglio Nazionale delle Ricerche (ITIA-CNR) (I), Zanussi Elettromeccanica S.p.a. (I), MASMEC S.R.L. (I).

TECHNICAL APPROACH

The PRODCHAIN project develops a toolbox, which gives significant support, especially for SME, in reorganizing their customer-supplier business processes to the needs of nowadays globally acting production networks. The toolbox incorporates best practices for typical customer-supplier-relationships and company types, which can be determined due to company characteristics and performance indicators.

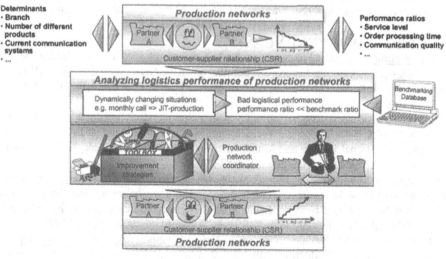

PRODCHAIN Toolbox

MAIN RESULTS
The most significant results of PRODCHAIN include:

Achievements in VE-related organisation. PRODCHAIN investigated various
types of VE in the production environment, ranging from Engineer-to-Order to
Make-to-Stock. The focus of PRODCHAIN has been the organization of the
customer-supplier relationships between various types of companies in the VO and
the integration of their business processes. Hereby, special attention has been given
to the most critical inter-company business processes and how they effect the overall
effectiveness of the production network.

Achievements in VO modelling. The PRODCHAIN project modeled entire
production networks in order to understand the processes within the networks. The
outcome has been the PRODCHAIN model, a generic model, which is based on the
SCOR methodology of the Supply Chain Council. The model, which is a
decomposition of processes is needed to form the performance measurement system
accordingly and to achieve precise definitions of performance indicators.

Achievements in performance measurement. While pursuing the improvement of
the logistic performance of globally acting production and logistics networks, the
focus of PRODCHAIN has been on the measurement and improvement of the inter-
company logistic performance, i.e. the logistic performance of customer-supplier
relationships and of the network itself, and not only the isolated performance of a
single company. A performance measuring system has been developed, which takes
into account the various types of companies in a supply chain.

Achievements on benchmarking. In parallel to the definition of a performance
measurement system a benchmarking study has been conducted to build up a
benchmarking database. This benchmarking study has been an anonymous
benchmarking, which takes the different characteristics of the product, the market
and the companies into account. The benchmarking database enables a comparison
of networks across different branches and types of manufacturing systems.

SELECTED REFERENCES
1. Supporting Enterprise Engineering in Production Networks. Stich. V. Weidemann, M.;
   Roesgen, Robert; In: Enterprise Engineering in the Networked Economy. (Weber
   F., Pawar K. S., Thoben K.-D. – Editors) CRi Digital, Nottingham 2003, pp.
   475-478.
2. Business Process Integration of Customer-Supplier-Relationships in Production
   Networks, Schumacher R.; Weidemann, M.; In: Human Factors in
   Organisational Design and Management – VII (Luczak H., Zink, K.J. – Editors)
   IEA Press Santa Monica 2003, S. 287-292.
3. Decision Support for improvement of logistics performance in production
   networks. Stich, Volker; Weidemann, Martin, In: Challenges and Achievements
   in E-business and E-work, Brian Stanford-Smith, Enrica Chiozza, Mireille Edin
   (Eds.), ISBN 1 58603 284 4. IOS Press, Amsterdam 2002, pp. 638-645.
4. PRODCHAIN: Development of a decision support methodology to improve
   performance in production networks. WWW page. http://www.prodchain.net.

Contributor: M. Weidemann – wei@fir.rwth-aachen.de

PRODNET II: Production Planning and Management in an Extended Enterprise

PROJECT SUMMARY

The PRODNET project designed and developed a prototype of an open horizontal infrastructure to support industrial virtual enterprises. Among the design requirements, special attention was put on flexibility, the need to cope with the heterogeneity of legacy systems, and the integration of available and emerging standards. One of the main aspects considered was the flow of orders between nodes and the monitoring of their evolution. The focus of this work was set on the specific needs of the small and medium size enterprises (SME) that may constitute a VE, but the achieved results can be as well applied to large companies.

Program: ESPRIT (European Commission) **Duration:** Oct 1996 – Oct 1999
Consortium: CSIN Lda (P) [Administrative management], New University of Lisbon (P) [Technical coordinator], University of Amsterdam (NL), Federal University of Santa Catarina (BR), ESTEC Lda (P), Lichen Informatique (F), Miralago SA (P), ProSTEP (D), Herten (BR), UNINOVA (P).

TECHNICAL APPROACH

PRODNET followed a transaction-oriented approach for the design and development of its horizontal infrastructure. Each node within the PRODNET infrastructure consists of two distinct Modules; namely the *Internal Module* and the *PRODNET Cooperation Layer* (PCL). The Internal Module represents the various legacy systems and applications that run at the enterprise, such as ERP, CAD, and PDM systems, other engineering tools, etc. The PCL is the main component of the infrastructure and is responsible for supporting all interactions among VE partners.

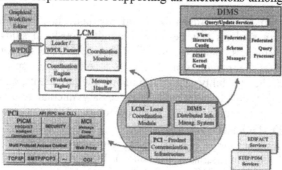

Main components of the PRODNET Cooperation Layer

Among others, some important features of the developed infrastructure are the support of safe communication, guarantee of information privacy and configurable levels of information access and visibility, support for EDIFACT and STEP standards and interoperability between these two standards, identification and development of necessary extensions to legacy systems such as an ERP system in order to operate in a VE environment, support for exchange of quality-related information, and orders status monitoring and follow up.

MAIN RESULTS

The most significant results of PRODNET include:

Achievements in VE-related activity coordination. PRODNET introduced a multi-level (hierarchical) activity coordination approach, that addresses the coordination problem at different levels of abstraction. Three levels were introduced in the developed architecture: the core activities coordination, the enterprise level (VE member) activity coordination, and the VE level (joint) activity coordination. In terms of implementation, an extended workflow-based engine was developed.

Achievements in integrated VE information management. An innovative distributed / federated information management approach was developed, which proved to provide particularly attractive features addressing some challenging information management criteria such as the openness, autonomy, heterogeneity, and information privacy, which are the main pre-conditions for trust building among SMEs involved in a VO domain. The approach includes a flexible export / import schema definition and a federated query mechanism.

Achievements in secure communications. The PRODNET communication infrastructure offers to the enterprise applications a transparent access to a diversified set of communication resources, increasing availability and contributing to reduce the communication costs. Message privacy, message integrity, and the guarantee of enterprise/users authentication for the communication between different enterprises are among the main features.

Achievements in distributed business process management. A knowledge-based decision support system provides an advanced distributed business processes (DBP) coordination functionality including DBP monitoring, conflict detection and support for conflict resolution, simulation and assessment of alternatives, and intra-organizational analysis of the VE in operation.

Achievements on the socio-organizational aspects. In parallel to the technical developments, an analysis was performed simultaneously to study the social and organizational impacts, and to identify the requirements for a successful implantation of the VE paradigm in SMEs. As a consequence, special attention was devoted to both the flexibility and configurability requirements, and to the study of required enterprise staff training and the necessary internal re-organization in the enterprise, in order to prepare for the implantation of a VE solution.

SELECTED REFERENCES

1. Infrastructures for Virtual Enterprises – Networking industrial enterprises, (L.M. Camarinha-Matos, H. Afsarmanesh – Editors), Kluwer Academic Publishers, ISBN 0-7923-8639-6, IFIP Vol. 153, Sep. 1999.
2. Hierarchical Coordination in virtual enterprise infrastructures, L.M. Camarinha-Matos, H. Afsarmanesh, C. Lima, *Journal of Intelligent and Robotic Systems*, Vol. 26, Issue 3/4, pp 267-287, Nov. 99, ISSN 0921-0296.
3. Flexibility and safety in a web-base infrastructure for virtual enterprises, L.M. Camarinha-Matos, H. Afsarmanesh, A. L. Osório, *International Journal of Computer Integrated Manufacturing* (Taylor & Francis), Vol. 14, N. 1, Jan 2001, pp 66-82.

Contributors: L. M. Camarinha-Matos – cam@uninova.pt
H. Afsarmanesh – hamideh@science.uva.nl

PROMINENCE: PROMoting Inter-European Networks of Collaborating Extended Enterprise

PROJECT SUMMARY

Many European SMEs within Extended Enterprises (EE) producing complex products have strong relations/networks with suppliers from countries in central Europe. Concerned EEs face enormous challenges during their daily multi-national orientated work. Anything that stops the flow of information, materials and money within a project between suppliers, partners, customers and employees will reduce their effectiveness and at the end their market share and in the future this context will be even more important because the decreasing slope of wages in Europe forces European EEs to orient themselves towards other low cost countries. Hence eastern partners of the EEs need to build up new competitive advantages in order to stay in the market as this development takes place. Prominence is focused on the management of Extended Enterprises that are established with small and medium-sized enterprises (SMEs) from eastern and western Europe. During the project, tools and methodologies are developed, that are targeted to help these companies managing their business in a more effective and profitable manner. Thereby the objective of Prominence is to give potential support to manage above mentioned challenge by a project managing software tool in connection with an e-business application, reachable and traceable via internet/intranet by all involved parties within an EE.

Program: Growth (European Commission)   **Duration:** Apr 2002 – Mar 2005
Consortium: SchlumbergerSEMA (E) [Administrative and Technical Management], LEOTECH Rapid Prototyping und Werkzeugbau GmbH (D), Cirp Informationssysteme und Rapid Prototyping GmbH (D), Centre for Computational Continuum Mechanics C3M (SL), Zanussi Elettromeccanica S.p.A. (I), FHP-Motors Hungary Kft (H), Moxy Engineering AS (N), Comelf SA (RO), RAAL (RO), ISOFIX S.L. (E), GOOD WORK (PL), University Stuttgart, Institute for Human Factors and Technology Management (D), Consiglio Nazionale delle Ricerche, Istituto di Tecnologie Industriali e Automazione (I)

TECHNICAL APPROACH

In Prominence a user and problem-oriented approach for the identification and evaluation of specific management areas for the extended inter-European SME was chosen.

1. Starting point is a survey and a collection of best practices of network of companies that are collaborating with modalities that are close to those experienced by the inter-European extended enterprises addressed by the Prominence project. The survey acts as a guideline and a starting point for the clear definition of the problem and for the conception of the improving methodologies.

2. Development and implementation of a set of management methods: A method concerning organizational perspectives for the implementation of one coherent and common working culture within the project involved extended enterprises, including strategic planning, project management and operational decision making. The

strategic planning includes future goals and decision of the direction of the long term planning. The project management speaks about an efficient management of project related work and project related goals, resource and capacity management and finally the operational decision making concerning management of the current needed action for running the daily business. A method concerning the collaboration and contains the initiation and establishment of the knowledge sharing, communication & organization and people & culture within the extended enterprise involved in the project, to let them grow together. The knowledge sharing covers information about common needs, standards, knowledge basis, agreements on exchange of information and ensuring the match of competencies. When we talk about communication & organization, the method includes distribution of responsibilities, contact persons, forms of communication, structural transparency and participation. People & culture contains aims for national and corporate culture, trust and commitment, the working together, team building perspectives and personal interactions. And third a logistical method for the implementation of an efficient logistic system between/within the extended enterprises involved in the project.

3. EE collaboration software tool (PRO-MAT): It is configured as an appropriate project managing software tool in connection with e-business application, operating over the Internet for the connection of all the companies within an extended enterprise. The software application gives solution to the detected extended enterprises issues and covers functionalities like project management, know-how transfer, logistics, communication and cultural management, system integration, orders and suppliers within Extended Enterprises.

MAIN RESULTS

The main contents and results of the project are:

- A Framework for the establishment and development of EEs in the defined environment
- A Best Practise Report on management and organisation of inter-European Extended SMEs
- Methodology and Reference model for the management of the Extended Enterprise
- A Software application designed to operate over the Internet for the support of the information exchange, the management of collaborative projects and the transfer of knowledge among the partners of the EE.

SELECTED REFERENCES

1. Prominence Project-Promoting Inter-European Networks of Collaborating Extended Enterprises. Boér CR, Bosani R, Dold C, Mauro P, Nøstdal R, Pierpaoli F, Ristol Jorba S. *In Proceedings of the ACS'02 - SCM Conference, October 23-25, Poland,* 2002
2. DEVELOPMENT AND MANAGEMENT OF EAST-WEST EUROPEAN EXTENDED ENTERPRISES, C. Dold, P. Mauro, R. Nøstdal, F. Pierpaoli, *Processes and foundations for virtual organization*; p. 467-474; ISBN 1-4020-7638-X, Kluwer Academic Publisher: Boston et al., 2004.

Contributor: Rita Nøstdal – rita.noestdal@iao.fraunhofer.de

Symphony: An integrated Set of Methods and Tools for Strategic and Operative Business Management Support for Knowledge-based, Adaptive SME

PROJECT SUMMARY

Symphony is an EU & Intelligent Manufacturing Systems (IMS) endorsed project which intends to provide SME, start-up companies and modular units of bigger companies with a dynamic management methodology with modular and integrated methods and tools that enable them to adapt rapidly to market, customer needs and technological changes. The Symphony project specifically addresses the needs of high-tech or service-oriented companies with a high amount of information in their value chain. These firms often operate in changing environments with high competitive pressure, forcing them to be knowledge-based and adaptive in order to build and to sustain competitive advantage.

Program: FP5 IST (European Commission), IMS **Duration:** Dec 2001 –Nov 2004
Consortium: Fraunhofer IAO (D) [Admin. and Techn. Management], CCSO (CH), ITIA - CNR (I), Universität Stuttgart (D), Cegos (F), Festo (D), GIC (D), IMIG (D), Eden Telecom (IL), Masmec (I), TTS (I), Cactus (E), CDN (E), Cézanne (I), Duvoisin-Groux (CH), Icare (CH), University of South Australia (AUS), Ecosol (AUS), CAMMS (AUS), E-Poly (CA).

TECHNICAL APPROACH

Due to new and far-reaching developments such as the emergence of networked organizational structures, information and knowledge-intensive markets and the further acceleration of business processes, SME are forced to take strategic decisions more often and in a more accurate way. For several reasons, strategic planning and implementation activities are barely formalized and often neglected in SME. This is where Symphony sets in. More specifically, its methods and tools should enable the target group to build and sustain competitive advantage in two ways:

- By understanding and assessing their position within the 'new' knowledge-based economic landscape, by enabling them to take the right strategic decisions and therefore to enhance their individual capacity to adapt.
- By growing and leveraging their internal (intangible) assets to exploit upcoming market opportunities, taking into account the fact that inter- and intra-firm networking have growing importance.

The first step iteration towards new tools and methods began with a review of state-of-the-art management concepts designed for SME as well as with a collection of good practices and new requirements for Symphony's industrial partners.

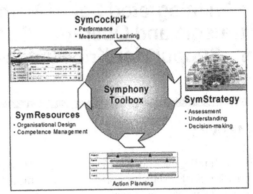

Figure 1: Overview Main Symphony Modules

The management toolbox itself is focused on a number concrete strategic problems that SME need to resolve (e.g. which resources to invest in). It is organized in a process-oriented way along a simple learning cycle (assess, decide, implement, monitor) to make it as user-friendly and comprehensive as possible. In contrast to other contemporary toolsets, Symphony guides SME not only through the decision-making process, but also facilitates the implementation and monitoring processes. Depending on the circumstances of the individual company, it is possible to use only parts of the toolset, if other tools/methods are already in use.

MAIN RESULTS

- A best practice study giving a differentiated overview on needs and constraints of knowledge-based, adaptive SMEs;
- SymStrategy - A collection of methods that facilitate strategy development and implementation for SME through a guided decision-making process.
- SymResources - An IT tool that enables SME managers to design their organisations according to their strategic goals, taking into account the development of the internal competencies and the organisation's integration into networks.
- SymCockpit - An IT tool that allows managers to assess the firm's current and past performance and potentials with regard to adaptability.
- A pragmatic implementation methodology to support an easy and time- and cost efficient implementation of the Symphony methods and tools.

SELECTED REFERENCES

1. A dynamic management methodology with modular and integrated methods and tools for knowledge-based adapted SMEs IMS project SYMPHONY; Meier,C.; Jehle, P.; Affolter, I.; Brouyère, L.; Merino, E.; Sciboz, L.; Roth, N.; Prieto, J.; Kemp,J. (2000): in: E.business: Key issues, Applications and technologies, edited by B. Stanford-Smith and P.T. Kidd., p. 680-686, IOS press, Amsterdam, 2000.
2. Symphony: www.symphony-village.org

Contributor: Mehmet Kürümlüoğlu – Mehmet.Kueruemlueoglu@iao.fhg.de

TeleCARE: A Multi-Agent Tele-Supervision System for Elderly Care

PROJECT SUMMARY

The IST TeleCARE project aimed at the design and development of a configurable infrastructure and a set of vertical services to support virtual communities in elderly support. The envisioned concept is the support for an integrated elderly care system, which consists of a number of organizations such as care centers / day centers, health care institutions, social security institutions, involving the cooperation of a number of human actors e.g. social care assistants, health care professionals, elderly people, and their relatives.

Program: IST (European Commission)   **Duration:** May 2001 – Apr 2004
Consortium: UNINOVA (P) [project coordinator], University of Amsterdam (NL), RoundRose Associates (UK), SKILL sa (E), Camera de Comercio de Navarra (E), Synkronix Ltd (UK).

TECHNICAL APPROACH

The TeleCARE approach resorts at the base to the Internet and mobile-agent technologies combined with a federated information management system. The following block diagram shows the TeleCARE infrastructure to support collaboration in the elderly care virtual organization. The *Basic Platform* is installed at each node of the TeleCARE network. The *Specialized Components* (vertical services) have a distributed implementation over the TeleCARE network.

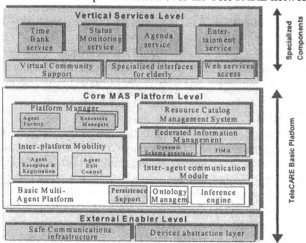

Main components of the platform: *External Enabler Level:* Supports the communication over the network and interfacing to the external (local) devices. *Core MAS Platform Level:* It is the main component of the basic platform. It supports the creation, launching, reception, and execution of stationary and mobile agents as well as their interactions. It also supports the storage and manipulation of distributed data and information, and provides a catalog of all devices and services supported in TeleCARE. *Services Level:* This is the application level.

MAIN RESULTS

The most significant results of TeleCARE include:

Achievements in virtual community. TeleCARE introduced the concept of professional virtual community (PVC) in the elderly care domain, contributing to support the concept of active aging. The specificities of the domain were taken into account when designing a support infrastructure and PVC-based vertical services.

Achievements in mobile agents platform. In order to cope with the privacy and robustness requirements of this application domain, several extensions were introduced in the AGLETS mobile agents platform, namely: some level of support for agents persistency, multi-level safety mechanisms (VPN, passport, biometric users' authentication), high-level mechanisms for agents localization and inter-agents communication.

Achievements in federated information management. TeleCARE combined the federated information management and the mobile agents paradigms rendering a novel architecture for distributed information management. This system shows a high degree of flexibility in terms of information visibility / access rights specification and enforcement, and federated query processing. Dynamic schema generation out of high-level ontologies is another important feature.

Achievements in services and resources cataloging. TeleCARE adopted a unified approach to catalog and grant access to services and resources following the WSDL (services) and UPnP (devices) standards.

Achievements in vertical services. A number of vertical services – e.g. life status monitoring, agenda reminder, time bank, entertainment – were developed using a truly distributed mobile-agent / federation based approach. Remote deployment of services and multi-user interfaces (for different kinds of users) are included. An integration between multi-agent and web server technologies is also developed.

SELECTED REFERENCES

1. Design of a virtual community infrastructure for elderly care, L. M. Camarinha-Matos, H. Afsarmanesh, *in* "Collaborative Business Ecosystems and Virtual Enterprises", Kluwer Academic Publishers, ISBN 1-4020-7020-9, May 2002.
2. A multi-agent based platform for virtual communities in elderly care, L. M. Camarinha-Matos, O. Castolo, J. Rosas in *Proceedings of ETFA '03 – 9th Int. Conf. On Emerging Technologies and Factory Automation*, ISBN 0-7803-7937-3, pp 421-428, Lisbon, Portugal, 16-19 Sept 2003.
3. TeleCARE: Collaborative virtual elderly support communities, L. M. Camarinha-Matos, H. Afsarmanesh, *Proceedings of TELECARE 2004*, Porto, Portugal, 13 April 2004.

Contributors: L. M. Camarinha-Matos – cam@uninova.pt
H. Afsarmanesh – hamideh@science.uva.nl

THINKcreative: Thinking network of experts on emerging smart organizations

PROJECT SUMMARY

The IST THINKcreative project aimed at identifying and characterizing emerging collaborative organizational forms, their required infrastructures, modeling formalisms, and software tools, as well as their associated socio-organizational, ethical and moral changes, within the time frame of 5, 10, and 15 years. Understanding the structure and associated behavior of these new collaborative forms as well as the required infrastructures, support tools, regulations and operating principles, economic models, and support institutions, are major research challenges. Motivated by these challenges, the THINKcreative project was launched as a "thinking network of experts on emerging smart organizations".

Program: FP5 IST (European Commission)   **Duration:** Jun 2001 – Mar 2004
Consortium: UNINOVA (P) [project coordinator], University of Amsterdam (NL), RoundRose Associates (UK), FhG-IAO (D), CAS Software (D), Czech Technical University (CZ), CeTIM (D), FhG-Fokus (D), Cranfield University (UK), Skandia (S), INESC P (P).

TECHNICAL APPROACH

This work is coordinated by a core team of 11 experts covering a wide spectrum of complementary expertise, including among others: VOs and collaborative systems, interoperation, knowledge and information management, software engineering, business process modeling, economy and management, social and ethical issues, and electronic business. Through a number of activities – focused workshops, regional workshops, discussion forum and panels, and a Delphi survey, a large number of other international experts and European industry leaders and visionaries were involved in the process.

THINK*creative* uses an adaptation of Delphi, combining the permanent core experts of the consortium with a large panel of experts gathered from different regions in Europe, as one of the instruments to identify major trends and likely future scenarios in collaborative forms. The panel of respondents was formed by 135 experts from industry (69 %) and academia (31 %), from the following countries: Portugal, Germany, The Netherlands, UK, Switzerland, Belgium, Czech Republic, Slovakia, France, Italy, and Sweden. A few participants from Mexico and USA were also involved in the survey.

A second mechanism to identify trends in organizational forms and related research needs was the organization of a series of workshops and discussion panels. These events were organized as consortium meetings (5) involving invited external experts, panels associated to international conferences (2), or as regional workshops (10) involving local industry and academic visionaries. In particular through the regional workshops, it was possible to involve more than 400 participants that otherwise would not travel abroad to attend any event in a major European city.

MAIN RESULTS
The most significant results of THINKcreative include:

Achievements in ICT infrastructures. THINKcreative identified the need for technology-independent reference models for support infrastructures of collaborative networked organizations, providing the framework for technical, organizational, and semantic interoperability. Multi-agent technology constitutes a promising contributor to the development of support infrastructures and services. Internet and web technologies, namely web services, represent a fast growing sector with large potential in inter-enterprise collaboration support but further developments in terms of supporting multi-party collaboration are necessary. A number of other emerging technologies e.g. grid, wireless communications, pervasive computing, location-aware and situation-aware environments for mobile users, are likely to provide important contributions but public funded research should avoid approaches that are too-biased by existing technologies.

Achievements in non-technologic areas. THINKcreative identified a set of research challenges in the socio-economic, organizational, and ethical areas. Topics such as entrepreneurship in creative economy, mechanisms to support creativity and innovation, planning and controlling organization performance, understanding emerging behavior, new business ethics and morality, are suggested.

Achievements in theoretical foundation. THINKcreative identified the urgent need to establish a sound theoretical foundation for collaborative networks. This foundation can start with theories and models developed in other disciplines, e.g. multi-agent systems, complexity theories, self-organizing systems, graph theory, network analysis and game theory, formal engineering methods, formal theories, temporal and modal logic, semiotics, dynamic ontologies, metaphors, and others. As no single formal modeling tool / approach adequately covers all modeling perspectives / needs in collaborative networks, interoperability among models is necessary. Given the increasing importance of the human aspects in collaborative networks, a new foundation for modeling social aspects is also required.

The results of THINKcreative are synthesized in a "green book" [1] that represents a suggested research agenda for collaborative networked organizations.

SELECTED REFERENCES
1. Collaborative Networked Organizations – Research agenda for emerging business models, L. M. Camarinha-Matos, H. Afsarmanesh (Eds.), Kluwer Academic Publishers, Mar 2004.
2. New collaborative organizations and their research needs, L. M. Camarinha-Matos, in Proceedings of PRO-VE'03 – Processes and Foundations for Virtual Organizations, Kluwer Academic Publishers, Oct 2003.
3. Towards a foundation for virtual organizations, L.M. Camarinha-Matos, A. Abreu, in Proceedings of Business Excellence 2003 – 1st Int. Conference on Performance measures, Benchmarking, and Best Practices in New Economy, Guimarães, Portugal, 10-13 Jun 2003.

Contributor: L. M. Camarinha-Matos – cam@uninova.pt

VDA: Virtual Destination Application

PROJECT SUMMARY

The main objective of the VDA project is to prove the technical viability of using a 3-D model of a tourist destination for its marketing and B2C-commerce of services: The possibility of visiting a famous destination through the Internet does motivate interest of the potential tourist for the presented destination. More importantly, it is possible to use VDA to offering entirely new products and services and thus create new markets and business models for the service industry. With VDA especially SMEs can directly offer services to worldwide customers, or become part of a value chain or service network for target groups like e.g. business travels or snowboarders.

Program: FP5 IST (European Commission)   **Duration:** Jan 2001 – Sep 2002
Consortium: CeTIM (D) [project coordinator], Institute for tourism and leisure, Chur (CH), Davos Tourismus (CH), Rothenburg Tourismus (CH), Echtzeit GmbH (D), Hotel Meistertrunk, Rothenburg (D), Hotel Roter Hahn, Rothenburg (D), Hotel Schranne, Rothenburg (D), Mittermeier, Rothenburg (D), Romantik-Hotel Markusturm, Rothenburg (D), Hotel Goldener Hirsch (D), Hotel Goldenes Fass, Rothenburg (D), Hotel Eisenhut, Rothenburg (D), Burghotel, Relais du Silence, Rothenburg (D)

TECHNICAL APPROACH

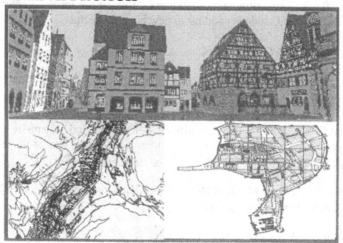

The consortium has developed a 3-D e-commerce platform for joint destination marketing that goes beyond the reach of the individual tourism businesses alone. The 3-D platform not only offers web-presentation of the local tourism businesses in the context of its destination but also serves as an integrating and organising platform for the local tourism network, which is considered as a crucial factor for successful take up of e-commerce. The main innovation of the Virtual Destination Project therefore was the increased understanding of success factors for e-business in tourism and best business practices in implementing it.

VDA was included in the show case book of successful eBusiness results of the FP 5 program.

MAIN RESULTS & RELATIONS TO VO CONCEPTS

The most significant VDA results related to VO concepts, were the idea to organise a virtual tourism business network through the 3-D city simulation web portal.

3-D Destination Web-Portal: Through the 3-D web-based city simulation, the destination businesses can collaborate virtually:

- Joint marketing: via World Wide Web the entire destination with its businesses can be coordinated through a single web interface, hence be accessed and marketed to the world wide customer.
- On-line virtual shopping mall: Through linking the individual e-business solutions with the 3-D web-portal, a virtual shopping complex can be easily established. With complex and taste dependent offerings as tourist services, the customer can review and experience his selection before the decision.
- Product assembly and service network for each traveller: The tourist can configure his or her own service package or select and adapt from standard packages. Through this, an individual VO network is assembled for each tourist serving his needs in the best way.
- Easy to expand: Due to the web-based nature, any new web-based coordination and communication application can be easily and quickly linked with the 3-D city simulation web-portal. This allows more complex activities to be organised, and also adding in new business partners.

SELECTED REFERENCES

1. Katzy, B. R. (1998). Designing and implementation of the Virtual Organisations, HICSS.

2. Kendall, K. E. (1997). "The significance of information systems research on emerging technologies: Seven information technologies that promise to improve managerial effectiveness." Decision Science 28(4): 775-791.

3. Snow, C. C., R. E. Miles, et al. (1992). "Managing the 21st Century Network Organizations." Organizational Dynamics(1): 5-20.

Contributors: Bernhard Katzy – Prof.Katzy@CeTIM.org
                     Gordon Sung – Gordon. Sung@CeTIM.org

VLAM-G: Grid-based Virtual Laboratory Amsterdam

PROJECT SUMMARY

The VLAM-G project designed and developed a prototype for a virtual laboratory environment dedicated to Grid-based distributed scientific and engineering experimentations. Special emphasis is given in the project to high-performance Grid-based distributed computing infrastructures, management of all experiment-related information, an execution engine for work-flow like definition of experiments, and uniform user interfaces for all access to the VLAM-G. The main focus of VLAM-G is on developing generic and reusable components to support sharing of hardware, software and information resources by multi-users, and extendibility of the environment for different scientific application cases. The two initial applications prototyped in VLAM-G were the DNA micro-array from the life sciences, and material analysis from the physics domain. However, the developed environment can also support other experimental science domains and applications.

Program: ICES/KIS-II (Dutch)   **Duration:** Jan 1999 – Jan 2003
Consortium: University of Amsterdam (NL) [project coordinator], Institute for Atomic and Molecular Physics (NL), The National Institute for Nuclear Physics and High Energy Physics (NL), Swammerdam Institute for Life Sciences (NL).

TECHNICAL APPROACH

The four-tier architecture of the VLAM-G is shown in Figure 1. *Application presentation tier* includes the user environments, which allow users to interact with the VLAM-G to use its facilities. The components of the *application toolkit tier* provide the generic VL functionality, on top of which application-specific functionality can be developed. *Grid services tier* provides the distributed resource management functionality using the Grid middleware technology.

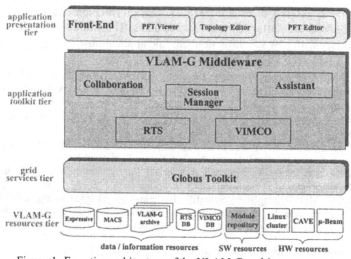

Figure 1. Four-tier architecture of the VLAM-G and its components

VLAM-G resources tier consists of the computing, networking, software, and storage resources that are made available to users and applications through the VLAM-G. The main components of the architecture are represented in Figure 1.

In VLAM-G, the steps involved in experiments are described by **studies,** using the **experiment templates.** Furthermore, the experiment's **topology** represents the computational aspects, defined in form of a data flow. In VLAM-G software **modules** are presented as self-contained elements. Therefore, users can define the topology of their experiments by simply connecting the related modules to each other, forming the data flow, which is then executed by the **Run Time System** on top of the available distributed Grid resources. The **VIMCO** component of the VLAM-G provides the necessary data models and functionality for storage and management of all experiment-related information. The **Front-End** consists of several uniform editors corresponding to different stages of experiment definition.

MAIN RESULTS

Achievements related to information management. The generic model developed for scientific/engineering experiments, uniformly represents multi-disciplinary and heterogeneous experiment-related information. The developed generic services, support management/manipulation of information while preserving access rights.

Achievements in distributed computing and work-flow like execution of experiments. Wrapping the processing functionality in self-contained modules allows for software reusability. The modules and their execution by the RTS component, hide the details of software engineering and Grid computing from its ordinary users.

Achievements related to collaboration and resource sharing. Base collaborative functionality is developed during the project for sharing hardware resources (through Grid), software resources (in form of reusable modules), and information resources (through uniform data models and access rights management).

Achievements related to user interfaces. All information and software resources in the VLAM-G are uniformly presented to users. This allows for easy extension of the laboratory with new scientific domains and applications.

SELECTED REFERENCES

1. VLAM-G: A Grid-based Virtual Laboratory. H. Afsarmanesh, R. G. Belleman, A. S. Z. Belloum, A. Benabdelkader, J. F. J. van den Brand, G. B. Eijkel, A. Frenkel, C. Garita, D. L. Groep, R. M. A. Heeren, Z. W. Hendrikse, L. O. Hertzberger, J. A. Kaandorp, E. C. Kaletas, V. Korkhov, C. T. A. M. de Laat, P. M. A. Sloot, D. Vasunin, A. Visser, and H. H. Yakali. *Scientific Programming,* 10 (2): 173-181, 2002.
2. The VL Abstract Machine: A Data and Process Handling System on the Grid. A. Belloum, Z. Hendrikse, D. Group, E. C. Kaletas, A. W. van Halderen, H. Afsarmanesh, and L. O. Hertzberger. *In Proceedings of the 9th International Conference and Exhibition on High-Performance Computing and Networking (HPCN Europe 2001),* 2001.
3. Modelling Multi-Disciplinary Scientific Experiments and Information. E. C. Kaletas, H. Afsarmanesh, and L. O. Hertzberger. *In Proceedings of the Eighteenth International Symposium on Computer and Information Sciences (ISCIS'03),* 2003.

Contributor: H. Afsarmanesh – hamideh@science.uva.nl
E. Kaletas – kaletas@science.uva.nl

VOmap: Roadmap Design for Collaborative Virtual Organizations in Dynamic Business Ecosystems

PROJECT SUMMARY

The IST VOmap project aimed at identifying and characterizing the key research challenges needed to fulfill the vision, required constituency, and the implementation model for a comprehensive European initiative on dynamic collaborative virtual organizations. The VOmap vision is that of an effective transformation of the landscape of European industry into a society of collaborative relationships.

Program: FP5 IST (European Commission)   **Duration:** Jul 2002 – Jun 2003
Consortium: UNINOVA (P) [project coordinator], University of Amsterdam (NL), FhG-IAO (D), CAS Software (D), CeTIM (D), VTT (FL), Virtuelle Fabrik (CH).

TECHNICAL APPROACH

The roadmapping work is coordinated by a core team of 7 experts covering a wide spectrum of complementary expertise, including among others: VOs and collaborative systems, interoperation, knowledge and information management, software engineering, business process modeling, economy and management, social and ethical issues, and electronic business. Through a number of activities – regional workshops, integration workshops, and written assessments – 100 experts (45% from industry, 45% from academia, 10% from other organizations) were involved.
In the elaboration of the roadmap five focus areas were considered:

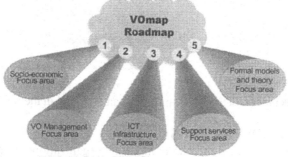

The work program comprised three main phases:
Phase 1: Elaboration of draft roadmap. To facilitate the focused discussions with a wide Support Group from different regions, it was necessary to first prepare an initial draft document, what was done by the core group.
Phase 2: Consultation and consensus building. During this phase the initial draft was thoroughly discussed in several iterations and in several (distributed) regional meetings/discussion panels with members of the Support Group. A Final Roadmap integrating all contributions was then made.
Phase 3: Wide dissemination and reinforcing links both inside and outside EU. A wider dissemination of results took place targeting other potential interested parties outside the Support Group.

MAIN RESULTS
The most significant results of VOmap include:

A roadmapping methodology. In spite of the growing interest in roadmapping and some existing successful examples the roadmapping is always performed by a group of specialists in the focus area, and unfortunately there is no real systematic roadmapping "approach" or even visioning "methodology" so far defined. Therefore VOmap developed a 10-step methodology that can be applied to other domains: (1) Characterize and consolidate the baseline, (2) Perceive trends and design scenarios, (3) Elaborate first vision statement and instantiations, (4) Fill the gap – where we are to where we wish to go, (5) Propose a plan of actions, (6) Verify the planned actions, (7) Plan the timing and other characterization of actions, (8) Finalize the definition of the roadmap chart, (9) Perform consultation and refinement, (10) Perform consolidation of the roadmap.

A roadmap for advanced VOs. A roadmap for the necessary integrated research and technological developments towards a new generation of virtual organizations is developed. This roadmap covers five specific focus areas of: Socio-economic, VO management, ICT infrastructure, Support Services, and Formal models and theories. For each focus area a number of strategic research actions are proposed. For each action three phases of activities are considered: (1) R&D, (2) Trials, and (3) Broad deployment. As an example, the following figure summarizes the suggested actions for the formal models and theories area:

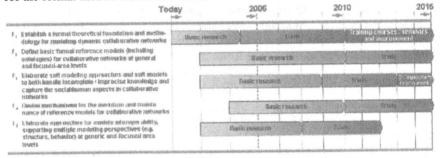

A detailed presentation of the VOmap results can be found in the references below.

SELECTED REFERENCES
1. A roadmap for strategic research on virtual organizations, L. M. Camarinha-Matos, Hamideh Afsarmanesh, in *Proceedings of PRO-VE'03 – Processes and Foundations for Virtual Organizations,* Kluwer Academic Publishers, Oct 2003.
2. A roadmapping methodology for strategic research on VO, L.M. Camarinha-Matos, H. Afsarmanesh, in Collaborative Networked Organizations – A research agenda for emerging business models, chap. 7.1, Kluwer Academic Publishers, ISBN 1-4020-7823-4, 2004.
3. A strategic roadmap for advanced virtual organizations, L.M. Camarinha-Matos, H. Afsarmanesh, H. Loeh, F. Sturm, M. Ollus, in Collaborative Networked Organizations – A research agenda for emerging business models, chap. 7.2, Kluwer Academic Publishers, ISBN 1-4020-7823-4, 2004.

Contributor: L. M. Camarinha-Matos – cam@uninova.pt

AUTHOR INDEX

SUBJECT INDEX